# AUTHORITY, CONTINUITY, AND CHANGE IN ISLAMIC LAW

Wael B. Hallaq is regarded as one of the leading scholars in the field of Islamic law. His latest book is about the function of authority in Islamic law, and how it is constructed, augmented, and utilized. In a comprehensive intellectual trawl through the intricacies of the law, the author demonstrates how that authority – at once religious and moral but essentially epistemic in nature – has always encompassed the power to motivate the processes of continuity and change. The role of the law schools in augmenting these processes cannot be doubted. However, as the author shows, it was the construction of the absolutist authority of the school founder, an image which he suggests was actually developed later in history, that maintained the foundations of school methodology and hermeneutics. The defense of that methodology, reasoned and highly calculated, in turn gave rise to an infinite variety of individual legal opinions, ultimately accommodating and legitimizing changes in the law. In this way, the author concludes that not only was Islamic law capable of change, but that the mechanisms of legal change were embedded in its very structure despite its essentially conservative nature. This book will be welcomed by specialists and scholars in Islamic law for its rigor and innovation.

WAEL B. HALLAQ is Professor at the Institute of Islamic Studies, McGill University. His many publications in the area of Islamic law include *A History of Islamic Legal Theories: An Introduction to Sunnī* uṣūl al-fiqh (1997) and *Law and Legal Theory in Classical and Medieval Islam* (1995).

# AUTHORITY, CONTINUITY, AND CHANGE IN ISLAMIC LAW

WAEL B. HALLAQ
*McGill University*

CAMBRIDGE
UNIVERSITY PRESS

CAMBRIDGE UNIVERSITY PRESS
Cambridge, New York, Melbourne, Madrid, Cape Town, Singapore, São Paulo

Cambridge University Press
The Edinburgh Building, Cambridge CB2 2RU, UK

Published in the United States of America by Cambridge University Press, New York

www.cambridge.org
Information on this title: www.cambridge.org/9780521803311



First published 2001
This digitally printed first paperback version 2005

*A catalogue record for this publication is available from the British Library*

ISBN-13 978-0-521-80331-1 hardback
ISBN-10 0-521-80331-4 hardback

ISBN-13 978-0-521-02393-1 paperback
ISBN-10 0-521-02393-9 paperback

To my mother
Samīra ʿĀqleh-Ḥallāq

# CONTENTS


*Preface* *page* ix

1 Juristic typologies: a framework for enquiry 1

2 Early *ijtihād* and the later construction of authority 24

3 The rise and augmentation of school authority 57

4 *Taqlīd*: authority, hermeneutics, and function 86

5 Operative terminology and the dynamics of legal doctrine 121

6 The jurisconsult, the author–jurist, and legal change 166

Summary and conclusions 236

*Bibliography* 242

*Index* 261

# PREFACE

To say that authority is the centerpiece of law is merely to state the obvious. Equally obvious therefore is the proposition that Islamic law – or any other law, for that matter – cannot be properly understood without an adequate awareness of the structure of authority that underlies it. It is this theme which constitutes the main preoccupation of the present work. In Islamic law, authority – which is at once religious and moral but mostly epistemic in nature[1] – has always encompassed the *power* to set in motion the inherent processes of continuity and change. Continuity here, in the form of *taqlīd*, is hardly seen as "blind" or mindless acquiescence to the opinions of others, but rather as the reasoned and highly calculated insistence on abiding by a particular authoritative legal doctrine. In this general sense, *taqlīd* can be said to characterize all the major legal traditions, which are regarded as inherently disposed to accommodating change even as they are deemed, by their very nature, to be conservative; it is in fact *taqlīd* that makes these seemingly contradictory states of affairs possible. For in law both continuity and change are two sides of the same coin, both involving the reasoned defense of a doctrine, with the difference that continuity requires the sustained defense of an established doctrine while change demands the defense of a new or, more often, a less authoritative one. Reasoned defense therefore is no more required in stimulating change than it is in preserving continuity.

In order to probe the substance and dimensions of these themes of continuity, change, and their relationship to authority, I have chosen to

[1] On these types of authority, see E. D. Watt, *Authority* (London and Canberra: Croom Helm, 1982), 45–54, 55–63; Richard T. De George, *The Nature and Limits of Authority* (Lawrence, Kans.: University of Kansas Press, 1985), 26–61, 191–209; Stanley I. Benn, "Authority," *Encyclopedia of Philosophy*, 8 vols. (New York: Macmillan Publishing Co., 1967), I, 215–18; Robert Peabody, "Authority," *International Encyclopedia of the Social Sciences*, ed. D. L. Sills, 17 vols. (New York: Macmillan and Free Press, 1968), I, 473–77.

examine the relatively compendious discursive construct called juristic typology which ranks legists according to the various levels of hermeneutical activity in which they are deemed competent to engage. This genre has the virtue of serving a double purpose, one of which is the inherent feature of self-representation. In speaking of the juristic structure of authority, of the various levels of its functioning, and of the limits of legal hermeneutics, it is instructive to listen to the voices emanating from within the tradition itself, for at a certain analytical level, self-perception is part and parcel of the objective reality which we have chosen to study. The other purpose, in contrast, is the harnessing of this typological genre for a critique that only outside observers of the tradition can proffer, since no participant in the tradition can advance such a critique and still remain part of that tradition. Subjecting the traditional account to a critical approach of this kind amounts to no less than deconstructing the historical imagination and inventions that were necessary to construct the authoritative edifice of the legal system and doctrine in the first place. No one, for instance, can at once question the almost mythological status of the eponyms of the four schools and still accept the fundamental assumptions of these typologies as anything more than linguistic structures needing to be decoded in a historiographical exercise. It is in virtue of such purposes that juristic typologies will serve to guide us as a framework for inquiry throughout this study.

One of the themes to be challenged, or at least questioned, in these typologies is the absolutist notion of a school founder. In chapter 2 I shall attempt to show, among other things, that while the image of a founding father was unquestionably essential for the school in constructing for itself an axis of authority, the abundantly available historical data serve to demonstrate that this image was a later creation and that the presumed founders of the four schools were far from having played these roles in their own times. This finding will further clarify the processes involved in the creation and construction of authority which was needed for the evolution and functioning of the schools. For our specific purposes, therefore, we shall be content to answer the question of *how* – rather than *why* – the imams' authority was constructed. This latter question will be the focus of another study currently in progress.[2]

In chapter 3 we shall trace the process by which the early multiple juristic voices of absolute *ijtihād* were progressively reduced to a relatively limited set of doctrines on which a special kind of authority was bestowed. The construction of the founder's authority, the reduction and

[2] See next note.

narrowing down of the early independent *ijtihādic* possibilities, and the final rise of *taqlīd* as an expression of loyalty to the schools are phenomena that share a single common denominator, namely, the augmentation of school authority without which the legal system could not have continued to exist, much less evolved or even thrived. The school as a doctrinal structure will therefore be shown to have constituted the very embodiment of this authority.

The inner dynamics of *taqlīd*, which represent the functional dominance of school authority, will constitute the main focus of chapter 4. A close examination of the activity of *taqlīd* and of the several types of discourse and reasoned arguments involved in this activity will make clear the many forms that school authority acquired. Within the confines of this activity, school authority could mean, at one end of the spectrum, the simple reproduction or mechanical application of authoritative doctrine, while at the other, it could involve the reenactment of a given authoritative opinion in the school, complete with all the ammunition of reasoned arguments and rhetorical discourse that the jurist could muster. But whether it was the former or the latter, nearly *ijtihādic*, type of *taqlīd* that was being advocated, or for that matter any degree of argument that lay between these two extremes, the defense of the school continued to be a central, if not the most important, goal of that activity.

In the final analysis, the defense of the school did not consist in a preoccupation with doctrinal trivia or with the mere collection and rehearsal of opinions. Rather, on a quite substantive level, it was a defense of methodology and hermeneutics, for the school itself was essentially founded upon a set of identifiable theoretical and positive principles, which in turn gave rise to an infinite variety of individual legal opinions and cases. These principles continued to serve as the foundation of the school as a substantive and authoritative legal entity, although the individual opinions and cases which constituted the practical and positivistic applications of these principles were subject to constant permutations. Cases and the opinions that governed them were regularly replaced by others, while the often undeclared principles from which they derived remained fairly constant.

The school was also defined by its substantive boundaries, represented by a massive bulk of particular cases and opinions that were articulated by the vast number of jurists who proclaimed loyalty to it in each generation, beginning with the presumed founders and their immediate followers, and ending with the jurists of later centuries. This arsenal of legal opinion represented, on the one hand, an imposing mass of doctrinal accretions, and on the other, a staggering plurality in the school's *corpus juris*. Now, this multiplicity of doctrinal narrative resulted in the development of a technical vocabulary designed to distinguish an authoritative hierarchy of legal opinion. In chapter 5, therefore, I explore what I call operative terminology whose function it was to determine which of the opinions governing a case carried the highest level of authority. For it was this terminology that designated the process by which a particular legal opinion was elevated from near obscurity or marginality to the highest, or one of the highest levels, of authoritative doctrine.

The inner dynamics of legal doctrine functioning under the rubric of operative terminology permitted the adaptation, *mutatis mutandis*, of legal opinions according to the requirements of time and place. And it is within the boundaries of this hermeneutical activity that much of the dynamic of legal change lay. In chapter 6 I shall argue that legal change was not incidental to Islamic law but that it was channeled through processes that were embedded in the very structures of the law. The chief agents mediating change through legitimization and formalization were the jurisconsult (*muftī*) and the author–jurist (*muṣannif*). The former created the link between social practices and the law, thereby articulating in piecemeal fashion the changing requirements of legal doctrine. No less important, however, was the function of the author–jurist who, together with the *muftī*, had the authority to create and fashion the authoritative legal text. Legal works of this kind encompassed not only the discursive body of the school's doctrine but also, and more specifically, that portion of the *corpus juris* which was deemed authoritative, for it was an integral part of the author–jurist's function to determine, on his own authority as well as on the authority of his associates, the standard and thus authoritative doctrine in his school. It was this authority possessed by the author–jurist that allowed him to mediate legal change as reflected in the juridical practices prevalent in his own social and regional milieu. In chapter 6, but also throughout the book, one of our chief concerns will continue to be the delimitation of the scope of authority associated with the most prominent legal offices, namely, the judge, the jurisconsult, and the author–jurist.

The nature of our enquiry dictates the investigation of sources that cover both the early and middle periods of Islam, a fairly long stretch of time indeed. In fact, our sources span the period from the second/eighth century to the thirteenth/nineteenth, a fact which inevitably imposes a caveat: The main focus of the book is the post-formative period which begins with the time when the schools had already reached maturity around the middle of the fourth/tenth century. The themes which will be raised here and which belong to the time-frame before the final consolidation of the schools are intended to highlight the processes by which authority was constructed in preparation for, and during, the post-formative period. It goes without saying that in the present work these themes are studied, not for their own sake, but in order to ascertain their respective roles in the construction of school authority. Similarly, the much later sources from the tenth/sixteenth century and afterwards are here utilized to illustrate the processes by which doctrinal authority was made to persist and respond to challenge, to ensure continuity as well as effect change. Thus, the issues raised in this book ultimately belong to the centuries that roughly fall between the fourth/tenth and the ninth/fifteenth.[3]

Still, the fact that this study encompasses over five centuries' worth of developments does raise the issue of generalization. Social and other historians of the Middle East have often attributed general characteristics to the subjects of their enquiry on the basis of a few case studies. In like manner, by failing to unravel the connections between these subjects and the society and culture in which they operated and out of which they emerged, the works of a number of historians appear to lapse into essentialism. Despite the fairly wide coverage of the present study, however, it avoids, by sheer necessity, these pitfalls. Insofar as the structure of legal authority is the focus of our enquiry, no jurist can be said to have articulated – or operated within – a concept of authority that was at variance with that of his peers and contemporaries. For jurists, by the nature of their function, were neither philosophers nor theologians who were largely free to innovate within their own intellectual traditions. Unlike the latter, jurists were bound by their legal culture, its demands, restrictions, and, above all, by the infrastructural social and cultural reality on the ground, a reality whose demands were neither binding nor restrictive in the case of theological, philosophical, or other types of intellectual discourse. In chapter 6 I will attempt to show that juristic doctrinal discourse succeeded in appropriating social reality by means of forging structural mechanisms that involved the functions of the jurisconsult and the author–jurist. The input of these latter functions, coupled with the findings – in chapter 5 – that the authoritative status of legal opinions was negotiated through considerations of social and mundane exigencies, demonstrate an organic connection between social practice and juristic

3 Answering the question why authority was constructed will involve us here in enquiries that are largely irrelevant to the issues under discussion. This question will form part of a study in progress that addresses the early formation of Islamic law, spanning the period extending from the first/seventh century to the middle of the fourth/tenth.

production of doctrine. At the end of the day, the latter emerges as a type of what has been called discursive practice.[4]

Be that as it may, the structure of authority does undergo diachronic change, a fact clearly attested by the transformations that took place during and after the consolidation of the legal schools. But the process of change in the structure of authority was certainly slow and was often rather subtle and seemingly imperceptible, a phenomenon that places certain constraints on the historian. For to diagnose and unravel the processes of change that were embedded in structures of juristic authority, a fairly long period of time must be subjected to scrutiny, and a wide variety of sources examined for this particular purpose. This is why an examination of juristic production covering several centuries is required, and, to make the processes of change clearer, sources from earlier and later periods are needed as well.

In my source coverage, there is admittedly a mild imbalance. I have attempted to draw evenly on works from the four schools. While this was largely possible, the Ḥanbalite legal literature was not always adequate for the task in hand. It will be immediately noted, for instance, that this school is absent from the list of juristic typologies, since no complete Ḥanbalite typology had been developed, at least insofar as I know. While in other parts of this study the Ḥanbalite presence is felt more, it almost never matches that of the other three schools. (The relative meagerness of Ḥanbalite sources is not only a function of the small size of the school in terms of the number of followers, but a historical phenomenon that has more serious dimensions still awaiting study.)

Finally, a word of thanks. In researching the subject of this book I have incurred a debt to my students who, as usual, have presented me with the challenge of having to answer their profound questions and to address their perspicacious comments. Adam Gacek, Salwa Ferahian, and Wayne St. Thomas of the Library of the Institute of Islamic Studies have been unfailingly helpful and supportive. Üner A. Turgay has been an ideal colleague and an extraordinarily supportive chair. My chief debt goes to Steve Millier whose library and editorial skills have been invaluable. To all these students and colleagues, I record my deepest gratitude.

4 Here, a distinction is to be drawn between the demands – in terms of the nature of sources – that are imposed on legal and social historians. For the latter, the connection between such sources and the realia of social practice are, admittedly, at best tenuous. But for the former, especially where structures of authority are concerned, they manifest these connections in no ambiguous manner.

# 1

# JURISTIC TYPOLOGIES: A FRAMEWORK FOR ENQUIRY

## I

A juristic typology is a form of discourse that reduces the community of legal specialists into manageable, formal categories, taking into consideration the entire historical and synchronic range of that community's juristic activities and functions. One of the fundamental characteristics of a typology is the elaboration of a structure of authority in which all the elements making up the typology are linked to each other, hierarchically or otherwise, by relationships of one type or another. The synchronic and diachronic ranges of a typology provide a synopsis of the constitutive elements operating within a historical legal tradition and within a living community of jurists. It also permits a panoramic view of the transmission of authority across types, of the limits on legal hermeneutics in each type, and of the sorts of relationships that are imposed by the interplay of authority and hermeneutics.

The evolution of the notion of the typology as a theoretical construct or conceptual model presupposes a conscious articulation of the elements that constitute them. To put it tautologically, since typologies purport to describe certain realities, these realities must, logically and historically speaking, predate any attempt at typification. And since Islamic juristic typologies presuppose, by virtue of their hermeneutical constitution, loyalty to the *madhhab* or legal school, then it is expected that no typology can be possible without positing a school structure.

Furthermore, and as a prerequisite to the formation of a typology, there must be developed a fairly sophisticated historical account of the school. In other words, no typology can be formulated without a substantial repertoire of the so-called *ṭabaqāt* (bio-bibliographical) literature. This literature, in its turn, totally depends on the conception of the *madhhab* as a doctrinal entity composed of jurist–scholars, their tradition of learning, and profession. The final formation of the schools was thus a precondition to the emergence of *ṭabaqāt* literature, just as this literature was a prerequisite for the rise of typologies.

Since the legal schools took shape by the middle of the fourth/tenth century,[1] and since the first *ṭabaqāt* works of the jurists seem to have been written by the end of the fourth/tenth century and the beginning of the fifth/eleventh,[2] we must not expect to find any typology emerging before the middle or end of the latter century. Indeed, it is no surprise that our sources have not revealed a typology prior to that of the distinguished Andalusian jurist Abū al-Walīd Muḥammad Ibn Rushd (d. 520/1126).

## II

One year before his death, the Cordoban jurist Ibn Rushd was called upon to answer what is in effect three questions:[3] First, what are the qualifications of the *muftī* in "these times of ours" according to the school of Mālik? Second, what is the status of the *qāḍī*'s ruling if he is a *muqallid* within the Mālikite school and if, in his region, no *mujtahid* is to be found? Should his rulings be categorically accepted, categorically revoked, or only provisionally accepted? Third, should the ruler – with respect to whom the *qāḍī*s are but *muqallids* – accept or revoke their decisions?

1 This is based on extensive research by this writer as well as on Christopher Melchert, *The Formation of the Sunni Schools of Law* (Leiden: E. J. Brill, 1997). See also nn. 1 and 3 of the preface, above.

2 It suffices here to quote one of the most important legal biographers in Islam, Tāj al-Dīn al-Subkī, who could not find a Shāfiᶜite biography earlier than the beginning of the fifth/eleventh century. In explaining his sources, he states: "I have searched hard and researched much in order to find those who wrote on *ṭabaqāt*. The first one who is said to have discoursed on that [subject] is the Imām Abū Ḥafṣ ᶜUmar Ibn al-Muṭawwiᶜī [d. 440/1048] . . . who wrote a book he entitled *al-Mudhahhab fī Shuyūkh al-Madhhab*. After him, the Qāḍī Abū al-Ṭayyib al-Ṭabarī [d. 450/1058] wrote a short work." See Subkī, *Ṭabaqāt al-Shāfiᶜiyya al-Kubrā*, 6 vols. (Cairo: al-Maktaba al-Ḥusayniyya, 1906), I, 114. Furthermore, in his *al-Majmūᶜ: Sharḥ al-Muhadhdhab*, 12 vols. (Cairo: Maṭbaᶜat al-Taḍāmun, 1344/1925), I, 40–54, Sharaf al-Dīn al-Nawawī devotes a section to *adab al-muftī* and there declares his debt to the works of Ibn al-Ṣalāḥ and ᶜAbd al-Wāḥid al-Ṣaymarī (d. 386/996), another Shāfiᶜite who wrote a work with the same title. But judging by the typology put forth by Nawawī, it is clear that his debt is exclusively to Ibn al-Ṣalāḥ, since nowhere in his discussion of the types of *muftī*s does he mention Ṣaymarī. On Ṣaymarī and his work, see Amīn b. Aḥmad Ismāᶜīl Pāshā, *Īḍāḥ al-Maknūn fī al-Dhayl ᶜalā Kashf al-Ẓunūn*, 6 vols. (repr., Beirut: Dār al-Kutub al-ᶜIlmiyya, 1992), I, 633.

3 Muḥammad b. Aḥmad Ibn Rushd, *Fatāwā Ibn Rushd*, ed. al-Mukhtār b. Ṭāhir al-Talīlī, 3 vols. (Beirut: Dār al-Gharb al-Islāmī, 1978), III, 1494–1504; Aḥmad b. Yaḥyā al-Wansharīsī, *al-Miᶜyār al-Mughrib wal-Jāmiᶜ al-Muᶜrib ᶜan Fatāwī ᶜUlamāʾ Ifrīqiyya wal-Andalus wal-Maghrib*, 13 vols. (Beirut: Dār al-Gharb al-Islāmī, 1401/1981), X, 30–35.

Ibn Rushd answered that the community of jurists consisted of three groups. The first had accepted the validity of Mālik's school by following it without knowledge of the evidence upon which the school's doctrine was based. This group concerned itself merely with memorizing Mālik's views on legal questions along with the views of his associates. It does so, however, without understanding the import of these views, let alone distinguishing those which are sound from those which are weak.

The second group deemed Mālikite doctrine valid because it had become clear to its members that the foundational principles on which the school was based were sound. Accordingly, they took it upon themselves to study and learn by heart Mālik's legal doctrines alongside the doctrines of his associates (*aṣḥāb*).[4] Despite the fact that their legal scholarship was not proficient enough to enable them to derive positive legal rulings from the texts of revelation or from the general precepts laid down by the founders, they also managed to learn how to distinguish between those views that accord with the school's principles and those that do not.

The third group also came to a deep and thorough understanding of Mālik's doctrine as well as the teachings of his associates. Like the second group, this group knew how to differentiate between the sound views that accord with the school's general precepts and those that are weak and therefore are deemed to stand in violation of these precepts. However, what distinguished the members of this group from those belonging to the other two is that they were able to reason on the basis of the revealed texts and the general principles of the school. Their knowledge encompassed the following topics: the legal subject matter of the Quran; abrogating and abrogated verses; ambiguous and clear Quranic language; the general and the particular; sound and weak legal *ḥadīth*; the opinions of the Companions, the Followers, and those who came after them throughout the Islamic domains; doctrines subject to their agreement and disagreement; the Arabic language; and methods of legal reasoning and the proper use in them of textual evidence.

Now in terms of their function, the members of the first group are disqualified from issuing *fatwā*s. True, they may have memorized the

[4] The term *aṣḥāb* (pl. of *ṣāḥib*) here means those who studied with Mālik, as well as those who happened, generations later, to follow his doctrines together with the doctrines of his immediate students. On *ṣuḥba* in the educational context, see George Makdisi, *The Rise of Colleges: Institutions of Learning in Islam and the West* (Edinburgh: Edinburgh University Press, 1981), 128–29; Michael Chamberlain, *Knowledge and Social Practice in Medieval Damascus, 1190–1350* (Cambridge: Cambridge University Press, 1994), 118–22; Jonathan Berkey, *The Transmission of Knowledge in Medieval Cairo* (Princeton: Princeton University Press, 1992), 34–35.

founding doctrines of the Mālikite school, but they have not yet developed the critical apparatus which allows one to discriminate between doctrines that are sound and those that are less sound. What they possess, in other words, is not *ʿilm*, i.e., the genuine understanding of the quality of textual evidence and the lines of legal reasoning through which legal norms are derived. All they have managed to do is to acquire by rote the school's doctrine, which permits them to issue *fatwās* only for themselves, that is, in situations where they are personally involved (*fī ḥaqqi nafsihi*). Should there be more than one opinion on the matter, then members of this group would be governed by the same rule applied to the layman (*ʿāmmī*), namely, that they are to accept one of the following options: (1) to adopt whichever opinion they deem suitable; (2) to investigate the credentials of the jurists who held these opinions so as to adopt the view of the most learned of them; and (3) to choose the most demanding of the available opinions in order to be on the safe side.

Since the members of the second group have distinguished themselves by a proficient knowledge of the school's doctrines and general precepts, they are qualified to give legal opinions lying within the doctrinal boundaries of the school of Mālik and his associates. In other words, they are not to attempt any form of *ijtihād* which may lead to the discovery of an unprecedented legal ruling.

By contrast, those belonging to the third group do have the freedom to exercise *ijtihād* since they have perfected the tools of original legal reasoning on the basis of the revealed texts. The qualifications permitting them to practice *ijtihād* are not a matter of quantitative memorization of legal doctrines; rather, they are the refined qualities of legal reasoning and an intimate knowledge of the Quran, the Sunna, and consensus. But how are these qualifications to be recognized? Ibn Rushd maintains that acknowledgment of an accomplished jurist who has reached such a distinguished level of legal learning must come from both the community of legal specialists in which he himself lives, and from the jurist himself. The judgment is thus both objective and subjective.[5]

Let us recall that the first question addressed to Ibn Rushd referred in part to the *muftī*'s qualifications during "these times of ours." It is remarkable, and quite significant for us – as shall become clear later – that Ibn Rushd did not view his own age as being any different from the ones preceding it, insisting that "the attributes of the *muftī* which he should fulfill do not change with the changing of times."[6]

[5] Ibn Rushd, *Fatāwā*, III, 1503. [6] Ibid.; Wansharīsī, *al-Miʿyār al-Mughrib*, X, 34.

Ibn Rushd's tripartite classification of *muftīs* is intended to prepare the ground for a reply to the first question, namely, What are the qualifications of the *muftī* according to Mālikite doctrine? The answer is that, in light of the classification set forth earlier, no one is entitled to issue *fatwās* – whether in accordance with Mālikite law or otherwise – unless he is able to investigate the textual sources of the law by means of the proper tools of legal reasoning. Put differently, if the jurist is unable to reach this level of competence, then no matter how extensive his knowledge of Mālikite law he lacks the necessary qualifications of a *muftī*. Thus, the prerequisite is the attainment of *ijtihād*, and *ijtihād*, Ibn Rushd seems to say, cannot be confined to any particular school or to boundaries preset by any other *mujtahid*, be he a contemporary, a predecessor or even the founder of a school.

As for the second question, the solution may be found in the discussion of the second category of jurists, namely, those who study and learn by heart the Mālikite doctrines and who are able to distinguish between sound and unsound opinions, but who are unable to derive positive legal rulings from the texts of revelation or from general precepts laid down by the masters. It is clear that Ibn Rushd places *qāḍīs* in this category by process of elimination, since they fit neither in the first category of *muqallids* nor in the third, which comprises only *mujtahids*. These *qāḍīs* are permitted to rule on cases already elaborated in Mālikite law, but in cases where there is no precedent they are obliged to seek the opinion of a *muftī* who is qualified to practice *ijtihād*, whether or not this *muftī* is to be found in the locality where the judge presides. Here, Ibn Rushd is merely acknowledging an age-old practice where jurists were in the habit of soliciting the opinion of a distinguished *muftī*.[7]

The third question Ibn Rushd answers summarily: If a *muqallid* presiding as a judge should rule on a matter requiring *ijtihād*, then his decision would be subject to judicial review. The ruler's duty is to decree that such judges should not dabble in matters involving *ijtihād* but should refer these matters to jurists who are properly qualified.[8]

The issues which gave rise to these questions were the subject of heated debate among the jurists of early twelfth-century Tangiers. Failing to persuade each other, these jurists addressed themselves to Ibn Rushd, at the time the most distinguished and recognized legal scholar in the

[7] Ibn Rushd's own *fatwās*, published in three volumes, reflect this reality. A large number of the *istiftā's* came from both *qāḍīs* and private individuals who resided in nearby and distant Spanish and North African locales. The present *fatwā*, for instance, came from Tangiers.

[8] Ibn Rushd, *Fatāwā*, III, 1504.

Mālikite school. The authority that Ibn Rushd carried was beyond dispute, whether during his lifetime or centuries thereafter. What he said was taken seriously, and his *fatwā*s and other writings became, over the course of the following centuries, authoritative statements that were incorporated into law manuals, commentaries, and super-commentaries.[9] The *fatwā* discussed above, for instance, was incorporated in a number of works, including Wansharīsī's *Miᶜyār*, Burzulī's *Nawāzil*, al-Mahdī al-Wazzānī's *Nawāzil*, Ibn Salmūn's *al-ᶜIqd al-Munaẓẓam*, and Ḥaṭṭāb's *Mawāhib al-Jalīl*.[10] The point to be made here is that Ibn Rushd's opinion continued to have relevance for centuries after his death, and as such it stood as an authoritative statement reflecting a juristic reality within the Mālikite school both during and long after the lifetime of this eminent jurist.

I shall reserve further commentary on Ibn Rushd's *fatwā* to a later stage in the discussion, but for now it is worth noting one significant aspect. The point of departure in this *fatwā* is that the limits of legal interpretation are confined to Mālikism, an assumption that seems implicit in the question posed by the jurists of Tangiers. The three questions they submitted to Ibn Rushd revolved exclusively around the tasks and hermeneutical skills of *muftī*s and *qāḍī*s. These were the parameters that Ibn Rushd accepted in his discussion of the first two types of jurists, whom he regarded as indeed obliged to conform to school doctrine since they lacked the tools of *ijtihād* (although the second type was still permitted to issue *fatwā*s). When he came to discuss the third type, however, Ibn Rushd parted company with his fellow jurists. In his eyes, the *muftī–mujtahid* was not bound by the limitations of the school, and his task (once the case proved to require *ijtihād*) entailed a direct confrontation with the revealed texts. Dependence on the opinions and doctrines of the predecessors – that is, on established authority – was no longer relevant nor needed at this stage. Even *muftī*s of the second type were not permitted to issue *fatwā*s "according to Mālik's school" unless they themselves were able, through independent means, to verify the opinions they cited from earlier authorities. That is to say, once *ijtihād* enters the picture, independence of mind becomes a must. This is the context for Ibn Rushd's leading statement, which is of

9 On the significance of incorporating *fatwā*s in law manuals and commentarial literature, see chapter 6, below.

10 Editorial references to these works are to be found in Ibn Rushd, *Fatāwā*, III, 1496–97. Ḥaṭṭāb discusses Ibn Rushd's *fatwā* in Muḥammad b. Muḥammad al-Ḥaṭṭāb, *Mawāhib al-Jalīl li-Sharḥ Mukhtaṣar Khalīl*, 6 vols. (Ṭarāblus, Libya: Maktabat al-Najāḥ, 1969), VI, 94–96.

particular significance for us: "The attributes of the *muftī* [–*mujtahid*] which he should fulfill do not change with the changing of times." Thus, the *ijtihād* of Mālik himself, and of the other founding masters of Mālikism, did not differ from that of later jurisprudents, including, probably, Ibn Rushd himself, who was known to have exercised *ijtihād* in a number of cases.[11]

If later *mujtahid*s were as qualified as the founding masters, however, did this mean that later *mujtahid*s could establish their own schools? To the best of my knowledge, Ibn Rushd does not address this question. But we can generally infer from his *ijtihād*ic activities[12] and writings that undertaking fresh *ijtihād* in one or more cases does in no way entail either the abandonment of a legal school or the establishment of a new one. For Ibn Rushd, this simply was not an issue. The three types of jurists he articulated operated entirely within the Mālikite system, with one significant exception. When *muftī*s of the third type encountered a case necessitating *ijtihād*, they dealt with it as independent *mujtahid*s, in the sense that they were not bound by the criteria which the founding masters had established for their own legal construction. This activity, however, though independent, did little to alienate them or their new opinions from the Mālikite school. On the contrary, the resulting opinions were added to the repertoire of the school's doctrine, and were memorized and debated in their turn by succeeding generations of jurists.

## III

About a century later, another major jurist was faced with a similar question. This was Abū ᶜAmr ᶜUthmān Ibn al-Ṣalāḥ (d. 643/1245), a Shāfiᶜite *muftī*, teacher, and author who lived in Damascus for a good part of his life.[13] Ibn al-Ṣalāḥ wrote at a time when the legal schools had already taken their final shape, which explains why he framed his discussion in terms of affiliation and loyalty to the school, and in a more developed and self-conscious manner than we found in Ibn Rushd.

11 See, for example, Wael B. Hallaq, "Murder in Cordoba: *Ijtihād*, *Iftā'* and the Evolution of Substantive Law in Medieval Islam," *Acta Orientalia*, 55 (1994): 55–83, and Burzulī's commentary on the *fatwā* of Ibn Rushd discussed here, in Ibn Rushd, *Fatāwā*, III, 1504–06.

12 See previous note.

13 See his biography in Taqī al Dīn b. Aḥmad Ibn Qāḍī Shuhba, *Ṭabaqāt al Shāfiᶜiyya*, ed. ᶜAbd al-ᶜAlīm Khān, 4 vols. (Hyderabad: Maṭbaᶜat Majlis Dā'irat al-Maᶜārif al-ᶜUthmāniyya, 1398/1978), II, 144–46; ᶜAbd al-Qādir b. Muḥammad al-Nuᶜaymī, *al-Dāris fī Tārīkh al-Madāris*, ed. Jaᶜfar al-Ḥusaynī, 2 vols. (Damascus: Maṭbaᶜat al-Taraqqī, 1367/1948), I, 20–21.

He begins by dividing the *muftīs* into two categories, independent (*mustaqill*) and dependent (*ghayr mustaqill*),[14] two terms that augur the emergence of a technical language through which juristic typification came to be articulated. The first category stands by itself, signaling the momentous achievement of the school founders. The second category encompasses four types to which a fifth informal type is added. Thus, all in all, Ibn al-Ṣalāḥ's typology consists of the following categories and types:

Category 1 (one type)
Category 2 (types 1, 2, 3, 4, and 5)

*Muftīs* of the first category, which he also identifies as absolute (*muṭlaq*), possess expert knowledge of *uṣūl al-fiqh*, which includes Quranic exegesis, *ḥadīth* criticism, the theory of abrogation, language, and the methods of exploiting the revealed texts and of deriving rulings therefrom. They are also knowledgeable in the realms of positive law (having mastered its difficult and precedent-setting cases), the science of disagreement (*khilāf*) and arithmetic. The *mujtahids* in this category must maintain these qualifications in all areas of the law, thereby distinguishing themselves from lesser *mujtahids*.[15]

Those who possess these lofty qualifications are able to dispense with the communal duty, the *farḍ al-kifāya*, which is incumbent upon all members of the community but discharged if certain members could fulfill it. They follow no one and belong to no school, the implication being – given the then current perception of the schools' history – that this definition applies to the founders of their own schools, the imams, who appeared on the scene during a fleeting moment in history. Ibn al-Ṣalāḥ declares these jurists long extinct, having left behind others to tread in their footsteps.

Those who follow in their path make up the second category, the dependent *muftīs* who are by definition affiliated with the founding masters, the imams. Ibn al-Ṣalāḥ falls short of making any explicit connection between the two types, but the connection seems to be assumed and appears to follow logically. The assumption is necessary because the entire community of *muftīs* is conceived here in terms of leaders and followers, of founding masters and succeeding generations of adherents who are progressively, in diachronic terms, inferior in knowledge to the

[14] Abū ʿAmr ʿUthmān b. ʿAbd al-Raḥmān Ibn al-Ṣalāḥ, *Adab al-Muftī wal-Mustaftī*, ed. Muwaffaq b. ʿAbd al-Qādir (Beirut: ʿĀlam al-Kutub, 1407/1986), 86 ff.
[15] Ibid., 89–91.

imams. This is perhaps why, in the course of the discussion, Ibn al-Ṣalāḥ changes the designation of the second category from *ghayr mustaqill* to *muntasib*, the affiliated *muftī*.

This second category is in turn divided into four (possibly five) types:

*Type 1*: Curiously, the first type is far from being a *muqallid*, i.e. one who follows the positive doctrine of the founding master or absolute *mujtahid*. Rather, this type of *muftī* possesses all the qualifications found in the absolute, independent *mujtahid*, and seems to equal him in every way. However, his affiliation with the latter is due to the fact that the *muftī* has chosen to follow his particular methods of *ijtihād* and to advocate his doctrines. In this context, Abū Isḥāq al-Isfarā'īnī (d. 418/1027) is on record as saying that this was the case with a number of *mujtahids* who affiliated themselves with the school founders not out of *taqlīd* but rather because they found the imams' methods of *ijtihād* most convincing. What he in effect means here is that the affiliation was created on the grounds that the *muftī* of the first sub-type happened to believe in the soundness of the *ijtihād* methods adopted by the absolute *mujtahid* because he had arrived independently at the same conclusions. *Taqlīd* plays no role here, because the adoption of the founder's *ijtihād* methods presupposes the existence of the quality of *ijtihād* which enables him to determine that the imam's methodology is the most sound.

This being the case, the distinction between these two types of *mujtahid* is drastically blurred, which raises, for instance, the question: Why should jurists of the second type "follow" the first if they are equally qualified? Or to put it another way: Why should those of the second type not establish their own schools? It is probably this ambiguity, or blurring of distinctions, that prompted Ibn al-Ṣalāḥ to interject a clarifying statement: The claim that the affiliated *mujtahids* are devoid of all strands of *taqlīd* is incorrect, for they, or *most of them* (*aktharuhum*), have not completely mastered the sciences of absolute *ijtihād* and thus have not attained the rank of independent *mujtahids*. This assertion seems to stand in flagrant contradiction to what Ibn al-Ṣalāḥ had said a little earlier, namely, that this kind of *muftī* possesses all the credentials of the absolute, independent *mujtahid* and stands on a par with him in nearly every way. The difficulty in accounting for the role of these *mujtahids* in the school hierarchy is underscored by Ibn al-Ṣalāḥ's qualification "most of them." This is significant since it allows for a certain blurring of distinctions between this type of *muftī* and the absolute *mujtahid*. Isfarā'īnī's assertion thus remains largely unaffected, while Ibn al-Ṣalāḥ's undifferentiated reality tends to accord with the facts of history, for we now know that the eponyms were not exclusively responsible for the rise and evolution of the schools.[16]

[16] A point we shall develop in chapter 2, below. See also Wael B. Hallaq, "Was al-Shafiʿi the Master Architect of Islamic Jurisprudence?" *International Journal of Middle East Studies*, 4 (1993): 587–605.

*Type 2*: The second type is the limited *mujtahid* (*muqayyad*) who is fully qualified to confirm and enhance the doctrines of the absolute *mujtahid*. His qualifications, however, do not allow him to step outside the principles and methods laid down by the imam of his school. He knows the law, legal theory, and the detailed methods of legal reasoning and linguistic analysis. He is an expert in *takhrīj*[17] and in deducing the law from its sources.[18] This last qualification becomes necessary because he is held responsible for determining the law in unprecedented cases according to the principles of his imam and of the school with which he is affiliated. Despite his ability to perform *ijtihād*, these qualifications of his are marred by a weakness in certain respects, such as in his knowledge of *ḥadīth* or in his mastery of the Arabic language. These weaknesses, Ibn al-Ṣalāḥ observes, have in reality been the lot of many *muftīs* who happened to be of this type. He also finds it easier to cite examples of such *muftīs* than he was when articulating the first type. He declares, for instance – without invoking the attestation of other authorities (as he did with Isfarā'īnī before) – that a certain class of eminent Shāfiʿite jurists did belong to this type, calling these latter *aṣḥāb al-wujūh* and *aṣḥāb al-ṭuruq*.[19]

The relationship existing between the revealed texts and the absolute *mujtahid* appears identical to that which links the imam's founding positive doctrines to the limited *mujtahid* of the second type. This latter, in other words, derives rulings for unprecedented cases on the basis of the imam's doctrines, just as his imam derived his own doctrines from the revealed sources. In rare cases, he may even embark on *ijtihād* in the same manner as the *muftī* of the first type does. At a later stage of the discussion, Ibn al-Ṣalāḥ develops this point. He argues that in unprecedented cases the limited *mujtahid* is permitted to conduct *ijtihād* in the same manner as the absolute *mujtahid*. Shāfiʿite *mujtahids* who have mastered the fundamental principles (*qawāʿid*) as laid down by Shāfiʿī, and who are fully trained in his methods of legal reasoning, are considered to have the same abilities as the absolute *mujtahid* does. In fact, Ibn al-Ṣalāḥ continues, such *mujtahids* may even be more capable than the absolute *mujtahid*, for they, we understand, have lived at a time when the fundamental school principles have long been prepared and established. Such tools as were available to them were never within the reach of the absolute *mujtahid*. Thus, Ibn al-Ṣalāḥ seems to say, they enjoy a definite advantage.

17 For a detailed account of *takhrīj*, see chapter 2, sections III–IV, below.

18 In fact, Jalāl al-Dīn al-Suyūṭī calls this type of jurist *mujtahid al-takhrīj* since the characteristic activity in which he is involved is that of *takhrīj*. See his *al-Radd ʿalā man Akhlada ilā al-Arḍ wa-Jahila anna al-Ijtihād fī Kulli ʿAṣrin Farḍ*, ed. Khalīl al-Mays (Beirut: Dār al-Kutub al-ʿIlmiyya, 1983), 116.

19 Norman Calder, "al-Nawawī's Typology of *Muftīs* and its Significance for a General Theory of Islamic Law," *Islamic Law and Society*, 4 (1996): 146, mistakenly defined *aṣḥāb al-wujūh* as "those [jurists] whose opinions are preserved." On this expression, see chapter 2, section III, below. On *aṣḥāb al-ṭuruq*, see chapter 5, section I, below.

It is important to realize that the license given to the limited *mujtahid* to perform the various activities of *ijtihād* is not mere theorization on the part of Ibn al-Ṣalāḥ. In a key sentence, he declares that the province of this *mujtahid*'s activities is acknowledged in both theory and practice. "This is the correct doctrine which has been put into practice, the haven of the *muftī*s for ages and ages."[20]

However, if the limited *mujtahid* finds that a ruling in a particular case has already been derived and elaborated by his imam, he must adopt it and ought not to question them by seeking textual evidence that might countervail or contradict it (*muʿāriḍ*). The ability to give preponderance to one piece of evidence over another belongs to the imam, who is seen as the real founder of the school. This is why the *fatwā* of the limited *mujtahid* of this type does not reflect his own juristic endeavor, but rather that of the imam. "He who applies [or adopts; *ʿāmil ʿalā*] the *fatwā* of the limited *mujtahid* is a *muqallid* of the imam, not of the limited *mujtahid* himself, since the latter relies in validating his opinion on the imam, for he is not acting independently in validating its attribution to the Lawgiver."[21] Authority here is hierarchical: *Direct confrontation with the revealed texts endows the hermeneutical enterprise of the imam with the highest level of authority.* A derivative hermeneutic therefore yields only derivative and subordinate authority. The derivative nature of this authority translates, formally, into affiliation, and substantively, into loyalty.

*Type 3*. Jurists of the third type are, expectedly, inferior to their counterparts of the second type: Ibn al-Ṣalāḥ calls them the "jurists who articulated the *wujūh* and *ṭuruq*" (*aṣḥāb al-wujūh wal-ṭuruq*).[22] The *muftī* of the third type has a trained intelligence, knows by heart the doctrines of the imam he follows (*madhhab imāmihi*), and is an expert in his methods and ways. These doctrines and methods he confirms, defends, refines, clarifies, reenacts, and makes preponderant, presumably over and against the doctrines of others. His qualifications, however, fall short of those posited for *muftī*s of the preceding types because he fails to match their knowledge in one or more of the following areas: (1) the authoritative law of the school, the *madhhab*;[23] (2) the methods of legal reasoning needed for the derivation of rulings; (3) *uṣūl al-fiqh* in all its aspects and details; and (4) a variety of tools needed for the practice of *ijtihād*, tools which the *aṣḥāb al-wujūh wal-ṭuruq* have perfected.

Who belonged to this type? Ibn al-Ṣalāḥ is even more specific about which jurists who fell into this group than he was about the first and second types. Here he introduces an explicit chronological element, hitherto absent from his typology. Many of the later jurists (*mutaʾakhkhirūn*) who flourished up to the end of the fifth/eleventh century were, according to him, of this category.

[20] Ibn al-Ṣalāḥ, *Adab al-Muftī*, 96: "*hādhā huwa al-ṣaḥīḥ al-ladhī ʿalayhi al-ʿamal wa-ilayhi mafzaʿ al-muftīn min mudadin madīda.*" On the significance of *ṣaḥīḥ* and *ʿamal*, see chapter 5, sections IV and VI, below.

[21] Ibn al-Ṣalāḥ, *Adab al-Muftī*, 95. [22] See n. 19, above.

[23] See chapter 5, section VI, below.

They were author–jurists (*muṣannifūn*)[24] who produced the magisterial works studied so assiduously by later generations of legal scholars, including, admittedly, the generation of Ibn al-Ṣalāḥ himself. Their juristic competence does not match that of their colleagues of the second type, but they did contribute to the ordering and refinement of the authoritative positive doctrine of the school, the *madhhab*. In their *fatwās*, they elaborated law in the same detailed manner as jurists of the second type did, or, at any rate, very close to it. Their competence in legal reasoning permitted them to infer rulings for new cases on the basis of established and already solved cases. In this respect, Ibn al-Ṣalāḥ states, they were not limited to certain types of legal reasoning, the implication being that their competence in this sphere was of a wide range.

*Type 4*: *Muftīs* belonging to this type are the carriers and transmitters of the *madhhab*. They fully understand straightforward and problematic cases, but their knowledge does not go beyond this stage of competence, for they are weak in establishing textual evidence and in legal reasoning. In issuing *fatwās*, they merely transmit the authoritative doctrine of the school as elaborated by the imam and his associates who are themselves *mujtahids* operating within the boundaries of their school. In referring to the latter authorities, Ibn al-Ṣalāḥ has in mind jurists belonging to the first category and types 1 and 2 of the second, for he uses a particular term, *takhrījāt*, when referring to that part of the school's authoritative doctrine which cannot be attributed to the imam's juristic activity. Since the sole juristic activity of type 2 is characterized as *takhrīj*, then *muftīs* of type 4 must transmit the doctrines of the imam, *muftīs* of type 1, and, by definition, those of type 2.

When *muftīs* of type 4 do not find in the school's doctrine answers to the questions facing them, they look for analogical cases that might provide solutions to the questions addressed to them. If they find such cases, and if they know that the analogy is sound (i.e., that differences between the cases are irrelevant),[25] then they transfer the rule of the established case to the new. Similarly, they may venture to apply, in a deductive manner, a general, well-defined school principle to the case at hand. Such opportunities are common, for it is unlikely that a jurist should encounter a case which has no parallel in the school or which does not conform to a general principle. However, should a *muftī* be incapable of reasoning on such a level, he should refrain from issuing *fatwās* when the answer has not been established in the school. Finally, *muftīs* of this type are unable to commit the entirety of the school's positive doctrines to memory. They can memorize most of the doctrines, but must be adequately trained in retrieving the rest from books.[26]

[24] On the author–jurist and his role in legitimizing legal change, see chapter 6, below.

[25] Commonly known as *qiyās ilghāʾ al-fāriq* or *qiyās nafī al-fāriq*. See Muwaffaq al-Dīn Ibn Qudāma, *Rawḍat al-Nāẓir wa-Junnat al-Munāẓir*, ed. Sayf al-Dīn al-Kātib (Beirut: Dār al-Kitāb al-ʿArabī, 1401/1981), 262–63; Jamāl al-Dīn Abū ʿAmr Ibn al-Ḥājib, *Mukhtaṣar al-Muntahā al-Uṣūlī* (Cairo: Maṭbaʿat Kurdistān al-ʿIlmiyya, 1326/1908), 132–33.

[26] Ibn al-Ṣalāḥ, *Adab al-Muftī*, 100.

In a subsequent discussion, related to, but not an integral part of the typology, Ibn al-Ṣalāḥ remarks that Imām al-Ḥaramayn al-Juwaynī (d. 478/1085) and others held the view that a jurist who is adept at *uṣūl* and knowledgeable in *fiqh* is not permitted, solely on that basis, to issue *fatwā*s.[27] Others are also reported to have maintained that a *muqallid* is not allowed to issue *fatwā*s in those areas of the law in which they are *muqallid*s. To be sure, there were those who opposed such views and were prepared to allow a *muqallid* with thorough knowledge of the imam's law (*mutabaḥḥiran fīhi*) to issue *fatwā*s in accordance with it. At this point, Ibn al-Ṣalāḥ interjects to explain that what is intended by the provision that a *muqallid* should not issue *fatwā*s is that he should not appear as though he is the author of the *fatwā*; rather, he should clearly attribute it to the *mujtahid* whom he followed on that particular point of law. Accordingly, Ibn al-Ṣalāḥ adds, "in the ranks of *muftī*s, we have counted *muqallid*s who are not true *muftī*s, but who have taken the places of others performing their tasks on their behalf. Thus, they have come to be counted amongst them. For example, they should say [when they are asked a question]: 'The opinion of Shāfiʿī is such and such.' "[28]

This preliminary discussion seeks to introduce, in a less conscious manner, what is in effect a fifth type. Ibn al-Ṣalāḥ explicitly observes that this type has nothing in common with the other categories of his typology, and yet at the same time refuses to assign it a formal place. This sub-type appears as subsidiary to the formal structure of the typology, its informality suggesting that it originated as an afterthought. Its exclusion from the formal structure of the typology is implicitly rationalized in the preliminary discussion where the main point made is that the true or quintessential *muftī* is the one who is himself able to reason independently, either by deriving legal rulings directly from the revealed texts (category 1 and types 1 and 2 of category 2) or by being knowledgeable in the methods of derivation and in the material sources so as to be able to verify the soundness of the opinions he issues (types 3 and 4). A person of the subsidiary type, however, possesses none of these qualities, for he is deficient (*qāṣir*) and all he has "studied is one or more books of the *madhhab* . . . If a layman does not find in his town anyone other than him, then he must consult him, for this is still better than a situation where the layman remains confused, having no solution to his problem."[29] If the town is devoid of *muftī*s, then the layman should turn to this *qāṣir* individual who must relay the solution

[27] Ibid., 101 f. [28] Ibid., 103. [29] Ibid., 104.

to the layman's problem as found in a reliable and trustworthy book. Here the layman would of course be following the opinion (*muqallidan*) of the imam, not that of the *qāṣir*. But if he cannot find an identical case in any written sources, then he should in no way attempt to infer its solution from what he might think to be similar cases in their pages.

Overall, then, Ibn al-Ṣalāḥ's typology encompasses six sorts of jurists, ranging from the independent *muftī*, the imam, down to the deficient jurist who is merely able to locate in the law books the cases about which he is asked. It is interesting that Ibn al-Ṣalāḥ's younger contemporary, Nawawī (d. 676/1277), reproduces, with a somewhat different arrangement of materials, the same typology, including the supplementary, informal discussion.[30] Like Ibn Rushd's typology, Ibn al-Ṣalāḥ's version became highly influential within and without the Shāfiᶜite tradition, more so than Nawawī's reproduction of it. In fact, it remained influential even after Suyūṭī reformulated it nearly three centuries later.[31]

## IV

Some three centuries after Ibn al-Ṣalāḥ and Nawawī, and perhaps shortly after Suyūṭī's lifetime, the Ottoman Shaykh al-Islām Aḥmad Ibn Kamāl Pāshāzādeh (d. 940/1533)[32] articulated a Ḥanafite typology of jurists in

[30] Calder, who studied Nawawī's typology in the larger context of his *Majmūᶜ*, curiously arrives at eight types altogether. He recognizes the first six, as I do. But he adds two more types for which I see no basis either in Ibn al-Ṣalāḥ or in Nawawī. The seventh type which Nawawī is said to have articulated is indeed not a type but rather a discussion I have characterized as preliminary to his less formal type 5 of the second category. The eighth type that Calder identifies is again not a type since it deals with laymen not *muftīs*, and *muftīs* are what the entire typology is all about. See Calder, "al-Nawawī's Typology," 148; cf. Nawawī, *al-Majmūᶜ*, I, 44–45.

[31] See, for instance, the widely quoted work of Shams al-Dīn Ibn Farḥūn, *Tabṣirat al-Ḥukkām fī Uṣūl al-Aqḍiya wa-Manāhij al-Aḥkām*, 2 vols. (Cairo: al-Maṭbaᶜa al-ᶜĀmira al-Sharafiyya, 1883), I, 51. For Suyūṭī's reformulation, see his *al-Radd*, 112–16. Suyūṭī, however, differs with Ibn al-Ṣalāḥ on the terminological definition of the first type in the second category. Whereas Ibn al-Ṣalāḥ uses the term "absolute" to describe *muftīs* of the first category, Suyūṭī argues that type 1 of the second category is also absolute, albeit affiliated: "*fa-hādhā muṭlaq muntasib lā mustaqill.*" Cf. Aḥmad b. ᶜAbd al-Raḥīm Shāh Walī Allāh al-Dahlawī, *ᶜIqd al-Jīd fī Aḥkām al-Ijtihād wal-Taqlīd*, ed. Muḥibb al-Dīn al-Khaṭīb (Cairo: al-Maṭbaᶜa al-Salafiyya, 1385/1965), 3–5.

[32] For his biography, see ᶜAbd al-Qādir al-Tamīmī, *al-Ṭabaqāt al-Saniyya fī Tarājim al-Ḥanafiyya*, ed. ᶜAbd al-Fattāḥ al-Ḥulw, 3 vols. (Cairo: Dār al-Rifāᶜī lil-Nashr, 1983), I, 355–57; Abū al-Ḥasanāt ᶜAbd al-Ḥayy al-Laknawī, *al-Fawāʾid al-Bahiyya fī Tarājim al-Ḥanafiyya* (Cairo: Maṭbaᶜat al-Saᶜāda, 1324/1906), 21–22; Muḥammad Amīn Ibn ᶜĀbidīn, *Ḥāshiyat Radd al-Muḥtār ᶜalā al-Durr al-Mukhtār: Sharḥ Tanwīr al-Abṣār*, 8 vols. (Beirut: Dār al-Fikr, 1979), I, 26.

which seven ranks (*ṭabaqāt*) are recognized.[33] The first is the rank of *mujtahids* in the Sharᶜ, consisting of the four imams, the founders and eponyms of the four legal schools. Also holding this rank are others "like them," almost certainly a reference to the eponyms of the schools that failed to survive. These eponyms established fundamental principles (*ta'sīs qawāᶜid al-uṣūl*) and derived positive legal rulings from the four sources, i.e., the Quran, the Sunna, consensus, and *qiyās*. They are independent, and follow no one, whether it be in the general principles and methodology of law (*uṣūl*) or in positive legal rulings (*furūᶜ*).

Second is the rank of *mujtahids* within the boundaries of the *madhhab*, such as Abū Ḥanīfa's students, especially Abū Yūsuf and Shaybānī. These latter were capable of deriving legal rulings according to the general principles laid down by their master, Abū Ḥanīfa. Despite the fact that they differ with him on many points of law, they nonetheless follow him in the fundamental principles he established. It is precisely in virtue of their adherence to the imam's fundamental principles that jurists of this rank are distinguished from other jurists – such as Shāfiᶜī – who also differed with Abū Ḥanīfa on individual points of law. Unlike this rank, however, Shāfiᶜī's differences extended even to fundamental principles, but then he is in a different rank altogether.

Third is the rank of *mujtahids* who practiced *ijtihād* in those particular cases that Abū Ḥanīfa did not address. Assigned to this rank, among others, are Abū Bakr al-Khaṣṣāf (d. 261/874),[34] Abū Jaᶜfar al-Ṭaḥāwī (d. 321/933),[35] Abū al-Ḥasan al-Karkhī (d. 340/951),[36] Shams al-A'imma al-Ḥulwānī (d. 456/1063),[37] Shams al-A'imma al-Sarakhsī (d. after 483/1090),[38] Fakhr al-Islām al-Pazdawī (d. 482/1089),[39] and Fakhr al-Dīn Qāḍīkhān (d. 592/1195).[40] These jurists, incapable of differing with Abū Ḥanīfa over either the methodology and theory of law (*uṣūl*) or positive legal rulings (*furūᶜ*), nonetheless solved unprecedented cases in accordance with the principles that the eponym had laid down.

[33] Ibn Kamāl's classification became highly influential in the Ḥanafite school, and was recorded in a number of widely read works. See Abū al-Wafā' Muḥammad al-Qurashī, *al-Jawāhir al-Muḍī'a fī Ṭabaqāt al-Ḥanafiyya*, 2 vols. (Hyderabad: Maṭbaᶜat Majlis Dā'irat al-Maᶜārif, 1332/1913), II, 558; Tamīmī, *al-Ṭabaqāt al-Saniyya*, I, 33–34; Ibn ᶜĀbidīn, *Ḥāshiya*, I, 77–78; Muḥammad Amīn Ibn ᶜĀbidīn, *Sharḥ al-Manẓūma al-Musammā bi-ᶜUqūd Rasm al-Muftī*, in his *Majmūᶜ Rasā'il Ibn ᶜĀbidīn*, 2 vols. (n.p., 1970), I, 11–12; Abū al-Ḥasanat ᶜAbd al-Ḥayy al-Laknawī, *al-Nāfiᶜ al-Kabīr: Sharḥ al-Jāmiᶜ al-Ṣaghīr* (Beirut: ᶜĀlam al-Kutub, 1406/1986), 9–11. References here are to the text of Qurashī's *al-Jawāhir al-Muḍī'a*.

[34] Zayn al-Dīn Qāsim Ibn Quṭlūbughā, *Tāj al-Tarājim fī Ṭabaqāt al-Ḥanafiyya* (Baghdad: Maktabat al-Muthannā, 1962), 7.

[35] Ibid., 8. [36] Ibid., 39. [37] Ibid., 35. [38] Ibid., 57–58.

[39] Ibid., 41. [40] Ibid., 22.

The fourth rank differs from the preceding three in that it is defined in terms of *taqlīd*, not *ijtihād*. Jurists of this rank are only capable of *takhrīj*, and are thus known as *mukharrijūn*.[41] Their ability to practice *takhrīj* is due to their competence in *uṣūl*, including knowledge of how rules were derived by the predecessors. It is their task to resolve juridical ambiguities and tilt the scale in favor of one of two or more opinions that govern a case. This they do by virtue of their skills in legal reasoning and analogical inference. Karkhī, Rāzī,[42] and, to some extent, the author of *Hidāya*,[43] belong to this rank, which seems a counterpart of the second sub-type advanced by Ibn al-Ṣalāḥ.

The fifth rank is that of *aṣḥāb al-tarjīḥ* who are also described by Ibn Kamāl as *muqallids*. Characterized as *murajjiḥūn*, they are able to address cases with two or more different rulings all established by their predecessors. Their competence lies in giving preponderance to one of these rulings over the other(s), on grounds such as its being dictated either by a more strict inference or by public interest. Abū al-Ḥasan al-Qudūrī (d. 428/1036)[44] and the author of *al-Hidāya*, Marghīnānī, for instance, are listed as belonging to this rank.

The sixth is the rank of *muqallids* who distinguish between sound and weak opinions, or between authoritative and less authoritative doctrines (*ẓāhir al-riwāya* and *al-nawādir*). What is characteristic of these *muqallids* is that they, as authors of law books, are careful not to include weak or rejectable opinions. Among the jurists belonging to this rank are the authors of the authoritative manuals (*mutūn*): Aḥmad Fakhr al-Dīn Ibn al-Faṣīḥ (d. 680/1281) who wrote *al-Kanz*;[45] ᶜAbd Allāh b. Mawdūd al-Mūṣilī (d. 683/1284) who wrote *al-Mukhtār*;[46] Ṣadr al-Sharīᶜa al-Maḥbūbī (d. 747/1346) who wrote *al-Wiqāya*;[47] and Aḥmad b. ᶜAlī Ibn al-Sāᶜātī (d. after 690/1291), the author of *Majmaᶜ al-Baḥrayn*.[48] (It is worth noting in passing that Ibn Kamāl identified most jurists who belonged to the fourth, fifth, and sixth ranks in terms of their works, works which represented their contribution to law and which became the yardstick of the quality of their hermeneutical activities. Here, it is

41 On *takhrīj* and the *mukharrijūn* (=*aṣḥāb al-takhrīj*), see chapter 2, section III, below.

42 Probably ᶜAlī b. Aḥmad Ḥusām al-Dīn al-Rāzī who died in 593/1196. See Ibn Quṭlūbughā, *Tāj al-Tarājim*, 42.

43 Shaykh al-Islām Burhān al-Dīn ᶜAlī b. Abī Bakr al-Marghīnānī (d. 593/1197). For his biography, see *al-Hidāya: Sharḥ Bidāyat al-Mubtadī*, 4 vols. (Cairo: Muṣṭafā Bābī al-Ḥalabī, n.d.), I, 3–9.

44 Ibn Quṭlūbughā, *Tāj al-Tarājim*, 7. 45 Ibid., 13. 46 Ibid., 31.

47 Carl Brockelmann, *Geschichte der arabischen Literatur*, 2 vols. (Leiden: E. J. Brill, 1943–49); 3 supplements (Leiden: E. J. Brill, 1937–42), suppl. 1, 646.

48 Ibn Quṭlūbughā, *Tāj al-Tarājim*, 6.

significant that they appear in the role of author–jurists as much as they are seen as *mujtahid*s or *muqallid*s.)

Finally, the seventh rank contains the lowliest *muqallid*s, including those who are poorly trained jurists, or who are incapable of "differentiating right from left."[49]

## V

Now let us examine the significance of these typologies within the context of our enquiry. We begin by noting two important anomalies. The first may be found in Ibn al-Ṣalāḥ's discussion of the first type of his category 2, which, incidentally, he does not label. Jurists of this type are neither founders nor followers, strictly speaking. He explicitly states that this type follows the imam neither in his *madhhab* nor in his methods and legal reasoning (*lā yakūnu muqallidan li-Imāmihi, lā fī al-madhhab wa-lā fī dalīlihi*).[50] If this is the case, then why should they even be included? The answer, I believe, lies in the unique history of the Shāfiʿite school, which appears to have been later consolidated by Ibn Surayj by incorporating into the school tradition the doctrines of a number of independent *mujtahid*s whose connection to Shāfiʿī seems tenuous. It should be noted that no trace of this ambiguous type can be found in either the Ḥanafite or the Mālikite typologies we have discussed here. In the latter, its absence is clear since Mālik and his associates are classed as indistinguishable equals in what would have otherwise been Ibn Rushd's fourth group. In the former typology, the second rank of jurists such as Abū Yūsuf, Shaybānī, and their peers follow Abū Ḥanīfa's path.

The second anomaly is Ibn Rushd's inverted classification, which begins with low-grade *muqallid*s and ends with *mujtahid*s par excellence, despite the fact that these latter, regardless of their legal creativity, ultimately operated within the boundaries of the Mālikite school. By contrast, Ibn al-Ṣalāḥ's and Ibn Kamāl's typologies begin with the highest ranked *mujtahid*s and descend to the lowest ranks.

It is undeniable that Ibn Rushd's inverted classification represents a deviation from the form of juristic taxonomy that dominated Islamic culture. All biographical and semi-biographical works dealing with jurists, theologians, traditionists, and others follow the chronological format, thus rendering Ibn Rushd's classification all the more anomalous. One possible explanation of this anomaly is the provenance of Ibn Rushd's typology, which seems to be one of, if not in fact, the earliest. Indeed, the

[49] Qurashī, *al-Jawāhir al-Muḍī'a*, 559. [50] Ibn al-Ṣalāḥ, *Adab al-Muftī*, 91.

juristic biographical tradition itself appears to have begun no earlier than a century or so before Ibn Rushd, which makes the argument in favor of his unprecedented typology quite persuasive.[51]

Because it is so early, Ibn Rushd's typology manifests a relatively weaker form of loyalty to the school tradition than later became the norm. An inverted typology conceptually and structurally tends to downgrade hierarchical authority, or, at the very least, is not acutely conscious of such an authority. The absence from it of any chronological element amounts to a virtual weakening of the chain of authority that mediates between the founding imam and his followers throughout the centuries. It should not be surprising then that Ibn Rushd does not elaborate a system of authority which is derivative in nature. Instead, the authority which is the focus of his typology is almost entirely hermeneutical. The types he elaborates are independent of each other, and are markedly disconnected in terms of an authoritative structure. Mālik "and his associates" are not introduced as a "group" in his classification, although, admittedly, they are constantly invoked. This omission may have been dictated by the nature of the question he was asked, although it remains true that the founding imam's distinct and prestigious status as advocated by both Ibn al-Ṣalāḥ and Ibn Kamāl is virtually absent from Ibn Rushd's scheme. It suffices to recall here his assertion that "the attributes of the *muftī* which he should fulfill do not change with the changing of times,"[52] implying that Mālik and his associates as well as all later *mujtahid*s of the third group (type) are equal in juristic competence.

The temporal proximity of Ibn Rushd to the final crystallization of the law schools, especially of Andalusian Mālikism, was a decisive factor that affected not only the degree to which the taxonomy was made elaborate, but also the historical consciousness that undergirded such a taxonomy. Whereas taxonomic elaborateness and historical consciousness are qualities largely absent from Ibn Rushd's typology, they dominate those of Ibn al-Ṣalāḥ and Ibn Kamāl. Ibn al-Ṣalāḥ wrote more than two centuries and a half after the formation of the Shāfiʿite school in the east, when a historical pattern of developments had by then become fairly clear. By his time, and certainly by Ibn Kamāl's day, historical consciousness of legal evolution, the structure of authority, and hermeneutical activity had become well defined. This consciousness is nearly absent from Ibn Rushd, obvious in Ibn al-Ṣalāḥ, and elaborate in Ibn Kamāl.

Ibn al-Ṣalāḥ's fifth type, which he introduces rather informally – leaving it extraneous to the typology itself – has its equivalent in Ibn

[51] See n. 2, above. [52] Wansharīsī, *al-Miʿyār al-Mughrib*, X, 34.

Kamāl's seventh and last rank, a rank not only articulated in a deliberate and conscious manner, but also formally integral to the typology. Furthermore, in what is equivalent to Ibn al-Ṣalāḥ's second type, Ibn Kamāl distinguished two ranks, one able to perform *ijtihād* in individual questions, the other limited to conducting *takhrīj*. In Ibn al-Ṣalāḥ both activities belong to the same type. This leaves us with the following parallels between the Shāfiʿite and Ḥanafite typologies: Category 1 equals rank 1; type 1 (of category 2) equals rank 2; type 3 equals rank 5; and type 4 equals rank 6.

Further comparison shows that Ibn al-Ṣalāḥ's category 1 and the first type of category 2, and Ibn Kamāl's ranks 1 and 2, are equivalent to what would have been Ibn Rushd's fourth group, although this must remain a matter for speculation. This is so because Ibn Rushd appears to deny the founding fathers any special characteristic, arguing in effect that later *mujtahid*s are no less qualified than these were. Admittedly, later *mujtahid*s are found to be affiliated, yet their *ijtihād* can often differ from that of the masters of the schools. With this affiliation in mind, Ibn Rushd's third group would then be equivalent to Ibn al-Ṣalāḥ's types 1 and 2. The second group is even less qualified, encompassing Ibn al-Ṣalāḥ's types 3, 4, and possibly 5. The first group would then be equivalent to Ibn al-Ṣalāḥ's type 5, with the difference that Ibn Rushd does not see them as entitled to issue *fatwā*s.

Perhaps the most salient feature of these typologies, especially the Shāfiʿite and Ḥanafite varieties, is that they sketch the diachronic and synchronic contours of Islamic legal history generally, and the development of the respective schools in particular. They sketch this history in terms of the authority and scope of hermeneutical activity, two separate domains that are nonetheless intimately interconnected. Interpretive activity may be more or less authoritative, and its scope may also be wide or narrow. But in Islamic legal history they stand in a relationship of correlation, for higher hermeneutical authority brings along with it a wider range of interpretive activity. The most absolute form of these two domains was the lot of the founding imams. As time went on, increasing numbers of jurists were to claim less and less competency in these domains. Indeed, diminishing returns in both authority and hermeneutics went hand in hand with an increasing dependency on former authority, although to a lesser extent on earlier *corpora* of interpretation. Synchronically, therefore, the function of these typologies is not only to describe, justify, and rationalize juristic activities of the past but also, and more importantly, to construct the history of the school as a structure of authority which is tightly interconnected in all its constituents. The structure that emerges is both hierarchical and pyramidical. In synchronic terms, then, the achievement is represented in the creation of a pedigree of authority that binds the school together as a guild.

Diachronically, the typologies justify the tradition in which the *muftīs* were viewed as founders of law schools as well as the sustainers of a continuous activity that connected the past with the present. But the connection was also made in concrete terms. The hermeneutics of one type or rank represented a legacy to the succeeding type and rank, a legacy to be accepted, articulated, elaborated, and further refined. The process began with absolute *ijtihād*, passing through more limited *ijtihād*, descending to *takhrīj*, and then ultimately *tarjīḥ* and other forms of interpretive activity. Participating at each of these stages was a group of identifiable jurists. Ibn Kamāl, for instance, recognized particular jurists as belonging to each of the ranks he proffered.

The typologies also function on the synchronic level, for they at once describe and justify the activities of *muftīs* both at and before the time that each typology, as a discursive strategy, came into being. For Ibn Rushd, the three groups he recognized were still active in his time; this is not only clear but indeed demonstrable, for Ibn Rushd himself was a supreme *mujtahid* in his own right.[53] To the exclusion of the first category of his typology, and perhaps the first type of the second, Ibn al-Ṣalāḥ's scheme also justifies and describes the range of juristic activities that prevailed during his time. Ibn Kamāl's typology, on the other hand, is more diachronically bound, and thus seems on the surface to be less susceptible to synchronic justification. Nonetheless, as in the case of Ibn al-Ṣalāḥ, ranks 5 to 7 did exist at all times subsequent to the formative period, and 3, and 4 could have conceivably existed at any time. Only ranks 1 and 2, being foundational, are unique, and thus represent a phenomenon that cannot be found repeated in later centuries.

The typologies may also serve as a description of the range of activities of a single jurist. The more accomplished the jurist, the greater the number of activities, across two or more types, in which he might have been involved. No doubt jurists operated within a system of authority, which means that *taqlīd* constituted the great majority of the cases with which they had to deal. But jurists of high caliber, such as Ibn al-Ṣalāḥ himself and Nawawī (as well as al-ᶜIzz Ibn ᶜAbd al-Salām [d. 660/1262] and, later, Taqī al-Dīn al-Subkī [d. 756/1355]) did deal with less common, rare, and difficult cases which required juristic competence of a more sophisticated, *ijtihād*ic type. Such jurists (including Ibn Kamāl

[53] See n. 11, above.

and Shaykh al-Islām Abū al-Suᶜūd [d. 982/1574]) did function at several levels. In Ibn al-Ṣalāḥ's classification, these latter operated as type 2 through 5, and possibly even type 1 jurists. In Ibn Kamāl's typology, they operated on the level of ranks 3–7. This multi-level functioning is partly attested by Ibn Kamāl's citation of names as examples of jurists who represented certain ranks. Marghīnānī, for instance, is cited as active at ranks 4 and 5, and Karkhī at ranks 3 and 4. We can easily assume that in Karkhī's case, he mastered all ranks between, and including, 3 and 7.

Karkhī's case is also instructive insofar as it demonstrates the interplay between *ijtihād* and *taqlīd*, both of which here acquire a multiplicity of meanings. For the *ijtihād* associated with rank 3 (the *mujtahid* in individual cases) is qualitatively different from that required in rank 4, and this, in turn, is to be differentiated from its counterparts in ranks 1, 2, and 5. Similarly, *taqlīd* operates on several levels. Ibn Kamāl's second rank is bound by *taqlīd* to the imam, but the quality of the *taqlīd* found there is entirely unlike that found, for instance, in rank 4, and certainly unrelated to that which ranks 6 and 7 practice. Thus, while *ijtihād* succeeds in maintaining a positive image, even in the middle ranks, *taqlīd* is, on one level, clearly a desirable practice in the higher ranks and an undesirable one in rank 7. Ibn al-Ṣalāḥ's informal fifth type also shares the same negative image, although Ibn al-Ṣalāḥ seems more charitable than Ibn Kamāl.[54] I say "on one level," because the level on which *taqlīd* is considered negative is one which is defined in terms of intellectual competence, accomplishment, and learning. On another level, *taqlīd* maintains a positive meaning, even in the lowest of ranks and types. This is the meaning of affiliation to the *madhhab*, a relationship in which the jurists of all ranks and types make a commitment to learn its doctrines, improve on them when possible, and defend them at all times. Adherence to the *madhhab* and an active defense of it constitute, respectively, the minimal and maximal forms of loyalty, and both represent varying levels of positive forms and meanings of *taqlīd*.

The positive senses of *taqlīd* transcend the province of *taqlīd* itself as narrowly defined, for if *ijtihād* has a positive image, it is ultimately because of the fact that it is backed up by *taqlīd*. To put it more precisely, except for the category (or type) of the imam, *ijtihād* would be an undesirable practice if it were not for *taqlīd*, for this latter perpetuates *ijtihād* which is quintessentially a creative, independent, and therefore

[54] It is in the sense where it is applied by jurists of the lower ranks that *taqlīd* was condemned. See chapter 4, section I, below.

positive activity. The only way the imams could have been conceived as establishing their schools was through absolute *ijtihād*, and if *ijtihād* were to continue to operate in the same absolute fashion in the absence of *taqlīd*, then there would have been no schools but a multitude of independent *mujtahids*. Thus it was *taqlīd* with respect to the imams' *ijtihād* that guaranteed the survival of the four schools, and, therefore, loyalty to them. *Taqlīd* was a necessary agent of mediating authority, and it was therefore a quality that permeated all types and ranks, except, of course, the first.[55]

It follows, therefore, that these typologies present us with a variety of layers of juristic activity, each of which involves the participation of one or more types of jurists. The elements we have identified are as follows:

(1) *Ijtihād*, which was, to varying degrees, the province of all jurists except those of the lower-middle and lowest ranks. In chapter 4 we shall encounter cases of *taqlīd* that bordered, if not encroached upon, the province of *ijtihād*. But equally importantly, we shall attempt to demonstrate, in chapter 2, that even the *ijtihād* of the founders, presumably absolute and wholly creative, fell short, in the final analysis, of such high and idealistic expectations.

(2) *Takhrīj*, a creative activity that involves a limited form of *ijtihād* whereby the jurist confronts the already established opinions of the imam and those of his immediate *mujtahid*-followers, not the revealed texts themselves. This activity, which resulted in a repertoire of new opinions, engaged jurists of the higher ranks, mostly those who came on the heels of the imams and of the early masters, but also, to a limited extent, a number of later jurists. The reasoning involved in *takhrīj* and its role in the early formation of the schools will be taken up in the second half of chapter 2.

(3) *Tarjīḥ* and all other forms of making certain opinions preponderant over others is an activity that engages, once again, the middle types, excluding the founders and the lowest rung of jurists. As we shall see in chapters 5 and 6, this activity was responsible for determining the authoritative opinions of the school at any stage of its history. This determination, which was to change from one period to another, was in turn itself instrumental in effecting legal change.

(4) *Taqlīd*, which is the province of jurists of all types and ranks, except, presumably, the first. For the sake of our analysis, we shall look at this activity as consisting of mainly two functions, depending on which sort of jurist is making use of it. The first is the function of maintaining authority within the *madhhab*, or, to put it differently, of maintaining loyalty. In this activity, jurists of the lower echelons are usually involved. The second function is that of defending the *madhhab*, an activity that engages the attention of the jurists belonging to the middle ranks and types. The founders and eponyms, by

[55] However, we shall in due course be compelled to question this theoretical postulate.

definition, had supposedly[56] no tradition to defend, while the lowest-ranking jurists were deemed intellectually and juristically incapable of putting forth a defense of the doctrines of their *madhhab*. In chapter 2 we shall challenge the typological assumption that ascribed to the founding imams such absolute originality. On the other hand, in chapter 4 we shall likewise show that *taqlīd* of the lowest form also involved defense of the *madhhab*.

(5) *Taṣnīf*, the activity of the author–jurist which characterizes all ranks and types except the lowest. This activity is not explicitly articulated in the typologies, but constitutes, nonetheless, a major feature in them. It is obliquely mentioned in ranks 4, 5, and 6 of Ibn Kamāl's typology, and in type 3 of Ibn al-Ṣalāḥ's. But it is assumed that all other higher ranks and types partook in the activity of writing. The author–jurist, therefore, emerges as a significant player in the field of juristic hermeneutics, whether as an absolute *mujtahid*, limited *mujtahid*, or even as a *muqallid* of the middle types. In chapter 6 we shall show the central role that the author–jurist played in sanctioning and formalizing legal change.

These typologies also enable us to identify four major players: the *muqallid*, the *muftī*, the *mujtahid*, and the author–jurist (*muṣannif*). None of these functions, as we have seen, constitutes an independent entity existing in complete isolation from the others. Indeed, each of these functions represents an activity that encroaches, at one level or another, upon the rest. The *muqallid* can be, though not in every case, by turns a *muftī*, a *mujtahid* of sorts, and an author. By the same token, a *mujtahid*, except theoretically in the case of an imam, can be a *muqallid*, and is always a *muftī* and, nearly always,[57] an author. The *muftī* can be a *muqallid*, an author, and a *mujtahid*. Similarly, the author can be a *muqallid*, a *mujtahid*, and a *muftī*, often at one and the same time.

Markedly absent from these typologies and from the discourse that informed them (with the partial exception of Ibn Rushd's) is the *qāḍī*. In chapters 3 and 6 we shall attempt to address the import of this omission when we discuss the hermeneutics which the *qāḍī*'s function involved.

56 See chapter 2, section II, below.

57 Among the four imams, Aḥmad Ibn Ḥanbal was the only one who was not an author–jurist. Shams al-Dīn Ibn Qayyim al-Jawziyya, a Ḥanbalite himself, acknowledges that Ibn Ḥanbal "disliked writing books" (*wa-kāna raḍiya Allāhu ʿanhu shadīda al-karāhiya li-taṣnīfi al-kutub*). See his *Iʿlām al-Muwaqqiʿīn ʿan Rabb al-ʿĀlamīn*, ed. Muḥammad ʿAbd al-Ḥamīd, 4 vols. (Beirut: al-Maṭbaʿa al-ʿAṣriyya, 1407/1987), I, 28. However, all Ibn Ḥanbal's immediate followers engaged in writing, as was the case with the followers of the other imams. See the last part of section II, chapter 2, below.

## 2

# EARLY *IJTIHĀD* AND THE LATER CONSTRUCTION OF AUTHORITY

## I

The creation of an archetype, i.e., an ideal authoritative model or standard to which all other types must conform or emulate, is undeniably a prime concern of juristic typologies. In the case of Islamic law, this archetype is the absolute *mujtahid* whose legal knowledge, presumed to be all-encompassing and wholly creative, is causally connected with the founding of a school. The school is not only named after him, but he is purported to have been its originator. The comprehensive and wide-ranging knowledge attributed to the absolute *mujtahid* is matched only by his assumed in-depth knowledge of, among other things, legal methodology or *uṣūl al-fiqh* (which is by necessity of his own creation), Quranic exegesis, *ḥadīth* criticism, the theory of abrogation, legal language, positive and substantive law, arithmetic, and the science of juristic disagreement.

The salient feature of the founders' *ijtihād*ic activity is no doubt the direct confrontation with the revealed texts, for it is only this deified involvement with the divine word that requires and presupposes thorough familiarity with so many important fields of knowledge. Even when certain cases require reasoning on the basis of established legal rules and derivative principles, the founding jurist's hermeneutic is held to be, in the final analysis, thoroughly grounded in the revealed texts. The founder's doctrine constitutes therefore the only purely juristic manifestation of the legal potentiality of revealed language. Without it, in other words, revelation would remain just that, revelation, lacking any articulation in it of the legal element. His doctrine lays claim to originality not only because it derives directly from the texts, but also because it is gleaned systematically, by means of clearly identifiable principles, from these sources. Its systematic character is seen as a product of a unified and cohesive methodology which only the founder could have forged; but a methodology, it must be asserted, that is itself inspired and dictated by revelation.

Now, what is striking about this typological conception of the founder *mujtahid* is its absoluteness not only in terms of credentials or epistemic, and indeed moral, authority,[1] but also in terms of chronological rupture with antecedents. At the juncture of this rupture, the precise point at which the most accomplished type of *mujtahid* is formed, the typology suffers from a memory loss, overlooking in the process the existence in reality of the founder's predecessors and his own immediate intellectual history. For it was with the latter that the *mujtahid*–imams formed a continuity, and of the former that they were necessarily a product. In the constructed typology, as perceived by the later legal profession, the founders became disconnected from previous generations of jurists as well as from a variety of historical processes that indeed culminated in the very achievements of the imams.[2]

## II

The following pages argue that this rupture did in fact take place and that it was certainly strategic and by no means fortuitous. As jurists, the founding fathers were highly accomplished, but not as absolutely and as categorically as they were made out to be. Dissociating them from the achievements of their past was only one of many ways to increase their prestige and augment the resumé of their accomplishments. But

[1] That the founders' authority also contained a strong moral element is abundantly attested by the *manāqib* literature. See, for instance, Aḥmad b. Ḥusayn Abū Bakr al-Bayhaqī, *Manāqib al-Shāfiʿī*, ed. Aḥmad Ṣaqr, 2 vols. (Cairo: Maktabat Dār al-Turāth, 1971), I, 260–385, 486–550, and passim; Shams al-Dīn Muḥammad b. Muḥammad al-Rāʿī, *Instiṣār al-Faqīr al-Sālik li-Tarjīḥ Madhhab al-Imām Mālik*, ed. Muḥammad Abū al-Ajfān (Beirut: Dār al-Gharb al-Islāmī, 1981), 139 ff., 167 ff., 173 ff.; Muḥammad b. Yūsuf al-Ṣāliḥī, *ʿUqūd al-Jummān fī Manāqib al-Imām al-Aʿẓam Abī Ḥanīfa al-Nuʿmān* (Hyderabad: Maṭbaʿat al-Maʿārif, 1394/1974), 211–31, 239–96. On epistemic and moral authority, see sources cited in the preface, n. 1.

[2] Shams al-Dīn b. Shihāb al-Dīn al-Ramlī, *Nihāyat al-Muḥtāj ilā Sharḥ al-Minhāj*, 8 vols. (Cairo: Muṣṭafā Bābī al-Ḥalabī, 1357/1938; repr. Beirut: Dār Iḥyā' al-Turāth al-ʿArabī, 1939), I, 41, reports, on the authority of Ibn al-Ṣalāḥ, that none other than the four imams may be followed, either in the issuing of *fatwā*s or in courtroom litigation. Representing the authority of school affiliation, this opinion of Ibn al-Ṣalāḥ became widely accepted by many later jurists of all four schools. Ḥaṭṭāb, *Mawāhib al-Jalīl*, I, 30, quotes Ibn al-Ṣalāḥ's statement and enhances it with another by Ghazālī (p. 31) who declares the founders' and schools' legal doctrines superior to those of earlier jurists. See also ʿAbd al-Raḥmān b. Muḥammad Bāʿalawī, *Bughyat al-Mustarshidīn fī Talkhīṣ Fatāwā baʿḍ al-A'imma min al-ʿUlamā' al-Muta'akhkhirīn* (Cairo: Muṣṭafā Bābī al-Ḥalabī, 1952), 274.

it was perhaps the only way to construct their supreme authority. True, they were *mujtahids* – or some of them were, at any rate – but not without qualification and certainly not absolutely. We shall try to show that none of them exercised *ijtihād* across the board, in each and every case they addressed or opinion they held. Indeed, we shall attempt to demonstrate that many of the opinions they held were inherited from other authorities.

Let us begin with Ḥanafism. In this school, and wholly in line with Ibn Kamāl's typology as we earlier outlined it,[3] the limits of hermeneutical activity were set by the imposition of a hierarchical taxonomy of legal authority,[4] at the top of which stood the doctrines of Abū Ḥanīfa (d. 150/767) and, immediately following, those of Abū Yūsuf (d. 182/798) and Shaybānī (d. 189/804).[5] Embodied in written narratives, these doctrines, known as *ẓāhir al-riwāya*, were transmitted through several channels by trustworthy and highly qualified jurists. A marginal number of cases (*masā'il*) belonging to the category of *ẓāhir al-riwāya* were also attributed to Zufar and al-Ḥasan b. Ziyād, two of Abū Ḥanīfa's foremost students.[6] Now, these doctrines were deemed binding, and no later *mujtahid*, however qualified he may have been, was permitted to reinterpret or diverge from them. For the Ḥanafites, they represented not only the highest authority in the school, but were chronologically the earliest. Some doctrines belonging to the later *mujtahids* were also deemed authoritative, but, in theory at least, they were second in prestige and were interpreted in light of the principles that Abū Ḥanīfa and his two distinguished students elaborated.[7]

Despite the authority which Abū Ḥanīfa carried as the eponym and ultimate founder of the school, its jurists could not wholly deny the

3 Chapter 1, section IV, above.

4 Fakhr al-Dīn Ḥasan b. Manṣūr al-Ūzajandī Qāḍīkhān, *Fatāwā Qāḍīkhān*, printed on the margins of *al-Fatāwā al-Hindiyya*, ed. and comp. al-Shaykh al-Niẓām et al., 6 vols., as vols. I–III (repr.; Beirut: Dār Iḥyā' al-Turāth al-ʿArabī, 1400/1980), I, 3; Wael B. Hallaq, "From *Fatwā*s to *Furūʿ*: Growth and Change in Islamic Substantive Law," *Islamic Law and Society*, 1 (February 1994): 39.

5 The fact that in terms of hierarchical authority Abū Ḥanīfa stood first did not mean that his opinion had precedence in all cases. When, for example, the two disciples held the same view, and the master held another, the jurist was allowed to adopt the opinion of the disciples. See ʿUmar b. ʿAbd al-ʿAzīz al-Ḥusām al-Shahīd Ibn Māza, *Sharḥ Adab al-Qāḍī*, ed. Abū al-Wafā al-Afghānī and Muḥammad Hāshimī (Beirut: Dār al-Kutub al-ʿIlmiyya, 1414/1994), 20. For various Ḥanafite opinions on the matter, see Ibn ʿĀbidīn, *Sharḥ al-Manẓūma*, 14 ff.

6 On ranking the five Ḥanafite masters in terms of hierarchical doctrinal authority, see ʿAlā' al-Dīn Muḥammad ʿAlī al-Ḥaṣkafī (al-ʿAlā'ī), *al-Durr al-Mukhtār*, printed with Ibn ʿĀbidīn's *Ḥāshiya*, I, 70–71.

7 Ibn ʿĀbidīn, *Ḥāshiya*, I, 70 ff.

obvious fact that Ḥanafite law, as it originated with Abū Ḥanīfa, owes a certain debt to his predecessors.[8] But this debt and the legal doctrine that it represented carried no real authority. In fact, the authorities from whom Abū Ḥanīfa appropriated his doctrine never formally entered into the orbit of authoritative doctrine, as schematized in the hierarchy of Ḥanafite law. As we have seen, the highest authoritative form of this law *begins* with Abū Ḥanīfa, not with anyone earlier. Furthermore, it is to be stressed that this recognition of indebtedness to the past was highly nominal, originating as it did in the desire to increase the founder's prestige and authority by the construction and articulation of a pedigree extending back, through the Followers and Companions, to the Prophet. Nevertheless, there is much historical truth to this construction. The Ḥanafite jurists articulated a genealogy, elegantly stated in both prose and verse, indicating the extent of Abū Ḥanīfa's debt: *Fiqh*, they said, "was planted by ᶜAbd Allāh Ibn Masᶜūd, irrigated by ᶜAlqama, harvested by Ibrāhīm al-Nakhaᶜī, threshed by Ḥammād, milled by Abū Ḥanīfa, kneaded by Abū Yūsuf, and baked by Shaybānī. The Muslims are nourished by his bread."[9]

The real debt owed to pre-Ḥanafite sources, on the one hand, and the construction of Abū Ḥanīfa's authority, on the other, created in Ḥanafism a serious doctrinal conflict. This conflict manifested itself in the emergence of a duality of doctrinal orientation. In a report classified as having the highest authority in the school, Abū Ḥanīfa is said to have remarked: "I refuse to follow (*uqallidu*) the Followers because they were men who practiced *ijtihād* and I am a man who practices *ijtihād*" (the Followers in this case being his immediate predecessors). Yet in another report which was relegated, in terms of authority, to a secondary status, Abū Ḥanīfa is said to have maintained the opposite view, accepting in particular the doctrines of the senior authorities among the Followers.[10]

These two contradictory reports raise a couple of important issues. The first is what their ranking was in terms of school authority. The anti-*taqlīd* position of the Followers emerged as superior to the other, a fact which attests to the dominance of the authority-construction process

[8] See, for instance, Abū Muḥammad Maḥmūd b. Aḥmad al-ᶜAynī, *al-Bināya fī Sharḥ al-Hidāya*, 12 vols. (Beirut: Dār al-Fikr, 1980), I, 52, who argues that the later commentators understood Marghīnānī's phrase "early reasoners" (*awā'il al-mustanbiṭīn*) to refer to Abū Ḥanīfa and his two students. He argues that the phrase was meant in a general way so as to include jurists earlier than Abū Ḥanīfa.

[9] Ibn ᶜAbidīn, *Ḥāshiya*, I, 49–50. The verse runs as follows: "*al-fiqhu zarᶜu bni Masᶜūdi wa-ᶜAlqamatu / ḥaṣṣāduhu thumma Ibrāhīmu dawwāsu; Nuᶜmānu ṭāḥinuhu Yaᶜqūbu ᶜājinuhu / Muḥammadun khābizu wal-ākilu al-nāsu.*"

[10] Ibn Māza, *Sharḥ Adab al-Qāḍī*, 19.

over acknowledgment of the debt to predecessors. The second is the relationship between these positions, on the one hand, and Abū Ḥanīfa's substantive law, on the other. The later Ḥanafites argued that the second position justified Abū Ḥanīfa's debt to the generation that immediately preceded him; whereas the first showed that when his opinions were identical to those held by the predecessors, it was because his otherwise independent *ijtihād* corresponded with theirs. It was further argued that this correspondence enhanced Abū Ḥanīfa's opinions and lent them added support and authority.[11] The focus, therefore, is Abū Ḥanīfa: authority resided in him however things might turn out, and whether or not he owed his predecessors any debt. If he adopted none of their opinions, then his authority as an independent *mujtahid* and a founder was categorically confirmed, and if he did in fact adopt them, then due to the authority bestowed upon him by Followers such as Nakhaᶜī (d. 96/714) and Ḥammād (d. 120/737), his authority as a *mujtahid* who reached conclusions identical to his predecessors was also confirmed.

As Abū Ḥanīfa's teacher, Ḥammād figures prominently in the former's doctrine. He, and to a lesser extent several others, appear either as links to earlier authorities, or as the ultimate reference. In a certain case pertaining to prayer, for instance, Abū Ḥanīfa explicitly adopts Ḥammād's opinion as his own.[12] The list of his indebtedness to Ḥammād can run long.[13] In another case involving prayer under threat (*ṣalāt al-khawf*), he espouses Nakhaᶜī's opinion, which the latter seems to have inherited in his turn from ᶜAbd Allāh Ibn ᶜAbbās (d. 68/687).[14] As a matter of interest, we should also note that Ibn Abī Laylā (d. 148/765), another presumably absolute *mujtahid* and an Iraqian authority, disagrees with Abū Ḥanīfa and upholds ᶜAṭā' b. Rabāḥ's opinion.[15] Here, both *mujtahid*s defer to earlier authorities. In addition to Ḥammād and Ibrāhīm al-Nakhaᶜī, ᶜAbd Allāh b. Jaᶜfar appears, to a lesser extent, as one of Abū Ḥanīfa's authorities.[16] Likewise, Ibn Abī Laylā's *ijtihād*ic authorities include al-Ḥakam, the Medinese jurists, and even Abū Ḥanīfa himself.[17] In a case involving preemption, for instance, he first adopted Abū Ḥanīfa's view then renounced it in favor of another opinion held by the Hijazi

[11] Ibid.
[12] Muḥammad b. Idrīs al-Shāfiᶜī, *Kitāb Ikhtilāf al-ᶜIrāqiyyīn*, in his *al-Umm*, ed. Maḥmūd Maṭarjī, 9 vols. (Beirut: Dār al-Kutub al-ᶜIlmiyya, 1413/1993), VII, 211.
[13] See, for instance, ibid., VII, 184–85 (a case of *wadīᶜa*), 218, 219 (cases of prayer), 223 (ritual purity), 230 (blood-money), and passim.
[14] Ibid., VII, 214.
[15] Ibid. ᶜAṭā' b. Rabāḥ (d. 114 or 115/732 or 733) was a Meccan jurist.
[16] See, e.g., ibid., VII, 237. [17] Ibid., VII, 176, 218, 227, 233.

jurists.[18] Abū Yūsuf, a companion of Abū Ḥanīfa and a student of his, also espoused certain of Ibn Abī Laylā's opinions.[19] In two penal cases, Shaybānī espouses opinions originally held by Nakhaᶜī and Ḥammād, but apparently passed on to him by Abū Ḥanīfa.[20]

Abū Yūsuf's and Shaybānī's doctrines can thus be attributed to three distinctly different sources: Abū Ḥanīfa's *ijtihād*ic teachings, the inherited tradition of other, mainly earlier, jurists, and their own *ijtihād*. Since both authorities were considered by the Ḥanafite school as carrying nearly equal weight to that of Abū Ḥanīfa himself, it becomes obvious that the latter cannot, in reality, be considered the school's actual founder. He owed as much, or nearly as much, to his predecessors as his two distinguished students owed to him. He was no more a founder or even an absolute *mujtahid* than were his immediate predecessors and younger contemporaries, such as Abū Yūsuf, Shaybānī, and al-Ḥasan b. Ziyād.

The evolution of Abū Ḥanīfa's authority as the most important figure in the school is best exemplified in the transformation that took place in the case of the tithe levied on cultivated land. Abū Yūsuf reports on the authority of Ibrāhīm al-Nakhaᶜī, through Ḥammād, that whatever grows on land, however small or large, is subject to a tithe. Abū Yūsuf then adds that Abū Ḥanīfa adopted this opinion (*kāna Abū Ḥanīfa ya'khudh bi-hādhā al-qawl*).[21] The later jurist Sarakhsī presents the matter as follows:

> The basis of the duty to pay tithe is God's statement [2:267]: "Spend of the good things which ye have earned, and of that which we bring forth from the earth for you." The meaning of "earned" is material wealth on which the alms-tax is paid. The meaning of the statement "that which we bring forth from the earth for you" is tithe. God also said [6:142]: "And pay the due thereof upon the harvest day." Likewise, the Prophet said: "Whatever land produces is subject to tithe."

[18] Ibid., VII, 176.

[19] Ibid., VII, 230. Abū Yūsuf's authority was likewise constructed by means of making him the only teacher of al-Ḥusayn b. Ḥafṣ who is reported to have introduced Ḥanafism to Iṣfahān, when in fact the latter studied under twenty-three scholars. Abū Yūsuf thus becomes the sole authority from which Iṣfahānī Ḥanafism was derived. Moreover, al-Ḥusayn studied only *ḥadīth* with Abū Yūsuf, but later sources claim the latter to have been his teacher of law. See N. Tsafrir, "The Beginnings of the Ḥanafī School in Iṣfahān," *Islamic Law and Society*, 5, 1 (1998): 2–3.

[20] Muḥammad b. al-Ḥasan al-Shaybānī, *Kitāb al-Aṣl al-Maᶜrūf bil-Mabsūṭ*, ed. Abū al-Wafā al-Afghānī, 5 vols. (Beirut: ᶜĀlam al-Kutub, 1990), IV, 439, 477. For other cases where Abū Yūsuf and Shaybānī followed the opinions of the Medinese and other jurists, see Ibn ᶜĀbidīn, *Sharḥ al-Manẓūma*, 1–53, at 31; Ibn ᶜĀbidīn, *Ḥāshiya*, I, 75.

[21] Yaᶜqūb b. Ibrāhīm Abū Yūsuf, *Kitāb al-Kharāj* (Beirut and Cairo: Dār al-Sharq, 1405/1985), 158.

> Abū Ḥanīfa's principle is that whatever grows in gardens and is meant to be cultivated of the land is subject to tithe, be it cereals, legumes, dates, herbs, chlorophyta (*wasma*), saffron, roses or dyeing plants (*wars*).[22] This is also the opinion of Ibn ʿAbbās. It is reported that when he was governor of Baṣra, he imposed the tithe on legumes, levying one measuring unit out of ten. Abū Ḥanīfa rationalized this opinion by the general Prophetic tradition "Whatever the heavens water and whatever the land produces is subject to tithe." He held the opinion that tithe, like *kharāj*, is an encumbrance on cultivable land. Just as the development of the land gives rise to the levy of *kharāj*, so does it give rise to tithe.[23]

Note here that Nakhaʿī, who appears in Abū Yūsuf as the original, authoritative source of the doctrine, has been entirely removed from Sarakhsī's reconstruction, and instead replaced by a cluster of revealed statements supplemented by the authority of Ibn ʿAbbās, a Companion. The function of inserting this authority subsequent to the Quranic and Apostolic citations is to give the otherwise unspecific and highly general stipulations of the Quran a clearly defined and precise meaning, a meaning that is determined by Ibn ʿAbbās's concrete practice. Thus, the latter's supplementary report is an exegetical exercise which permits the clarification and delimitation of the legal significance of the two Quranic verses.

In this passage, two more points are to be noted: on the one hand, there is a presentation of the revealed subject matter together with Sarakhsī's annotation; on the other, there is Abū Ḥanīfa and his opinion. The logical sequence of how authority proceeds directly from revelation to Abū Ḥanīfa's reasoning (partly manifested in the analogy with *kharāj*) becomes crystal clear. In this exercise of authority reconstruction, Sarakhsī erases the debt to Nakhaʿī, thereby dissipating the latter's authority altogether. Abū Ḥanīfa, on the other hand, emerges as the first and direct interpreter of revelation par excellence, a necessary condition of an absolute *mujtahid* and founder of a school.

At this juncture, a natural question poses itself perforce: Why did Abū Ḥanīfa – not Nakhaʿī, Ḥammād, or, for that matter, Abū Yūsuf or Shaybānī – become credited with founding the school, and henceforth achieve the status of an absolute *mujtahid*? A comprehensive answer cannot be offered at this point in time, especially as to the choice of Abū Ḥanīfa as putative founder of his school (or the choice of any of the other

[22] The *wasma* and *wars* are south Arabian plants whose leaves are used as dyes, the former imparting a green pigment and the latter a yellow one. See Jamāl al-Dīn Ibn Manẓūr, *Lisān al-ʿArab*, 15 vols. (repr.; Beirut: Dār Ṣādir, 1972), VI, 254, XII, 637.

[23] Muḥammad b. Aḥmad Abū Sahl al-Sarakhsī, *al-Mabsūṭ*, 30 vols. (Cairo: Maṭbaʿat al-Saʿāda, 1324–31/1906–12), III, 2.

presumed founders), given the state of our present knowledge. But it is fairly clear that Abū Ḥanīfa's rise to a status of founder had to do with the emergence of the concept of authority in law. In view of the near total aloofness of the state and of any of its organs from the domain of law, legal authority had to be anchored in a source, and this source was the arch-jurist as an individual legal personality. In other words, we cannot at this juncture explain why Abū Ḥanīfa specifically and the other eponyms were chosen to play the role of founder, but we do know that they fulfilled the requirements that were imposed by the idea of legal authority. In the case of Abū Ḥanīfa, he certainly emerged as an authority *ex post facto*; this is attested in a revealing remark made by Jāḥiẓ to the effect that Abū Ḥanīfa rose to importance after having virtually been a *persona non grata* (*ᶜaẓuma sha'nuhu baᶜda khumūlihi*).[24] It is significant that Jāḥiẓ, who died in 255/868, was, in terms of chronology, sufficiently close to the realities of Abū Ḥanīfa's immediate successors to be considered by us a reliable observer, and too early to have succumbed to the ideological biases of authority construction that developed in the period after him. Jāḥiẓ's evidence is bolstered by the credible testimony of ᶜAbd al-Raḥmān b. Mahdī who, around the very end of the second century A.H. (800–820 A.D.), observed that the most distinguished jurists of his time were Sufyān al-Thawrī, Mālik, Ḥammād b. Zayd, and ᶜAbd Allāh Ibn al-Mubārak.[25] Abū Ḥanīfa is conspicuously absent from this list.

The lack of any work by Abū Ḥanīfa himself, and the improvements and virtually indistinguishable contributions made by his two students on his behalf, makes Abū Ḥanīfa a difficult case study. In this respect, Mālik b. Anas (d. 179/795), the eponym of the Mālikite school, provides a better illustration of the process by which an early jurist was subsequently made an absolute *mujtahid* and a founder.

In the *Muwaṭṭa'*, Mālik himself is primarily a transmitter of earlier or contemporary doctrine, particularly the consensus of the Medinese jurists.[26] In certain instances though he maintains his own opinion, especially, one gathers, when the Quran or Prophetic Sunna elaborates

[24] Abū ᶜUthmān ᶜAmr b. Baḥr al-Jāḥiẓ, *Rasā'il*, ed. ᶜAbd al-Salām Hārūn, 2 vols. (Cairo: Maktabat al-Khānjī, 1964), II, 272.

[25] Abū Isḥāq Ibrāhīm b. ᶜAlī al-Shīrāzī, *Ṭabaqāt al-Fuqahā'*, ed. Iḥsān ᶜAbbās (Beirut: Dār al-Rā'id al-ᶜArabī, 1970), 94.

[26] Mālik was under the influence of several leading jurists, including Ibn Shihāb al-Zuhrī, Ibn Hurmuz, Zayd b. Aslam, Abū al-Zinād, Abū al-Aswad Yatīm ᶜUrwa, Ayyūb al-Sikhtyānī, Rabīᶜa b. Abī ᶜAbd al-Raḥmān, Yaḥyā b. Saᶜīd al-Anṣārī, Mūsā b. ᶜUqba, and Muḥammad b. ᶜAjlān. Shams al-Dīn Muḥammad Ibn Farḥūn, *al-Dībāj al-Mudhahhab fī Maᶜrifat Aᶜyān ᶜUlamā' al-Madhhab* (Beirut: Dār al-Kutub al-ᶜIlmiyya, 1417/1996), 79–80.

certain legal themes. An example in point is the issue of a woman's right to inheritance within the family. Here Mālik renders his own opinion while relying on the Quran and Prophetic Sunna.[27] Less frequently do we find him formulating legal norms on the basis of Prophetic Sunna alone.[28] In still other instances, Mālik can be found to espouse an opinion with neither the textual evidence nor legal reasoning in justification of the opinion.[29] Even if we assume that such opinions were his own, that is, that they were reached by him through *ijtihād* – an assumption, we shall see, that is largely unwarranted – it remains the case that the totality of these opinions is comparatively marginal in the *Muwaṭṭa'*.

It is often clear that not all opinions stated by Mālik in the *Muwaṭṭa'* are his own,[30] although it is also often the case that the picture is not very clear. In certain instances, Mālik is made to state opinions that initially seem to be his, when it later transpires that they are not. In a case pertaining to alms-tax, for instance, Mālik states an opinion which he later qualifies with the formula "This is the best I have heard."[31] Were it not the best he had heard, it is highly probable that he would have avoided making any remark. Similarly, in a case involving preemption, an opinion is introduced by the oft-used formula "Mālik said" (*qāla Mālik*). Having stated the opinion, Mālik falls silent, and Yaḥyā, the most renowned transmitter and narrator of the *Muwaṭṭa'*,[32] interjects himself with another *qāla Mālik* formula that is followed by yet another of Mālik's common formulas, namely, "This is the opinion which we hold" (*wa-hādhā al-amr ʿindanā*).[33] Of special importance in this phrase is the last word, *ʿindanā*, which is in the plural and which refers to the Hijazi jurists in general and the Medinese in particular. It turns out here too that the opinion is not Mālik's. The expression of a collective opinion varies in detail and

27 Mālik b. Anas, *al-Muwaṭṭa'* (Beirut: Dār al-Jīl, 1414/1993), 462.

28 Ibid., 467. For a detailed study of the *Muwaṭṭa'*'s hierarchy of doctrine, see Yasin Dutton, *The Origins of Islamic Law: The Qur'an, the Muwaṭṭa' and Medinan ʿAmal* (Richmond: Curzon, 1999).

29 E.g. ibid., 452, 461, 464, 756, and passim.

30 This is consistent with the well-known and oft-quoted report that Mālik refrained from giving, or at least was reluctant to offer, his own opinions on all questions addressed to him: Ibn Farḥūn, *Dībāj*, 69–70. This reluctance is said to have been motivated by piety, but it is just as likely that it was due to the fact that Mālik did not always have an answer to give, much less his *own* answer. In this context, it is perhaps fruitful to compare this account with Mālik's own student, Ḥārith b. Asad, who did not issue *fatwās* because he, by his own admission, often did not know the answers: ibid., 176. What could be acknowledged in the case of Ḥārith, however, would have been unthinkable in that of Mālik, since an admission of ignorance would have flagrantly contradicted the epistemic authority so carefully built around him by his school.

31 Mālik, *Muwaṭṭa'*, 251, 267, 282, 771, and passim.

32 Ḥaṭṭāb, *Mawāhib al-Jalīl*, I, 6 (l. 14).

33 Mālik, *Muwaṭṭa'*, 624, also at 584.

emphasis, and the significance of these variations is not always clear.[34] The following statements illustrate its various uses:

1. "I have long observed jurists in our region follow this opinion."[35]
2. "This is what I heard from the jurists, and have long observed Muslims practice the matter in this manner in our midst."[36]
3. "This is the opinion which the jurists have been adopting in our midst."[37]
4. "The opinion on which we reached consensus, and which is not subject to disagreement, and which I have long observed the jurists follow in our region is . . ."[38]
5. "The opinion on which we have reached a consensus, and the *sunna* on which there is no disagreement, and what I have long observed the jurists follow in our region is . . ."[39]

Such statements refer to anonymous practice and agreement, without attaching to them the name of any particular jurist. They accompany no less than one-eighth (13 percent) of the opinions in *al-Muwaṭṭa'*, judging by an inventory of the chapter on sales, a rather important part of the work.[40] Our count furthermore shows that 27 percent of the opinions are attributed to earlier jurists, notably Saᶜīd Ibn al-Musayyib, Yaḥyā b. Saᶜīd, Ibn Shihāb, and Salmān b. Yasār.[41] Some 21 percent of the opinions are based on revealed texts, mostly Prophetic Sunna. The remainder, 39 percent, are opinions voiced by Mālik without authority, be it textual or personal. As we have seen earlier, we can in no way be sure that the source of such opinions is Mālik himself. This means that the corpus of Mālik's own opinions must be much smaller than 39 percent, and that both the *ḥadīth* and juristic material which he transmitted constitute far more than 61 percent of the *Muwaṭṭa'*'s contents – that is, if we go by our statistical count in the chapter on sales. A random investigation of the rest of the *Muwaṭṭa'*, though admittedly impressionistic, tends to confirm this

[34] Ibid., 245, 452, 453, 454, 455, 456, 458, 459, 460, 461, 463, 755, 756, 757, 759, 761, 763, 768, 769, and passim.

[35] Ibid., 464: "*wa-ᶜalā dhālika adraktu ahl al-ᶜilm bi-baladinā.*"

[36] Ibid., 688: "*fa-hādhā al-ladhī samiᶜtu min ahl al-ᶜilm wa-adraktu ᶜamal al-nās ᶜalā dhālika ᶜindanā.*"

[37] Ibid., 583: "*wa-hādhā al-amr al-ladhī lam yazal ᶜalayhi al-nās ᶜindanā.*"

[38] Ibid., 459: "*al-amr al-mujtamaᶜ ᶜalayh ᶜindanā al-ladhī lā ikhtilāfa fī-hi wal-ladhī adraktu ᶜalayhi ahl al-ᶜilm bi-baladinā . . .*"

[39] Ibid., 463: "*al-amr al-mujtamaᶜ ᶜalayh ᶜindanā wal-sunna al-latī lā ikhtilāfa fī-hā wal-ladhī adraktu ᶜalayhi ahl al-ᶜilm bi-baladinā . . .*"

[40] Ibid., 539–93.

[41] Ibid., 682, 684, 745, 747, 748, 750, 751, 752, 753, 758 (and passim, for Ibn al-Musayyib); 456, 676, 669, 680, 681, 743, 775 (and passim, for Ibn Saᶜīd); 676, 743, 744, 746, 755 (and passim, for Ibn Shihāb); 456, 687, 744, 749, 753 (and passim, for Salmān b. Yasār).

estimate, which may in fact be overgenerous in its appraisal of Mālik's own contributions.

These results are substantially corroborated by Ibn Uways's report of Mālik's own, revealing explanation of what he attempted to do in the *Muwaṭṭa'*, a report that is in all likelihood authentic though seldom encountered in Mālikite works:

> Indeed, most of the contents of the book are not my opinions but rather those which I heard (*samāʿī*) from many leading scholars. Their opinions were so many that they overcame me (*ghalabū ʿalayya*). But their opinions are the ones which they took from the Companions, and I in turn took these opinions from these leading scholars. They are a legacy which devolved from one age to another till these times of ours. When I say "My opinion," so it is. [When I say] "The matter subject to agreement," it means that matter on which they [the scholars] reached a consensus. When I say "The matter as we have it," (*al-amr ʿindanā*) it means the matter which constitutes the practice in our midst and region, which jurists apply, and with which both laymen and scholars are familiar. When I say "Some scholars [held]," then it is an opinion that some scholars espoused and to which I am inclined. If I have not heard (*lam asmaʿ*) an opinion [on a matter] from them, then I exercise my *ijtihād* according to the doctrine of someone I have met, so that [my *ijtihād*] does not swerve from the ways (*madhhab*) of the Medinese. If [on a given matter] there is no opinion to be heard [at all], then I will formulate an opinion by conducting *ijtihād* on the basis of the Sunna and in accordance with the jurists' doctrines, as well as with the practices of our region since the time of the Prophet.[42]

These pronouncements cannot be unauthentic, not only because of the unlikely possibility that they would have been put with flagrant impunity in the mouth of Mālik by later jurists of the school, but also because they quite simply undermine the very authority giving structure to the school itself, which furthermore explains why these declarations did not gain much notoriety in Mālikite literature. Mālik himself admits his vast debt to the authority and legacy of the Medinese and his own predecessors, and this he does readily. It was his followers, especially during the period of the school's formation, who sought, consciously or not, to minimize this debt.

Now, in the space of slightly over half a century after Mālik's death, the Mālikite jurists succeeded in promoting Mālik to a status of a chief authority, a status that put him well on his way to being made the founder of the school. This process of what we term authority construc-

[42] Aḥmad Bābā al-Tinbaktī, *Nayl al-Ibtihāj bi-Taṭrīz al-Dībāj*, ed. ʿAbd al-Ḥamīd al-Harāma (Ṭarāblus, Libya: Kulliyyat al-Daʿwa al-Islāmiyya, 1989), 295–96; Ibn Farḥūn, *Dībāj*, 72–73.

tion manifests itself in the *Mudawwana*, a work associated with the name of ᶜAbd al-Salām b. Saᶜīd al-Tanūkhī, known as Saḥnūn (d. 240/854). In this work, Mālik appears as one of the foremost authorities on law. He is held up as the author of juristic doctrines and opinions, whether or not he truly formulated them himself. Surprisingly, many of the opinions in the *Muwaṭṭa'* which Mālik merely transmitted on the authority of his predecessors or anonymous contemporaries appear in the *Mudawwana* as his own. Consider the following examples:

1. "Yaḥyā told me that Mālik heard (*samiᶜa*) that blood-money should be paid within the span of three or four years. Mālik said: Three years is the best I have heard concerning this matter."[43] It is obvious here that this is not Mālik's own opinion, though he quotes it quite approvingly. In the *Mudawwana*, the opinion becomes Mālik's: "Saḥnūn was asked: 'Over how many years should the blood-money be paid according to Mālik's opinion?' Saḥnūn said: 'In three years.'"[44]
2. "Yaḥyā told me that Mālik heard (*balaghahu*) that if the faculty of hearing in both ears is completely lost [due to injury], then the full blood-money is due." This opinion from the *Muwaṭṭa'*[45] is, again, clearly not formulated by Mālik himself. But in the *Mudawwana* it is transformed into Mālik's own opinion. Interestingly, it is introduced thus: "Mālik said: If hearing in both ears is completely lost [due to injury], then the full blood-money is due."[46]
3. "Yaḥyā told me that Mālik said: The opinion on which we have reached a consensus (*al-amr al-mujtamaᶜ ᶜalayhi ᶜindanā*) is that if a man buys linen in one town, then carries it into another and sells it for a profit, the price of the linen should not include the costs of commissions, or of packaging, loading, or storage. The transportation fees, however, should be considered an integral part of the linen's price (*yuḥsab fī aṣl al-thaman*) and do not constitute a profit. If the seller informs the buyer of these [additional] costs, and he bargains with him as to obtain compensation, and if the buyer accepts [to make payment], then all is well (*fa-lā ba'sa bi-hi*)."[47] This, obviously, is not Mālik's own opinion but one which emerged out of a consensus reached by the Medinese jurists. Again, in the *Mudawwana*, the opinion is attributed to Malik himself. It is restated in a nearly identical form, but the opening line is different and, for that matter, revealing: "Mālik said concerning linen bought in one town and transported into another: *I opine* (*arā*) that . . ."[48] The exclusive attribution to Mālik is emphatically manifest.

[43] Mālik, *Muwaṭṭa'*, 743.
[44] Mālik b. Anas, *al-Mudawwana al-Kubrā*, ed. Aḥmad ᶜAbd al-Salām, 5 vols. (Beirut: Dār al-Kutub al-ᶜIlmiyya, 1415/1994), IV, 567.
[45] Mālik, *Muwaṭṭa'*, 748. [46] Mālik, *Mudawwana*, IV, 563.
[47] Mālik, *Muwaṭṭa'*, 581.
[48] Mālik, *Mudawwana*, III, 238 (italics mine). The original phrasing is even more revealing: "*qāla Mālik fī al-bazz yushtarā fī balad fa-yuḥmal ilā baladin ākhar, qāla arā an lā* . . ."

It is obvious, beyond a shadow of doubt, that Mālik, here and elsewhere, is made responsible not only for unattributed opinions (which, as we have seen, do not necessarily belong to him) but also for opinions that clearly originate with other, identifiable authorities, be they individual or collective (i.e., Medinese consensus). Mālik's role is thus transformed by the later Mālikites from being a transmitter in the *Muwaṭṭa'* into that of the foremost authority for what was then emerging as the Mālikite school.[49]

The change in Mālik's role and image is by no means identical to that which occurred in the case of Abū Ḥanīfa, for the Mālik of the *Muwaṭṭa'* functioned also in the role of a traditionist, unlike Abū Ḥanīfa. But it is well-nigh certain that great many of the opinions which the latter transmitted from Ḥammād, Nakhaᶜī, and others were later attributed to him. All the schools, not only the Mālikites, contributed to this process of authority construction. In the later sections of this chapter we shall see that this process was further enhanced by attributions to the founder of opinions garnered not only from their predecessors but also from their successors. The construction of the founders' authority *qua* founders and imams drew on sources both prior and subsequent to them.

Like Abū Ḥanīfa and Mālik, the figure of Muḥammad b. Idrīs al-Shāfiᶜī (d. 204/820) was subjected to the same process. But unlike Mālik, Shāfiᶜī appears much less as a transmitter of *ḥadīth* and legal opinion and more as a jurist holding opinions of his own. This is the impression left upon a casual reader of his *magnum opus*, *al-Umm*, which consists substantially of unattributed opinions, statements of legal norms formulated without textual support or legal reasoning. However, a careful study of this work reveals that Shāfiᶜī was no less indebted to his predecessors than

[49] It is quite significant that Mohammad Fadel, who has studied the Mālikite school closely but who has not addressed the issue of what I have called authority construction, makes the following remark with regard to Ibn al-Qāsim (d. 191/866) who was considered, together with Saḥnūn, the most reliable transmitter of Mālik's doctrine:

> It was impossible to rely solely on Ibn al-Qāsim's teachings, for there were many issues of law for which Ibn al-Qāsim could not *attribute* an opinion to Mālik. This obliged later jurists to use the opinions of Mālik's other disciples, who often *attributed* positions to Mālik on precisely those cases for which Ibn al-Qāsim had not been able to provide a solution. More importantly, however, Ibn al-Qāsim's privileged position as the authoritative transmitter of Mālik's doctrine seems to have been developed at a later date. Presumably, for the first centuries of Mālikite jurisprudence, opinions had been evaluated on the basis of their individual worth and not on the *authority* of the transmitter of that opinion.

See his "The Social Logic of *Taqlīd* and the Rise of the *Mukhtaṣar*," *Islamic Law and Society*, 4 (1996), 218 (italics mine). Note here that Fadel senses, but does not articulate, the process of authority construction in the Mālikite school.

were Mālik and Abū Ḥanīfa. It is often the case that when the doctrine or opinion is standard and shared by the community of jurists, Shāfiʿī relates it without attributing it to any particular authority. A typical example of this can be seen in the case of hiring beasts for the purpose of transporting goods:

> Shāfiʿī said: If a man hires a beast [to use for transportation] from Mecca to Marw,[50] but he travels with it [only] to Medina, then he must pay the hiring fees agreed upon for traveling to Marw . . . If the beast perishes, he must pay the hiring fees to Marw plus the value of the beast. If it came to suffer from a defect while he is traveling with it – such as a wound in the rear, blindness, etc. – and this defect has affected its performance, he may return it [to its owner from whom] he is entitled to receive the equivalent value of the defective part.[51]

This opinion certainly circulated prior to Shāfiʿī, as attested by the early authorities cited in the *Mudawwana*.[52] The same type of evidence may be found in two opinions concerning collective homicide of the kind initially caused by bodily injury, such as severing of a limb. Shāfiʿī presents the opinions without textual support or legal reasoning, and gives no juristic authority for them. Yet the same opinions had already surfaced, with some variation, in the *Muwaṭṭa'*.[53] Similarly, Shāfiʿī acknowledges no authority or textual evidence in favor of the opinion that the full amount of blood-money becomes due when the sense of hearing is completely impaired as a result of bodily injury.[54] Yet it turns out that this opinion is stated in the *Muwaṭṭa'* as having been heard by Mālik from another authority.[55]

Much of *al-Umm* is made up of such opinions.[56] At times, however, the opinions are clearly defended in terms of consensus or, alternatively, in terms of the absence of disagreement. Concerning the law of rent and hire, Shāfiʿī, like most later *muqallids*, argues that it is justified by the Sunna, the practice of a number of Companions, and the "absence, as far as I know, of disagreement on it among the jurists of all regions

[50] In the text the city is called Marr, a place name which I could not locate in the standard geographical dictionaries. The context suggests that it is a distortion of Marw, a city in Khurasan.

[51] Shāfiʿī, *Umm*, IV, 29. [52] Mālik, *Mudawwana*, III, 486–87.

[53] Shāfiʿī, *Umm*, VI, 42, 59; Mālik, *Muwaṭṭa'*, 760, 762, 743, respectively.

[54] Shāfiʿī, *Umm*, VI, 89. [55] Mālik, *Muwaṭṭa'*, 748.

[56] This perhaps explains Shāfiʿī's requirement that for a jurist to qualify as a *muftī*, he must master, among other things, the legal doctrines of his predecessors and contemporaries (*aqāwīl ahl al-ʿilm qadīman wa-ḥadīthan*). See his *Kitāb Ibṭāl al-Istiḥsān* in *Umm*, VII, 497.

including ours."[57] In many instances, Shāfiʿī's sole defense or justification is the absence of disagreement, which implies, or is made to imply, the existence of consensus.[58] Less often, he explicitly states that two or more opinions exist concerning a particular case. In the matter of death resulting from bodily injury, Shāfiʿī introduces two opinions after the formula "*qīla*" (it was held).[59] It is clear that he had formulated neither of the two opinions himself. Here Shāfiʿī is practicing *taqlīd*, in precisely the same manner as his followers have practiced it for centuries since his death.

Shāfiʿī practiced another form of *taqlīd* frequently resorted to by later jurists belonging to all the four schools, namely, the reenactment of *ijtihād* which later came to be known as *ittibāʿ*.[60] By Shāfiʿī's time, it had become a firmly established doctrine that if a man wished to marry a fifth wife, he had to divorce one of the first four, in accordance with the Quranic verse 4:25. The interlocutor asks Shāfiʿī if other jurists have held this opinion, whereupon Shāfiʿī replies that the Quranic evidence is sufficient. But he then admits that others did hold this opinion, and proceeds to give two chains of authority, one consisting of ʿAbd al-Majīd → Ibn Jurayj → Abū al-Zubayr → Jābir, and the other including the first two of these names followed by Ṭāwūs who transmitted it on the authority of his father.[61]

The reluctance of Shāfiʿī to admit his propensity to *taqlīd* may be observed sporadically throughout *al-Umm*. With regard to the question of a gift made under coercion by a wife to her husband, he criticizes Abū Ḥanīfa's opinion and offers instead that of Ibn Abī Laylā. Having done so, he states his own opinion, which is identical to that of the latter.[62] That he states his opinion without providing its textual basis, and without explaining his own legal reasoning in justification of it, suggests that Shāfiʿī either adopted Ibn Abī Laylā's opinion as it is, or, what is more likely, accepted it in the way of *ittibāʿ*. In either case, he is not the originator of the opinion, even though he lets us assume that it is his own, independent doctrine.

Nonetheless, Shāfiʿī does at times acknowledge his debt to other jurists. With regard to the question of dedicating alms-giving as a charitable trust, Shāfiʿī again attacks Abū Ḥanīfa's opinion, and introduces, this time, the argument propounded by Abū Yūsuf and Shaybānī who disagreed with their mentor – a phenomenon of frequent occurrence among the three Ḥanafite authorities. Shāfiʿī admits – this time not so reluctantly – that Abū Yūsuf's reasoning in favor of an alternative opinion is exquisite

[57] Shāfiʿī, *Umm*, IV, 30.
[58] Ibid., IV, 30, 33, 109, 143; V, 6, 10–11, 16, 313, and passim. [59] Ibid., VI, 43.
[60] See chapter 4, section I, below. [61] Shāfiʿī, *Umm*, V, 15. [62] Ibid., IV, 73.

and that it proved superior to his own. At the end of the statement, Shāfiᶜī intimates that he sides with, or adopts, Abū Yūsuf's opinion.[63] This example can be found repeated on a number of occasions,[64] but the following is representative:

> Shāfiᶜī said: Some jurists maintained that if a man left [an inheritance of] 300 dinars, then his two sons would divide it between themselves, each receiving 150 dinars. One of the two then acknowledges that a [third] man is his brother, but the other denies this claim. What I recall of the early Medinese opinion (*qawl al-Madaniyyīn al-mutaqaddim*) is that the [third] man's filiation is not acknowledged and that he receives no amount whatsoever [of the inheritance]. This is so because the brother [who made the claim] did not acknowledge a debt to him, nor did he leave him a bequest. Rather, he merely claimed that he is entitled to inherit. If he could prove that he has a right to the inheritance, then he should inherit and he will also be liable to the payment of blood-money.[65] But since this relationship cannot be established, he cannot inherit. This, in my view, is the soundest opinion.[66]

In order to become the final authority in his school, Shāfiᶜī was required to shed the image of a *muqallid*,[67] a process of authority construction to which both Abū Ḥanīfa and Mālik were subjected. One example should suffice to make our point. With regard to land rent, Shāfiᶜī holds an opinion that he explicitly attributes to the chain of authority: Mālik → Ibn Shihāb → Saᶜīd Ibn al-Musayyib. It was not long after Shāfiᶜī's death that he was made responsible for this opinion.[68] In his *Mukhtaṣar*, Ibrāhīm al-Muzanī (d. 264/877) states the same opinion, but there attributes it, without the slightest ambiguity, to Shāfiᶜī.[69]

As obvious as is the *ex post eventum* construction of the authority of these three imams, it appears to have been even more flagrant in the case of Aḥmad Ibn Ḥanbal (d. 241/855). Abū Ḥanīfa and Shāfiᶜī were admittedly jurists of the first caliber (although one might incidentally

63 Ibid., IV, 69–70.

64 Ibid., V, 3; VI, 45 (a verbatim restatement of *Muwaṭṭa'*, 645–46); VII, 7, and passim.

65 Being the closest agnate, he is liable to the payment of blood-money should one of his brothers commit murder. The right to inheritance and the obligation to pay blood-money are defined, by the operation of the law, as the functions of agnatic relationships.

66 Shāfiᶜī, *Umm*, VI, 276–77.

67 This image is borne out by the *manāqib* literature which assigned to Shāfiᶜī, in a gradual fashion, the role of the master architect of legal theory. On these developments in the *manāqib* genre, see Hallaq, "Was al-Shafiᶜi the Master Architect?" 599–600.

68 Shāfiᶜī, *Umm*, IV, 30.

69 Ibrāhīm al-Muzanī, *Mukhtaṣar*, published as vol. IX of Shāfiᶜī's *Umm*, IX, 139.

remark that the eighth-century Taqī al-Dīn al-Subkī, among others, possessed a far more acute legal mind). Mālik does not appear to have stood on par with them as a legal reasoner or as a seasoned jurist. But he was jurist of a sort, nonetheless. Ibn Ḥanbal was none of these things. He was in the first place a traditionist and theologian, and his involvement with law as a technical discipline was rather minimal. This much of his background is acknowledged by followers and foes alike. Among the latter, the well-known Ṭabarī refused to acknowledge him as a jurist apparently because "he never taught law, and never had law students."[70] Even as late as the fifth/eleventh century, this perception persisted in some circles, probably among certain of the Ḥanbalites themselves.[71] In their various works on the legal and learned professions, Ibn Qutayba, Maqdisī, Ṭaḥāwī, al-Qāḍī al-Nuᶜmān, Dabbūsī, and al-ᶜAlā' al-Samarqandī neglected even to include him, although Maqdisī listed him among the traditionists.[72] Ibn ᶜAbd al-Barr wrote a whole treatise on the virtues of the schools' founders – at least those schools that had survived by his time – but Ibn Ḥanbal was not one of them.[73] Abū Bakr Ibn al-Athram, a Ḥanbalite, is reported to have said that he used to study law and the science of legal disagreement (*khilāf*) until he came to sit in the circle of Ibn Ḥanbal, at which time he categorically abandoned this course of learning in favor of *ḥadīth*.[74] The later Ḥanbalite jurist Ṭūfī openly acknowledged that Ibn Ḥanbal "did not transmit legal doctrine, for his entire concern was with *ḥadīth* and its collection."[75] This image of Ibn Ḥanbal was so pervasive that it never faded away for many centuries to come.[76]

[70] See the introduction to Abū Jarīr Jaᶜfar al-Ṭabarī's *Ikhtilāf al-Fuqahā'* (Beirut: Dar al-Kutub al-ᶜIlmiyya, 1980), 10.

[71] ᶜAbd al-Raḥmān Shihāb al-Dīn Ibn Rajab, *Kitāb al-Dhayl ᶜalā Ṭabaqāt al-Ḥanābila*, 2 vols. (Cairo: Maṭbaᶜat al-Sunna al-Muḥammadiyya, 1952–53), I, 156–57, quoting Ibn ᶜAqīl's observation that some of the younger legal scholars, most probably law students, thought Ibn Ḥanbal lacking in juristic skills. He argues to the contrary, however, which is to be expected from a later Ḥanbalite who is, by definition, a loyalist.

[72] Ṭabarī, *Ikhtilāf*, 15–16. For al-Qāḍī al-Nuᶜmān b. Muḥammad (d. 351/962), see his *Kitāb Ikhtilāf Uṣūl al-Madhāhib*, ed. Muṣṭafā Ghālib (Beirut: Dār al-Andalus, 1973), 66. Speaking of the Sunnī community of jurists, Nuᶜmān (ibid., 127) reports that they claimed consensus to be limited to Mālik, Abū Ḥanīfa, Shāfiᶜī, Awzāᶜī, and their fellow jurists.

[73] Ibid., 16.

[74] Muḥammad b. Abī Yaᶜlā al-Baghdādī Ibn al-Farrā', *Ṭabaqāt al-Ḥanābila*, ed. M. H. al-Fiqī, 2 vols. (Cairo: Maṭbaᶜat al-Sunna al-Muḥammadiyya, 1952), I, 72, 296.

[75] Najm al-Dīn al-Ṭūfī, *Sharḥ Mukhtaṣar al-Rawḍa*, ed. ᶜAbd Allāh al-Turkī, 3 vols. (Beirut: Mu'assasat al-Risāla, 1407/1987), III, 626–27: "*fa-innahu kāna lā yarwī tadwīn al-ra'y bal hammuhu al-ḥadīth wa-jamᶜuhu.*"

[76] Manṣūr b. Yūnus Ibn Idrīs al-Bahūtī (d. after 1046/1636), *Kashshāf al-Qināᶜ ᶜan Matn al-Iqnāᶜ*, 6 vols. (Beirut: ᶜĀlam al-Kutub, 1983), VI, 21.

Ibn Ḥanbal thus emerges as less of a founder than any of the other three eponyms. A traditionist par excellence, he was by definition preoccupied with *ḥadīth*, not law. We may suppose, only because of the later developments which made of Ḥanbalism a legal school, that he did address some legal problems and that he rendered legal opinions mostly in terms of *ḥadīth*. This is probably the nucleus with which his followers worked, and which they later elaborated and expanded.[77] It is therefore not an exaggeration to assert that the bare beginnings of legal Ḥanbalism are to be located in the juristic activities of the generation that followed Ibn Ḥanbal, associated as it is with the names of Abū Bakr al-Athram (d. 261/874), ʿAbd Allāh al-Maymūnī (d. 274/887), Abū Bakr al-Marrūdhī (d. 275/888), Ḥarb al-Kirmānī (d. 280/893), Ibrāhīm b. Isḥāq al-Ḥarbī (d. 285/898), and Ibn Ḥanbal's two sons Ṣāliḥ (d. 266/880 ?) and ʿAbd Allāh (d. 290/903).[78] (It is curious that Ibn al-Athram is said to have been a central figure in the early development of legal Ḥanbalism when his study of law came to a halt once he entered Ibn Ḥanbal's circle.) But these scholars, among other less major figures, are said to have been no more than bearers of Ibn Ḥanbal's opinions and doctrines. None of them, for instance, constructed a complete, or even near complete, system of the eponym's legal subject matter. It was left to Aḥmad b. Muḥammad Abū Bakr al-Khallāl (d. 311/923) to bring what was seen as the master's dispersed doctrines together. Khallāl was reported to have traveled widely in search of Ibn Ḥanbal's students who heard him speak of matters legal, and he was in touch with a great number of them, including Ibn Ḥanbal's two sons and Ibrāhīm al-Ḥarbī.[79] Ibn al-Farrā', a major biographer and a jurist of the Ḥanbalite school, remarks that Khallāl's collection of the eponym's opinions was never matched, either before or after.[80]

It would not be then an exaggeration to argue that, had it not been for Khallāl's enterprise and ambition, the Ḥanbalite school would never have emerged as a legal entity. For to do so, Ibn Ḥanbal would have

[77] Ibn Ḥanbal's marked lack of interest in law and legal questions does not tally with the fact that later Ḥanbalite works routinely report two or three opinions (usually known as *riwāyāt*) which Ibn Ḥanbal is said to have held with regard to a single case. The only conceivable explanation, as far as I can see, is that these *riwāyāt* were later attributions by his followers, but attributions made by means other than *takhrīj* (which we shall discuss shortly in this chapter).

[78] Muwaffaq al-Dīn Ibn Qudāma, *al-Kāfī fī Fiqh al-Imām Aḥmad b. Ḥanbal*, ed. Ṣidqī Jamīl and Yūsuf Salīm, 4 vols. (Beirut: Dār al-Fikr, 1992–94), I, 10; Ibn al-Farrā', *Ṭabaqāt*, II, 12. The fact that Subkī (*Ṭabaqāt*, II, 26) gives al-Ḥarbī a biographical notice suggests that Ibn Ḥanbal's students were not trained exclusively – nor even principally – under him, as is also evidenced in the case of Ibn al-Athram.

[79] Ibn al-Farrā', *Ṭabaqāt*, II, 12–13. [80] Ibid., II, 113.

had to furnish a wide range of legal doctrine and opinion, and in this task he certainly needed help. This help came from his followers and particularly the generation that succeeded them. They, like the Ḥanafites, Mālikites, and Shāfiʿites before them, attributed to their eponym opinions that he held or was thought to have held, whether or not these opinions originated with him as a *mujtahid*. In the case of Ibn Ḥanbal, a charismatic theologian and traditionist and the hero of the *Miḥna*, the clothing of his personality with legal authority was a much less difficult task both to undertake and accomplish, and this despite his notoriously imperfect record as a jurist.

The construction of authority around the figures of the presumed founders must also be viewed in the larger context of the development of Islamic law. Multifarious in nature and evolving from the outset as a jurists' law, legal authority during the first two centuries of Islam was dispersed and diluted. There were many jurists who advocated doctrines that were made up of various elements, some belonging to their predecessors and older contemporaries, and some of their own making. It is important to realize, as we have shown in some detail above, that none of these jurist-founders constructed his own doctrine singlehandedly, as the later typologies – and tradition at large – would have us believe. In fact, Ibn Ḥanbal's case is in itself an argument precisely to the contrary. But the argument can be taken still further: If Ibn Ḥanbal was transformed, despite all the odds, into a school founder, then it is no surprise that any one of the major *mujtahids* during this early period could have become a founder too.

Throughout the second/eighth and third/ninth centuries, juristic authority was so widely dispersed that it was unable to fulfill the requirements and demands of legal evolution. Authority, by definition, must have a clearly defined locus, and to be effective, it must be perceived to be such. Both these conditions were fulfilled in the person of the jurist–scholar who was made, through a process of authority attributions, the founder of a school. Even in later centuries, with the stupendous doctrinal accretions of later followers, the founder's authority remained the most significant, although the entirety of his doctrine, both attributed and original, was insufficient to meet the exigencies of later judicial application and unable to sustain singlehandedly the entire school. Although in later centuries the founder remained the most sanctified legal figure in the school, he remained little more than *primus inter pares*. The authoritative school doctrine, the *madhhab*, consisted of opinions originating with various jurists. But all these jurists and the opinions they held were enlisted under the nominal tutelage of the founder. The creation of authority in the figure of the founder was part of the wider effort to construct the school's authority, one of the greatest achievements of Islamic law.

## III

We have already intimated that the process of authority construction did not only involve the dissociation of the eponyms from the contributions of their predecessors, to whom they were indebted. The process also entailed augmenting the authority of the supposed founders by attributing doctrines to them which they may never have held. It is the juristic constitution of these doctrinal contributions and the manner in which they underwent the process of attribution that will occupy us in the following pages.

It may at first glance seem a contradiction to speak of *ijtihād* as part of the *muqallid*'s activity, but this is by no means the case. We have seen in chapter 1 that the typologies acknowledge a group of jurists who stood below the rank of the absolute *mujtahids*, a group that was distinguished by the dual attribute of being *muqallids* to the founding imam and, simultaneously, *mujtahids* able to derive legal norms through the process of *takhrīj*.[81] Virtually overlooked by modern scholarship,[82] this important activity was largely responsible for the early doctrinal development of the personal schools, its zenith being located between the very beginning of the fourth/tenth century and the end of the fifth/eleventh, although strong traces of it could still be observed throughout the following centuries.[83]

[81] The origins of this term's technical meaning are by no means easy to reconstruct. None of the second/eighth-century jurists, including Shāfiʿī, uses the term in any obvious technical sense. To the best of my knowledge, the first semi-technical occurrence of it is found in Muzanī's *Kitāb al-Amr wal-Nahy*, where the author uses the term *makhraj* (lit. an outlet) to mean something like a solution to a problem, a way, that is, to get out of a problem through legal reasoning. It is quite noticeable, however, that Muzanī employs the term while taking Shāfiʿī's doctrine into account, which in this treatise is nearly always the case. See his *Kitāb al-Amr wal-Nahy*, in Robert Brunschvig, "Le livre de l'ordre et de la défense d'al-Muzani," *Bulletin d'études orientales*, 11 (1945–46): 145–94, at 153, 156, 158, 161, 162, and passim. Incidentally, it is noteworthy that *takhrīj* as a way of reasoning is not expounded, as a rule, in works of legal theory. As a technical term, it appears in none of the major technical dictionaries, e.g. Tahānawī's *Kashshāf Iṣṭilāḥāt al-Funūn* and Jurjānī's *Taʿrīfāt*.

[82] The only work that allocates some discussion to the later, not early, activity of *takhrīj* is, to the best of my knowledge, Sherman Jackson, *Islamic Law and the State: The Constitutional Jurisprudence of Shihāb al-Dīn al-Qarāfī* (Leiden: E. J. Brill, 1996), 91–96. Jackson deals with this issue from the limited perspective of Qarāfī and, at any rate, addresses neither the structure of reasoning involved in this activity nor its role in early legal evolution.

[83] See nn. 130–32, below.

According to Ibn al-Ṣalāḥ, the limited *mujtahid* exercises *takhrīj* on either of two bases: a particular text of his imam where a specific opinion is stated or, in the absence of such a text, he confronts revelation and derives from it a legal norm according to the principles and methodology established by his imam. This he does while heeding the type and quality of reasoning that is habitually employed by the imam,[84] and in this sense *takhrīj* exhibits the same features as the reasoning which constitutes the conventional, full-fledged *ijtihād* of the arch-jurist. In both types of *takhrīj*, however, conformity with the imam's legal theory and the general and particular principles of the law is said to be the prime concern.

The first type became known as *al-takhrīj wal-naql*, while the second, being a relatively more independent activity, was given the unqualified designation *takhrīj*. This latter involves reasoning, among many things, on the basis of general principles, such as the principle that necessity renders lawful what is otherwise illicit, or that no legal obligation shall be imposed beyond the limit of endurance or optimal capability. In this type of activity, the limited *mujtahid* takes these principles as his rule of thumb and solves problems accordingly.

The following example, from Ḥanbalite law, illustrates the activity of *al-takhrīj wal-naql*: If someone intends to perform prayer while wearing ritually impure clothes – the assumption being that ritually pure clothes are not available at the time – he or she must still pray but must also repeat the prayer when the proper apparel can be had. This is said to have been Ibn Ḥanbal's opinion. Another reported opinion of his concerns prayer in a ritually impure place. He held, contrary to the first case, that if someone prays in such a place, he need not pray again in compensation. In the later Ḥanbalite school, the principle emerged that both the ritual purity of the location of the prayer and the clothes worn while performing this duty constitute a condition for the validity of prayer. This being so, the two issues become cognate and, therefore, subject to mutual consideration. In other words, the legal norms attached to the two cases become interchangeable, thus creating two contradictory legal norms for each. Najm al-Dīn al-Ṭūfī explains how this comes about:

> The stipulation that wearing ritually impure clothes requires repetition of the prayer is a legal norm that is transferred (*yunqal*) to the [issue of] place. So a new legal norm emerges in the case of place (*yatakharraj fī-hi*). The stipulation that praying in a ritually impure place does not require repetition of the prayer is a legal norm that is transferred to [the issue of]

[84] Ibn al-Ṣalāḥ, *Adab al-Muftī*, 97.

clothes. Accordingly, a new legal norm emerges in the case of clothes. This is why each of the two cases will have two legal opinions, one held by the founder, the other reached by *al-naql* (*wal-takhrīj*).[85]

On the authority of Majd al-Dīn Ibn Taymiyya (d. 652/1254), the grandfather of Taqī al-Dīn, Ṭūfī reports another case of *takhrīj wal-naql*: A bequest given in handwriting is considered valid in the opinion of the imam. But the attestation of a bequest in handwriting is considered null and void if the witnesses are left ignorant of its particulars. The invalidity of the testimony thus renders the bequest itself void. The reasoning we have observed in the case of prayer prevails here too, since the common denominator is the handwritten bequest. The outcome of this reasoning is that each case will acquire two contradictory legal norms, one of validity, the other of nullity.[86]

During the post-formative period of the schools, when the authority of the founder imam was at last considered undisputed, the activity of *al-takhrīj wal-naql* came to be restricted, in terms of source material, to the imam's or his followers' opinions. In actual fact, however, and before the formation of the schools as guilds, this was by no means the case. The early Shāfiᶜite jurist Ibn al-Qāṣṣ (d. 335/946) reports dozens, perhaps hundreds, of cases in which *takhrīj* was practiced both within and without the boundaries of the imam's legal principles and *corpus juris*. (In fact he acknowledges, despite his Shāfiᶜite affiliation, that his work *Adab al-Qāḍī* is based on both Shāfiᶜī's and Abū Ḥanīfa's doctrines.)[87] In the case of a person whose speaking faculty is impaired (*akhras*), Shāfiᶜī and Abū Ḥanīfa apparently disagreed over whether or not his testimony

[85] Ṭūfī, *Sharḥ Mukhtaṣar al-Rawḍa*, III, 641: "*wa-man lam yajid illā thawban najisan ṣallā fī-hi wa-aᶜāda, naṣṣa ᶜalayhi. Wa-naṣṣa fī-man ḥubisa fī mawḍiᶜ najis fa-ṣallā, annahu lā yuᶜīd. Fa-yatakharraj fī-himā riwāyatān wa-dhālika li'anna ṭahārat al-thawb wal-makān kilāhumā sharṭ fī al-ṣalāt. Wa-hādhā wajh al-shabah bayna al-mas'alatayn. Wa-qad naṣṣa fī al-thawb al-najis annahu yuᶜīd, fa-yanqul ḥukmahu ilā al-makān, wa-yatakharraj fī-hi mithluhu, wa-naṣṣa fī al-mawḍiᶜ al-najis ᶜalā annahu lā yuᶜīd, fa-yanqul ḥukmahu ilā al-thawb al-najis, fa-yatakharraj fī-hi mithluhu, fa-lā jarama ṣāra fī kulli wāḥidatin min al-mas'alatayn riwāyatān, iḥdāhumā bil-naṣṣ wal-ukhrā bil-naql.*"

[86] Ibid., III, 642.

[87] Abū al-ᶜAbbās Aḥmad b. Abī Aḥmad al-Ṭabarī Ibn al-Qāṣṣ, *Adab al-Qāḍī*, ed. Ḥusayn Jabbūrī, 2 vols. (Ṭā'if: Maktabat al-Ṣiddīq, 1409/1989), I, 68. The absence of schools, and therefore of school loyalty, during the second/eighth and third/ninth centuries also explains the cross-influences between and among the schools' founders. Thus we should not consider unlikely the report that when Abū Yūsuf and Shaybānī met Mālik, they abandoned nearly one-third of the doctrine which they had elaborated in Kūfa in favor of Mālik's doctrine: Rāᶜī, *Intiṣār al-Faqīr*, 204. Despite the propagandist uses that were made of this report, it can still be considered authentic in light of what we know about interdoctrinal influences.

might be accepted if he knows sign language (*ya'qil al-ishāra*). Ibn Surayj (d. 306/918), a distinguished Shāfiᶜite and Ibn al-Qāṣṣ's professor, conducted *takhrīj* on the basis of these two doctrines, with the result that two contradictory opinions were accepted for this case: one that the testimony is valid, the other that it is void.[88] What is most interesting about Ibn al-Qāṣṣ's report is that Ibn Surayj's activity was deemed to fall within the hermeneutical contours of the Shāfiᶜite school. He reports Ibn Surayj to have reached these two solutions "according to Shāfiᶜī's way" (*fa-kharrajahā Abū al-ᶜAbbās Ibn Surayj ᶜalā madhhab al-Shāfiᶜī ᶜalā qawlayn*).[89] A similar attribution may be found in the case of the *qāḍī*'s (un)equal treatment of the plaintiff and defendant in his courtroom. Ibn al-Qāṣṣ reports that "the opinion of Shāfiᶜī is that the *qāḍī* should not allow one of the two parties to state his arguments before the court without the other being present. Ibn Surayj produced this opinion by way of *takhrīj*" (*qālahu Ibn Surayj takhrījan*).[90] Ibn Surayj's *takhrīj* becomes Shāfiᶜī's authoritative opinion.

Drawing on Abū Ḥanīfa's doctrine appears to have been a frequent practice of Ibn Surayj.[91] The former held, for instance, that if four witnesses testify that an act of adultery took place, but all disagree as to the precise location in the house in which the act took place, then the *ḥadd* punishment should be inflicted nonetheless. Admittedly, Abū Ḥanīfa's reasoning is dictated by *istiḥsān*,[92] since *qiyās* does not allow for the penalty of *ḥadd* when doubt exists; rather it demands that the penalty only be meted out when all witnesses agree on the specific location in which the act was said to have taken place. Now, in another case of adultery, the authoritative doctrine of the Shāfiᶜite school held that if two witnesses testify that a man had sexual intercourse with a consenting woman, and

88 Ibn al-Qāṣṣ, *Adab al-Qāḍī*, I, 306. 89 Ibid.

90 Ibid., I, 214. See also Subkī, *Ṭabaqāt*, II, 94–95.

91 And on Shaybānī's doctrine as well. It should not come as a surprise then that Ibn Surayj, the most illustrious figure of the Shāfiᶜite school after Shāfiᶜi himself, and the one held responsible for the phenomenal success of Shāfiᶜism, should be remembered in Shāfiᶜite biographical literature as having elaborated his legal doctrine on the basis of Shaybānī's law and legal principles. In the very words of Shīrāzī, Ibn Surayj "*farraᶜa ᶜala kutub Muḥammad ibn al-Ḥasan*," i.e., he derived positive legal rulings on the basis of Shaybānī's doctrine. It is perhaps because of this that the later Shāfiᶜites expressed some reservations about the nature of Ibn Surayj's doctrines. One of the oft-quoted utterances is that made by Abū Ḥāmid al-Isfarā'īnī who said that "we go along with Abū al-ᶜAbbās [Ibn Surayj] on doctrine generally, but not on matters of specifics" (*naḥnu najrī maᶜ Abī al-ᶜAbbās fī ẓawāhir al-fiqh dūna al-daqā'iq*). See Shīrāzī, *Ṭabaqāt*, 109; Ibn Qāḍī Shuhba, *Ṭabaqāt*, I, 49.

92 On *istiḥsān*, see Wael B. Hallaq, *A History of Islamic Legal Theories* (Cambridge: Cambridge University Press, 1997), 107–11, and passim.

two other witnesses attest that he raped her, then he would not be deemed liable to the death penalty dictated by *ḥudūd*. Following the principles of *takhrīj* as outlined above, Ibn Surayj transferred the legal norm in the Ḥanafite case to the Shāfiʿite one, the result being that if doubt exists as to whether sexual intercourse occurred as rape or by mutual consent, the man should suffer capital punishment regardless.[93]

Ibn al-Qāṣṣ too exercised *takhrīj*, harvesting for his school the fruits cultivated by the Ḥanafites and other jurists, including Shaybānī and Mālik.[94] His *takhrīj* is more often than not based on Shāfiʿī's doctrine along with Ḥanafite opinion, but he frequently relies on Abū Ḥanīfa's opinions exclusively[95] and comes up with derivative opinions that he and his successors considered to be of Shāfiʿite pedigree. This practice of borrowing from the doctrinal tradition of another school and attributing the confiscated opinion to one's own school and its founder was by no means limited to the Shāfiʿites. It is not uncommon, for instance, to find Ḥanbalite opinions that have been derived through *takhrīj* from exclusively Ḥanafite, Mālikite, and/or other sources.[96] But if the activity of *takhrīj* routinely involved dipping into the doctrinal reservoir of other schools, the Shāfiʿites could be considered the prime innovators, for, as Ṭūfī testifies, they were particularly given to this activity.[97]

But the Ḥanafites were not far behind. Earlier in this chapter, we discussed in passing the first level of the hierarchical taxonomy of Ḥanafite legal doctrine. In this taxonomy, there exist three levels of doctrine, each level consisting of one or more categories. The highest level of authoritative doctrine, known as *ẓāhir al-riwāya* or *masāʾil al-uṣūl*, is found in the works of the three early masters, Abū Ḥanīfa, Abū Yūsuf,

93 Sayf al-Dīn Abū Bakr Muḥammad al-Qaffāl al-Shāshī, *Ḥulyat al-ʿUlamāʾ fī Maʿrifat Madhāhib al-Fuqahāʾ*, ed. Yāsīn Darārka, 8 vols. (Amman: Dār al-Bāzz, 1988), VIII, 306.

94 Ibn al-Qāṣṣ, *Adab al-Qāḍī*, I, 105, 106, 109–10, 112, 114, 136, 146, 195, 198, 213, 251, 253–54, 255; II, 359, 423, and passim. See also nn. 84–87, above.

95 Ibid., I, 112, 213; II, 359, 420, 447, and passim. See, for instance, ibid., I, 251; II, 417, for exclusive reliance on Abū Ḥanīfa and his two students.

96 ʿAlāʾ al-Dīn ʿAlī b. Muḥammad b. ʿAbbās al-Baʿlī, *al-Ikhtiyārāt al-Fiqhiyya min Fatāwā Shaykh al-Islām Ibn Taymiyya* (Beirut: Dār al-Fikr, 1369/1949), 15. Ibn al-Mundhir (d. 318/930) is frequently cited in Ḥanbalite works as an authority, although he was not a Ḥanbalite. In fact, he was said by biographers to have been an independent *mujtahid*, although he is also said to have been a distinguished member of the Shāfiʿite school and heavily involved in *takhrīj* according to Shāfiʿism. On Ibn al-Mundhir, see Nawawī, *al-Majmūʿ*, I, 72; Subkī, *Ṭabaqāt*, II, 126–29.

97 Ṭūfī, *Sharḥ Mukhtaṣar al-Rawḍa*, III, 642. Ṭūfī's explanation is that Shāfiʿī's doctrine, having often included more than one opinion for each case, gave rise to a rich activity of *takhrīj*.

and Shaybānī.[98] What gives these works the authority they enjoy is the perception that they were transmitted through a large number of channels by trustworthy and highly qualified jurists. A marginal number of cases belonging to this category of doctrine are attributed to Zufar and al-Ḥasan b. Ziyād. The second level is termed *masā'il al-nawādir*, a body of doctrine also attributed to the three masters but without the sanctioning authority either of highly qualified transmitters or a large number of channels of transmission.[99] The third level consists of what is termed *wāqiʿāt* or *nawāzil*, cases that were not addressed by the early masters and that were solved by later jurists. These cases were new and the jurists who were "asked about them" and who provided solutions for them "were many."[100] Of particular significance here is the fact that the great majority of these cases were solved by means of *takhrīj*.[101] Among the names associated with this category of Ḥanafite doctrine are ʿIṣām b. Yūsuf (d. 210/825), Ibrāhīm Ibn Rustam (d. 211/826), Muḥammad b. Samāʿa (d. 233/848), Abū Sulaymān al-Jūzajānī (d. after 200/815), Aḥmad Abū Ḥafṣ al-Bukhārī (d. 217/832), Muḥammad b. Salama (d. 278/891), Muḥammad b. Muqātil (d. 248/862 ?), Naṣīr b. Yaḥyā (d. 268/881), and al-Qāsim b. Sallām (d. 223/837).[102]

That *takhrīj* was extensively practiced over the course of several centuries is a fact confirmed by the activities and writings of jurists who flourished as late as the seventh/thirteenth century.[103] Although the

[98] The works embodying the doctrines of the three masters are six, all compiled by Shaybānī. They are *al-Mabsūṭ*, *al-Ziyādāt*, *al-Jāmiʿ al-Kabīr*, *al-Jāmiʿ al-Ṣaghīr*, *al-Siyar al-Kabīr*, and *al-Siyar al-Ṣaghīr*. See Ibn ʿĀbidīn, *Ḥāshiya*, I, 69. However, in his *Sharḥ al-Manẓūma*, 17–18, Ibn ʿĀbidīn introduces Ibn Kamāl's distinction between *ẓāhir al-riwāya* and *masā'il al-uṣūl*, a distinction which he draws in turn on Sarakhsī's differentiation. The former, according to Ibn Kamāl, is limited to the six works enumerated. The latter, on the other hand, may include cases belonging to *nawādir*, which constitutes the second category of doctrine.

[99] These works include Shaybānī's *Kīsāniyyāt*, *Hārūniyyāt*, and *Jurjāniyyāt*; Ibn Ziyād's *Muḥarrar*; and Abū Yūsuf's *Kitāb al-Amālī*.

[100] Ibn ʿĀbidīn, *Ḥāshiya*, I, 69. See also Ḥājjī Khalīfa, *Kashf al-Ẓunūn ʿan Asāmī al-Kutub wal-Funūn*, 2 vols. (Istanbul: Maṭbaʿat Wakālat al-Maʿārif al-Jalīla, 1941–43), II, 1281.

[101] Ibn ʿĀbidīn, *Ḥāshiya*, I, 50; Ibn ʿĀbidīn, *Sharḥ al-Manẓūma*, 25; Shāh Walī Allāh, *ʿIqd al-Jīd*, 19.

[102] Ibn ʿĀbidīn, *Ḥāshiya*, I, 69.

[103] Ibn Abī al-ʿIzz al-Ḥanafī, *al-Ittibāʿ*, ed. Muḥammad ʿAṭā' Allāh Ḥanīf and ʿĀṣim al-Qaryūṭī (Amman: n.p., 1405/1984), 62. For a general history of *takhrīj* – to be used with caution – see Yaʿqūb b. ʿAbd al-Wahhāb Bāḥusayn, *al-Takhrīj ʿInda al-Fuqahā' wal-Uṣūliyyīn* (Riyadh: Maktabat al-Rushd, 1414/1993). Ibn al-Ṣalāḥ, who died in 643/1245, asserts that the practice of *takhrīj*, when an already established opinion is nowhere to be found, "has been prevalent for ages" (*yajūzu lil-muftī al-muntasib an yuftī fī-mā lā yajiduhu min aḥkāmī al-waqā'iʿi manṣūṣan ʿalayhi li-Imāmihi bi-mā yukharrijuhu ʿalā madhhabihi, wa-hādhā huwa al-ṣaḥīḥ al-ladhī ʿalayhi al-ʿamal wa-ilayhi mafzaʿ al-muftīn min mudadin madīda.*" See his *Adab al-Muftī*, 96.

activity itself was known as *takhrīj*, its practitioners in the Shāfiᶜite school became known as *aṣḥāb al-wujūh*.[104] In the Ḥanafite, Mālikite, and Ḥanbalite schools, however, the designation *aṣḥāb al-takhrīj* persisted, as attested in the terminological usages of biographical dictionaries and law manuals. In addition to the names we have already discussed, the following is a list of jurists who are described in these dictionaries as having seriously engaged in *takhrīj*:

1. The Shāfiᶜite Ibrāhīm al-Muzanī, whose *takhrīj* was so extensive that the later Shāfiᶜite jurists distinguished between those of his opinions that conformed to the school's hermeneutic (and were thus accepted as an important part of the school's doctrine), and those that did not.[105] These latter, however, were still significant enough to be considered by some jurists sufficient, on their own, to form the basis of an independent *madhhab*.[106]
2. ᶜAlī Ibn al-Ḥusayn Ibn Ḥarbawayh (d. 319/931), claimed by the Shāfiᶜites, but a student of Abū Thawr and Dāwūd Ibn Khalaf al-Ẓāhirī.[107]
3. Muḥammad b. al-Mufaḍḍal Abū al-Ṭayyib al-Ḍabbī (d. 308/920), a student of Ibn Surayj and a distinguished Shāfiᶜite.[108]
4. Abū Saᶜīd al-Iṣṭakhrī (d. 328/939), a major jurist of *aṣḥāb al-wujūh*.[109]
5. Zakariyyā b. Aḥmad Abū Yaḥyā al-Balkhī (d. 330/941), "one of the distinguished Shāfiᶜites and of the *aṣḥāb al-wujūh*."[110]
6. The Ḥanbalite ᶜUmar b. al-Ḥusayn al-Khiraqī (d. 334/945), who engaged extensively in *takhrīj* but whose writings containing his most creative reasoning were destroyed when his house was reportedly consumed by fire.[111] His *Mukhtaṣar*, however, which survived him long enough to have an influence, contained many cases of his *takhrīj* which he nonetheless attributed to Ibn Ḥanbal.[112]
7. The Shāfiᶜite ᶜAlī b. Ḥusayn Abū al-Ḥasan al-Jūrī (d. ca. 330/941), considered one of the *aṣḥāb al-wujūh*.[113]
8. Ẓāhir al-Sarakhsī (d. 389/998), a major Shāfiᶜite jurist. Yet, despite being one of the *aṣḥāb wujūh*, little of his doctrine, according to Nawawī, was transmitted.[114]

104 Ibn al-Ṣalāḥ, *Adab al-Muftī*, 97.
105 Muḥyī al-Dīn Sharaf al-Dīn b. Yaḥyā al-Nawawī, *Tahdhīb al-Asmā' wal-Lughāt*, 3 vols. (Cairo: Idārat al-Tibāᶜa al-Munīriyya, 1927), I, 285; Ibn Qāḍī Shuhba, *Ṭabaqāt*, I, 8; Subkī, *Ṭabaqāt*, I, 243–44.
106 Nawawī, *Tahdhīb*, I, 285; Ibn Qāḍī Shuhba, *Ṭabaqāt*, I, 8.
107 Subkī, *Ṭabaqāt*, II, 301–02. 108 Ibn Qāḍī Shuhba, *Ṭabaqāt*, I, 66.
109 Ibid., I, 75. 110 Ibid., I, 76.
111 Ismāᶜīl b. ᶜUmar Ibn Kathīr, *al-Bidāya wal-Nihāya*, 14 vols. (Beirut: Dār al-Kutub al-ᶜIlmiyya, 1985–88), XI, 228.
112 See the editor's introduction to Shams al-Dīn Muḥammad b. ᶜAbd Allāh al-Miṣrī al-Zarkashī, *Sharḥ al-Zarkashī ᶜalā Mukhtaṣar al-Khiraqī*, ed. ᶜAbd Allāh b. ᶜAbd al-Raḥmān al-Jabrīn, 7 vols. (Riyadh: Maktabat al-ᶜUbaykān, 1413/1993), I, 47–48.
113 Subkī, *Ṭabaqāt*, II, 307. 114 Nawawī, *Tahdhīb*, I, 192.

9. The Ḥanafite Abū ʿAbd Allāh Muḥammad b. Yaḥyā b. Mahdī al-Jurjānī (d. 398/1007), the teacher of Qudūrī and Nāṭifī, who was deemed one of the *aṣḥāb al-takhrīj*.[115]
10. ʿAbd Allāh b. Muḥammad al-Khawārizmī (d. 398/1007), one of the *aṣḥāb al-wujūh* and considered a leading jurist of the Shāfiʿite school.[116]
11. Yūsuf b. Aḥmad Ibn Kajj (d. 405/1014), a prominent Shāfiʿite jurist who is considered one of the most exacting of the *aṣḥāb al-wujūh* (*min aṣḥāb al-wujūh al-mutqinīn*).[117]
12. ʿAbd al-Raḥmān Muḥammad al-Fūrānī Abū al-Qāsim al-Marwazī (d. 461/1068), who is described as having articulated "good *wujūh*" in the Shāfiʿite *madhhab* (*wa-lahu wujūh jayyida fī al-madhhab*).[118]
13. Al-Qāḍī Ḥusayn b. Muḥammad al-Marwazī (d. 462/1069), a major figure in the Shāfiʿite school and one of the *aṣḥāb al-wujūh*.[119]
14. ʿAbd al-Raḥmān Ibn Baṭṭa al-Fayrazān (d. 470/1077), a Ḥanbalite jurist who is described as having engaged in *takhrīj* in a variety of ways (*kharraja al-takhārīj*).[120]
15. Abū Naṣr Muḥammad Ibn al-Ṣabbāgh (d. 477/1084), considered by some as an absolute *mujtahid* and a towering figure of the *aṣḥāb al-wujūh* in the Shāfiʿite school.[121]
16. The Mālikite Abū Ṭāhir b. Bashīr al-Tanūkhī (d. after 526/1131), whose *takhrīj* was said by Ibn Daqīq al-ʿĪd to be methodologically deficient.[122]
17. The famous Ḥanafite jurist and author Burhān al-Dīn al-Marghīnānī (d. 593/1196), the author of the famous *al-Hidāya* and one of the *aṣḥāb al-takhrīj*.[123]

The biographical works took special notice not only of those who engaged in *takhrīj*, but also of those who specialized in or made it their concern to study and transmit the doctrines and legal opinions derived through this particular juristic activity. We thus find that Aḥmad b. ʿAlī al-Arānī (d. 643/1245), a distinguished Shāfiʿite, excelled in the transmission of the *wujūh* that had been elaborated in his school.[124] Similarly, the biographers describe the Shāfiʿite ʿUthmān b. ʿAbd al-Raḥmān al-Naṣrī (d. 643/1245) as having had penetrating knowledge (*baṣīran*) of the doctrines elaborated through *takhrīj*.[125]

Ṭūfī's remark that the Shāfiʿites engaged in *takhrīj* more than did the other schools is confirmed by our general survey of biographical works. In Ibn Qāḍī Shuhba's *Ṭabaqāt*, for instance, there appear some two dozen major jurists who engaged in this activity, only a few of whom we have

115 Laknawī, *al-Fawāʾid al-Bahiyya*, 202.
116 Ibn Qāḍī Shuhba, *Ṭabaqāt*, I, 144. 117 Ibid., I, 197. 118 Ibid., I, 266–67.
119 Nawawī, *Tahdhīb*, I, 164–65. 120 Ibn Rajab, *Dhayl*, I, 26–27.
121 Ibn Qāḍī Shuhba, *Ṭabaqāt*, I, 269–70. 122 Ibn Farḥūn, *Dībāj*, 87.
123 Ibn ʿĀbidīn, *Sharḥ al-Manẓūma*, 49; Qurashī, *al-Jawāhir al-Muḍīʾa*, II, 559.
124 Ibn Qāḍī Shuhba, *Ṭabaqāt*, II, 125. 125 Ibid., II, 145.

listed above.[126] Our survey of the biographical dictionaries of the four schools also shows that the Shāfiᶜites and Ḥanbalites could each boast a larger number of jurists who engaged in this activity than the other two schools combined.[127] On the other hand, of all four schools, the Mālikites are said to have engaged in this activity the least.[128]

The Shāfiᶜite involvement in *takhrīj* seems to have reached its zenith in the fourth/tenth and fifth/eleventh centuries, the last jurists associated with it, according to Ibn Abī al-Damm, having been Maḥāmilī (d. 415/1024), Māwardī (d. 450/1058), and Abū al-Ṭayyib al-Ṭabarī (d. 450/1058).[129] But Ibn Abī al-Damm's claim cannot be fully or even substantially confirmed by data from either biographical dictionaries or works of positive law. During the later centuries – especially after the fourth/tenth – the activity in the Shāfiᶜite school continued, albeit with somewhat diminished vigor.[130] In the other schools, it also found expression in later doctrines, as attested in the juristic production of two towering Ḥanbalite figures, Ibn Qudāma (d. 620/1223) and Taqī al-Dīn Ibn Taymiyya (d. 728/1327),[131] as well as in the writings of a number of Ḥanafite and Mālikite jurists.[132]

[126] Ibid., I, 99–100 (Ibn Abī Hurayra), 149 (Muḥammad b. al-Ḥasan al-Astrabādhī), 152 (Muḥammad Abū Bakr al-Ūdanī), 154 (Muḥammad b. ᶜAlī al-Māsarujsī), 177 (Abū al-Qāsim al-Ṣaymarī), 207 (al-Ḥasan Abū ᶜAlī al-Bandanījī), 221 (Muḥammad b. ᶜAbd al-Malik al-Marwazī), 233 (al-Ḥusayn b. Muḥammad al-Qaṭṭān), 241 (Abū al-Ḥasan al-Māwardī), 262 (Abū al-Rabīᶜ Ṭāhir b. ᶜAbd Allāh al-Turkī), 264–65 (Abū Saᶜd al-Nīsābūrī), 266–67 (ᶜAbd al-Raḥmān al-Fūrānī al-Marwazī).

[127] In addition to those listed by Ibn Qāḍī Shuhba (previous note), see Nawawī, *Tahdhīb*, I, 92–94, 113, 164, 238. For the Ḥanbalites, see Zarkashī, *Sharḥ*, I, 28 ff.

[128] This is the claim of Qarāfī. See Rāᶜī, *Intiṣār al-Faqīr*, 169. Qarāfī's claim, it must be noted, does find initial support in the sources, notably in Ibn Farḥūn's *Dībāj*.

[129] Ibrāhīm b. ᶜAbd Allāh Ibn Abī al-Damm, *Adab al-Qaḍā' aw al-Durar al-Manẓūmāt fī al-Aqḍiya wal-Ḥukūmāt*, ed. Muḥammad ᶜAṭā' (Beirut: Dār al-Kutub al-ᶜIlmiyya, 1987), 40.

[130] See, for example, Taqī al-Dīn ᶜAlī al-Subkī, *Fatāwā al-Subkī*, 2 vols. (Cairo: Maktabat al-Qudsī, 1937), I, 324; II, 468, 525; Subkī, *Ṭabaqāt*, VI, 186 ff., 193. Sharaf al-Dīn al-Nawawī, who died in 676/1277, is still speaking of *takhrīj*. See his *al-Majmūᶜ*, I, 68.

[131] See Nawawī, *al-Majmūᶜ*, I, 68; Bāḥusayn, *Takhrīj*, 266 (quoted from Muwaffaq al-Dīn Ibn Qudāma, *al-Mughnī*, 12 vols. (Beirut: Dār al-Kitāb al-ᶜArabī, 1983), IX, 131); Ṭūfī, *Sharḥ Mukhtaṣar al-Rawḍa*, III, 628; Ibn al-Ṣalāḥ, *Adab al-Muftī*, 126, is still speaking of *takhrīj*. So is ᶜAlī b. Sulaymān b. Muḥammad al-Mirdāwī, *Taṣḥīḥ al-Furūᶜ*, printed with Shams al-Dīn Muḥammad Ibn Mufliḥ, *Kitāb al-Furūᶜ*, ed. ᶜAbd al-Sattār Farrāj, 6 vols. (Beirut: ᶜĀlam al-Kutub, 1405/1985), I, 51.

[132] ᶜAlā' al-Dīn Abū Bakr Ibn Masᶜūd al-Kāsānī, *Badā'iᶜ al-Ṣanā'iᶜ fī Tartīb al-Sharā'iᶜ*, 7 vols. (Beirut: Dār al-Kitāb al-ᶜArabī, 1982), I, 2, where he makes a preliminary remark to the effect that his book examines legal cases and the modes of their *takhrīj* according to the principles and general precepts laid down presumably by the founding fathers (*yataṣaffaḥ . . . aqsām al-masā'il wa-fuṣūlahā wa-takhrījahā ᶜalā qawāᶜidihā wa-uṣūlihā*); W. B. Hallaq, "A Prelude to Ottoman Reform: Ibn ᶜĀbidīn on Custom

## IV

Be that as it may, there is no doubt that *takhrīj* constituted, in the authoritative doctrinal structure of the four schools, the second most important body of legal subject matter – second, that is, to the actual doctrines of the eponyms, and second only when disentangled from the eponym's *corpus juris*. For it was often the case that attributions to the imam became indistinguishably blended with their own doctrine or at least with what was thought to be their own doctrine (a qualification that has been established in the previous section). We have thus far seen a number of examples which make it demonstrably clear that the *takhrīj* of later authorities becomes the property of the eponyms. This process of attribution, it is important to stress, did not go unnoticed by the jurists themselves. They were acutely aware of it not only as a matter of practice, but also as a matter of theory. Abū Isḥāq al-Shīrāzī, a Shāfiᶜite jurist and legal theoretician, devotes to this issue what is for us a significant chapter in his monumental *uṣūl* work *Sharḥ al-Lumaᶜ*. The chapter's title leaves us in no doubt as to the facts: "Concerning the Matter that it is not Permissible to Attribute to Shāfiᶜī what his Followers have Established through *takhrīj*."[133]

Shīrāzī observes that some of the Shāfiᶜites did allow such attributions, a significant admission which goes to show that this process was recognized as a conscious act,[134] unlike that of attributing to the eponyms the opinions of their predecessors. Shīrāzī reports furthermore that proponents of the doctrine defended their position by adducing the following argument: The conclusions of *qiyās* are considered part of the Sharīᶜa, and they are thus attributed to God and the Prophet. Just as this is true, it is also true that the conclusions of *qiyās* drawn by other jurists on the basis of Shāfiᶜī's opinions may and should be attributed to Shāfiᶜī himself. Shīrāzī rejects this argument though, saying that the conclusions of *qiyās* are never considered statements by God or the Prophet himself. Rather, they are considered part of the religion of God and the Prophet (*dīnu*

and Legal Change," proceedings of a conference held in Istanbul, May 25–30, 1999 (New York: Columbia University Press, forthcoming). See also the Mālikite Ḥaṭṭāb, *Mawāhib al-Jalīl*, I, 41. On the discourse of the Mālikite Qarāfī concerning the theory of *takhrīj*, see Jackson, *Islamic Law and the State*, 91–96. Jackson remarks that "Qarāfī himself engages in this practice on occasion" (p. 96).

133 Abū Isḥāq Ibrāhīm b. ᶜAlī al-Shīrāzī, *Sharḥ al-Lumaᶜ*, ed. ᶜAbd al-Majīd Turkī, 2 vols. (Beirut: Dār al-Gharb al-Islāmī, 1988), II, 1084–85: "*Fī annahu lā yajūz an yunsab ilā al-Shāfiᶜī mā kharrajahu aḥad aṣḥābihi ᶜalā qawlihi.*"

134 The controversy and its relevance are still obvious at least two centuries after Shīrāzī wrote. See Ibn al-Ṣalāḥ, *Adab al-Muftī*, 96–97.

*Allāh wa-dīnu Rasūlihi*).[135] Besides, Shīrāzī continues, even this attribution in terms of religion is inadmissible, for neither Shāfiʿī nor any of the other founding *mujtahid*s have their own religion.

Shīrāzī then cites another argument advanced by his interlocutor: If the eponym holds a certain opinion with regard to one case, say, the proprietorship of a garden, then his opinion about another case, such as the proprietorship of land surrounding a house, would be analogous. The implication here, in line with the first argument, is that an analogous opinion not necessarily derived by the eponym belongs nonetheless to him, since the principles of reasoning involved in the case dictate identical conclusions. Shīrāzī counters by arguing that there is in effect a qualitative difference between the interlocutor's example, which is analogical, and *takhrīj*, which always involves two different, not similar, cases. Analogical cases, Shīrāzī argues, may be attributed to the eponym despite the fact that one of them was not solved by him. But when the two cases are different, and when one of them was solved by another jurist, no attribution of the latter to the eponym should be considered permissible.[136]

Ṭūfī provides further clarification of Shīrāzī's argument. If the eponym established a certain legal norm for a particular case, and also explicated the rationale (*ʿilla*) which led him to that norm, then all other cases possessing this identifiable *ʿilla* should have the same norm. In this sense, the eponym's doctrine, used to solve the first case, can be said to have provided the solution of the latter ones, even though the eponym may not have even known of their existence. In other words, the latter cases can be attributed to him.[137] On the other hand, should he solve a case without articulating the *ʿilla* behind it, and should he not predicate the same legal norm he derived for this case upon what appears to be an analogous case, then his doctrines (*madhhab*) in both cases must be seen as unrelated. The disparity is assumed because of the distinct possibility that he would have *articulated* a different *ʿilla* for each case or set of cases. But, Ṭūfī adds, many jurists (*al-kathīr min al-fuqahā'*) disregarded such distinctions and permitted the activity of *takhrīj* nonetheless.[138]

Ṭūfī's testimony, coupled with that of Shīrāzī, is revealing. It not only tells of the presence of a significant juristic–interpretive activity that dominated legal history for a considerable period, but also discloses the

[135] Shīrāzī, *Sharḥ al-Lumaʿ*, II, 1084. [136] Ibid., II, 1085.

[137] Ṭūfī, *Sharḥ Mukhtaṣar al-Rawḍa*, III, 638: "*idhā naṣṣa al-mujtahid ʿalā ḥukm fī mas'ala li-ʿilla bayyanahā fa-madhhabuhu fī kulli mas'ala wujidat fī-hā tilka al-ʿilla ka-madhhabihi fī hādhihi al-mas'ala.*" See also the introduction to Zarkashī, *Sharḥ*, I, 28 ff.

[138] Ṭūfī, *Sharḥ Mukhtaṣar al-Rawḍa*, III, 639.

methodological issues that such activity involved. The penchant to attribute doctrines to the eponym constituted ultimately the crux of the controversy between the two sides. Curiously, the theoretical exposition of *takhrīj* did not account for the contributions of authorities external to the school of the founder. The recruitment of Ḥanafite doctrine and its assimilation into the Shāfiᶜite school was not, for instance, given any due notice. In fact, because the theoretical elaboration of *takhrīj* appeared at a time when the schools had already reached their full development, it must not have been in the best interest of the affiliated jurists to expose their debt to other schools. We might conjecture that the debt was to a large extent reciprocal among all the schools, which explains why no jurist found it opportune or wise to expose the other schools' debt to his own. His own school, one suspects, would have been equally vulnerable to the same charge.

## V

It is therefore clear that *ijtihād* through *takhrīj* was a dominant interpretive activity for several centuries and that at least a fair number of jurists were in the habit of attributing the results of their juristic endeavors to the founders.[139] This process of attribution, which is one of back-projection, both complemented and enhanced the other process of attribution by which the founder imams were themselves credited with a body of doctrines that their predecessors had elaborated. This is not to say, however, that both processes were of the same nature, for one was a self-conscious act while the other was not. The process of crediting the presumed founders with doctrines which had been constructed by their predecessors was never acknowledged, whether by legal practitioners or theoreticians. Islamic legal discourse is simply silent on this point. Attributions through *takhrīj*, on the other hand, were widely acknowledged.

The explanation for this phenomenon is not difficult: The attribution of later opinions to a founder can be and indeed was justified by the

[139] See the statement of the Ḥanbalite Ibn Qāsim in this regard, quoted in Zarkashī, *Sharḥ*, I, 31–32. This process of attribution gave rise to an operative terminology which required distinctions to be made between the actual opinions of the imams and those that were placed in their mouths. Ibn ᶜĀbidīn, for instance, argues that it is improper to use the formula "Abū Ḥanīfa said" (*qāla Abū Ḥanīfa*) if Abū Ḥanīfa himself had not held the opinion. The *takhrījāt* (pl. of *takhrīj*) of the major jurists, he asserts, must be stated with the formula "Abū Ḥanīfa's *madhhab* dictates that . . ." (*muqtaḍā madhhab Abī Ḥanīfa kadhā*). See his *Sharḥ al-Manẓūma*, 25.

supposed fact that these opinions were reached on the basis of a methodology of legal reasoning constructed in its entirety by the presumed founder. The assumption underlying this justification is that the founder would have himself reached these same opinions had he addressed the cases which his later followers encountered. But he did not, for the cases (*nawāzil*) befalling Muslims were deemed to be infinite. Here there are two distinct elements which further enhance the authority of the presumed founder at the expense of his followers. First, it makes their interpretive activity, or *ijtihād*, seem derivative but above all mechanical: all they need to do is to follow the methodological blueprint of the imam. This conception of methodological subservience permeates not only the juristic typologies but also all structures of positive law and biographical narrative; that is, the doctrinal, interpretive, and sociological make-up of the law. As we shall see in chapter 4, positive law depended on the identification of the imam's principles that underlie individual legal norms just as much as it depended on a variety of other considerations emanating from, and imposed upon them by, their own social exigencies. Similarly, the biographical narrative, a central feature of Islamic law, was thoroughly driven by hierarchical structures which would have no meaning without the juristic foundations laid down by the arch-figure of the imam. The second element is the wholesale attribution to the founder imam of creating an entire system of legal methodology that constitutes in effect the juridical basis of the school. I have shown elsewhere that legal theory and the methodology of the law emerged as an organic and systematic entity nearly one century after the death of Shāfiᶜī and a good half-century after the death of the last of the eponyms whose school has survived, namely, Ahmad Ibn Ḥanbal.[140] The fact of the matter is that both legal theory (*uṣūl al-fiqh*) and the principles of positive law (also known as *uṣūl*)[141] were gradual developments that began before the presumed imams lived and came to full maturity long after they perished.

Given the prestige and authority attached to the figure of the founder imams, it was self-defeating to acknowledge their debt to their immediate predecessors who were jurists like themselves.[142] That link had to be suppressed and severed at any expense. It had to be replaced by another link in which the imams confronted the revealed texts directly, as we have seen

[140] Hallaq, "Was al-Shafiᶜi the Master Architect?" 587 ff. [141] See chapter 4, below.

[142] We have already seen that Abū Ḥanīfa was associated with the highly authorized statement that "I refuse to follow (*uqallidu*) the Followers because they were men who practiced *ijtihād* and I am a man who practices *ijtihād*." This statement, especially in light of the authoritative status it acquired in the school, must have been intended to defy any admission of debt. See n. 10, above.

in the instructive example provided by Sarakhsī concerning the levy of the tithe.[143] Obviously, the link with the immediately preceding jurists could not have been dwelt upon, much less articulated as a theoretical issue. *Takhrīj*, on the other hand, was articulated in this manner, and therein lies the difference.[144]

143 See section II, above. One implication of our finding in this chapter pertains to the controversy among modern scholars over the issue of the gate of *ijtihād*. Against the age-long notion that the gate of *ijtihād* was closed – a notion advocated and indeed articulated by Schacht – it has been argued that this creative activity continued at least until late medieval times. See Wael B. Hallaq, "Was the Gate of Ijtihād Closed?" *International Journal of Middle East Studies*, 16 (1984): 3–41. Norman Calder has argued that "Schacht will be correct in asserting that the gate of *ijtihād* closed about 900 [A.D.] if he means that about then the Muslim community embraced the principle of *intisāb* or school affiliation. Hallaq will be correct in asserting that the gate of *ijtihād* did not close, if he distinguishes clearly the two types of *ijtihād* – independent and affiliated." See Calder, "al-Nawawī's Typology," 157. Now, if our findings are accepted, then Calder's distinction – previously suggested by others – becomes entirely meaningless, for it never existed in the first place. If there was ever a claim in favor of closing the gate of *ijtihād*, it could have meant one thing and one thing only, i.e. precluding the possibility of a new school, headed, of course, by an imam who would have to offer a legal methodology and a set of positive legal principles qualitatively different from those advocated by the established schools.

144 The findings of this chapter find corroboration in several quarters, each approaching the same general theme from a completely different angle. See Hallaq, "Was al-Shafiʿi the Master Architect?" reprinted in Wael B. Hallaq, *Law and Legal Theory in Classical and Medieval Islam* (Variorum: Aldershot, 1995), article VII, including the addenda; Melchert, *Formation of the Sunni Schools*; and Jonathan E. Brockopp, "Early Islamic Jurisprudence in Egypt: Two Scholars and their *Mukhtaṣars*," *International Journal of Middle East Studies*, 30 (1998): 167 ff. To these writings one may cautiously add Norman Calder, *Studies in Early Muslim Jurisprudence* (Oxford: Clarendon Press, 1993); cautiously, because Calder makes too much of the evidence available to him. For critiques of this work, see the sources cited in Harald Motzki, "The Prophet and the Cat: On Dating Mālik's *Muwaṭṭa'* and Legal Traditions," *Jerusalem Studies in Arabic and Islam*, 22 (1998): 18–83, at 19, n. 3.

## 3

# THE RISE AND AUGMENTATION OF SCHOOL AUTHORITY

## I

That the so-called founders were not truly absolute *mujtahids*, and that they did not exercise *ijtihād* across the board, is a finding that has serious implications. So does our conclusion, in chapter 2, that the authority of the so-called founders was largely a later creation, partly drawn from attributions to the eponyms by their successors, and partly a later denial of the significant contributions made by the earliest jurists to the formation of the eponyms' doctrines. One important implication of these findings is that the schools that were attributed to the imams did not rely on their talents as high-caliber *mujtahids* or, at any rate, as *mujtahids* of a special kind. There were many jurists like them during the formative period, which began at the end of the first/seventh century and continued till the middle of the fourth/tenth. Obviously, not one of them, founder of a school or not, constructed his doctrine out of a sociological and legal–jurisprudential vacuum. They studied law with previous generations of legal scholars and transmitted from them a cumulative doctrine which encompassed both authoritative and less authoritative opinions. Of course, they reformulated part of this cumulative doctrine, and hence contributed to the creation of *khilāf*, the *corpus juris* of disagreement. But they also transmitted intact to the next generation of legal scholars a substantial part of the doctrine they received from their teachers or senior colleagues. The extent of their ingenuity and creativeness in reformulating part of the received doctrine was certainly common in all the founders, as well as in many others who were not fortunate enough to be designated as founders of schools by later historical forces. For as we saw in the preceding chapter, it was these complex forces, rather than the distinctive contributions of the imams themselves, that transformed some of them into school founders.

This explains in part why Ibn Ḥanbal emerged as a founder when Muzanī, a far more skillful and creative jurist, did not. Despite the ideological biases of later biographical literature in favor of a fairly unified and strictly authoritative school doctrine, Muzanī still appears to have been a jurist–rebel in the Shāfiᶜite tradition. Perhaps more than any other jurist of this school, he is associated with what was termed *tafarrudāt*, a frequently used designation which, when said of a jurist, indicates that he diverged from the mainstream doctrine of the school. So we can quite safely infer that the term must have come into being after the emergence of an authoritative school doctrine, or *madhhab*, properly speaking. For it is frequently emphasized in the biographical literature of the Shāfiᶜite school that Muzanī's *tafarrudāt* are not considered part and parcel of Shāfiᶜite doctrine.[1] In fact, he is reported to have authored a whole treatise "according to his own *madhhab*, not according to that of Shāfiᶜī."[2] His divergences from Shāfiᶜī's doctrine were so many that Marwazī (d. 304/916) felt compelled to write a substantial treatise (*mujallad ḍakhm*) in an attempt to reconcile the doctrines of the two, perhaps by bringing Muzanī's doctrine closer to that of Shāfiᶜī, at least to the extent that this was possible. The discourse of the biographies suggests that a major preoccupation of Marwazī in this work was to smooth the edges of Muzanī's critique (*iᶜtirāḍāt*) of Shāfiᶜī. But despite his best efforts, he seems to have been unable to bring himself to side consistently with Shāfiᶜī, and is reported to have frequently found Muzanī's opinion superior to that of the former.[3] It is interesting to note in this context that half a century after Marwazī's death, when school doctrine had reached a fuller stage of development, the distinguished Abū Bakr al-Fārisī (d. 349/960) attacked Muzanī in favor of Shāfiᶜī.[4]

Thus in the eyes of later *madhhab*-oriented jurists, Muzanī was anything but a loyal student. Abū Bakr al-Fārisī's attack was to demonstrate this much. But during the pre-*madhhab* era, in which Muzanī flourished, unrestricted juristic maneuvering was still quite possible. By virtue of the force of maintaining tradition, both early and later perceptions combined to create a dual image of Muzanī. Juwaynī and Rāfiᶜī are reported to have said that Muzanī's *tafarrudāt* constitute part of his own, independent *madhhab*, whereas his *takhrīj*, in which he conforms to Shāfiᶜī, has precedence over any other juristic doctrine within the latter's *madhhab*, and

[1] Subkī, *Ṭabaqāt*, I, 243; Ibn Qāḍī Shuhba, *Ṭabaqāt*, I, 8 (on the authority of Ibn Kajj [d. 405/1014]).
[2] Nawawī, *Tahdhīb*, I, 285; Subkī, *Ṭabaqāt*, I, 245–46.
[3] Ibn Qāḍī Shuhba, *Ṭabaqāt*, I, 71. [4] Ibid., I, 94–95.

thus "inescapably belongs to the Shāfiᶜite school."[5] *Takhrīj* aside, Rāfiᶜī argues, "the man is responsible for an independent school" (*fal-rajul ṣāḥib madhhab mustaqill*).[6] But failing to attract any following, a Muzanite school was not to be.

It is not our intention here to explain why circumstances did not favour the rise of Muzanism, as they did Shāfiᶜism or Ḥanbalism, among others. Nor is it even within the reach of our knowledge to answer this question at present. It is sufficient for us to note that, at least in part, Muzanī's case resembles that of numerous other early *mujtahid*s whose juristic accomplishments were superior to those of some of the school founders, yet did not receive the same recognition.

For Muzanī was not alone. Independent *mujtahid*s continued to rise to the challenge of formulating the law. Their names and extraordinary activities have been recorded in some detail in biographical literature, despite the "ideological" biases that these later works exhibited in favor of school affiliation. Not only Muzanī, but also Ḥarmala (d. 243/857), another student of Shāfiᶜī, is said to have reached such a level of legal learning and accomplishment as to have been considered responsible for a school of his own.[7] Another Iraqian jurist whose training combined elements of Kūfan doctrine and Shāfiᶜī's teachings was Ibrāhīm b. Khālid Abū Thawr (d. 240/854), whose *tafarrudāt* were not accepted by the later Shāfiᶜites because he "had his own *madhhab*."[8] Among the Mālikites who demonstrated a strong tendency towards independent reasoning we find Aḥmad b. Ziyād and Saᶜīd b. Muḥammad Ibn al-Ḥaddād (both appear to have flourished around the end of the third/ninth century), who are reported to have categorically refused to bow to the authority of the masters without allowing their own reasoning to adjudicate first.[9]

To this list of independent *mujtahid*s we must add the very distinguished group of jurists known as the "Four Muḥammads" (*al-Muḥammadūn al-Arbaᶜa*), namely, Muḥammad b. Jarīr al-Ṭabarī (d. 310/922), Muḥammad b. Isḥāq Ibn Khuzayma al-Nīsābūrī (d. 311/923), Muḥammad b. Naṣr al-Marwazī (d. 294/906), and Muḥammad b. Ibrāhīm Ibn al-Mundhir al-Nīsābūrī (d. 318/930).[10] All four were considered absolute *mujtahid*s

[5] Ibid., I, 8; Nawawī, *Tahdhīb*, I, 285: "*idhā tafarrada al-Muzanī bi-ra'y fa-hwa ṣāḥib madhhab wa-idhā kharraja lil-Shāfiᶜī qawlan fa-takhrījuhu awlā min takhrīj ghayrihi wa-hwa multaḥiq bil-madhhab lā maḥāla.*"

[6] Ibn Qāḍī Shuhba, *Ṭabaqāt*, I, 8. [7] Suyūṭī, *al-Radd*, 188.

[8] Ibn Qāḍī Shuhba, *Ṭabaqāt*, I, 3–4.

[9] Abū ᶜAbd Allāh Muḥammad b. Ḥārith al-Khushanī, *Quḍāt Qurṭuba* (Cairo: Dār al-Kutub al-Miṣriyya, 1982), 282, 201–02.

[10] Subkī, *Ṭabaqāt*, II, 20–26, 126–30, 130–35, 135–40; Ibn Qāḍī Shuhba, *Ṭabaqāt*, I, 60, 62; Suyūṭī, *al-Radd*, 189; Shīrāzī, *Ṭabaqāt*, 86–87.

who developed independent legal doctrines that were seen later as consisting of a large number of *tafarrudāt*.[11] This phenomenon presents us with a problem in Islamic legal history because their contributions appear to have been no less independent-minded and significant than those of the four founders; nevertheless, they never succeeded in establishing schools of their own, or at least none that managed to survive. Admittedly, this problem cannot be separated from the quandary we have already discussed, namely: Why did Abū Ḥanīfa, Mālik, Shāfiʿī, and Ibn Ḥanbal emerge as imams and founders? Why, moreover, to complicate matters further, did their schools succeed when others failed? To attempt to answer these questions, however, would take us beyond our present enquiry.[12]

Still another problem raised by the Four Muḥammads is their place in the doctrinal configuration of the four schools, from which they were not largely dissociated. We have already seen that Ibn al-Mundhir al-Nīsābūrī figures prominently in later Ḥanbalite doctrine,[13] and all four were at the same time considered, rather ambivalently, members of the Shāfiʿite school.[14] Yet Ṭabarī did succeed in attracting followers and had, for a short time at least, a school which was recognizably separate from its Shāfiʿite parent.[15] Similarly, Ibn Khuzayma appears to have had his own followers, most notably Daʿlaj b. Aḥmad al-Sajzī (d. 351/962) who "used to issue *fatwā*s according to Ibn Khuzayma's *madhhab*."[16] The *qāḍī* Abū Bakr Aḥmad b. Kalīl, on the other hand, did not issue *fatwā*s according to the *madhhab* of Ṭabarī, although he was his student and one of his associates (*aḥad aṣḥābihi*). Instead, Ibn Kalīl is said to have disagreed with his mentor, choosing to follow instead a distinct *madhhab* that consisted of a combination of various doctrines.[17]

The foregoing is merely a sampling of the biographical notices and data dedicated to the jurists who flourished by the end of the formative period, that is, roughly speaking, by the middle of the fourth/tenth century. The picture that emerges is one of plurality. The so-called independent

[11] Subkī, *Ṭabaqāt*, II, 139. See also sources cited in previous note.

[12] See preface, n. 3, above.

[13] See Ibn Qudāma, *Mughnī*, XI, 259, 263, 271, 272, 277, 281, and passim. See also the editor's references to Ibn Qudāma's *Mughnī* in Muḥammad b. Ibrāhīm al Nīsābūrī Ibn al-Mundhir, *al-Ijmāʿ*, ed. ʿAbd Allāh al-Bārūdī (Beirut: Dār al-Jinān, 1986), 182 ff., 187 ff., 191 ff., 201 ff., and passim.

[14] Subkī, *Ṭabaqāt*, I, 244; II, 126, 139; Ibn al-Nadīm, *al-Fihrist* (Beirut: Dār al-Maʿrifa lil-Ṭibāʿa wal-Nashr, 1398/1978), 302.

[15] See Ibn al-Nadīm, *Fihrist*, 326–29, who places Jarīrism on a par with the other schools. See also Suyūṭī, *al-Radd*, 189.

[16] Subkī, *Ṭabaqāt*, II, 222.

[17] Suyūṭī, *al-Radd*, 190.

*mujtahids*, the likes of Abū Thawr, Muzanī, and the Four Muḥammads, are not only said to have created their own doctrines but also contributed to those of schools not their own. All of them developed, albeit to varying degrees, their own legal doctrines. Yet all of them were recruited to provide doctrinal support in the Shāfiᶜite school. Ibn al-Mundhir, one of the Four Muḥammads, was appropriated even more extensively in the Ḥanbalite school.[18]

## II

This ubiquitous plurality became increasingly circumscribed by the beginning of the fourth/tenth century, as evidenced by the data contained in biographical collections. Around this time, the school as a guild began to crystallize, for it was not long thereafter that the school came to be universally recognized as an authoritative structure. But a distinction must be made at this point between two fairly separate developments with regard to the evolution of the school, or at least its usual designation, *madhhab*. The word *madhhab* meant a number of different things, depending on how the word was used and in what particular context. One sense of the word indicated personal affiliation to the doctrine of an imam, a meaning which had fully emerged and been solidified by the middle of the fourth/tenth century. Perhaps a more important sense of the term was its signification of the positive and theoretical doctrine of the imam in particular and of his followers in general. In this sense, therefore, the *madhhab* acquired the meaning of "a school's authoritative doctrine," a meaning that was only later to emerge in its final form, perhaps as late as the end of the sixth/twelfth century. But the process by which this sense developed was a lengthy one, with the fourth/tenth and fifth/eleventh centuries proving to be the period of its most significant growth.

Whereas the earlier period (which had ended, so to speak, by the middle of the fourth/tenth century) was one of almost indistinguishable plurality, the century or two immediately succeeding it witnessed a significant narrowing of doctrinal possibilities. We demonstrated earlier how this plurality allowed for the easy appropriation of various doctrines as one's own. Ibn Surayj, for instance, perhaps the most important figure in the Shāfiᶜite school after Shāfiᶜī himself, and the jurist responsible for the spread and success of the school,[19] is said to have written a work

[18] See n. 13, above.

[19] See Hallaq, "Was al-Shafiᶜi the Master Architect?" 595 ff.; Melchert, *Formation of the Sunni Schools*, 87 ff.

in which he derived his doctrine from Shaybānī's, not Shāfiʿī's, system (*farraʿa ʿalā kutub Muḥammad b. al-Ḥasan*).[20] This appropriation could not, and indeed did not, occur in the later period. Like Ibn Surayj, Ibn al-Qāṣṣ (d. 335/946) belonged to the Shāfiʿite school, but in his book *Adab al-Qāḍī* he, by his own admission, combined the doctrines of Shāfiʿī and Abū Ḥanīfa.[21] Yet another eloquent testimony to this unbounded plurality was the uncertainty of the young Muḥammad b. Naṣr al-Marwazī at the outset of his career as to which imam to follow, Abū Ḥanīfa, Mālik, or Shāfiʿī.[22] Later on in life, of course, he became an independent *mujtahid*. Nevertheless, Marwazī's uncertainty is indicative of the impertinence of the *madhhab* as an authoritative doctrinal entity. Rising students did not see any need or feel any pressure to bind themselves to a *madhhab*, a situation which was soon to change. While the young Marwazī faced the dilemma of having to choose an imam to study and follow (in this case Shāfiʿī),[23] students of the late fourth/tenth and fifth/eleventh centuries did not face such uncertainties or even choices, for they lived in a world where they already had to belong to a *madhhab* before embarking on a career in law.

The emergence of a personal and doctrinal *madhhab* by no means spelled the end of *ijtihād*. Elsewhere, I have shown that the reported closure of the gate of *ijtihād* was no more than a myth,[24] to be interpreted, if taken seriously, as a closure of the possibility of creating new schools of law in the manner the imams were said to have forged their own *madhhabs*. In light of our findings in the previous chapter, the *doctrine* of the closure of the gate can now be seen as an attempt to enhance and augment the constructed authority of the founding imams, and had little to do with the realities of legal reasoning, the jurists' competence, or the modes of reproducing legal doctrine.

Even during the post-formative period, that is, during the second half of the fourth/tenth century and the fifth/eleventh, a number of *mujtahids* continued to forge their own legal doctrines. ʿAbd Allāh b. Ibrāhīm Abū al-Faḍl al-Maqdisī (d. 480/1087) was reported to have risen to the rank of *mujtahid*.[25] So apparently did Ibrāhīm b. Muḥammad b. Mihrān

[20] Shīrāzī, *Ṭabaqāt*, 109; Ibn Qāḍī Shuhba, *Ṭabaqāt*, I, 49.
[21] Ibn al-Qāṣṣ, *Adab al-Qāḍī*, I, 68: "*fa-allaftu kitābī hādhā fī adab al-qāḍī ʿalā madhhab al-Shāfiʿī wal-Kūfī*," the latter being an unequivocal reference to Abū Ḥanīfa.
[22] Subkī, *Ṭabaqāt*, II, 23.
[23] This is reported, of course, in Shāfiʿite biographical works (cf. Subkī, *Ṭabaqāt*, II, 23), but the credibility of this account must be questioned.
[24] Hallaq, "Was the Gate of Ijtihād Closed?" 3 ff.
[25] Ibn Qāḍī Shuhba, *Ṭabaqāt*, I, 291.

Abū Isḥāq al-Isfarā'īnī (d. 418/1027), the famous jurist and theologian.[26] But these were affiliated *mujtahids* who operated within the boundaries of their schools. From this point on, *ijtihād*, however creative it might have been, was performed within at least a nominal school structure. In other words, even though a jurist's activity may have amounted to so-called independent *ijtihād*, the activity was deemed to fall within the hermeneutical contours of the school, just as the outcome of this sort of *ijtihād* was said to be a contribution to the school's substantive doctrine. The example of Abū Muḥammad al-Juwaynī (d. 438/1064), the father of Imām al-Ḥaramayn, may be somewhat extreme, but it does illustrate our point. Juwaynī the father was clearly a Shāfiᶜite who wrote some of the more important and influential works in the school. Yet he was also recognized as a *mujtahid* who consciously stood, or attempted to place himself, outside the boundaries of any school. It is reported that he wrote, or at least began to write (*sharaᶜa fī kitāb*),[27] a work entitled *al-Muḥīṭ* in which he intended, quite deliberately, to transcend the limits of the Shāfiᶜite school by discounting its specific doctrines altogether.[28] Juwaynī's radical position is instructive because despite all his attempts at promoting his own juristic agenda and nonconformity, he continued to be counted among the staunch Shafiᶜites who unquestionably belonged to the school. At the same time, it is not without significance that immediately following this account of Juwaynī's doctrinal dissent, Subkī reports that the traditionist Abū Bakr al-Bayhaqī, a fervent advocate of Shāfiᶜī,[29] severely criticized Juwaynī, arguing that the ultimate authority for everything the latter taught was none other than Shāfiᶜī himself.[30] Here, again, we witness not only a defense of the constructed authority of the imam, but also to some extent a denial of the significance and weight of any attempt to step outside the boundaries of school authority.[31]

[26] Ibid., I, 158–59; Shīrāzī, *Ṭabaqāt*, 124.

[27] We know that he completed the first three volumes of the work, which were read by Abū Bakr al-Bayhaqī. See Subkī, *Ṭabaqāt*, III, 209–10.

[28] Ibid., III, 209: "*kāna al-Shaykh Abū Muḥammad qad sharaᶜa fī kitābin sammāhu al-Muḥīṭ, ᶜazama fī-hi ᶜalā ᶜadam al-taqayyud bil-madhhab wa'annahu yaqif ᶜalā mawrid al-aḥādīth lā yataᶜaddāhā wa-yatajannab jānib al-taᶜaṣṣub lil-madhāhib.*" See also Suyūṭī, *al-Radd*, 190.

[29] Evidenced in his *Manāqib al-Shāfiᶜī*. See also Hallaq, "Was al-Shafiᶜi the Master Architect?" 599–600.

[30] Subkī, *Ṭabaqāt*, III, 210.

[31] Of Muḥammad b. Aḥmad b. Sulaymān al-Aswānī (d. 335/946), Subkī reports that he wrote a two-volume work on the basis of Shāfiᶜī's doctrine, but throughout the book objected to certain of the latter's views. Subkī adds that his objections themselves were open to criticism and reconsideration, and that the later jurists subjected them to "correction" (*taṣḥīḥ*). See his *Ṭabaqāt*, II, 108. On *taṣḥīḥ*, see chapter 5, section IV, below.

This denial is also manifested in a language critical of divergences from school doctrine, a language that became technical in nature. In addition to *tafarrudāt*, the chief term made to carry the burden of divergences from the authoritative doctrine was *gharīb*, usually employed in the plural form *gharā'ib*. Thus, while ᶜAbd al-Wāḥid b. Muḥammad al-Shīrāzī (d. 486/1093) was credited with the distinction of having contributed to the spread of the Ḥanbalite school, his biographers could not overlook the fact that he produced "many *gharā'ib* in the law."[32] The same was the case with Aḥmad b. Muḥammad al-Qaṭṭān (d. 359/969) and ᶜAbd al-ᶜAzīz al-Jīlī (d. 632/1234).[33] The latter is said to have been an expert in the authoritative doctrine of the school, but his commentary on Ghazālī's *Wajīz* contained many *gharā'ib*; because of this he was rumored, especially among law students, to be a weak jurist. Nawawī and Ibn al-Ṣalāḥ also caution that in his *tafarrudāt*, which is most probably a reference to his divergences, Jīlī is not to be considered a reliable authority.[34]

Similarly, during the same period, which begins around the middle of the fourth/tenth century, the biographical works inaugurate a new terminology that was widely used in defining the achievements of jurists, terminology that is utterly absent from writings belonging to the third/ninth or second/eighth century. Now, jurists are often described as carriers of the *madhhab*, not in the sense of personal authority but rather as keepers and promoters of a shared authoritative doctrine. An example of this emerging terminology appears in the case of the Ḥanbalite ᶜAbd al-Khāliq b. ᶜĪsā al-Hāshimī (d. 470/1077) who is said to have "excelled in the *madhhab*" (*baraᶜa fī al-madhhab*).[35] Another characterization is intimate knowledge of the school doctrine (*kāna ᶜārifan fī al-madhhab*), associated with such figures as the Ḥanbalite Ṭalḥa b. Ṭalḥa al-ᶜĀqūlī (d. 512/1118).[36] The Ḥanafite Bakr b. Muḥammad al-Zarnajrī (d. 512/1118) was considered exemplary in his knowledge (by heart) of the *madhhab*, and was for this reason nicknamed the Little Abū Ḥanīfa.[37] ᶜAbd al-Wāḥid al-Ṣaymarī (d. 386/996) was counted among the pillars of the Shāfiᶜite school of his day, one of his most notable qualities being that he memorized and was well versed in the doctrine of his school (*ḥāfiẓan lil-madhhab*).[38]

32 Ibn Rajab, *Dhayl*, I, 70. 33 Ibn Qāḍī Shuhba, *Ṭabaqāt*, I, 96; II, 93–94.

34 Ibid., II, 94. 35 Ibn Rajab, *Dhayl*, I, 16.

36 Ibid., I, 138–39.

37 Laknawī, *al-Fawā'id al-Bahiyya*, 56: "(*kāna*) *yuḍrab bi-hi al-mathal fī ḥifẓ al-madhhab, wa-kāna ahl baladihi yusammūnahu bi-Abī Ḥanīfa al-Aṣghar.*"

38 Subkī, *Ṭabaqāt*, II, 243.

With this development, the *madhhab* became an object to be studied, memorized, excelled in. When Imām al-Ḥaramayn al-Juwaynī fled persecution in his home city of Nīshāpūr and found himself in the Hijaz, he spent the four years of his stay there teaching, issuing *fatwās*, and "collecting" the various doctrines of the school (*yajmaᶜ ṭuruq al-madhhab*).[39] Finding the best opinions of the *madhhab* was already considered an accomplishment much to be desired; thus, during the period under question, a number of works were written in an effort to bring together those opinions. The treatises of Abū ᶜAbd Allāh Muḥammad b. Yaḥyā b. Mahdī al-Jurjānī (d. 398/1007),[40] Abū Ḥāmid al-Marwazī (d. 362/972), Abū ᶜAlī al-Ṭabarī (d. 350/961),[41] and Ṣaymarī, were among the great many works that proliferated during and after this period. Once again, the extraordinarily rich biographical and bibliographical data covering the third/ninth century lack any reference to works on such topics.

Immediately after the formative period, the search for authoritative opinions became a notable yet common activity. Thus, Subkī makes special mention of Muḥammad b. ᶜAbd Allāh Ibn Waraqa al-Bukhārī (d. 385/995) who used to espouse the sound *wujūh* of the *madhhab*, namely those reached through *takhrīj*.[42] It is also reported that ᶜAbd al-Raḥmān al-Fūrānī (d. 461/1068), whom we encountered earlier as one of *aṣḥāb al-wujūh*,[43] was credited for his admirable ability to pin down the sound opinions (*saḥīḥ*) of the *mukharrijūn*, a task which he performed in his work *al-Ibāna*. It is revealing that he was credited by the biographers as having been one of the first, if not the first, to engage in this activity.[44] Revealing, because such a piece of information suggests to us that *taṣḥīḥ*, which is the designation for establishing the correct school opinion on a matter,[45] could not have arisen in a context where there was no authoritative school doctrine, i.e., a *madhhab*. To say that there is a sound opinion is thus also to say that there are others which are either unsound or less sound. More importantly, it is to say that there exists an established doctrine, a standard doctrinal yardstick against which the sound can be measured against and separated from the less sound. This yardstick is the *madhhab* which began to emerge in the beginning of the fourth/tenth century. But the process that carried the *madhhab* to a full maturity was a lengthy one, spanning another two or three centuries.

[39] Ibn Qāḍī Shuhba, *Ṭabaqāt*, I, 275. [40] Ḥājjī Khalīfa, *Kashf al-Ẓunūn*, I, 398.
[41] For the last two, see Shīrāzī, *Ṭabaqāt*, 114, 115. [42] Subkī, *Ṭabaqāt*, II, 168.
[43] See chapter 2, section III (no. 12), above.
[44] Ibn Qāḍī Shuhba, *Ṭabaqāt*, I, 266; Subkī, *Ṭabaqāt*, III, 225.
[45] See chapter 5, section IV, below.

## III

In order to gauge this development, we shall now turn from the evidence provided in biographical dictionaries to works of legal theory and substantive law. We shall follow this development through two channels, represented in the criteria of *ijtihād* and *taqlīd*. For to follow or abide by the *madhhab* as a doctrinal entity was a manifestation of *taqlīd*; nay, it was *taqlīd* pure and simple (although we shall see in the next chapter that *taqlīd* was much more than following another's opinion without questioning).

Two of the most important juristic roles in the Islamic legal system were undoubtedly the *muftī* and the *qāḍī*, the jurisconsult and magistrate. How their juristic functions related to *ijtihād* and *taqlīd* throughout the centuries is an issue that represents and illustrates the evolution of the *madhhab* as an authoritative and binding doctrine. These two domains, then, will constitute the bulk of our enquiry throughout the rest of this chapter.[46]

Shāfiʿī does not explicitly state that a jurisconsult must be capable of *ijtihād*. However, he enumerates the branches of knowledge in which the jurist must be proficient in order to qualify as a *muftī*. It turns out that these branches are precisely those at which the *mujtahid* must be adept, and include skilled knowledge of the Quran, of Prophetic Sunna, the Arabic language, the legal questions subject to consensus, and the art of legal reasoning (*qiyās*).[47]

More than two centuries later, the requirement remained unchanged. Abū al-Ḥusayn al-Baṣrī (d. 436/1044) explicitly maintains that for a jurist to qualify as a *muftī*, he must be a *mujtahid*. Now, to reach the rank of *ijtihād*, an all-encompassing knowledge of legal reasoning is a prerequisite. Baṣrī, however, subsumes virtually all branches of rational and textual knowledge under the category of legal reasoning, since reasoning about the law, he argues, requires expert knowledge of the revealed texts, of the sciences that treat them – such as the abrogation and transmission of Prophetic traditions – and of the methods of establishing and verifying the *ratio legis* (*ʿilla*).[48] Only when all these sciences and texts have been mastered may one be permitted to issue *fatwās*. The sole exception to this

[46] The following section on *iftāʾ* and its relationship to *ijtihād* draws in part on my article "*Iftāʾ* and *Ijtihād* in Sunnī Legal Theory: A Developmental Account," in Muhammad Khalid Masud et al., eds., *Islamic Legal Interpretation: Muftīs and their Fatwās* (Cambridge, Mass.: Harvard University Press, 1996), 33–43.

[47] Shāfiʿī, *Kitāb Ibṭāl al-Istiḥsān*, 492, 497.

[48] Abū al-Ḥusayn al-Baṣrī, *al-Muʿtamad fī Uṣūl al-Fiqh*, ed. Muhammad Hamidullah et al., 2 vols. (Damascus: Institut Français, 1964–65), II, 929–31.

is a jurist who is adept at such sciences and textual evidence as pertain to the law of inheritance. He is allowed to issue *fatwās* in this area alone, since inheritance and bequests rarely bear on other branches of the law. With this sole exception, each jurisconsult must fulfill the requirement of *ijtihād*, the implication being that a jurisconsult, when asked to issue a *fatwā*, must not follow the teachings of other jurists but should instead formulate his own opinion.[49]

This mode of issuing *fatwās* is to be distinguished from the response to a layman's request in which a jurisconsult–*mujtahid* merely states an opinion formulated by other jurists concerning an issue (*al-iftā' bil-ḥifẓ*). In such an instance, the jurisconsult must comply with the request and must name the authority who held that opinion. In all other cases, *iftā'* clearly means for Baṣrī the exercise of *ijtihād*, for if a jurisconsult issues a *fatwā* through *taqlīd*, namely, by following the authority and opinions of others, then he is said to be a *muqallid*. According to Baṣrī, the logical conclusion of allowing a *muqallid* to practice *iftā'* is grave, since it means that laymen, who can never be anything more than *muqallids*, can conceivably issue *fatwās*, whether for themselves or for others, on the basis of the writings of earlier jurists – a conclusion that is utterly objectionable.[50]

Baṣrī's discourse is rather representative of fifth/eleventh-century writings on the issue. Abū Isḥāq al-Shīrāzī (d. 476/1083) lists the sciences and texts the jurisconsult must master, and these are again identical to those required of *mujtahids*.[51] The Mālikite Abū al-Walīd al-Bājī (d. 474/1081) insists, after having given a similar list of sciences, that any jurist who falls short of mastering even one of these fields of legal knowledge cannot be permitted to practice *iftā'*.[52] Māwardī for his part predicates *iftā'* on the attainment of *ijtihād*.[53] Similarly, Imām al-Ḥaramayn al-Juwaynī not only uses the terms "*muftī*" and "*mujtahid*" interchangeably but also states that jurists by and large have always required that a *muftī* possess a thorough knowledge of both the texts containing the law and the methods of legal reasoning that are necessary for deriving rules for novel legal cases. In addition, it is required that he be adept at exegesis and language, and though he need not memorize the Prophetic traditions, he must be able to locate the materials he requires to solve the case in hand. Finally, he must be well versed in legal theory (*uṣūl al-fiqh*) which lays

49 Ibid., II, 932. 50 Ibid.
51 Shīrāzī, *Sharḥ al-Luma'*, II, 1033.
52 Abū al-Walīd b. Khalaf al-Bājī, *Iḥkām al-Fuṣūl fī Aḥkām al-Uṣūl* (Beirut: Dār al-Gharb al-Islāmī, 1986), 722.
53 ʿAlī Muḥammad b. Ḥabīb al-Māwardī, *Adab al-Qāḍī*, ed. Muḥyī Hilāl Sarḥān, 2 vols. (Baghdad: Maṭbaʿat al-Irshād, 1391/1971), I, 637.

down the methodology and principles of the law.[54] In his rather short work, *al-Waraqāt*, Juwaynī clearly summarizes his view of the matter by saying that the *muftī* must be fully able to practice *ijtihād*.[55]

In his work *al-Mankhūl*, the Shāfiʿite Abū Ḥāmid al-Ghazālī (d. 505/1111) discusses the qualifications of the *mujtahid* in the first sub-chapter of *Kitāb al-Fatwā*, a clear indication of the interchangeability – in terms of hermeneutical function – between *iftāʾ* and *ijtihād*. In this chapter, he declares that "the jurisconsult is he who has complete mastery of the Sharīʿa rules embedded in the revealed texts as well as of those discovered by means of legal reasoning."[56] This statement, coupled with two other remarks of a similar nature,[57] makes it clear that Ghazālī follows his predecessors in affirming that to be a jurisconsult is to be nothing less than a *mujtahid*.

About a century or so after Ghazālī, an interesting and instructive change was to occur in the theoreticians' discourse on the issue. Although the Shāfiʿite Sayf al-Dīn al-Āmidī (d. 632/1234) approaches the problem from the same angle as did his predecessors, and although he insists in the beginning of his work *al-Iḥkām* on the same qualifications for the jurisconsult,[58] he later allocates a separate space to the question (*Masʾala*) of "whether or not a non-*mujtahid* is permitted to issue *fatwā*s according to the school of a *mujtahid*." Immediately thereafter, he adds the significant phrase "as it is the custom nowadays."[59] After having discussed the disagreements among jurists with regard to the matter, he argues that a *mujtahid* within a school (*mujtahid fī al-madhhab*) who is knowledgeable of the methodology of the independent *mujtahid* (*mustaqill*) he follows, and who is capable of deriving rules in accordance with this methodology and defending his positions in scholarly debates, is entitled to practice *iftāʾ*. In support of this opinion, Āmidī claims the existence of an indubitable consensus.[60]

Three significant changes are evident in Āmidī's discourse. First, he speaks of juristic disagreement over the qualifications of the jurisconsult,

[54] Imām al-Ḥaramayn al-Juwaynī, *al-Burhān fī Uṣūl al-Fiqh*, ed. ʿAbd al-ʿAẓīm Dīb, 2 vols. (Cairo: Dār al-Anṣār, 1400/1980), II, 1332–33.

[55] Imām al-Ḥaramayn al-Juwaynī, *al-Waraqāt fī ʿIlm Uṣūl al-Fiqh*, printed with Aḥmad b. Qāsim al-ʿAbbādī, *Sharḥ ʿalā Sharḥ al-Maḥallī ʿalā al-Waraqāt* (Surabaya: Sharikat Maktabat Aḥmad b. Saʿd b. Nabhān, n.d.), 14.

[56] Abū Ḥāmid Muḥammad b. Muḥammad al-Ghazālī, *al-Mankhūl min Taʿlīqāt al-Uṣūl*, ed. Muḥammad Ḥasan Haytū (Damascus: Dār al-Fikr, 1980), 463, 465. See also his *al-Mustaṣfā min ʿIlm al-Uṣūl*, 2 vols. (Cairo: al-Maṭbaʿa al-Amīriyya, 1324/1906), II, 391.

[57] Ghazālī, *Mankhūl*, 478 (ll. 2, 9–10).

[58] Abū al-Ḥasan ʿAlī Sayf al-Dīn al-Āmidī, *al-Iḥkām fī Uṣūl al-Aḥkām*, 3 vols. (Cairo: Maṭbaʿat ʿAlī Ṣubayḥ, 1968), III, 245.

[59] Ibid., III, 254. [60] Ibid., III, 255.

a disagreement that before the sixth/twelfth century must have been, if it existed at all, so marginal that no author we know of even cared to mention it. While Abū Ḥusayn al-Baṣrī and "other legal theoreticians" are said by Āmidī to have supported the side demanding *ijtihād*, no particular name is associated with the other side of the controversy. Again, Āmidī's account of the juristic disagreement suggests that the "other side" was, by his time, still relatively marginal. Second, according to Āmidī, a less than independent *mujtahid* may occupy the office of *iftā'*, whereas earlier jurists (with the partial exception of Baṣrī) assumed that unqualified *ijtihād* was indispensable. Third, in Āmidī's work and in others, we find, significantly, a new section or chapter exclusively devoted to discussing the permissibility (or impermissibility) of issuing *fatwā*s by a jurisconsult who lacks the qualifications of a *mujtahid*.[61]

Although Āmidī's discourse denotes a change in attitude towards the qualifications of the jurisconsult, he nonetheless continues to insist that the rank requires that a jurist be a *mujtahid fī al-madhhab*. A younger contemporary of Āmidī, however, goes further. The Mālikite Ibn al-Ḥājib (d. 646/1248) concedes that a jurist who is "knowledgeable of a *madhhab* and is able to reason correctly, but who is not himself a *mujtahid fī al-madhhab*" is nonetheless entitled to issue *fatwā*s.[62]

By the middle of the seventh/thirteenth century, the theoretical concession allowing *muqallid*s to fulfill the duty of *iftā'* seems to have become commonplace. Al-ᶜIzz Ibn ᶜAbd al-Salām (d. 660/1262), issuing a *fatwā* of his own on the question of who is entitled to be a jurisconsult, takes the position that if independent *ijtihād* cannot be attained, then the jurisconsult may be a *mujtahid fī al-madhhab*. Failing this, he may still issue a *fatwā* on points of law where he feels, beyond a shade of doubt, that he is competent. Should the case under review fall within an area of the law where he is not so competent, but where he has rarely been mistaken and the likelihood of an error is quite slim, then he is still entitled to act as a jurisconsult. In all other cases, Ibn ᶜAbd al-Salām insists, he should be banned from doing so.[63]

[61] In addition to Āmidī, see, for example, Ibn Amīr al-Ḥājj, *al-Taqrīr wal-Taḥbīr: Sharḥ ᶜalā Taḥrīr al-Imām al-Kamāl Ibn al-Humām*, 3 vols. (Cairo: al-Maṭbaᶜa al-Kubrā al-Amīriyya, 1317/1899), III, 346 ff.; ᶜAḍud al-Dīn al-Ījī, *Sharḥ Mukhtaṣar al-Muntahā al-Uṣūlī*, ed. Shaᶜbān Muḥammad Ismaᶜīl, 2 vols. (Cairo: Maṭbaᶜat al-Kulliyyāt al-Azhariyya, 1973–74), II, 308 ff.; Muḥammad b. ᶜAlī al-Shawkānī, *Irshād al-Fuḥūl ilā Taḥqīq al-Ḥaqq min ᶜIlm al-Uṣūl* (Surabaya: Sharikat Maktabat Aḥmad b. Nabhān, n.d.), 269.

[62] Jamāl al-Dīn Abū ᶜAmr Ibn al-Ḥājib, *Muntahā al-Wuṣūl wal-Amal fī ᶜIlmayy al-Uṣūl wal-Jadal*, ed. Muḥammad al-Naᶜsānī (Cairo: Maṭbaᶜat al-Saᶜāda, 1326/1908), 165.

[63] Wansharīsī, *al-Miᶜyār al-Mughrib*, XI, 110.

Ibn Daqīq al-ʿĪd (d. 702/1302), however, is reported to have gone so far as to maintain that

> predicating *futyā* on the attainment of *ijtihād* leads to immense difficulties (*ḥaraj ʿaẓīm*) as well as to a situation in which people will indulge themselves in their own pleasures. Therefore, we hold that if the jurisconsult is just (*ʿadl*) and is knowledgeable of the school of the *mujtahid* whom he cites in his *fatwā*, then this is sufficient . . . Indeed, in these times of ours, there is a consensus on this type of *fatwā*.[64]

The great majority of theoreticians who flourished subsequently to the figures we have so far discussed make the same concession to the *muftī–muqallid* in their writings. These later works, it should be remarked, are either indirectly based on theories expounded during the fifth/eleventh century or commentaries on such theories. By probing the changes and modifications that the later commentators make in their commentaries and super-commentaries, we learn not only something about the rise of *taqlīd* and the monopoly of the *madhhab*, but also how later legal scholarship negotiated its relationship with the cumulative authority of the tradition.

Juwaynī, we have already seen, equated the jurisconsult with the *mujtahid*. Commenting on his short work *al-Waraqāt*, Jalāl al-Dīn al-Maḥallī (d. 864/1459) follows in his footsteps. But in his super-commentary on Maḥallī, ʿAbbādī stops at the phrase "the jurisconsult, namely, the *mujtahid*" which appears in the original text and, obviously, in Maḥallī's commentary. This phrase, ʿAbbādī argues, lends itself to two interpretations: that the jurisconsult must be a *mujtahid* or that he may be a *mujtahid* if it is possible for him to be one. Immediately thereafter, ʿAbbādī goes on to say that the second interpretation is the more likely one.[65] Later on in his discussion, ʿAbbādī returns to the issue. He quotes the works of a number of predecessors in this regard, but, significantly, none of the them is earlier than that of Āmidī. After discussing the concession the latter made to the jurisconsult who is a *mujtahid fī al-madhhab*, he proceeds to cite Tāj al-Dīn al-Subkī (d. 771/1369), who has, he says, a number of followers on this issue. According to ʿAbbādī, Subkī maintains that the bone of contention lies with the question of whether the "*mujtahid al-fatwā* who is adept at the school of an imam and who can give preponderance to one legal opinion of that imam over

[64] Cited in Ibn Amīr al-Ḥājj, *al-Taqrīr*, III, 348; Shawkānī, *Irshād al-Fuḥūl*, 270.

[65] Aḥmad b. Qāsim al-ʿAbbādī, *Sharḥ ʿalā Sharḥ al-Maḥallī ʿalā al-Waraqāt*, printed on the margins of Shawkānī, *Irshād al-Fuḥūl*, 230: "*yuḥtamal irādat ittiḥādihimā mafhūman wa-irādat ittiḥādihimā mā ṣadaqā, wa-laʿalla al-thānī aqrab*."

another" can engage in *iftāʾ*. The correct view, Subkī maintains, is that he may do so out of necessity, such as when a *mujtahid* is not to be found. ʿAbbādī also maintains that in another work Subkī allows a *muqallid* to issue *fatwā*s even if he is not able to give preponderance to one view over another. Furthermore, such a jurisconsult is under no obligation to name the authorities whose doctrines he cites – a clear departure from the doctrines of early jurists, such as, for instance, Juwaynī. ʿAbbādī quotes an anonymous commentator on Subkī as saying that this sort of *iftāʾ* had been the prevailing practice in more recent times (*al-aʿṣār al-mutaʾakhkhira*). In what seems to be an attempt to bolster Subkī's view, ʿAbbādī quotes a certain commentator, most probably Nawawī, who essentially makes the same argument.[66]

In ʿAbbādī's super-commentary there are at least three issues worth noting. First, it is instructive that in his discussion the author engages Subkī and Āmidī rather extensively. In doing so, it is clear that ʿAbbādī must have hoped to mitigate the strict demands laid down centuries before by Juwaynī and his peers. Second, the sequence of quoting later authors parallels an increasing adjustment to a reality in which jurisconsults were by and large *muqallid*s. Thus Āmidī, the first to be cited, admits the *iftāʾ* of a *muqallid fī al-madhhab*, while the commentator on the *Muhadhdhab*, being last, goes as far as to permit a *muqallid* par excellence to practice *iftāʾ*. Third, ʿAbbādī interprets (not without reason) Subkī's expression "*mujtahid al-fatwā*" as referring to a *muqallid*.

It is to be noted in passing that in his work *Jamʿ al-Jawāmiʿ*, Subkī allows a *muqallid* to engage in *iftāʾ*, provided he is knowledgeable of the means by which the doctrines of his school were reached.[67] Needless to say, Subkī deems legitimate the *iftāʾ* of the jurist known to Āmidī as a *mujtahid fī al-madhhab*. Maḥallī, who comments on Subkī's work, adds that the practice of issuing the latter type of *fatwā* was long the prevailing practice and had never been censured or challenged. When speaking of the former type, the *fatwā* of the *muqallid*, he also notes that "it has been prevalent in recent times."[68]

Commenting on both Maḥallī and Subkī, Bannānī (d. 1199/1784) observes that a jurisconsult who is knowledgeable in the law of his school but cannot derive rulings for new legal cases is commonly called by the jurists a *mujtahid al-fatwā*. Bannānī, to be sure, realizes that a contradiction is entailed by the expression and its technical denotation, but he does

[66] ʿAbbādī, *Sharḥ*, 244–45.

[67] ʿAbd al-Raḥmān b. Jād Allāh al-Bannānī, *Ḥāshiya ʿalā Jamʿ al-Jawāmiʿ*, 2 vols. (Bombay: Molavi Mohammed B. Gulamrasul Surtis, 1970), II, 397.

[68] Ibid., II, 397, 398.

not bother to offer any explanation.[69] However, in his super-commentary on Bannānī, Shirbīnī explains that the expression is merely conventional and does not connote the ordinary meaning of the term.[70]

The changes and modifications brought about by ʿAbbādī to Juwaynī's doctrine are by no means singular. A similar modification may be observed in Ījī's (d. 756/1355) commentary on Ibn al-Ḥājib's *Muntahā*. Following Ibn al-Ḥājib, Ījī discerns four views held by the jurists as to the legitimacy of *iftāʾ* by *muqallids*, and he agrees with the first view which permits a *muqallid* to practice *iftāʾ*, provided he has mastered the teachings of his school and is able to reason properly. He upholds this view on the grounds that "at all times, and repeatedly, jurisconsults who are not *mujtahids* have issued *fatwās*. No one has abjured this [practice] and thus it has been subjected to consensus."[71] Ījī's claim that a consensus has been reached is serious, for to invoke the authority of this sanctioning instrument is tantamount to asserting that the legitimacy of the practice lies beyond the realm of probability. But Ījī's claim of epistemic certainty for this view is difficult to substantiate, since he himself acknowledges that the jurists disagreed over the matter. In fact, this is precisely the objection Taftāzānī raises against Ījī. In his super-commentary on Ījī's *Sharḥ*, he insists that such a consensus has not been reached, since there were jurists who abjured this practice.[72]

Furthermore, Ījī does not subscribe to the second view held by a certain group of jurists, namely, that a *muqallid* can serve as a jurisconsult if and only if a *mujtahid* is nowhere to be found. Nor does he accept the third view which allows a *muqallid* to issue *fatwās* whatever his professional qualifications. And he obviously rejects the fourth view which denies *muqallids* any role in this capacity. In addition to supporting his argument on the basis of consensus, Ījī adds (aiming particularly at those who argue that a *muqallid* is merely a layman) that if the *muqallid* is adept at the doctrines of his school, then he is not a layman ignorant of legal science but is, rather, sufficiently qualified to perform the tasks that *iftāʾ* involves.[73]

The four views reported by Āmidī, Ibn al-Ḥājib, and Ījī seem to have become an integral part of juristic discourse, at least beginning with the early seventh/thirteenth century. In his commentary on Bayḍāwī's (d. 685/1286) *Minhāj al-Wuṣūl*, Asnawī (d. 772/1370) speaks of the same views, but adds a new element to the issue. He maintains that the controversy recorded by Āmidī and Ibn al-Ḥājib had to do with the *muqallid* of a living *mujtahid*, and that the issue of a jurisconsult who is a *muqallid*

69 Ibid., II, 389. 70 Ibid. 71 Ījī, *Sharḥ*, II, 308.
72 Ibid., II, 308 (ll. 35–36). 73 Ibid., II, 308–09.

of a dead *mujtahid* is altogether different. On this last point, another controversy had arisen, and it seems that there were two main sides to the question. The first maintained that it is not lawful for a *muftī–muqallid* to follow the doctrine of a dead *mujtahid*, since the latter has, in effect, no opinion (*lā qawla la-hu*) to be accounted for by the succeeding jurists – the reason for this being that such an opinion does not count in the consensus of a later generation. However, a living *mujtahid* who holds an opinion that differs from all other opinions can prevent a consensus from taking place. Therefore, since the opinions of a dead *mujtahid* cannot be taken into consideration, the *muftī* should not resort to them in issuing *fatwās*.[74]

The second party, on the other hand, argued for the validity of *iftā'* according to the doctrine of a dead *mujtahid*. One of its spokesmen was Bayḍāwī himself who held in justification of this position that "since *mujtahids* do not exist in the present age, consensus has been concluded on the practice of this kind of *iftā'*."[75] Asnawī, however, maintains that Bayḍāwī's line of argument is weak, because consensus may be reached only by *mujtahids*, and since these no longer exist, any alleged consensus is invalid. The correct justification of this position, he argues, is that the barring of such a practice is detrimental to the welfare of society. Whatever the reasoning behind their positions, both Bayḍāwī and Asnawī adopted the view that a jurisconsult may be a *muqallid* whether the *mujtahid* he follows be dead or alive.[76]

The four positions articulated by the legal theoreticians cannot properly be understood without reference to diachronic developments. The first position dominated legal discourse from the second/eighth to the fifth/eleventh century, when jurisconsults, in order to qualify for the office of *iftā'*, were required in theory to be *mujtahids*. The second, advocated by Āmidī, among others, reflected the concession made by a large group of theoreticians to a reality in which, it was thought, *mujtahids* of the highest caliber, the imams and their equals, no longer existed, and that the task had to fall to *mujtahids* whose legal activity was confined to the application of a methodology already established by the founders. The third accepted a *muqallid* in the role of a jurisconsult, but only when a *mujtahid* was not available. The fourth approved of the *muftī–muqallid*, whether or not a *mujtahid* was to be found.

[74] Jamāl al-Dīn ʿAbd al-Raḥmān al-Asnawī, *Nihāyat al-Sūl fī Sharḥ Minhāj al-Wuṣūl*, 3 vols. (Cairo: Muḥammad ʿAlī Ṣubayḥ, n.d.), III, 331–32.

[75] ʿAbd Allāh b. ʿUmar al-Bayḍāwī, *Minhāj al-Wuṣūl ilā ʿIlm al-Uṣūl*, 3 vols., printed with Ibn Amīr Ḥajj, *al-Taqrīr*, III, 331 (ll. 4–7).

[76] Asnawī, *Nihāyat al-Sūl*, III, 327–32.

Chronologically, the third position in all likelihood preceded the fourth. But that the first position emerged prior to the second, and the first prior to the others, seems beyond doubt. The appearance in later legal literature of a chapter devoted to the legality (*jawāz*) of the *muqallid*'s *iftā'*, and its complete absence from works written prior to and during the fifth/eleventh century, is alone a cardinal piece of evidence that demonstrates the transformation from *ijtihād* to *taqlīd*. To this evidence may be added the fact that the fifth/eleventh-century theorists were unanimous in their stipulation that a jurisconsult had to be a *mujtahid*. Furthermore, they reported no opinion held by any of their predecessors to the contrary.

If the chronology of the four positions is correct, as the evidence indicates, then it is possible to use their diachronic emergence as an indicator of the Muslim jurists' evolving perception of their profession, if not of the objective changes that occurred in the structure of legal authority. It is important to note that the majority of legal theoreticians did not fail to follow a certain pattern when discussing who was qualified to act as a jurisconsult. As a rule, they begin with the requirement of *ijtihād*, be it limited or absolute, and then they go on to lower the bar to admit those possessed of the least amount of legal knowledge they deemed acceptable. For the early theoreticians, only the fully qualified *mujtahid* had the right to practice *iftā'*; for Āmidī and others, it was the *mujtahid fī al-madhhab*; and for the majority of later theoreticians, it was ultimately *taqlīd* that constituted the minimal requirement, though most of them, quite significantly, first began by stipulating *ijtihād*.

Whatever requirements obtained in each period, they were in complete accord with the practices prevailing on the ground. We have seen that the argument from *wuqū*ᶜ (the actual practice of the immediate and distant past)[77] was central in justifying the *iftā'* of the jurist who was less than a *mujtahid*. In fact, this argument was used, though unsuccessfully, to invoke a consensus in legitimizing the *muftī–muqallid*. The use of such a discursive argumentation was by no means restricted to the issue under consideration, for the legal theoreticians resorted to it when dealing with a number of other controversies. Its deployment, therefore, reveals two interrelated features of legal theory, namely, that this theory reflected the realities of legal practice and legal developments, yet at the same time tended to lag behind in doing so. The reason for this belated reaction was

[77] On the theoretical and epistemological role of the argument from *wuqū*ᶜ, see Abū Isḥāq Ibrāhīm al-Shāṭibī, *al-Muwāfaqāt fī Uṣūl al-Aḥkām*, ed. Muḥyī al-Dīn ᶜAbd al-Ḥamīd, 4 vols. (Cairo: Maṭbaᶜat Muḥammad ᶜAlī Ṣubayḥ, 1970), I, 12.

that legal theory reflected established phenomena and institutionalized trends, and its function in part was to rationalize the law as it developed, allowing for the inevitable twists and turns that the law undergoes.[78]

The fifth/eleventh century marks the end of the period in which the activity of *takhrīj* was extensively practiced. This is also the period which in legal theory is identified with *ijtihād*, a general label which encompasses, among other methods, the inferential processes constituted by *takhrīj*. This is not to say, of course, that the sort of *ijtihād* that involved direct confrontation with the revealed texts had already ceased by the end of this period. Elsewhere we have shown that this is by no means the case.[79] It was these activities, which began much earlier, that gave rise to the view that a jurisconsult must be a *mujtahid*. But beginning with the fourth/tenth century, and continuing through the fifth/eleventh, we observe a corollary development which gave shape to the *madhhab* as an authoritative doctrine. Now, juristic activity was to become confined to the boundaries set by the achievements of past generations whose doctrines represented a legacy to the future. These achievements constituted the *madhhab* by which the jurisconsult, it was thought, had to be guided. Āmidī's theoretical representation reflects this attitude. The *madhhab* as both an authoritative doctrine and a monopolizing entity continued to assert itself long after the fifth/eleventh and sixth/twelfth centuries, a fact of paramount importance. This assertion of authority was to give rise to the third and fourth theoretical positions, namely, that a jurisconsult might be a pure *muqallid*. In works of substantive law, this position was clearly articulated by the pronouncement, clearly expressed in all later works, that any *fatwā* issued on the basis of an opinion not fully recognized in the school is invalid.[80]

## IV

In addition to the evidence found in biographical dictionaries and the treatises of theoreticians, this transformation in the structure of authority is reflected in works of positive law, a genre that distinguishes itself

[78] On this theme of rationalization and justification, see Wael B. Hallaq, "Considerations on the Function and Character of Sunnī Legal Theory," *Journal of the American Oriental Society*, 104 (1984): 679–89.

[79] Hallaq, "Was the Gate of Ijtihād Closed?"; Hallaq, "Murder in Cordoba."

[80] See, for instance, Ḥaṭṭāb, *Mawāhib al-Jalīl*, VI, 91 (ll. 9–11); Ibn ʿĀbidīn, *Sharḥ al-Manẓūma*, 51; Ibn Farḥūn, *Tabṣirat al-Ḥukkām*, I, 18, 53; Bāʿalawī, *Bughyat al-Mustarshidīn*, 274. On the authority of opinions within the school, see chapter 5, below.

from each of the foregoing sources in different yet fundamental respects. Unlike biographical dictionaries, works of positive law do not address the totality of the professional activities and achievements of the jurists themselves. Rather, they represent statements about the law as a transmitted, cumulative tradition, bringing together authoritative doctrines of both the distant and the recent past. And unlike theoretical works which articulate a descriptive–prescriptive philosophical discourse of the law, they are concerned, quite concretely, with the applied law itself – a point we shall take up in the final chapter. Thus there is a particular value in the manner in which works of positive law reflect the socio-legal reality on the ground.

With this in mind, we shall examine how these works demonstrate, in terms of authority, the transformation that occurred in another central legal role, i.e., the *qāḍī*. But before proceeding with this matter, a question must be posed. Why did works of legal theory regularly omit a discussion of the *qāḍī*'s professional credentials when it did provide a consistent body of discourse related to the jurisconsult? The answer is that since the prime concern of legal theory is the elaboration of a methodology of legal reasoning and interpretation for the purpose of constructing legal norms, it was natural that it should turn to the *muftī* who was deemed the legal reasoner par excellence. The *qāḍī qua qāḍī*, on the other hand, was not seen in this way. The *muftī* solved, or attempted to solve, new and difficult cases, while the *qāḍī* applied the solutions in his court. The locus of legal and hermeneutical creativity was thus the *muftī*, whereas the *qāḍī* applied the law much as a bureaucrat applies administrative rules. The *muftī* worked with textual and doctrinal evidence – the stuff of hermeneutics – but the *qāḍī* applied ready-made solutions, reached by the *muftī*, to particular cases, after having heard the evidence.[81] That the office of the *qāḍī*, as a legal role,[82] was not deemed a province of legal reasoning and hermeneutical activity explains why his juridical credentials were not addressed by theoretical works.

This omission also explains a duality in the discourse of positive legal works with regard to the *qāḍī*'s professional credentials, particularly those pertaining to competence in *ijtihād*. As early as the second/eighth century, it was recognized that the *qāḍī* might or might not be a highly competent jurist, which, as we have seen, was not the case with the *muftī*. During this early period, the *muftī*, as a type, was considered the ultimate

[81] Shihāb al-Dīn al-Qarāfī, *al-Iḥkām fī Tamyīz al-Fatāwā ʿan al-Aḥkām wa-Taṣarrufāt al-Qāḍī wal-Imām*, ed. ʿIzzat al-ʿAṭṭār (Cairo: Maṭbaʿat al-Anwār, 1967), 29–30.

[82] On distinguishing between and among legal roles, see chapter 6, below.

authority, which, by definition, precludes the possibility of him turning to higher authorities – at least insofar as theoretical types go. The *qāḍī*, on the other hand, was never viewed through the same lens. In his *al-Umm*, Shāfiʿī already encourages *qāḍīs* to seek legal counsel from an authority that "has adept knowledge of the Quran, the Sunna, and the jurists' doctrines and their opinions. He must be able to reason (*yaʿrif al-qiyās*) . . . and [must master] the Arabic language."[83] These fields of competence, we have seen, are precisely those that Shāfiʿī set for the *mujtahid*. The *qāḍī* then is strongly advised to seek the counsel of the *mujtahid* who is at one and the same time the *muftī*.

Shāfiʿī's earnest recommendation falls short of listing all the realistic credentials expected of the *qāḍī* during or even after his time. In a period in which *ijtihād* was a lively activity,[84] there certainly were many *qāḍīs* who were competent as *mujtahids*, a fact abundantly attested by our biographical and theoretical works. Thus the *qāḍī* was required to seek legal advice only when he was unable to reach decisions for the more difficult cases presented to him in his courtroom. This duality in the *qāḍī*'s credentials explains the order and arrangement of discourse in works of positive law in general and those pertaining to *adab al-qāḍī* in particular. In his commentary on Khaṣṣāf (d. 261/874), the Ḥanafite Jaṣṣāṣ (d. ca. 370/981) argues that the *qāḍī* should be knowledgeable in legal interpretation so as to be able to derive rulings from the revealed texts. This appears as the first order of preference. Jaṣṣāṣ however immediately qualifies this statement by saying that to guard against risky decisions, the *qāḍī* must seek the counsel of jurists by listening to their opinions on the cases presented to him in the courtroom. Only then should he determine which is the soundest and most suitable opinion for the case in hand.[85] Elsewhere in the book, Jaṣṣāṣ makes it clear that the advising jurists are "the people of *ijtihād*."[86]

Thus far, the doctrinal authority of the *qāḍī* seems to emanate either from his own ability to reason or from the *mujtahid* who offers him counsel. We may also assume that "seeking advice" also meant the advice of jurists who were not *mujtahids*. But even then, the counsel of such

[83] Shāfiʿī, *Umm*, VI, 287.

[84] This translates into the characterization that *ijtihād* was seen to have been rampant because the schools had not yet been finally formed. This is not to say that the activity ceased later on, but that it was controlled by the hermeneutical imperatives of the school so that it lost its independent and even undomesticated character.

[85] Abū Bakr Aḥmad b. ʿAlī al-Jaṣṣāṣ, *Sharḥ Kitāb Adab al-Qāḍī*, ed. Farḥāt Ziadeh (Cairo: Qism al-Nashr bil-Jāmiʿa al-Amrīkiyya, 1978), 37–39. See also Ibn al-Mundhir, *Iqnāʿ*, 410, who expresses the same views.

[86] Jaṣṣāṣ, *Adab al-Qāḍī*, 42–43, 101–02, 105, 106.

jurists will have to depend, in the final analysis, on the authority of a *mujtahid* whose opinion is thought to be the best solution to the case presented at court. In Jaṣṣāṣ, it is to be noted, no mention is yet made of a binding *madhhab*.

By the time of Māwardī (d. 450/1058), the *madhhab* as a doctrinal entity was well on the rise. Māwardī begins by stressing the *qāḍī*'s need for good advice: "In the *qāḍī*'s assembly, no one should be present with the litigants unless he is involved in the case. For we prefer (*fa-innanā nastaḥibb*) that the assembly not be devoid of witnesses and jurists. The *qāḍī* should seek the counsel of the jurists . . . because counsel is recommended in matters that are not conclusive (*al-umūr al-mushtabaha*)."[87] Note here that the presence of the jurists in the courtroom is considered pertinent and germane to litigation. The jurists are placed on a par with persons directly "involved in the case." Seeking their advice becomes all the more urgent in matters that are ambiguous, i.e., cases over which the jurists have disagreed due to the fact that the pertinent textual evidence is itself capable of more than one interpretation. In other words, where there is no certainty – usually cases that are not sanctioned by consensus – counsel is highly advisable.[88]

Citing with approval Shāfiʿī's discussion of the qualifications of court advisors, Māwardī summarizes these by saying that "in short, any one whose *iftā'* is deemed acceptable in the law can be consulted by the *qāḍī* . . . He should thus fulfill the conditions required of the *muftī*, not the *qāḍī*."[89] Having said this, he proceeds to enumerate these conditions, of which the most prominent is competence in *ijtihād*. Once these conditions are met, the jurist can issue *fatwā*s and provide counsel to the *qāḍī*.[90]

Conducting a discussion of the controversial cases, and personally disputing (*munāẓara*) them with the jurists serve to assist the *qāḍī* in finding his way to *ijtihād*. If he arrives on his own at a solution to the case, he must render judgment according to his solution, not theirs. His councilors must not voice any objections once he renders a decision, for he is as much entitled to exercise *ijtihād* as they are entitled to their own opinions.[91] It is in this spirit that Māwardī argues in favor of the *qāḍī*'s right to apply the results of his own *ijtihād*, even though they may be at variance with the opinions established by the founder of the school to which he belongs. If he happens to be a Shāfiʿite, for instance, and

[87] ʿAlī Muḥammad b. Ḥabīb al-Māwardī, *al-Ḥāwī al-Kabīr fī al-Furūʿ*, ed. Maḥmūd Maṭarjī et al., 24 vols. (Beirut: Dār al-Fikr, 1994), XX, 98, 100.
[88] Ibid., XX, 102. [89] Ibid., XX, 103. [90] Ibid., XX, 104. [91] Ibid., XX, 102.

his *ijtihād* leads him to deduce an opinion that had previously been held authoritative by the Ḥanafites, then he is permitted to apply it to litigants appearing in his court.[92]

Māwardī's account thus far represents the dominant position assumed by jurists up to his time. But as the product of a period characterized by the rise of the *madhhab* as an authoritative doctrine, Māwardī was also bound to feel the pressure that this relatively recent development generated. Some jurists, appearing to be in the minority at the time,[93] held that "the schools nowadays have become well established (*istaqarrat al-madhāhib*) and the imams followed in these schools have become known. Therefore, no one who is affiliated with a school is allowed to render judgment in accordance with [the doctrine of] another school." Māwardī retorts, significantly, that although sound opinion justifies this position, the principles of the law do not, because the judge must render judgment according to his own *ijtihād*, not that of others.[94] What is significant about this rebuttal is that it implies a certain concession which Māwardī made to his opponent: He admits, albeit qualifiedly, the legitimacy of the opposing view, a view that was sanctioned by the force of actual legal practice.

Māwardī's discourse reflects a stage of transformation in which old positions – reflecting fundamental structural developments – were still fervently maintained while new positions were gradually appearing and evolving, but with terminal force. It must have seemed to Māwardī that these were ephemeral positions, reflecting an equally contingent reality. Little did Māwardī know that the exceptions and minority positions of his time would become the dominant voice.

92 Ibid., XX, 75, 226. Such opinions could still be heard a generation or more after Māwardī. Abū Bakr al-Ṭurṭūshī (d. 520/1126) also held the view that

> No Muslim is obligated to follow [the opinion] of the one to whose doctrine he is affiliated in regard to legal cases and judgments. Thus, one who is a Malikite is not obligated to follow in his rulings the opinion of Mālik. The same is applicable to the rest of the schools. Indeed, the judge decides cases on the basis of whatever rule his reasoning leads him to.

Cited in Fadel, "Social Logic of *Taqlīd*," 213.

93 In two different contexts in which this particular issue is raised, Māwardī uses the term "*baʿḍ*," once in conjunction with "*fuqahā*'" (jurists) and the other time with "*aṣḥabuna*" (our associates or colleagues). In either case, *baʿḍ* is mostly used to refer to the singular, a fact which significantly reduces the weight of the claim, and certainly justifies the assumption that it was a minority who adopted this position. For the two contexts, see his *al-Ḥāwī al-Kabīr*, XX, 75, 227.

94 Ibid., XX, 75, 227: "*wa-hādhā wa-in kāna al-ra'y yaqtaḍīh fa-uṣūl al-sharʿ tunāfīh li-anna ʿalā al-ḥākim an yaḥkum bi-ijtihādi nafsih wa-laysa ʿalayhi an yaḥkum bi-ijtihādi ghayrih.*"

Another step in the transition from *ijtihād* to *taqlīd* was taken, half a century or so later, by the Ḥanafite al-Ḥusām al-Shahīd Ibn Māza (d. 536/1141) who wrote a commentary on Khaṣṣāf's work *Adab al-Qāḍī*. In the opening chapter, Ibn Māza follows Jaṣṣāṣ in requiring the *qāḍī* to be a *mujtahid*, and discusses in some detail the justification for this requirement.[95] Later in the work he returns to this issue in more detail, initially restating what he had already said in the opening section: *ijtihād* is required of the *qāḍī*. But Ibn Māza offers, in a somewhat oblique manner, a significant variation on Jaṣṣāṣ's theme. The *qāḍī*, he begins to say, must judge according to the Quran and the Sunna, for "we have been commanded to follow" these sources. Should he not find the law in these two sources, the *qāḍī* must turn to the Companions' consensus. If they disagree on the matter under scrutiny, then he is free to exercise his own *ijtihād* in finding the soundest opinion. Should the Companions have no opinion at all on the issue, he turns to the Followers, treating their doctrines in the same manner as he would treat those of the Companions. In the absence of any guidance from the Followers, he must exercise his own *ijtihād* in formulating a legal norm that is applicable to the case in which he is the presiding judge. But if he is no *mujtahid*, then he must consult a *muftī* who is, by definition, a *mujtahid*.[96] At this point, Ibn Māza abruptly introduces another theme involving "that on which our associates (*aṣḥābunā*) have agreed and disagreed." By "associates" Ibn Māza means the founding masters, especially Abū Ḥanīfa, Abū Yūsuf, and Shaybānī. If these three have agreed on a matter, then the *qāḍī* cannot diverge from their opinions, whether or not he is a *mujtahid*. Should the three masters disagree, then the preference is for Abū Ḥanīfa's opinion, since he was engaged in legal activity at the time of the Followers.[97]

Note here that Ibn Māza still labors under the same duality of doctrinal orientation as did Māwardī before him, but gives it added force and tension. Māwardī rejected, though lukewarmly, the minority opinion in favor of following the *madhhab*. Ibn Māza, on the other hand, upholds the doctrine of the three masters – but only when they are in agreement – as the ultimate doctrine to be followed, whether the *qāḍī* is a *mujtahid* or not. When the transition to the *madhhab* reached its full measure, the Ḥanafites, like all the other schools, demanded that the *qāḍī* follow the authoritative doctrine of the school, were it held by Abū Ḥanīfa or by any other jurist.[98]

[95] Ibn Māza, *Sharḥ Adab al-Qāḍī*, 4–5. [96] Ibid., 17–18. [97] Ibid., 19–20.
[98] See, for example, Ibn ʿĀbidīn, *Sharḥ al-Manẓūma*, 51.

But the near abandonment of *ijtihād* in favor of a complete monopoly of the *madhhab* required two more steps to be taken, steps that are manifestly evident in the changing discourse relative to the *qāḍī*'s credentials. The first of these steps is represented in the discourse of the Shāfiᶜite jurist and judge Ibn Abī al-Damm (d. 642/1244). In his *Kitāb Adab al-Qaḍā'* he observes that according to the *madhhab* of "our imam," the judge must be an absolute *mujtahid* (*mujtahid muṭlaq*), which means that he must have masterly knowledge of the Book, the Sunna, consensus, *qiyās*, the jurists' doctrines (*aqāwīl al-nās*), and the Arabic language. At this point, Ibn Abī al-Damm expounds in some detail what each of these fields of knowledge entail in terms of sub-specialties, e.g., abrogation, ambiguity, transmission, authenticity, etc. Of particular interest is the requirement to master the art of legal reasoning: The *qāḍī* must, among other things, be adept at deducing or inducing legal norms from their relevant sources, as well as being an astute reasoner, an expert in exploiting legal indicants and knowledge in the methods of linguistic inference.[99]

"Having said this," Ibn Abī al-Damm continues, "you must know that these qualities are rarely found in any of the jurists of our time. Indeed, no absolute *mujtahid* exists nowadays in the entire universe." This is so despite the fact that learned people have compiled books about all sorts of disciplines, ranging from the science of traditions and their transmission to exegesis, law, and legal theory.

> The early scholars have filled the land with treatises which they authored and designed, [an accomplishment] which rendered these sciences much more accessible, and made it easier for the later jurists to learn law . . . Yet, in none of the Islamic regions is there to be found an absolute *mujtahid*. Indeed, there is not even any affiliated *mujtahid* whose opinions can be considered the result of *takhrīj* according to the doctrine of the Imam.[100]

This deplorable state of affairs, Ibn Abī al-Damm thought, was symptomatic of a general deterioration in the ability of people to attain sophisticated kinds of knowledge. What is interesting here is the fact that he saw this deterioration as an intentional act of God.[101] Elsewhere, we have shown the connection that was made between the perceived absence of *ijtihād* and this sense of deterioration, a belief that was eschatologically required for the approaching Day of Judgment.[102]

Ibn Abī al-Damm provides a list of *mujtahids* who made distinguished contributions to the Shāfiᶜite school, but the last of these lived in the fifth/

[99] Ibn Abī al-Damm, *Adab al-Qaḍā'*, 36–37. [100] Ibid., 37. [101] Ibid., 38.
[102] W. B. Hallaq, "On the Origins of the Controversy about the Existence of Mujtahids and the Gate of Ijtihād," *Studia Islamica*, 63 (1986): 129–41.

eleventh century. The achievements of the past, though highly admired and appreciated by Ibn Abī al-Damm, cannot be replicated. In summing up the matter, our author maintains, absolute and limited *ijtihād* were two requirements expected of the *qāḍī* in earlier epochs when each region in the Islamic world could boast a group of *mujtahid*s fit to serve for judgeship and *iftā'*. Given that "in our own times the world is devoid of *mujtahid*s, it should be asserted in a conclusive manner" that it is permissible to appoint a person who is characterised by:

(1) Knowledge of one of the *madhhab*s of the imams. That is to say, he should have knowledge of the dominant views in his school (*ghālib madhhabihi*), of the imam's doctrines, and of the opinions deduced by *takhrīj* and of those of his followers. He should have a good mind, natural intelligence, sound thinking, and should memorize the *madhhab*. His sound judgment should outweigh his errors, and he should be able to readily retrieve the masters' opinions (*mustaḥḍiran li-mā qālahu a'immatuhu*).

(2) Ability to deduce the significations of words from transmitted texts; to know the methods of reasoning which permit him to conduct *qiyās*; finally, he should be equipped with the methods of weighing textual indicants and their systematic ordering. "He who possesses these qualities, no less, is fit, in these times of ours, to be appointed to judgeship. The judicial decisions and *fatwā*s of anyone who possesses these qualities should be deemed valid, for these qualities are rare nowadays."[103]

Ibn Abī al-Damm's discourse presents us with a number of important issues. In the second passage quoted above, his understanding of what *ijtihād* meant has in it a certain measure of amplification, perhaps even a mythical dimension. The dominance of the *madhhab*, though not readily obvious in this particular discussion of his, precludes in his mind the presence of total, absolute *ijtihād*, a type of juristic activity that belonged to the founders who are inimitable. Even limited *ijtihād* belonged to the generations of the past. His age and the juristic activities in which he and his contemporaries engaged were no match, he realized, for their counterparts in the past. His age, in other words, suffered from a decline that is associated with eschatological concerns. Yet he who must qualify for judgeship should be skillful in the art of legal reasoning which entails, among other things, a certain degree of textual knowledge that permits competent hermeneutical engagement. Since this activity amounts in effect to nothing less than *ijtihād*, one begins to wonder about the textual strategy devised by Ibn Abī al-Damm. For he, on the one hand, patently argues that *ijtihād* ceased to be a quality required of *qāḍī*s, while, on the

[103] Ibn Abī al-Damm, *Adab al-Qaḍā'*, 41.

other hand, he insists that the *qāḍīs*, said to be in effect *muqallids*, must engage in a juristic activity of the type that *ijtihād* requires.[104]

The solution to this seeming contradiction lies in the relationship between passages 1 and 2 above. Ibn Abī al-Damm has in effect said nothing that his immediate predecessors and successors have not said: *Ijtihād* is always welcome if it can be attained, but following the *madhhab*'s doctrines comes first in order of importance. This is precisely why his discussion in passage 1 wholly pertains to knowledge of the masters' doctrines and the ability to retrieve it readily. And although the numbering of the passages is artificial (being my own) the order and logical progression of the discussion remains entirely faithful to Ibn Abī al-Damm's mode of presentation. The *madhhab* and the doctrines of which it consists is the immediate occupation of the *qāḍī*; thereafter, and as a secondary stage, comes direct hermeneutical engagement with the law. Ibn Abī al-Damm's discourse is therefore an assertion of the authority of the established *madhhab*, with all that this meant and consequently entailed in terms of an intellectual manipulation of the law and legal reasoning.

The second and final step in the transition to *taqlīd* was largely a matter of articulating, in more conscious terms, the relationship of the prerequisites of *ijtihād* and *taqlīd*. The Mālikite Ibn Farḥūn (d. 799/1396) opens his discussion of this topic by stating that the majority of jurists held that if the *qāḍī* attained the rank of *ijtihād*, then he must follow the authority of no one. Indeed, this had become a fundamental tenet, shared by all jurists of the four schools and dictated by the permanence of the notion that new problems and cases will continue to befall the Muslim community and that as long as these problems remain unsolved, the duty imposed upon the community of Muslims will not be considered disposed.[105]

Having made this brief statement concerning *ijtihād*, Ibn Farḥūn immediately moves on to a lengthy discussion of the "*qāḍī* who does not belong to the folk of *ijtihād*." Here, he quotes Māzarī (d. 536/1141):

> The question [that a *qāḍī* should be a *mujtahid*] has been discussed by the scholars of the past, when knowledge during their era was abundant and widespread, and when many of them were preoccupied with deducing legal norms and with disputation according to the [principles of the] schools. But in our own age, in the entire expanse of the [Islamic] domains, there is no jurist who has reached a level of intellectual reflection enabling him to

[104] It will be noted that on the interpretation of this passage, I disagree with Sherman Jackson, *Islamic Law and the State*, 157–59.

[105] Ibn al-Ṣalāḥ, *Adab al-Muftī*, 95–96.

> attain the rank of *ijtihād*, a jurist who has expert knowledge of legal theory, of language, traditions [etc.] . . . The Maghreb in this age of ours is entirely devoid of such qualifications . . . Therefore, forbidding in these times the appointment of a *muqallid*–judge would lead to the paralysis of the law and would cause chaos, sedition, and strife. And there is no place for these [things] in the law.[106]

The *qāḍī–muqallid*, Ibn Farḥūn maintains, is then obliged to seek counsel and to follow the school's masters through *taqlīd*. As a *muqallid*, he should adopt those opinions that seem to him, after investigation, the most sound. On the authority of Māzarī, Ibn Farḥūn advances the view that it is the *mashhūr* (widespread) opinion that the *qāḍī–muqallid* should follow.[107] If he seeks counsel, he should, again after search and enquiry, ask the most learned. It is significant that "the most learned" no longer meant a jurist capable of *ijtihād*, for in keeping with the development that culminated in the concession to allow a *muqallid* to function as a jurisconsult, the most learned could now be a *muqallid*, a view which Ibn Farḥūn adopts from Māzarī.[108] This secondary development stands in sharp contrast to the earlier requirement that a *muftī* must be a *mujtahid*. Thus, when a difficult case presented itself to the *qaḍī–muqallid*, he had now to seek the counsel of a *muftī–muqallid* who was obliged in turn to render an opinion deemed, by the judgment of the school, authoritative; and this was the *mashhūr* opinion.[109]

The functions of *qaḍā'* and *iftā'* thus underwent a well-nigh identical process of transformation from *ijtihād* to *taqlīd*. The culmination of this process is best summarized by Bāᶜalawī (fl. around 1245/1830) who, with full approval, quotes one of Bāfaqīh's *fatwā*s:

> Neither the judge nor the jurisconsult should swerve from the imam's doctrine, for [if a judge rules] according to any other doctrine, his decision will be revoked (*yunqaḍ*). Ibn al-Ṣalāḥ reported that a consensus has been reached to the effect that no judgment should diverge from the *madhhab*. And this view was adopted by the later jurists (*wa-iᶜtamadahu al-muta'akhkhirūn*) . . . It is well known that the *madhhab* is a transmitted doctrine by which the *muqallids* are bound and outside of which they cannot traverse. It is for this reason that no *qāḍī* or *muftī* can forgo the doctrines preponderated (*murajjaḥ*) by the two Shaykhs, Nawawī and Rāfiᶜī.[110]

106 Ibn Farḥūn, *Tabṣirat al-Ḥukkām*, I, 18–19.
107 Ibid., I, 45, 51. On the *mashhūr*, see chapter 5, section V, below.
108 Ibn Farḥūn, *Tabṣirat al-Ḥukkām*, I, 29.
109 Ibid., I, 18, 53 (on the authority of Shihāb al-Dīn al-Qarāfī).
110 Bāᶜalawī, *Bughyat al-Mustarshidīn*, 274.

Considered to have pinned down the authoritative doctrine of the Shāfiᶜite school, Nawawī and Rāfiᶜī's magisterial compilations become now the final frame of reference for both the *qāḍī* and the *muftī*. Similarly, each of the other three schools came to adopt certain works as embodying their authoritative doctrine, considered equally binding upon both the *muftī* and the *qāḍī*.

## V

In conclusion, it cannot be overemphasized that the transition from *ijtihād* to *taqlīd* that we have surveyed here had little to do with the actual credentials and achievements of the jurists, and still less with the perception of the declining glory of Islam, properly so-called *fasād al-zamān*.[111] It is quite instructive (though in no way ironic) that Māzarī, who unequivocally argued that no jurist of his time could attain the rank of *ijtihād*, was himself considered a *mujtahid*. And it is even more instructive for our purposes that he was at the same time considered exemplary in having never issued a *fatwā* that departed from the *mashhūr* doctrine of his school.[112] The transition, therefore, represented a development in the growth of legal authority, a development, I wish to claim, that was ineluctable. The process through which *taqlīd* came to dominate was not a causal phenomenon, but rather symptomatic of a more fundamental and monumental event, namely, the rise and final coming to maturity of the *madhhab*. *Taqlīd*, therefore, was an external expression of the internal dynamics that came to dominate and characterize the *madhhab* as both a doctrinal entity and a hermeneutical engagement – dynamics that will be taken up in detail in the next chapter. The construction of what came to be the imam's authority, the dramatic reduction and narrowing down of the independent *ijtihād*ic possibilities of the third/ninth and fourth/tenth centuries, and the final rise of *taqlīd* as an expression of loyalty to the schools are phenomena that share one common denominator: the centrifugal polarization of authority without which no law can exist. The *madhhab* was the very embodiment of this authority.

[111] An issue raised by Ibn Abī al-Damm, as we have seen above. See also Hallaq, "The Origins of the Controversy," 136 ff. In this context, it should be mentioned that our findings here constitute in part a revision of the findings in this article.

[112] Ibn Farḥūn, *Tabṣirat al-Ḥukkām*, I, 51.

# ☙☙ 4 ☙☙

## *TAQLĪD*: AUTHORITY, HERMENEUTICS, AND FUNCTION

### I

As a term denoting the acceptance of legal authority, *taqlīd* has had a complex history. During the second/eighth century, it generally meant the acceptance of the Companions' legal teachings as well as those of the Followers (*tābiᶜūn*) who had attained a ripe age during the time of the Companions.[1] Later on, the term's connotation underwent change, and acquired the meaning of following the authority of a *mujtahid*, whether or not he was the founder of a school. However, this general sense of the term, which was to remain fairly constant throughout the centuries, carried with it at least one major ambiguity. On the one hand, it was used in the sense of following the *mujtahid*'s authority without questioning either his textual evidence or the line of reasoning he adopted in a particular case. In this sense, the term was also applicable to the act of following the totality of the founder's legal doctrines as a methodologically systematic structure, without the *muqallid* being bound by all the individual opinions within the corpus of those doctrines. Ḥanafite *muqallids*, for example, were never bound by all of Abū Ḥanīfa's opinions, whether or not they were genuinely his, and regularly drew on the doctrines of several authorities affiliated with the school. On the other hand, the term was also employed to indicate loyalty to a legal doctrine but with full knowledge, on the part of the *muqallid*, of the means by which this doctrine was derived. Generally speaking, *uṣūl al-fiqh* works employed the term in the first sense, and regarded *taqlīd* as almost exclusively the province of the layman.[2] This phenomenon may be explained by the fact

[1] See Abū Bakr Aḥmad b. ᶜUmar al-Khaṣṣāf's *Kitāb Adab al-Qāḍī* in Ibn Māza, *Sharḥ Adab al-Qāḍī*, 18; Joseph Schacht, *The Origins of Muhammadan Jurisprudence* (Oxford: Clarendon Press, 1950), 18, 32.

[2] Ibn al-Ḥājib, *Mukhtaṣar*, 140–41; Ibn Qudāma, *Rawḍat al-Nāẓir*, 343–45; Fakhr al-Dīn al-Rāzī, *al-Maḥṣūl fī ᶜIlm al-Uṣūl*, 2 vols. (Beirut: Dār al-Kutub al-ᶜIlmiyya, 1408/1988), II, 527 ff. See also Ḥaṭṭāb, *Mawāhib al-Jalīl*, I, 30.

that the discourse of *uṣūl* was in part preoccupied with laying down an *ijtihād*ic methodology in which there is no room for *taqlīd* among the jurists targeted by this discourse.[3] When this type of *taqlīd* is predicated of a professional jurist, it carries a sense of scorn and condemnation. The many treatises, tracts, and chapters entitled *fī dhamm al-taqlīd* (in condemnation of *taqlīd*) were directed at such jurist–*muqallids* and were common to all times and all legal schools.[4]

The second type of *taqlīd* is seen to operate more in connection with loyalty to the school and within the context of the bindingness of authoritative legal doctrines.[5] In Ibn Rushd's and Ibn al-Ṣalāḥ's typologies, this *taqlīd* is associated with all but the lowest levels, i.e. groups 2 and 3 in the former's classification, and types 1–4 (of category 2) in the latter's.[6] In Ibn Kamāl's scheme, it is explicitly associated with ranks 4–6.[7] Only Ibn Rushd's first group, Ibn al-Ṣalāḥ's fifth type, and Ibn Kamāl's seventh rank are associated with the first sort of *taqlīd*, i.e., the one that came to be condemned in certain quarters.

Synchronically and diachronically, *taqlīd* was regularly practiced in both senses of the term. Which of the two senses was intended when the term was used depended on the context and frame of reference. Ambiguities no

3 This also explains why the jurist *muqallid* is not discussed in *uṣūl al-fiqh* works. See the sources cited in previous note.

4 Especially the Mālikites, Ḥanbalites, and Shāfiᶜites, and to a lesser degree the Ḥanafites. See ᶜAbd al-Wahhāb b. ᶜAlī Ibn Naṣr al-Mālikī, *al-Muqaddima fī al-Uṣūl*, printed with ᶜAlī b. ᶜUmar Ibn al-Qaṣṣār, *al-Muqaddima fī al-Uṣūl*, ed. Muḥammad al-Sulaymānī (Beirut: Dār al-Gharb al-Islāmī, 1996), 300 ff.; Abū al-Wafā' Muḥammad Ibn ᶜAqīl, *Kitāb al-Funūn*, ed. George Makdisi, 2 vols. (Beirut: Dār al-Mashriq, 1970–71), II, 602–10; Ibn Qayyim al-Jawziyya, *Iᶜlām al-Muwaqqiᶜīn*, II, 168–260; Muzanī, *Mukhtaṣar*, IX, 3; Suyūṭī, *al-Radd*, 196, 117, 120, where he mentions a number of prominent jurists who wrote in condemnation of *taqlīd*, including Muzanī, Zarkashī, Ibn Ḥazm, Ibn ᶜAbd al-Barr, Ibn Abī Shāma, Ibn Qayyim al-Jawziyya, al-Majd al-Shīrāzī, and the Shāfiᶜite jurist Ibn Daqīq al-ᶜĪd, who wrote a treatise titled *al-Tasdīd fī Dhamm al-Taqlīd*.

In his *Jāmiᶜ Bayān al-ᶜIlm wa-Faḍlihi wa-mā Yanbaghī fī Riwāyatihi wa Ḥamlihi*, 2 vols. (Cairo: Idārat al-Ṭibāᶜa al-Munīriyya, n.d.), II, 109–19, Ibn ᶜAbd al-Barr (d. 463/1070) adduces in condemnation of *taqlīd* a number of Quranic verses and Prophetic traditions, and claims the existence of a consensus among all jurists as to its invalidity. He seems to draw a distinction between *taqlīd* and *ittibāᶜ*. For the jurist, the former is forbidden, whereas the latter is permitted. "If evidence obliges you to follow someone's opinion, then you are a follower of his (*muttabiᶜūhu*), for [this kind of] following (*ittibaᶜ*) is permitted in religious matters, but *taqlīd* is forbidden" (p. 117). *Taqlīd*, he continues, is adopting an opinion without knowledge, which is the opposite of *ittibāᶜ*. See also Suyūṭī, *al-Radd*, 120–22.

5 See Ḥaṭṭāb, *Mawāhib al-Jalīl*, I, 30–31, 37, on the authority of Mālikite and Shāfiᶜite jurists, including Ghazālī and Ibn al-Ṣalāḥ.

6 See our discussion in chapter 1, sections II–III, above.

7 See chapter 1, section IV, above.

doubt persisted, which explains why some later jurists attempted to disambiguate the usage by resorting to the term *ittibāᶜ* (lit. following) to denote the second sense of the term, where the *muqallid* accepts the authority of the *mujtahid*, not blindly, but with adequate – if not full – understanding of the latter's evidence and reasoning, and out of juristic loyalty to him.[8]

## II

If the spectrum of *taqlīd* encompassed these two extremes of juristic competence in the school's doctrines, then *muqallid*s as well as *mujtahid*s (even of Mālik's and Shāfiᶜī's caliber) partook in it. This chapter seeks to demonstrate the dynamics of *taqlīd*, which, as we shall see, may at times border on the juristic activity associated with *ijtihād*, and yet at others constitutes nothing more than the mere reproduction of the predecessors' doctrine. But in the majority of cases, the activity of *taqlīd* may be located between these two extremes. At both ends of the spectrum, and at each point in between, *taqlīd* represented a juristic function and was dictated by a purpose. In the context of a single case or legal doctrine, it could function at one or more levels of meaning, thus bestowing on the case or doctrine a texture that was horizontally multi-layered and vertically composite. In the pages of the average juristic text or law manual, the author–jurist inevitably indulges in every variety of *taqlīd*, ranging from simple restatement of authority to quasi-*ijtihād* of a sort.

Let us illustrate. In the chapter dealing with damages in the contractual obligations of hire, the Mālikite jurist Ḥaṭṭāb records the following opinion:

> In his *Ṭurar*, he [Ibn ᶜĀt][9] said that in Ibn Lubāba's *Muʾallafa*[10] [it is stated that] if the [hired] shepherd wounds the goats once, twice and thrice, and the owner does not hold him responsible for damages, [showing this] by remaining silent and by being content with him, he [the owner] has no right to hold him liable to damages should he wound a goat thereafter.[11]

This statement consists of straightforward reproduction of a doctrine reported by a jurist on the authority of yet another jurist. Ḥaṭṭāb records it in the context of a discussion about a variety of types of hire contract

[8] Ibn Qayyim al-Jawziyya, *Iᶜlām al-Muwaqqiᶜīn*, II, 171, 178 ff.; Suyūṭī, *al-Radd*, 120–22; Ibn Naṣr, *Muqaddima*, 302.

[9] Aḥmad b. Hārūn b. Aḥmad b. Jaᶜfar Ibn ᶜĀt al-Shāṭibī (d. 609/1212).

[10] Muḥammad Abū ᶜAbd Allāh b. ᶜUmar Ibn Lubāba al-Qurṭubī (d. 314/926).

[11] Ḥaṭṭāb, *Mawāhib al-Jalīl*, V, 430.

which may result in damage claims. He offers neither commentary on, nor direct explanation of, the rationale behind it. However, there is little reason to doubt Ḥaṭṭāb's understanding of both the relevance and nature of Ibn Lubāba's opinion, for he quotes it, along with dozens of other opinions, to elaborate the principles involved in damages pertaining to such contracts.

The very fact that an opinion is introduced in a highly specific context indicates the reason for which it was introduced in that particular context. In other words, one can safely assume that whenever an opinion is cited, the rationale behind it would have been known, and thus it constitutes either an illustration or an application of a principle. However, principles are rarely, if ever, articulated. They appear for the most part to have been taken for granted, thereby rendering their explication unnecessary.[12] This absence constitutes a salient feature of Islamic legal discourse, especially in treatises written prior to the fifth/eleventh century. As an example, consider the following question addressed to Ibn Rushd:

> A judge borrowed from the revenues of mosque endowments (*aḥbās*) in order to build platforms (*maṣāṭib*) around the grand mosque, although he had knowledge that the revenues of the grand mosque would not have the surplus [needed] to pay back the debt. Should he be held liable for damages or not?
> Answer: He is not to be held liable for damages.[13]

Although Ibn Rushd's answer does not explicitly cite another's opinion, he is implicitly basing himself on an authoritative Andalusian–Mālikite principle to the effect that the surplus of endowments may be spent on other endowments when the latter are in the red. Ibn Rushd functions here as a *muqallid*, but not without understanding the significance of the case in question and its relation to the principle of which the case is only an instance of its application.

Ḥaṭṭāb's and Ibn Rushd's examples provide two illustrations only of a large body of cases and opinions which are cited as instances of applications of certain principles without articulation of these latter. It is difficult to explain why this is so,[14] but it seems that shorter works tend to avoid any explication of the cases or opinions, just as they are silent on the principles from which they were derived or of which they are instances

[12] Later on in this chapter, we shall qualify this generalization with regard to later works which exhibited a certain tendency to articulate principles. See section IV, below.

[13] Ibn Rushd, *Fatāwā*, III, 1268.

[14] See section IV, below, where a partial explanation is attempted. See also Baber Johansen, "Casuistry: Between Legal Concept and Social Praxis," *Islamic Law and Society*, 2, 2 (1995), 154–56.

of application.[15] At times, we find this to be the case even in longer works, which suggests to us that certain of these principles were deemed so obvious and so little in need of explanation that they were taken for granted. The majority of principles, however, were not explicitly stated because they apparently could not be captured in an adequately concise manner. Instead, in order to convey the full implications of these principles, the range of, and exceptions to, their application, they were commonly illustrated through cases, or types of cases.

Be that as it may, principles which do not admit of exceptions underlie the cases and opinions, whether they are explicitly articulated or assumed. In fact, the cases and opinions are most often cited, not for their own sake, but rather as illustrations of the principle and/or of its application. True, they are intended to provide examples for solving future problems, but this remains secondary to their function as practical examples of a principle's application. This striving to elucidate the principles often appears to be the desideratum of juristic discourse in works of positive law. Even in such a condensed work as the *Mukhtaṣar* of the Ḥanafite Ṭaḥāwī, this is clearly the case. Consider the following example:

> Concerning a rented house whose owner has sold it [to other than the tenant] before the end of the lease, Abū Ḥanīfa and Muḥammad [b. Ḥasan al-Shaybānī] said: the tenant has the right to bar the buyer from purchasing it and to nullify the sale. If the tenant does nullify the sale [before the end of the lease], then the sale becomes irrevocably void. However, if he does not do so and the lease period expires, then the sale remains in effect. This is the old opinion of Abū Yūsuf.
>
> Those who wrote down Abū Yūsuf's views (*aṣḥāb al-imlā'*)[16] related that [later] he held the opinion that the tenant has no right to nullify the sale, and that renting the house is tantamount to its having a defect (*ʿayb*) in it. If the buyer is aware of the defect [i.e., the lease], then the owner will not be liable, and the former has the right to possess the property after the lease period has expired. If he was not aware of the defect, he has the option (*khiyār*) either to cancel the sale due to the defect which he later found, or to accept it.
>
> Muḥammad reported that Abū Ḥanīfa held the view that the tenant has no right to void the sale of the house, but if he allows the sale to go into effect, then the remaining period of his lease would be canceled.

[15] Some authors explicitly admit that their works do not permit the exploration of principles, lines of reasoning, etc. See, e.g. Ibn Ghānim b. Muḥammad al-Baghdādī, *Majmaʿ al-Ḍamānāt* (Cairo: al-Maṭbaʿa al-Khayriyya, 1308/1890), 3.

[16] That is, students who copied down Abū Yūsuf's lectures. See Ibn ʿĀbidīn, *Sharḥ al-Manẓūma*, 17, where he remarks that the Shāfiʿites call this type of *imlā'* a *taʿlīqa*. On the *taʿlīqa*, see Makdisi, *Rise*, 114–21, 126–27.

> Abū Ḥanīfa's first opinion was reported by persons other than Muḥammad. Those who recorded the views of Abū Yūsuf reported this opinion from him on the authority of Abū Ḥanīfa. Among them is Kaysānī who reported it to us from his father, from Abū Yūsuf, from Abū Ḥanīfa himself. It is more in line with Abū Ḥanīfa's doctrines and principles (*uṣūl*) which he [Abū Yūsuf] did not dispute.[17]

In dealing with the sale of a rented residential property, Ṭaḥāwī finds himself here compelled to discuss three different opinions within the school, each of them enjoying varying weight since they were held or reported by the three early masters, Abū Ḥanīfa, Abū Yūsuf, and Shaybānī. The first paragraph above states what Ṭaḥāwī seems to have considered the main tradition in the school – at least the one behind which he intends to throw his full support. In the second, Ṭaḥāwī introduces a competing opinion, held by Abū Yūsuf. In the third, a contradictory opinion is attributed by Shaybānī to Abū Ḥanīfa, but an opinion that contradicts the latter's position cited in the first paragraph. In the fourth paragraph, Ṭaḥāwī neutralizes Shaybānī as a transmitter of Abū Ḥanīfa's opinion and establishes in favor of the first opinion (stated in the first paragraph) an alternative and superior chain of transmission on the authority of Kaysānī, Kaysānī's father, and Abū Yūsuf. Ṭaḥāwī also declares Abū Ḥanīfa's first opinion superior to both Abū Ḥanīfa's other opinion and to Abū Yūsuf's competing view by virtue of the fact that the first opinion is in line with the general principles laid down by Abū Ḥanīfa himself and presumably accepted by his two so-called disciples. The principle underlying this opinion, however, is only alluded to, not articulated. One can infer that Abū Ḥanīfa held it as a principle, and not merely as an opinion, that the tenant must be protected and must thus be given precedence over a potential or prospective buyer during the period of his tenancy. Ṭaḥāwī's claim that Abū Ḥanīfa's opinion stands in line with his own principle, which Abū Yūsuf did not dispute, further weakens the latter's opinion by implying that it is not in line with the authoritative Ḥanafite tradition which he himself accepted.

In this case it is clear that Ṭaḥāwī's approach to deciding in favor of a certain opinion is one of comparing and contrasting. The comparison is taken still further to show the relative weakness of all opinions except one, namely, that which was being advocated. Among all of the opinions which no doubt have some merit, this particular opinion emerges as distinctly superior, not because it was held by any given jurist but rather

[17] Abū Jaʿfar Aḥmad b. Muḥammad al-Ṭaḥāwī, *Mukhtaṣar*, ed. Abū al-Wafā al-Afghānī (Cairo: Maṭbaʿat Dār al-Kitāb al-ʿArabī, 1370/1950), 130–31.

because it conforms, more than any other, to the authoritative principles of the school.

Comparing and contrasting opinions in an effort to reduce them, through elimination, to a single opinion based on one principle was not necessarily typical, nor was it done in such obvious ways as Ṭaḥāwī adopted in this case. Sarakhsī, for instance, writes:

> The *qāḍī* who receives a written instrument from another *qāḍī* must ask the bearer [i.e. witnesses] to testify that the instrument is truly that of the sending *qāḍī* [named] and that the seal is his. This is so because the [receiving] *qāḍī* has no knowledge [of the case] and thus two witnesses are needed as proof. He should have the instrument read before them and should testify to its contents. It is the principle of Abū Ḥanīfa – may God bestow mercy upon him – that in order for the instrument to be legally valid as a basis of judicial decisions, it is a condition that the witnesses know its contents. This was the old opinion of Abū Yūsuf, but he rescinded it and held that if the witnesses testify that the instrument truly belongs to the sending *qāḍī* and that the seal set on it is his, the [receiving] *qāḍī* should accept it, even though they may not know its contents. This is the opinion of Ibn Abī Laylā – may God have mercy on him – the reason for it being that the instrument may deal with matters that the two judges [the sending and the receiving] do not wish any one else to know; and this is why the instrument is sealed.[18]

Here, two opinions are set apart by two different rationales. Abū Yūsuf's change of mind seems enhanced by the fact that Ibn Abī Laylā had held the same opinion. But naming Ibn Abī Laylā, a non-Ḥanafite, as a supporting authority may not have been to Abū Yūsuf's advantage, after all. On the other hand, by employment of a stylistic device, Abū Ḥanīfa's opinion is made to dominate, first by referring to it approvingly as the standard doctrine of the school, and second by mentioning it at the outset, as though it were the default opinion. Once this is done, the authority holding the opinion is named and other competing opinions are then introduced.

However, it is not always the case that one opinion or principle must be made the preponderant one. At times, two or more opinions or principles are stated as equally valid. Qudūrī writes that "according to Abū Ḥanīfa, common property (*mushāᶜ*) is not rentable, but both of them [Abū Yūsuf and Shaybānī] held that it is."[19] These two general rules

[18] Sarakhsī, *Mabsūṭ*, XV, 95.

[19] Aḥmad b. Muḥammad b. Jaᶜfar al-Qudūrī, *Mukhtaṣar*, ed. Kāmil ᶜUwayda (Beirut: Dār al-Kutub al-ᶜIlmiyya, 1418/1997), 104.

or principles are simply stated by Qudūrī without further comment, as if to permit the jurist or judge to pick either of the two as the basis for deducing a rule or a decision. The equal validity of both positions seems to have persisted in the Ḥanafite school. The later Ottoman jurist Ibrāhīm al-Ḥalabī states these two opinions in the same distanced fashion, giving no one opinion precedence over the other.[20]

Similarly, ʿAlāʾ al-Dīn al-Samarqandī reports a disagreement among the Ḥanafites as to the time when *zakāt* is to be paid. Thaljī and Abū Bakr al-Jaṣṣāṣ appear to have maintained that it is payable at any time within the period for which it is due. But Shaybānī and Karkhī opined that it is payable at the very beginning of the period. Having stated these two positions, Samarqandī concludes by saying that "ultimately, the matter is subject to disagreement as to whether it is payable immediately or at a later time."[21] Now, as was the case in the rentability of common property, the issue is disagreement over principles which are the product of varying interpretations of the revealed texts. Individual cases are decided one way or another depending on which principle is applied. The apparently equal status of the two competing principles permits the jurist or judge a liberal choice. Any attempt to tip the scale in favor of one as opposed to the other, however, entails an examination of the textual and other evidence by which each was derived. But this, technically speaking, no longer lies within the province of *taqlīd*, and a discussion of it must therefore be postponed until chapter 5.

To stipulate principles as the foundation of deduction is equivalent to stipulating axiomatic postulates that underlie a class of cases. These postulates are not principles in the sense that they do not constitute general propositions from which rules are inferred deductively. Rather, they represent only one, albeit important, element among the totality of premises from which the rule is inferred. Just as the choice of one principle over another determines a different rule for the same case, so does the acceptance of one axiomatic position affect the manner in which a case is solved. And just as in the case where principles may be stipulated without making an attempt to render one of them preponderant over the other, axiomatic positions are normally stated without any clear effort to argue in favor of one position over another. The Shāfiʿites, for instance, disagree on the fee which the bathhouse keeper charges. Shāshī puts the crux of the matter thus:

[20] Ibrāhīm b. Muḥammad al-Ḥalabī, *Multaqā al-Abḥur*, ed. Wahbī al-Albānī, 2 vols. (Beirut: Muʾassasat al-Risāla, 1409/1989), II, 162.

[21] ʿAlāʾ al-Dīn al-Samarqandī, *Tuḥfat al-Fuqahāʾ*, 3 vols. (Damascus: Dār al-Fikr, 1384/1964), I, 558–59.

> Our associates have disagreed concerning the amount charged by the bath keeper. Is it the price of water, an entrance fee, a rental fee for the bucket [used for washing], or a fee for valetry? Some of them opined that it is the price of water, that the bath keeper valets as a volunteer, and that he only lends the bucket. Others maintained that the amount represents a [cover] fee for entrance, rental of the bucket, and valetry. Therefore, the customer is not liable to damages pertaining to the bucket [if it is destroyed]. But if the clothes [of the customer] are destroyed [while in the custody of the bath keeper], is the bath keeper liable to damages? On this, there are two opinions.[22]

The point of this passage, which is part of a larger discussion on the liability for damage to rented property, is not to formulate any casuistic rule but rather to state the entire range of opinions which are themselves definitions of what the bathhouse keeper's fee is. Each opinion, which allocates the fee in a particular manner, entails a conclusion about liability for damaged property that is different from other conclusions because the latter are based on different allocations of the fee. If one accepts that the fee represents the price of the water, then the customer is responsible for damages if the bucket is destroyed, because he borrowed it but did not rent it. If it is borrowed, then the benefit accrues to the borrower, not the bucket owner. Accordingly, the bucket owner is not held liable to damages, because – to put it tautologically – he derived no benefit by lending it. But if one accepts that the amount represents a rental fee for the bucket, then the user is not liable because the bathhouse keeper benefits from the rental fee.[23]

Now, the same questions and opinions are also introduced toward the very end of the passage concerning the bathhouse keeper's liability if the customer's clothes are ruined. Again, as in the case of the bucket, two opinions are stated, or rather intimated, in this regard. The brevity of Shāshī's discussion, and the cursory manner in which he glosses over the last opinions about clothing, are, together with other stylistic elements, all indicative of a profound familiarity with an age-old issue that hardly merits discussion beyond a synopsis. Shāshī's passage, therefore, is no more than a summary of the axiomatic postulates that are distinctly known to lead to a variety of solutions in the law of damages.

In the majority of the cases and opinions thus far discussed, there may be detected a penchant for comparing and contrasting, with a marked effort to isolate a particular opinion by identifying it with an accepted or authoritative principle. Normally, the principles that dominate in a

[22] Shāshī, *Ḥulyat al-ʿUlamāʾ*, V, 448. [23] See Māwardī, *al-Ḥāwī al-Kabīr*, IX, 256.

school tend to support opinions that have themselves become authoritative, though a number of major jurists may hold different opinions. Consider the following example, also from Shāshī's work:

> [The case of a person who] hands (*yadfa*ᶜ) a piece of cloth to someone else, and the latter sews it [into a dress] without mentioning his fee, has four opinions: The first is that he [the owner of the cloth] is obliged to pay the fee. This is Muzanī's opinion. The second opinion is that if he told him [the tailor] "sew the garment," then he is obliged to pay; but if he [the tailor] began his work and later said "pay me so that I will sew it," then he is not obliged [to pay him]. This is Abū Isḥāq's opinion.[24] The third opinion is that if the craftsman [=tailor] has been known to charge a fee for sewing, then he should be paid. If he has not been known to do so, then payment is not necessary. This is Abū al-ᶜAbbās [Ibn Surayj]'s opinion. The fourth, which is the authoritative opinion in the school (*madhhab*), is that in none of these cases is he entitled to a fee.[25]

In his opening statement, Shāshī makes it clear that the act of handing over the garment was not accompanied by any formal exchange of words, such as, for instance, offer and acceptance. It is precisely the absence of such a formality that gives rise to a problematic that constitutes the nexus of the entire juristic disagreement. Each of the four opinions expressed is based on a previous assumption or a principle. Muzanī appears to consider the transaction, if it can be regarded as such, as an implied offer and acceptance, a consideration which justifies the opinion that the owner of the garment stands obligated to pay the tailor a fee. Abū Isḥāq, on the other hand, requires that the offer be explicitly stated, whereas acceptance comes into effect by the implied fact that the tailor has begun his work on the dress. Ibn Surayj deals with the matter in different terms. He accepts the transaction as an implied contract if it is customarily known that the man is a professional tailor who charges fees for his labor. The authoritative doctrine of the school, however, is that a contract in matters of rent and hire is not deemed to be in effect if offer and acceptance were not explicitly stated at the outset. This explains why Shāshī, when citing the fourth opinion of the *madhhab*, is careful to add the clause "in all cases."

What Shāshī has done here, as is often the case, is to cite all relevant opinions which represent the application of different principles. By so doing, he shows, without much elaboration, how each of the different

[24] Presumably Abū Isḥāq Ibrāhīm al-Shīrāzī (d. 476/1083).

[25] Shāshī, *Ḥulyat al-ᶜUlamāʾ*, V, 455. See also Zayn al-Dīn Ibn Nujaym, *al-Ashbāh wal-Naẓāʾir* (Calcutta: al-Maṭbaᶜa al-Taᶜlīmiyya, 1260/1844), 134.

opinions is undergirded by a different presupposition. But in this case he also accomplishes another task, namely, to assert that the fourth opinion differs from the rest due to the fact that it is based on a principle which has become authoritative in the school. He does not state the principle, and certainly does not openly assert its authoritative nature. Instead, he implies, without allowing for ambiguity, that because the fourth opinion is the *madhhab* – i.e., the authoritative doctrine – then the principle on which it is based is, *a fortiori*, the authoritative principle of the school. (Incidentally, note that two of Shāshī's authorities are jurists who lived a century or more after Shāfiʿī, while those responsible for determining the authoritativeness of the fourth opinion belong to an even later period, from the middle of the fourth/tenth century and thereafter, when the Shāfiʿite school had already reached its final formation.)

In both examples, of the bathhouse keeper and of the tailor, Shāshī can be characterized as having been highly elliptic, leaving much to the realm of the implied. He states opinions, here and elsewhere, without their respective principles, and principles without their various applications or interpretations. Such is the case with many other jurists. It is worth remarking in passing that this phenomenon is more a mark of avoiding having to state the obvious than being a simple restatement of doctrines whose rationalization and justification are not within reach. In longer works, authors tend to expand on such matters, as does, for instance, Nawawī in his expansive *Rawḍa*,[26] where he deals with most of the matters addressed by Shāshī.

It is often the case that opinions are very carefully articulated, which is also true of the reasoning that underlies them. The Ḥanafite work *al-Fatāwā al-Hindiyya* offers illustrative examples, one of which is the following:[27]

> If a man hires a beast in order to use it for the transportation of a stipulated quantity of barley, but uses it instead to transport the same quantity of wheat, then he is liable to pay the beast's value in damages if it perishes, and is not bound to pay the hiring fee [to its owner]. This is the opinion of all [Ḥanafite jurists], because wheat is heavier, more solid and denser than barley. His doing so is tantamount to having used it to transport stones or iron.
>
> The situation would be different if he were to hire it for the transportation of ten dry measures of barley and instead uses it to transport eleven such measures [of the same commodity]. If he does so, he would

[26] Muḥyī al-Dīn Sharaf al-Dīn al-Nawawī, *Rawḍat al-Ṭālibīn*, ed. ʿĀdil ʿAbd al-Mawjūd and ʿAlī Muʿawwaḍ, 8 vols. (Beirut: Dār al-Kutub al-ʿIlmiyya, n.d.), IV, 306 ff.

[27] *Al-Fatāwā al-Hindiyya*, IV, 490–91.

be liable [only] to a portion of the damages[28] [if the beast perished and] if it is [deemed] capable of carrying that [commodity], because what has been transported is of the same species as that which has been stipulated [in the contract of hire].

If it is stipulated that he will transport ten dry measures of wheat, but he instead uses it to transport ten dry measures of barley, then, according to *istiḥsān*, he is not liable to damages [if the beast perishes] . . . If, on the other hand, he stipulates [the commodity] to be barley, but he instead uses it for the transportation of the same quantity of wheat, then he is liable to damages. The governing principle (*aṣl*) is that if the commodity transported is other than that which was stipulated [in the contract], and that if the two commodities are of the same weight, but the former occupies a smaller space on the back of the beast than that which the latter would have occupied, then he [who hires the beast] would be liable to damages because the commodity actually transported would harm the beast more than the commodity stipulated [in the contract]. This would be tantamount to a situation in which wheat or barley is stipulated, but then iron or stones of the same stipulated weight are transported instead. If, on the other hand, the commodity actually transported occupies a larger space on the back of the beast than that which was stipulated,[29] then he is not liable to damages because this [distribution of load] is easier for the beast . . . Such is the opinion given in *fatwās* (*wa-bi-hādhā yuftā*). This is from *al-Ẓahīriyya*.[30]

If he hires a beast in order to use it for the transportation of barley, but instead loads one saddlebag with wheat and the other with barley, and the beast perishes, our associates held that he is liable to damages equal to one half of [its] value and one half of the hiring fee. This is according to *al-Yanābīʿ*.[31] The governing principle [here] is that if the hirer violates the stipulation [in the contract] by loading the beast with the same material stipulated or something lighter in weight, then he is not liable to damages because the [owner's] acceptance of a certain [potential] harm means acceptance of a lower degree of harm. But if he violates the stipulation by raising the level of [potential] harm above that which was stipulated, and if the beast perishes, then he would be liable to damages, but not to the payment of the fee, if the materials he transports were of a kind different from that which was stipulated. If it were of the same kind, then he would be liable to an amount of damages proportionate to that part of the load in excess of what was stipulated, as well as to the hiring fee. This is so because the beast will have perished due to both an act for which he received

[28] Equal to one-tenth of the beast's actual value.

[29] It being understood here that the two commodities are equal in weight.

[30] By Muḥammad Ẓahīr al-Dīn b. Aḥmad al-Ḥanafī al-Walwālijī who died in 710/1310. See Ḥājjī Khalīfa, *Kashf al-Ẓunūn*, II, 1230.

[31] *Al-Yanābīʿ* was written by Muḥammad b. ʿAlī al-Shiblī (d. 769/1367).

> permission [from the owner] and an act for which he did not receive such permission. Damages are thus distributed in relative proportion. However, if he loads the beast beyond its capability, then he is liable because he was not permitted to do so. Iron is more harmful than cotton because it gathers in one spot on the back of the beast, whereas cotton spreads out. This is cited in *al-Ikhtiyār Sharḥ al-Mukhtār.*[32]

This is a fairly elaborate exposition which relates exclusively to damage liability for hired beasts. As may be observed, the preoccupation of the authors is not with textual attestations from the Quran or the Sunna, but rather with authoritative principles that have dominated the school. At least two such principles are explicitly cited, and they constitute the major premises which prompt the lines of reasoning adopted in this case. The essential point here is that both overloading the hired beast with a commodity that has been stipulated in the contract and loading it with a commodity of a denser quality but of the same weight stipulated will render the hirer liable for damages.

Another salient feature in this passage is the authority through which these principles and the law of which they form a part are mediated. Four authorities are cited: The first, given at the outset, is effectively the totality of the major Ḥanafite scholars; the second is *al-Ẓahīriyya*, by Muḥammad b. Aḥmad al-Ḥanafī (d. 710/1310); the third is *al-Yanābīᶜ*, by Muḥammad b. ᶜAbd Allāh al-Shiblī (d. 769/1367); and the fourth is *al-Ikhtiyār*, by ᶜAbd Allāh b. Mawdūd al-Mūṣilī (d. 683/1284). It is worth noting that the last three are relatively late, and are cited by title, not by their respective authors. Of this phenomenon we shall say something later.[33] For now it suffices to say that the activity of *taqlīd* involved here is not confined to the citation or repetition of what earlier authorities held to be true. The authority that is being transmitted cannot be confined to a casuistic repetition of cases. If casuistry is involved, it is to illustrate principles around which the law revolves. The authority being transmitted through *taqlīd* therefore is one that has at its center the articulation of principles which constitute the foundation underlying a changing array of cases to which these principles constitute applications. It is the principles and certainly not the individual cases that constitute the backbone of *taqlīd.* True, the majority of the jurists did not occupy themselves with the manner in which these principles were derived,

[32] *Al-Mukhtār* was written by ᶜAbd Allāh b. Maḥmūd b. Mawdūd al-Mūṣilī (d. 683/1284). He wrote a commentary on his own book which he titled *al-Ikhtiyār li-Taᶜlīl al-Mukhtār* (5 vols. [Cairo: Muṣṭafā Bābī al-Ḥalabī, 1951]) and the reference here is very probably to this commentary. See vol. II, 51 ff.

[33] See the next section of this chapter and chapter 6, section VIII, below.

although it remains true that many of those evolved with time and cannot be traced to a direct source or a conscious act of *ijtihād*. But the great majority of them, as is attested in the pages of hundreds of treatises written on the subject, understood the significance of the principles and knew how to apply them. For they were *muqallid*s, and this is precisely what *taqlīd* meant. Furthermore, the object of loyalty here is not even the earliest authorities of the school, a phenomenon we have already observed in Shāshī. One searches in vain for the names of Abū Ḥanīfa, Abū Yūsuf, Shaybānī, Zufar, and other early authorities. Instead, it is the later jurists, and in particular the later treatises *qua* treatises, that occupy center stage.

I have said that in this example the preoccupation of the authors is not with the manner in which the principles and the rules were derived from the revealed texts. This is because such principles were not extracted directly from such sources; rather, they represent juristic elaborations on the basis of earlier elaborations that were themselves probably derived from these sources. This is precisely what Ibn Kamāl meant when he declared the chief credential of the middle ranks of jurists to be loyalty to the founder's *uṣūl*.[34] But when the principles were perceived as emanating directly from the revealed sources, the *muqallid*s were not shy to venture upon examining such sources.

In his discussion of pilgrimage as a religious duty, Nawawī makes the following argument:[35]

> Pilgrimage is one of the pillars and duties of Islam, for it was related upon the authority of Ibn ʿUmar – may God be pleased with him and with his father – that he said: "I heard the Messenger of God – may God bestow peace upon him – say: 'Islam was founded upon five things; the *shahāda* that there is no god but God, performance of prayer, payment of the *zakāt*, pilgrimage to the House and the fasting of Ramadan.'" With regard to the lesser pilgrimage (*ʿumra*), there are two opinions [by Shāfiʿī]. In the new opinion,[36] he considered the lesser pilgrimage a duty on the basis of what ʿĀ'isha reported. She said: "I asked: 'O messenger of God, should women participate in *jihād*?' The Prophet said: 'Yes, a *jihād* in which no killing is involved – pilgrimage and the lesser pilgrimage.'" In the old opinion,

[34] Qurashī, *al-Jawāhir al-Muḍī'a*, II, 558–59.

[35] In his *al-Majmūʿ*, a commentary on Abū Isḥāq al-Shīrāzī's *Muhadhdhab*, which was to remain incomplete despite the later efforts of Taqī al-Dīn al-Subkī and others. See Jalāl al-Dīn ʿAbd al-Raḥmān al-Suyūṭī, *al-Minhāj al-Sawī fī Tarjamat al-Imām al-Nawawī*, printed with Nawawī, *Rawḍat al-Ṭālibīn*, I, 63–64.

[36] As is well known, Shāfiʿī often held two opinions on the same matter: the so-called "Old" doctrine he reportedly espoused before his migration to Egypt, and the "New" one that he formulated while in Egypt. On this, see Nawawī, *al-Majmūʿ*, I, 65 ff.

Shāfiʿī did not consider it a duty on the grounds of Jābir's tradition that the Prophet, when asked if the lesser pilgrimage was a duty, replied: "No, but if you perform it, it is better for you." The correct opinion is the first [i.e., the new one], because the latter tradition was not reported directly from the Prophet (*rafaʿa*)[37] by Ibn Lahīʿa, and what he narrated exclusively on his own authority is weak.

*Commentary*: Ibn ʿUmar's tradition was narrated by Bukhārī and Muslim. In the two *Ṣaḥīḥs*,[38] the tradition was reported with the variants "pilgrimage and the fasting of Ramadan" as well as "the fasting of Ramadan and pilgrimage." Both are sound, for the conjunctive "and" does not necessitate a particular order of things. Ibn ʿUmar heard it twice, and he reported it with the two variants. If the author [i.e., Shīrāzī] used this tradition as evidence and did not use God's words "People owe God the pilgrimage to the House,"[39] it is because he wanted to show that pilgrimage is a pillar, and this meaning is found in the Prophetic tradition, not in the Quranic verse.

ʿĀ'isha's tradition was related by Ibn Māja, Bayhaqī, and others through sound chains of transmission. Ibn Māja related the tradition according to the conditions set by Bukhārī and Muslim.[40] In favor of the lesser pilgrimage being a duty, Bayhaqī reported, on his own authority, on the authority of Abū Razīn al-ʿAqīlī, the Companion – may God be pleased with him – that he [Abū Razīn] said to the Prophet: "O messenger of God, my father can perform neither pilgrimage nor the lesser one, nor can he ride a caravan." The Prophet said: "Then perform pilgrimage and lesser pilgrimage on his behalf." Bayhaqī said: "Muslim b. al-Ḥajjāj said: 'I heard Aḥmad Ibn Ḥanbal say: "Concerning the duty to perform the lesser pilgrimage, I do not know a better and more sound tradition than this report of Abū Razīn."' " These are Bayhaqī's words. This tradition of Abū Razīn is sound, and was narrated by Abū Dāwūd, Tirmidhī, Nasā'ī, Ibn Māja, and others through sound chains of transmission. Tirmidhī said: It is a tradition of the *ḥasan–ṣaḥīḥ* type.[41]

37 *Marfūʿ* is a tradition on the authority of one of the Companions to the effect that the Prophet said or did something. The fact that a Companion attested to the words or deeds of the Prophet makes the tradition "lifted" to the level of the Prophet, in contradistinction with a transmission from a Successor who could not have possibly met the Prophet. See Abū ʿAmr ʿUthmān b. ʿAbd al-Raḥmān Ibn al-Ṣalāḥ, *Muqaddimat Ibn al-Ṣalāḥ wa-Maḥāsin al-Iṣṭilāḥ*, ed. ʿĀ'isha ʿAbd al-Raḥmān (Cairo: Dār al-Maʿārif, 1989), 193; G. H. A. Juynboll, "Rafʿ," *Encyclopaedia of Islam*, new (2nd) edition (Leiden: E. J. Brill, 1960– ), VIII, 384–85.

38 By Bukhārī and Muslim. 39 Quran 3:97.

40 For these conditions, see Ibn al-Ṣalāḥ, *Muqaddima*, 170.

41 This combination of terms is unique to Tirmidhī. It refers to the *isnād* of a tradition, so that if a tradition is reported through two chains of transmission, one being *ṣaḥīḥ* (sound) and the other *ḥasan* (good), it was termed a *ḥasan–ṣaḥīḥ* tradition. See James Robson, "Varieties of the *Ḥasan* Tradition," *Journal of Semitic studies*, 6 (1961), 49 ff.; Ibn al-Ṣalāḥ, *Muqaddima*, 185.

As for Jābir's tradition, it was narrated by Tirmidhī as one of a group of traditions on the authority of Ḥajjāj who is Ibn Arṭa'a, on the authority of Muḥammad Ibn al-Munkadir, on the authority of Jābir that the Prophet was asked about whether or not the lesser pilgrimage is a duty. He said: "It is not, but if you perform it, it is better for you." Tirmidhī said: "This tradition is of the *ḥasan–ṣaḥīḥ* type." Tirmidhī reported that Shāfiᶜī said: "The lesser pilgrimage is a duty, and I know of no one who permitted it to be otherwise. There is nothing in it which proves it to be a voluntary act." He also said: "Jābir's tradition was reported on the authority of the Prophet, but it is weak and cannot sustain an argument. Moreover, we have been told that Ibn ᶜAbbās deemed the lesser pilgrimage a duty." This is the end of Tirmidhī's statement.

Tirmidhī's claim that this tradition is of the *ḥasan–ṣaḥīḥ* type cannot be accepted. One should not be misled by Tirmidhī's statement concerning this tradition because the traditionists agree that it is weak. Its weakness is due to the fact that it turns on al-Ḥajjāj Ibn Arṭa'a, for he is its sole transmitter. Tirmidhī reported it on his authority, although Ḥajjāj, by the agreement of the traditionists, is a weak transmitter and a forger. In his tradition, he said "*from* (*ᶜan*) Muḥammad Ibn al-Munkadir." There is no disagreement [among the traditionists] that if a [person known to be a] forger uses the word *ᶜan*, then his transmission should not be considered credible.[42]

Now, the author's [i.e., Shīrāzī's] statement "because the latter tradition [of Jābir] was reported directly from the Prophet by Ibn Lahīᶜa, and what he narrated exclusively on his own authority is weak" has been criticized on account of the fact that he had erred with regard to it. This is so, because the one who reported it from the Prophet was not Ibn Lahīᶜa but al-Ḥajjāj Ibn Arṭa'a, as we have already mentioned. The author was also criticized for his statement that "what Ibn Lahīᶜa narrated exclusively on his own authority is weak," because Ibn Lahīᶜa is weak whether he narrates a tradition alone or together with others.[43]

The crux of this long discussion is simply whether the performance of pilgrimage and the lesser pilgrimage are mandatory acts or not. Here, three juristic voices can be identified: Shāfiᶜī, Shīrāzī, and Nawawī himself.

[42] A tradition that was transmitted, at any link, through the use of "*ᶜan*" was considered by a number of *ḥadīth* scholars to be "interrupted" (*munqaṭiᶜ*), unless it can be established that the two scholars creating that link are both trustworthy (in this case defined as having never been involved in *ḥadīth* forgery, *tadlīs*) and that they had been in the *ṣuḥba* of each other for a reasonably long period of time. Al-Ḥajjāj b. Arṭa'a failed to meet the first condition, to say the least. See Ibrāhīm b. ᶜAbd Allāh al-Qāsimī, *Taqrīb Iṣṭilāḥ al-Muḥaddithīn min Afhām al-Ṭālibīn* (Kerala: Dār al-Hilāl lil-Kutub al-Islāmiyya, 1985), 48. On *ṣuḥba*, see chapter 1, n. 4, above.

[43] Sālim ᶜAbd al-Ghanī al-Rāfiᶜī, *Mukhtaṣar al-Majmūᶜ: Sharḥ al-Muhadhdhab*, 8 vols. (Jedda: Maktabat al-Sawādī, 1995), VII, 6–9.

A rudimentary form of *taqlīd* would have been satisfactorily accomplished had Nawawī merely stated the accepted opinions of Shāfiʿī, namely, that both pilgrimage and the lesser pilgrimage are obligatory. These opinions could have been stated in a straightforward manner; e.g., "According to Shāfiʿī, pilgrimage and the lesser pilgrimage are obligatory duties." Instead, the discussion is opened by the introduction of competing opinions, expressed in contradictory traditions, and, to complicate the matter further, Shāfiʿī's old opinions are also cited.

Now, the point of advancing all these divergent opinions is to show that out of all the conceivable solutions to the problem, Shāfiʿī's (new) solutions are the most convincing.[44] This was the intent of Shīrāzī when he dealt with the issue, and it was likewise the intent of Nawawī who found Shīrāzī's reasoning to be wanting in certain respects. Nawawī reconstructs the authority supporting Ibn ʿUmar's tradition by anchoring it in the two *Ṣaḥīḥ*s of Muslim and Bukhārī. ʿĀ'isha's tradition is supported by the authority of the collections made by Ibn Māja and others, but ultimately this authority derives from the fact that Ibn Māja sorted out this tradition according to Muslim's and Bukhārī's conditions.[45] In favor of the obligatory nature of the lesser pilgrimage, Nawawī introduces an impressive array of traditionist authorities, including Ibn Ḥanbal, Bayhaqī, Abū Dāwūd, Nasā'ī, Ibn Māja, and Tirmidhī. But the latter's authority is disputed when it comes to Jābir's tradition, which he considers sound. Shāfiʿī, on the one hand, and the anonymous collectivity of the traditionists, on the other, are cited in refutation of Tirmidhī's position. Furthermore, Nawawī subjects Shīrāzī himself to criticism, charging him with having erred in his evaluation of Ibn Lahīʿa as a traditionist.

[44] Rehearsing a range of opinions was widely recognized as having the benefit of showing that, of all conceivable opinions, the one being defended is the most convincing or sound. In a revealing passage, Ṭūfī explains why old and obsolete opinions of the masters are listed in law books alongside recognized and authoritative opinions. Logic, he says, requires that obsolete opinions which are by definition not part of practice (*mā lā ʿamala ʿalayh lā ḥājata la-hu*) should not be rehearsed in these books, for that would in effect be a waste of time. However, such opinions are included for another reason, namely, to demonstrate the methods by which a variety of opinions pertaining to a single case are derived. Such a demonstration allows the reasoner to compare and contrast the relevant and obsolete opinions as well as the interpretive methods that lie behind them. This comparative analysis will in turn permit him to choose the most convincing of the opinions, an analytical process known as *tarjīḥ*. Although Ṭūfī happened to be speaking of old vis-à-vis new opinions, the principle of rehearsing a variety of opinions, old and new, from within and without the school, had the same function. See his *Sharḥ Mukhtaṣar al-Rawḍa*, III, 626.

[45] See n. 40, above.

Nawawī's *taqlīd* in this case is of the best kind. He is loyal to both Shāfiʿī and the mediating authority, Shīrāzī. Examining the tradition closely, he insists on the obligatory nature of pilgrimage and the lesser pilgrimage. But in affirmation of this loyalty, he goes beyond it to re-examine the textual evidence sustaining the tradition, with the result that it is given an extra weight. *Taqlīd* here is not only an intelligent application of principles, as we have seen earlier, but a reenactment of *ijtihād*. Nawawī, like Shīrāzī before him, traced the evidence and hermeneutics used by Shāfiʿī. Both of them reproduced it, and both improved on it. This undeniably creative activity cannot, nonetheless, be characterized as *ijtihād*, but rather as the highest manifestation of *taqlīd*, calculated, pondered, analyzed, and finally ratified. It is not *ijtihād* par excellence because it is not an independent act of reasoning and interpretation. But it is an eloquent expression of what has been termed *ittibāʿ*, an intelligent and creative type of *taqlīd* by which an earlier *ijtihād* is reenacted, defended, and, in most cases, improved.

## III

To describe this type of *taqlīd* as intelligent and creative by no means implies that other types are, in these respects, inferior. The hermeneutical activity that engaged Nawawī was in effect a confrontation with the revealed texts through the mediating authority of Shāfiʿī and Shīrāzī. No principles of the type we encountered in earlier cases were involved. The case of pilgrimage, whether greater or lesser, did not lend itself to such levels of abstraction. Pilgrimage is either an obligatory duty or it is not. In the other examples we encountered earlier, on the other hand, principles constituted the backbone of *taqlīd*. The jurists of the post-formative period, namely, the successors of the imam in Ibn al-Ṣalāḥ's and Ibn Kamāl's typologies, were not interested in vindicating principles as they would be seen to derive from the revealed texts. As a rule, they were taken for granted. Part of the reason why this was the case is that some of these principles were derived from earlier principles or assumptions which were the product of juristic thought that found no more than a tenuous connection with the revealed texts. The case of overloading hired beasts exemplifies principles of this sort.

But an explanation for the lack of interest shown by jurists in the connection between principles and textual support must be sought in the notion of loyalty to one's school. This loyalty would not have been the same had the jurists found it necessary to vindicate the school's principles at every stage of reproducing doctrine. Loyalty meant precisely the acceptance of these principles – though not necessarily unquestioningly – and more importantly, it meant applying them to individual cases. Whatever the legal question or case might have been, it was nothing more than an instance to which a principle was applied.

Nonetheless, loyalty also meant a defense of the principles as well as of the hermeneutics of the school.[46] And here lies another important feature of *taqlīd*. Generally speaking, *taqlīd* of the defensive type operated on two levels: the defense of one authority within the school over and against another, and the defense of the school as a whole or an individual authority in it against (an)other school(s) as a collective entity, or against an individual authority or authorities belonging to another school or schools. Three examples should suffice to illustrate our point, the first of which is taken from the Ḥanafite Sarakhsī:[47]

> According to us [the Ḥanafites], the *qāḍī* should not inflict a corporal punishment, be it Quranic (*ḥadd*) or discretionary (*taᶜzīr*), nor should he physically punish a person on behalf of another, in the precinct of the mosque. Shāfiᶜī, may God bestow mercy upon him, held the opinion that the *qāḍī* may do so if he does not [thereby] sully the mosque because the act of being in the mosque represents nearness to God and obedience to Him. Since these are the intended purposes of the mosque, then punishment is merely the tail end of his duties as a judge. And since he is permitted to sit in judgment in the [yard of the] mosque, he is therefore permitted to complete the adjudication of his cases including the meting out of punishments there.
>
> The argument in support of our [Ḥanafite] position is the tradition from the Prophet who said: "No Quranic punishments are to be meted out in the mosques." In Makḥūl's tradition, the prophet said: "From your mosques, keep away your boys, your madmen, your shouts, your disputes, your meting out of Quranic punishments, your sword drawing and your trading . . . ." It was reported that ᶜUmar – may God be pleased with him – ordered that a man be physically punished, and told the person to whom he gave this order: "Take him out of the mosque, then strike him." Furthermore, the Prophet was not reported to have himself ordered the infliction [in the mosque] of a Quranic punishment upon anyone, because he abhorred sullying the mosque and the shouting of the person being punished once he is stricken.

[46] In fact, treatises – wholly or in part – were written explicitly for the purpose of defending a particular school and of showing its superiority to the others. See, for example, Rāᶜī, *Intiṣār al-Faqīr*, especially at 199 ff.; Ibn Farḥūn, *Dībāj*, 11–16; Abū al-Mu'ayyad Muwaffaq al-Dīn b. Aḥmad al-Makkī, *Manāqib al-Imām al-Aᶜẓam Abī Ḥanīfa*, 2 vols. (Hyderabad: Maṭbaᶜat Majlis Dā'irat al-Maᶜārif al-Niẓāmiyya, 1321/1903), I, 38 and passim.

[47] Sarakhsī, *Mabsūṭ*, XV, 107.

This passage represents a vindication of the Ḥanafite position vis-à-vis that of Shāfiʿī in particular and, through him, that of the Shāfiʿite school in general. Sarakhsī presents Shāfiʿī's stance as one based on a general line of reasoning, deriving from the basic assumption that the mosque's function is to bring Muslims closer to God as well as to show obedience to Him. Since the *qāḍī* seeks to achieve these ends, then bringing his work to completion by inflicting punishment on convicted criminals becomes permissible. It is irrelevant to our purposes here whether this is the full extent of Shāfiʿī's position or reasoning on the matter. The point is that Sarakhsī sets up Shāfiʿī's position only to knock it down with what is in effect impressive textual evidence.

The second example, from a Shāfiʿite source, provides a somewhat more complicated picture. The issue at stake is whether pilgrimage should be performed instantaneously (*ʿalā al-fawr*) or whether it can be deferred to a later time (*ʿalā al-tarākhī*). On the authority of Shīrāzī, Nawawī states:

> We have already mentioned that our school's doctrine (*madhhabunā*) is that it can be deferred to a later time. This opinion was held by Awzāʿī, Thawrī, and Muḥammad b. al-Ḥasan [al-Shaybānī]. Māwardī reported it on the authority of Ibn ʿAbbās, Anas, Jābir, ʿAṭā', and Ṭāwūs, may God be pleased with them all. Mālik and Abū Yūsuf opined that it is to be performed instantaneously. It is also the opinion of Muzanī and the majority of Abū Ḥanīfa's followers. Abū Ḥanīfa himself did not hold a view with regard to this question.
>
> In favor of their opinion, the latter argued by citing God: "Perform pilgrimage and the lesser pilgrimage for the sake of God."[48] This is a command (*amr*) and commands make instantaneous performance [of the thing commanded] necessary.[49] They also adduced the tradition reported by Mihrān b. Ṣafwān on the authority of Ibn ʿAbbās – may God be pleased with both – that the Prophet said: "He who wants to perform pilgrimage must hurry." This tradition was narrated by Abū Dāwūd on his own authority, on Mihrān's authority, but this Mihrān is unknown (*majhūl*). Ibn Abī Ḥātim said: "Abū Zurʿa was asked about him [Mihrān], and he replied: 'I do not know him except through this tradition.'" They also adduced the aforementioned tradition:[50] "He who is not prevented from pilgrimage due to poverty, incurable illness, or a tyrant, will die either as a Jew or as a Christian, whichever he chooses."
>
> Shāfiʿī and our associates, [on the other hand], argued that the command to perform pilgrimage was revealed after the migration [to Medina],

[48] Quran 2:196.

[49] On commands and the imperative form, see Hallaq, *History*, 47–56.

[50] Introduced earlier in the chapter on pilgrimage. Rāfiʿī, *Mukhtaṣar al-Majmūʿ*, VII, 22.

as well as after the Prophet conquered Mecca in Ramadan, 8 A.H. He left Mecca in Shawwāl the same year, and left behind as a governor ᶜAttāb b. Asīd. Muslims began to perform pilgrimage in the year 8 A.H. upon the Prophet's command. Meanwhile, the Prophet, together with his wives and most of his Companions, were all living in Medina. He conducted the raid on Tabūk in the year 9 A.H., and left Tabūk before making the pilgrimage. He sent Abū Bakr – may God be pleased with him – to perform pilgrimage on his behalf in the same year, despite the fact that he, his wives, and the majority of his Companions were able to go on pilgrimage and were pre-occupied with neither war nor any thing else. Later on, in the year 10 A.H., he, his wives, and Companions all went on pilgrimage, which shows that it may be deferred.[51]

In the first paragraph, Nawawī opens his discussion with a statement of the school's doctrine and immediately marshals a prestigious list of jurists who held that doctrine. Even a leading Ḥanafite, Shaybānī, makes an appearance here. To give this position added support, a number of Companions are cited as having held the same doctrine. On the other hand, the Mālikites and the Ḥanafites, against whose position Nawawī is arguing here, are made to appear as holding the minority opinion by adopting the opposite doctrine. Mālik and Abū Yūsuf, together with Muzanī, are made to appear isolated when compared with the extensive list of names already set forth. Even Abū Ḥanīfa cannot come to their aid since he himself is said never to have formulated an opinion on the matter. The sheer number and weight of voices in favor of, or against, a position are seen here as constituting in themselves an argument.[52] Although Nawawī's discourse in the first paragraph has the appearance of an objective accounting of those who stood for and against the allowability of deferring pilgrimage, it is nothing less than an attempt to score a point by showing that his camp enjoyed the weighty support of the most illustrious Companions and jurists, including, of course, Shāfiᶜī himself.

In the second paragraph, a Quranic verse and two traditions are cited in favor of the Mālikite and Ḥanafite positions. Nawawī, apparently drawing upon the authority of Shīrāzī, undermines Abū Dāwūd's tradition by invoking Abū Zurᶜa's testimony against it. The other tradition, related on the authority of Abū Umāma, has also been shown – in a previous discussion of pilgrimage – to have a weak chain of transmission.[53] In favor of the Shāfiᶜite position, Nawawī gives a relatively detailed

[51] Ibid., VII, 37–38.

[52] This form of argument had become accepted since the second/eighth century. See Schacht, *Origins*, 14 and n. 2 therein.

[53] Rāfiᶜī, *Mukhtaṣar al-Majmūᶜ*, VII, 22–23.

historical account of how the Prophet, his wives, and Companions deferred going on pilgrimage. What Nawawī manages to accomplish here is not only to reproduce the authoritative doctrine of his school, but also to put forth an eloquent defense of it vis-à-vis the Ḥanafites first, and the Mālikites second. As with Sarakhsī's *taqlīd*, Nawawī's version here amounts to nothing short of a defense of the *madhhab*.

Our third example, pertaining to the permissibility of eating the flesh of horses, also comes from Nawawī:

> We have already mentioned that our doctrine is that it is permissible and that it is not reprehensible (*lā karāhata fī-hi*). This opinion was held by most scholars, including ʿAbd Allāh b. al-Zubayr, Faḍāla b. ʿUbayd, Anas b. Mālik, Asmā' bint Abī Bakr, Suwayd b. Ghafla, ʿAlqama, Aswad, ʿAṭā', Shurayḥ, Saʿīd b. Jubayr, al-Ḥasan al-Baṣrī, Ibrāhīm al-Nakhaʿī, Ḥammād b. Abī Sulaymān, Aḥmad [Ibn Ḥanbal], Isḥāq [Ibn Rāhawayh], Abū Yūsuf, Muḥammad (al-Shaybānī), Dawūd (b. Khalaf), and others. Others found it reprehensible, including Ibn ʿAbbās, al-Hakam, Mālik, and Abū Ḥanīfa. The latter held that he who eats it is blameworthy, but it [the act] cannot be called impermissible. In defense of this position, he adduced the Quranic verse [16:8] "Horses, mules, and donkeys are intended for you to ride, and for ornament." [Abū Ḥanīfa argued that] God did not mention eating them, whereas, in the preceding verse, He did mention the eating of grazing livestock. Abū Ḥanīfa also adduced the tradition of Ṣāliḥ b. Yaḥyā b. al-Miqdām from his father from his grandfather from Khālid b. al-Walīd who said: "The Messenger of God forbade [eating] the meat of horses, mules, and donkeys and all predatory animals." This tradition was reported by Abū Dāwūd, Nasā'ī, and Ibn Māja on the authority of Taqiyya b. al-Walīd who transmitted it from Ṣāliḥ, from Yaḥyā b. al-Miqdām b. Maʿdyakrib from his father, from his grandfather from Khālid [b. al-Walīd]. The leading *ḥadīth* scholars agree that this is a weak tradition, and some held that it was abrogated. Dāraquṭnī and Bayhaqī have reported, through a chain of transmission, on the authority of Mūsā b. Hārūn al-Ḥammāl, that he said that this tradition is weak. He also said that neither Ṣāliḥ b. Yaḥyā nor his father are known [to be reliable transmitters] except through their transmission on the authority of Ṣāliḥ's grandfather. Bukhārī said that this tradition is questionable (*fī-hi naẓar*). Bayhaqī said that the tradition's chain of transmission is confused; and as if this were not enough, it is contradicted by [other] traditions transmitted by trustworthy [authorities] concerning the horse's flesh. Khaṭṭābī also said that the tradition's chain of transmission is questionable, since the chain of Ṣāliḥ b. Yaḥyā b. Miqdām from his father from his grandfather is confused. Abū Dāwūd said that this tradition was abrogated. Nasā'ī maintained that the tradition which permits [eating the flesh of horses] is more sound. Even if we grant that it is a sound tradition, it is likely to have been abrogated

because the permission expressed in the [other] sound tradition suggests that abrogation took place.

In support of their position, our associates adduced the tradition of Jābir who said: "During the battle of Khaybar, the Prophet forbade the consumption of the flesh of domestic donkeys and permitted that of horses." Bukhārī and Muslim reported this tradition in their *Saḥīḥ*s . . . Jābir also said: "We traveled with the Messenger of God and used to eat the flesh of horses and drink their milk." Dāraquṭnī and Bayhaqī reported this tradition with a sound (*ṣaḥīḥ*) chain of transmission. In [yet another] report from Jābir, they are said to have eaten the flesh of horses during the Prophet's lifetime. Asmā' bint Abī Bakr reported that "we used to eat the horse's flesh during the lifetime of the Prophet." Bukhārī and Muslim reported this tradition. She also said that "we slaughtered a horse during the lifetime of the Prophet and ate it."

As for our rebuttal of the others' argument on the basis of the Quranic verse, it is the same as Khaṭṭābī's as well as our associates' response: That the mention of riding and ornament does not mean that their benefits are limited to just that. If he specifically mentioned these two [benefits], it is because they are most important when it comes to the horses' use. God, for example, said [Q. 2:173]: "I forbade unto you carrion, blood, and swine flesh." Only the flesh of the swine was mentioned because it is the more important, but Muslims are in universal agreement (*ajmaʿa*) that the pig's lard, blood, and all other parts are forbidden. This is also why God did not mention the horse as a means of transporting objects, although he did mention it in the case of grazing beasts [16:7]: "And they bear your loads for you." This [omission] does not entail that horses should not be used for transportation of objects. To our interpretation of this verse must be added the evidence from the sound traditions we have adduced in favor of the permissibility of consuming the horse's flesh, in addition to [the fact] that there is no sound evidence to the contrary (*ʿadam al-muʿāriḍ al-ṣaḥīḥ*).[54]

This kind of strategy in defending the *madhhab* should by now be clear. Nawawī's main target is seemingly Abū Ḥanīfa, and subsidiary to him stood Mālik and other less major figures of authority. Again, in an effort to promote the validity of his school's doctrine regarding the permissibility of consuming horsemeat, he marshals a long list of authorities which includes leading Companions and Followers, and, to score a point, none other than Abū Ḥanīfa's own disciples. The single tradition cited in support of the impermissibility of this act meets with Nawawī's devastating critique, leaving it in veritable ruins. In the same vein, Nawawī advances an evincive argument against Abū Ḥanīfa's interpretation of the Quranic verse 16:8. At the end of the day, the Shāfiʿite position is not

[54] Nawawī, *al-Majmūʿ*, IX, 4–5.

only vindicated but proven to be unquestionably superior to the only other alternative that was held by Abū Ḥanīfa and Mālik.

Needless to say, the defense of the *madhhab* as a dominant attitude in the elaboration of positive law appeared as a feature of legal discourse only subsequent to the formation of the legal schools. But this attitude should not be expected to surface in every case the jurists discussed. Some cases were unique to the schools, and did not therefore require either contestation or defense. A fertile ground for polemic was furnished by the older cases and questions that the schools, or most of them at any rate, shared. This common ground did not extend to the solutions they gave them. Not only did the principles which they applied to the same cases vary, but a single principle could receive diverging interpretations, thus leading to further differences in positive doctrine which in turn required defense.

Loyalty to the school with which one was affiliated never waned and, if anything, became all the more entrenched in both normative juristic activity and in the jurists' psyches. On the other hand, loyalty was not limited to a particular figure in one's school. While jurists were constantly and consistently loyal to their schools as collective entities, no jurist was loyal constantly and consistently, in every respect and detail of doctrine, to any single authority within his school. Loyalty of this sort never existed in reality, which is a powerful testimony to the liberal nature of *taqlīd*.

A jurist did express nominal loyalty to the so-called founder of his school, not because he adopted the latter's doctrines exclusively, but because he and his doctrines epitomized the unique nature of the school, in its positive law, juristic character, theological stance, and, most importantly, methodological and hermeneutical approaches. But once loyalty to the school was manifested, no jurist felt bound to accept the entirety of the founder's positive legal doctrines. The Ḥanafites, for instance, gave Abū Yūsuf and Shaybānī priority over Abū Ḥanīfa when the two agreed with each other and at the same time differed from him. In fact, in those cases where the interests of society were served better by the application of a particular rule, that rule would have priority even though it might not have been held by Abū Ḥanīfa.[55] But whatever the theory behind the distribution of authority may have been, jurists in reality never felt irrevocably bound by the founder's doctrines. And generally speaking, the later the period, the more true this proposition is. Loyalty to several authorities is exemplified in the work of the Ḥanafite jurist al-Mūṣilī,

[55] Qāḍīkhān, *Fatāwā*, I, 3; Ibn ʿĀbidīn, *Ḥāshiya*, I, 70 ff.; Ibn ʿĀbidīn, *Nashr al-ʿUrf fī Bināʾ Baʿḍ al-Aḥkām ʿalā al-ʿUrf*, in Ibn ʿĀbidīn, *Majmūʿat Rasāʾil*, II, 114–47, at 130 ff., and passim.

who, like the majority of his fellows in that school, declares at the outset that in his book he opted for "Abū Ḥanīfa's doctrine" (*qawl Abī Ḥanīfa*).[56] What the reader finds instead is a rich blend of doctrines emanating from many different authorities, including Abū Yūsuf, Shaybānī, Zufar, Karkhī, Abū al-Layth al-Samarqandī, Shams al-A'imma al-Sarakhsī, and anonymous "later jurists" (*muta'akhkhirūn*).[57] Similarly, Ṭaḥāwī opens his work with the following statement: "In this book of mine, I have compiled legal issues which one can neither afford to ignore nor fall short of learning. The answers I have chosen for these issues derive from the doctrines of Abū Ḥanīfa al-Nuᶜmān b. Thābit, Abū Yūsuf Yaᶜqūb b. Ibrāhīm al-Anṣārī, and Muḥammad b. al-Ḥasan al-Shaybānī."[58] Nevertheless, Ṭaḥāwī does take into consideration the doctrines of other authorities, as shown in the following example:

> Concerning a husband and his wife who disagree over the matter of [ownership of] their household effects given that they are free[59] and still living in matrimony. Abū Ḥanīfa – may God be pleased with him – held the opinion that whatever possessions in the house normatively belong to males shall be the husband's. The husband shall take an oath acknowledging his wife's claim to them. Whatever possessions normatively belong to females shall be the wife's. The wife shall take an oath acknowledging her husband's claim to them. Whatever possessions in the house that normatively belong to both males and females shall be the husband's. The husband shall take an oath acknowledging his wife's claim to them. If one of the spouses were to die, the solution would be the same as above, with the exception that possessions [equally] belonging to males and females shall revert to the surviving spouse.
>
> Abū Yūsuf – may God be pleased with him – held the same view as that of Abū Ḥanīfa, whether the spouses are both alive or one of them dies. But he opined that the husband should give his wife that portion of the possessions which specifically belongs to women in an amount equal to that given to women as a marriage gift (*mā yujahhaz bi-hi*). The remainder goes to the husband.
>
> Muḥammad – may God be pleased with him – held the view that whether they are both alive or one has died the [division of possessions] should be as Abū Ḥanīfa stipulated for them if they were both alive.
>
> It is reported that Zufar – may God be pleased with him – held the view that the possessions should be divided equally between the two, each taking an oath acknowledging the other's claim. This is the opinion which we adopt. It is also reported that Zufar held another opinion.[60]

[56] Mūṣilī, *Ikhtiyār*, I, 6.
[57] See, for instance, the chapter on hire and rent in ibid., II, 50–62.
[58] Ṭaḥāwī, *Mukhtaṣar*, 15. [59] I.e. not slaves. [60] Ṭaḥāwī, *Mukhtaṣar*, 228–29.

Despite the fact that Abū Ḥanīfa, Abū Yūsuf, and Shaybānī were held up as the highest authorities in the Ḥanafite school, and despite the fact that Zufar himself was known to have held yet another opinion, Ṭaḥāwī chose to adopt Zufar's position which required that household property be divided into equal shares. Such an example can be multiplied at will,[61] drawn from all the four schools. Ṭaḥāwī's example suffices to make the point, however.

In light of the terseness of Ṭaḥāwī's *Mukhtaṣar*, and the notorious difficulties in reconstructing legal practice at any particular time or place, it is difficult to explain why Ṭaḥāwī opted for Zufar over and against the three major Ḥanafite authorities. It may have been strictly a matter of legal reasoning, regarding whose logic and structure the text is (unsurprisingly) silent. But it may well have been a matter of practical necessity, rationalized, *ex post eventum*, by a particular line of reasoning.

Opinions dictated by a dominant practice are often referred to in legal texts in a pronounced manner. Generally speaking, in abridgments like that of Ṭaḥāwī, there is no room for detailed justification either of the opinions adopted by the author or of other jurists' opinions that he rehearses. But in larger works, practice and its imperatives are often explicitly acknowledged as determining the outcome of cases. This can certainly be documented in the Ḥanafite, Shāfiʿite, and Mālikite schools, and probably in certain Ḥanbalite texts. As we shall see below in chapter 5, practice often held a paramount position in determining the extent of authority bestowed on a particular opinion or doctrine. A jurist's choice of an opinion as the most authoritative was frequently justified by the fact that it was sanctioned by practice, was adopted by judges, or, as we have seen earlier in *al-Fatāwā al-Hindiyya*, used in the issuing of *fatwā*s.[62]

Since practice necessarily differed in certain areas of the law from one region to another,[63] the authority that a particular practice bestowed upon a certain case often differed as well. The western Mālikite jurist Ibn Farḥūn articulates this phenomenon rather clearly. He argues that when a jurist declares that a particular point of law has been dictated by a certain practice, he should not be understood to have made a universal statement but rather a statement applying to a particular region or place. Practice and prevalent customs determine which doctrine is to be applied and which not. This principle, Ibn Farḥūn maintains, has been adopted by

61 Ibid., 394, 405, 410, and passim. 62 See chapter 5, section VI, below.
63 See, for example, Wael B. Hallaq, "Model *Shurūṭ* Works and the Dialectic of Doctrine and Practice," *Islamic Law and Society*, 2, 2 (1995): 109–34; Wael B. Hallaq, "*Qāḍīs* Communicating: Legal Change and the Law of Documentary Evidence," *al-Qanṭara*, 20 (1999).

the Shāfiᶜites as well.[64] He quotes the Shāfiᶜite Ibn al-Ṣalāḥ has having argued that if practice happened to be in agreement with one of Shāfiᶜī's old doctrines, which are otherwise considered obsolete, then that opinion would become authoritative. He also speaks of the prominent eastern Mālikite jurist Ibn ᶜAbd al-Salām who held an opinion concerning the law of interdiction (*ḥajr*) which was apparently considered less than authoritative but became so because it reflected the practice of a region, presumably his.[65]

In the Ḥanafite school, the link between doctrines adopted and the exigencies of practice is also made consciously and clearly. It is a tenet of Ḥanafism that whenever Abū Ḥanīfa has on his side one of his two disciples, the opinion he holds is considered authoritative and as such it must be applied.[66] This tenet, however, is subject to important exceptions. For instance, the later Ḥanafites are recognized as having been empowered to diverge from both Abū Ḥanīfa's opinion and that of one of his disciples in favor of the minority opinion of the other disciple. The justification for this divergence is usually attributed to the requirements of practice.[67] Even the relatively marginal authority of Zufar is at times chosen over and against the three founding authorities, as we saw in Ṭaḥāwī's last example. Ṭaḥāwī did not care to explain the reasons why Zufar's opinion is made preponderant in certain cases. But Shāh Walī Allāh did. The opinions of Zufar that were favored in the school over those of Abū Ḥanīfa, Abū Yūsuf, and Shaybānī were simply more realistic and practicable.[68] Zufar's pronouncement that the sick can pray while sitting was favored over all other opinions in the school precisely on such grounds. Reporting what seems to have been an average Ḥanafite doctrine, Walī Allāh argues that any opinion in the school which takes note of human welfare and public interest in any particular era may be applied, the implication being that it may be applied despite the existence of competing authoritative doctrines.[69]

Ḥaṭṭāb affords us another detailed example from the Mālikite school, an example which assigns to the events of everyday life further legal significance:

> In the chapter on hire, Burzulī stated that "Ibn Abī Zayd [al-Qayrawānī] was asked about a hired builder whose work on a [given] day is interrupted

[64] Ibn Farḥūn, *Tabṣirat al-Ḥukkām*, I, 49. See also chapter 5, section VI, below.
[65] Ibn Farḥūn, *Tabṣirat al-Ḥukkām*, I, 49.
[66] Ibn Māza, *Sharḥ Adab al-Qāḍī*, 19; Ibn ᶜĀbidīn, *Ḥāshiya*, I, 71.
[67] Shāh Walī Allāh, *ᶜIqd al-Jīd*, 28. [68] Ibid.
[69] Ibid., 29: "*wa-yajūz lil-mashāyikh an ya'khudhū bi-qawli wāḥidin min aṣḥābinā ᶜamalan li-maṣlaḥat al-zamān.*"

> due to the falling of rain. He held the view that the builder is entitled to a portion of the payment equal to the time he worked. He does not receive payment for the remainder of the day [during which he did not work]. Saḥnūn held the same opinion. But others opined that the builder is entitled to all of the fee because he is not responsible for the stoppage of the work." Ibn ᶜArafa said that in his *Wathā'iq*, Saḥnūn held the opinion that if the falling of rain causes the work of a hired builder, a hired harvester, or other laborers to cease, then he is entitled to all the fee, not only that portion for which he actually worked, because he is not responsible for the stoppage of the work. These disagreements, Ibn ᶜArafa said, have no bearing upon the cases that we have encountered in our city of Tunis, because the custom there has decreed that contracts of hire become null and void upon the fall of heavy rain.[70]

The implication of the last few words in this passage is that in the event of rainfall a hired person would cease to be entitled to any fee because the contract was rendered void by, and upon, the occurrence of such an event. What is remarkable here is that not only are none of the Mālikite authorities in this passage reported to have held an opinion corresponding with the Tunisian practice, but Ibn ᶜArafa, himself a major Mālikite jurist, declares the aforementioned doctrines of the school to have nothing to do with that locale's practice.

In chapters 5 and 6, we shall have more than one occasion to explain the relationship between authoritative doctrines and legal practice in more detail. It will become obvious that the relevance of this practice to legal doctrine was taken for granted by all the schools. True, the relationship may appear to us more pronounced in the Mālikite school of the west, but the other schools, especially the Ḥanafite and the Shāfiᶜite, no doubt recognized it just as readily.

## IV

Before concluding this chapter, one important matter remains to be discussed. We have observed how *taqlīd* operated on a variety of levels. The spectrum in which it functioned ranged from a simple reproduction of doctrine to a full reenactment of legal reasoning and textual evidence which one or another of the early masters adopted. Preoccupation with principles and defense of the school's doctrine also turned out to be the heart and soul of *taqlīd*. But this is not all. An integral part of the activity of *taqlīd* manifested itself in a less conscious manner, which perhaps

[70] Ḥaṭṭāb, *Mawāhib al-Jalīl*, V, 432–33.

explains the silence over it in the juristic typologies we discussed in the first chapter. This is the evolution, during the so-called era of *taqlīd*, of a new type of discourse which differed from its predecessor in both kind and quality. Just as *taqlīd*'s major occupation was with the articulation of *applied* principles, it was necessary to raise the early casuistic method of exposition to a higher plane by formulating discourse of a more general applicability. In other words, the straightforward listing of cases proved insufficient as the exclusive method of exposition. Inductive generalization was introduced as a supplement, but not necessarily as a substitute, to casuistry. Whereas the founders' work was characterized by a strong, indeed exclusive, tendency toward casuistry, the *muqallids* systematized the endless instances of casuistry into a set or sets of general principles that governed the major issues involved in each area of the law.

There is no doubt that the evolution from a case-by-case style of exposition to a principle-based method of generalization indicates a higher degree of development within a system. The founding masters were occupied with solutions to individual questions, mostly coming to them through the medium of *istiftā'*, i.e., the soliciting of a *fatwā*. This explains why the early authors of legal treatises, whether of the abridged or comprehensive type, presented their subject matter on a case-by-case basis, without the noticeable presence of generalizations. Cases were lined up one after the other, from the beginning of the section or chapter down to its end. Such a style of exposition lacked a cogent structure, except for the evenness of the casuistic coverage.

Later works, however, almost universally exhibit a hierarchical structure, wherein general definitions and at times principles are stated at the outset, plus individual cases that both aid in the articulation of principles and teach the techniques of applying the principles to these cases.[71] While the logical connection between individual cases is not obvious in earlier works, the connection between the generalizations and individual cases is readily clear in later expositions. These cases, having inductively given rise to generalizations, came in their turn to be subsumed under these same principles.

To illustrate this tendency toward generalization, we shall compare two Ḥanafite texts, one from the end of the third/ninth century and the very beginning of the fourth/tenth, and the other from the middle of the seventh/thirteenth century. This choice does in no way suggest that by the beginning of the fourth/tenth century no advance whatsoever had been made toward generalization, nor should it be understood to mean

[71] Cf. Johansen, "Casuistry," 137 ff.

that the trend of generalization reached maturity by the middle of the seventh/thirteenth. Perhaps some rudimentary beginnings were made by the beginning of the fourth/tenth century, and it is highly likely that the trend continued unabated after the seventh/thirteenth. The two texts selected merely represent the transition from strict casuistry to a generalizing style of exposition, a transition, we must stress, that occurred entirely within the boundaries of *taqlīd*.

In our first text by Ṭaḥāwī, the chapter on hire and rent begins with the following:

> If a man rents from another man a house or [hires] a slave or any other thing, and it is delivered to him without the lessor stipulating that the price [or fee] must be paid immediately [upon delivery], then the lessor has no right to demand of the lessee immediate payment of the rent price. Instead, the lessee must pay the rent for each phase that has lapsed during the period of the rent. This is Abū Ḥanīfa's, Abū Yūsuf's, and Muḥammad's opinion, which we adopt.[72]

Note that despite the rudimentary nature of this opinion, an attempt is made to lump together all instances in which *ijāra* (rent and hire) is involved, be the object hired a house, a slave, or otherwise. The choice of a house in illustration of this principle was no doubt intended to cover the rent of immovable property where the lessee benefits from residing in the property itself. The example of a slave, however, covers those instances in which hire, not rent, is involved, with the understanding that the hirer benefits from the services which the slave offers. This lumping together of objects represents an advance over a more casuistic classification of cases in which houses, slaves, and other objects appear individually as the exclusive locus of the opinion. Yet, notwithstanding this attempt at grouping similar cases, the opinion still lacks the basic features of generalization.

Ṭaḥāwī continues his exposition by introducing five more opinions which are related to the same theme of rent payment. Immediately following these we find an opinion pertaining to damages to rented property: "If someone hires a beast in order to take it to a stipulated place, but he takes it to a point beyond that place, he would be liable to damages [equal to its value] as of the time he went beyond the stipulated place. He must also pay the hire fee."[73] Ṭaḥāwī then returns to his discussion of payment of rent, only to reintroduce opinions pertaining to damage liability. The logical connection between the opinions when presented in the order that Ṭaḥāwī imposes is at times convincing, but at many others it seems tenuous. Thus, in addition to eschewing for the most part

[72] Ṭaḥāwī, *Mukhtaṣar*, 128. [73] Ibid., 128.

generalizations, Ṭaḥāwī's discussion lacks rigor in its organization of the subject matter.

The style of exposition is characteristically that of "He who does X, Y, and Z, is entitled to (or owes) P, Q, and R." But the terms in which the whole discourse is presented are very concrete and of a limited scope, typified by such statements as "He who rents a house for the duration of a year to begin in the future, [his] rent contract is valid."[74] Although the house is used to represent immovable property, and the specification of one year to represent any agreed-upon time-frame, the examples are nonetheless caught in a confined conception of legal applicability. Logically, they are more suitable for subsumption under general propositions than they are capable of functioning as major premises in syllogistic inferences.

Ṭaḥāwī's exposition stands in sharp contrast to our second text, that of the Ḥanafite jurist ᶜAbd Allāh b. Mawdūd al-Mūṣilī. In the chapter on hire and rent, Mūṣilī opens with a definition of the term *ijāra*. (In sharp contrast, Ṭaḥāwī offers no such definition.) *Ijāra*, Mūṣilī states, "is the sale of *manāfiᶜ*," i.e. the enjoyment of services and usufruct. This type of sale, he continues, is permitted – despite the imperatives of *qiyās* – because society needs it (*li-ḥājat al-nās*).[75] For, by definition, since usufruct and services do not exist the moment a contract is concluded, there can be no sale, for the law requires that the object being sold be in existence on completion of the transaction.

Having defined *ijāra*, and having established its juristic status as a consensual entity[76] (in contradistinction to one arrived at through legal reasoning), Mūṣilī begins to state certain general principles:

> Usufruct and objects of hire [and rent: *ujra*] must be known (*maᶜlūma*).[77] Things permitted to have a price are permitted to be objects of lease, and their lease may be invalidated by violating the prerequisites (*shurūṭ*).[78] The right to cancelation,[79] to inspection,[80] and to rescission due to

[74] Ibid., 131. [75] Mūṣilī, *al-Mukhtār lil-Fatwā*, printed with his *Ikhtiyār*, II, 50.

[76] On society's needs as a consensual entity, see Hallaq, "*Qāḍīs* Communicating," sections I and VI.

[77] That is, they must be known to have a potential existence.

[78] In this sense, *shurūṭ* are the general prerequisites for the validity of a legal act. See Joseph Schacht, *An Introduction to Islamic Law* (Oxford: Clarendon Press, 1964), 118. On the prerequisites of *ijāra*, see Marghīnānī, *Hidāya*, III, 231 ff.

[79] The Arabic terminology is *khiyār al-sharṭ* which is a stipulated contractual right of the buyer or lessee to the cancelation of the contract within a certain period of time, usually no more than three days. See Marghīnānī, *Hidāya*, III, 27 ff.

[80] The Arabic terminology is *khiyār al-ruʾyā* which is the buyer's or lessee's right to cancel the contract upon seeing the object he bought, rented, or hired, the assumption here being that he had not seen the object at the time of concluding the contract. See Marghīnānī, *Hidāya*, III, 32 ff.

> defect[81] are all affirmed in the [law of] *ijāra*. It is also voidable and rescindable. Usufruct is defined by stipulating the period, as in [renting a] residential house or a cultivable land for a stated period; or by specification, as in dyeing or tailoring a dress, or as in hiring a beast for the transportation of a specific thing, or for riding it to a particular destination; or by gesture (*ishāra*), as in [hiring someone] to carry *this* food [to which one points].[82]

Note that this passage is free of casuistry and contains instead generalized statements that are applicable to the whole range of *ijāra*. Instead of introducing particular examples from which generalizations may be inductively inferred, the discourse here has almost universal applicability, and forms the basis of an entire range of deductive possibilities. And instead of identifying anew the conditions and prerequisites for the validity of an *ijāra* contract through the elaboration of individual cases which embody such conditions (a feature of Ṭaḥāwī's work), Mūṣilī simply creates a link to the well-known chapter on sales (*buyūʿ*) by making the latter applicable to the former. Furthermore, he defines the means by which the usufruct may be known through a universal language (e.g., stipulation of time and specification of service), although he introduces particular examples in order to illustrate them. Logically, this discourse represents a reversal of that adopted by Ṭaḥāwī and the early masters, a reversal in the sense that Ṭaḥāwī moved from particulars to universals (which he and his contemporaries were unable to articulate), whereas Mūṣilī, more than three centuries later – and having articulated such universals – moved from these universals to particulars representing mere instances of the universals.

However, immediately thereafter, Mūṣilī reverts to a discussion of individual cases. At first glance, the uniqueness of each of these cases makes any abstraction on their basis impossible. But in the second section, he attempts once more to establish generalizations. Here he distinguishes two types of hired persons, the common (*mushtarak*) and the private (*khāṣṣ*).[83] The *mushtarak*, he states, is not entitled to a fee until he performs the task for which he was hired, e.g. a tanner or a builder who is hired to do a particular job. The property upon which he is hired to work is held by him as if in trust (*amāna*), the implication here being that if the property is destroyed, he is not liable to damages unless he himself caused its destruction. The *khāṣṣ*, on the other hand, is someone who is hired for a particular duration to perform a service. He is entitled to a fee upon

[81] *Khiyār al-ʿayb* is the buyer's or lessee's right to return the object he bought, hired, or rented due to a defect in it, thereby effecting the cancelation of the contract. See Marghīnānī, *Hidāya*, III, 35 ff.

[82] Mūṣilī, *Ikhtiyār*, II, 51. [83] Ibid., II, 53.

concluding the contract, even though he may not have started his work yet. Now, articulating a distinction between these two types as central entities was important, for such a distinction in turn determined the types of damage liability in the law of hire and rent. In Mūṣilī, the distinction is pronounced and occupies a central place in his doctrine on the subject. In Ṭaḥāwī, on the other hand, it is virtually absent,[84] although Ṭaḥāwī, like his predecessors, knew of it.[85]

These distinctions are followed by other general principles pertaining, *inter alia*, to the payment of rental and hiring fees. What is characteristic of Mūṣilī's discourse here and elsewhere is the close logical relationship between the generalizing statements and casuistry. As soon as a generalizing proposition is made it is followed either by supporting or excepting particulars. The former are apparently intended to illustrate the generalization as well as to provide concrete instances of its applicability. The latter, on the other hand, are introduced in order to exclude certain rules or cases from a general principle. There are, of course, other individual cases and opinions whose logical connection to the generalizations is at best tenuous. But these had been passed down through generations of juristic exposition as a group of cases which did not lend themselves to abstraction.

The available literature does not permit us to determine with any measure of accuracy the period in which the transition from pure casuistic exposition to generalization took place. But it seems safe to assume that once the schools had taken form by the middle of the fourth/tenth century, generalization as a hermeneutical activity became a viable pursuit. This assumption is warranted by the fact that an essential element in the evolution of the schools was the articulation of a set of positive doctrines recognized by the members of each school as authoritative. This is precisely what the term *madhhab* signified – a body of positive legal cases that were acknowledged as authoritative and as making up the doctrinal, though not necessarily personal, constitution of the school.[86] And once these doctrines were deemed authoritative, they were elaborated and studied as applications of predetermined principles, principles from which they had issued but which had not yet been explicitly articulated. We have seen that one of *taqlīd*'s major preoccupations was precisely

[84] In the middle of a discussion, Ṭaḥāwī defines in a cursory manner only the *khāṣṣ* type, saying that it is "he who is hired for a known period" (*huwa al-musta'jar ʿalā mudda maʿlūma*): *Mukhtaṣar*, 130.

[85] Ibid., 129 (l. 12), 130 (l. 1). See also Māwardī, *al-Ḥāwī al-Kabīr*, IX, 254.

[86] The other principal meaning of the term *madhhab* was the personal constitution of the school, namely, a body of individual jurists who declared their loyalty to an eponym, although they were not obliged to follow his doctrines in every case. In this sense, then, affiliation with an eponym was in part, if not largely, a nominal, not a substantive, one.

the articulation of these principles. It should come as no surprise then that this evolution toward generalization was intimately connected with the *muqallids*' constant preoccupation with principles which we have demonstrated in the case studies presented earlier in this chapter.

Nor does the achievement of *taqlīd* stop here. The very centrality of the principles that permitted generalization in juristic discourse also gave rise to another significant development subsequent to the appearance and entrenchment of the generalizing mode of exposition. This development, which began after the fifth/eleventh century, is represented by the emergence of new types of legal discourse, such as *qawāʿid*[87] and *al-ashbāh wal-naẓā'ir*.[88] These types embody a systematic construction of higher general principles that derived from a variety of sources, including individual cases and lower general principles of the kind we have encountered in this chapter.[89]

## V

All in all, we have demonstrated that *taqlīd* is far from the blind following of an authority, as a number of major Islamicists have claimed. True, there were always jurists at the lowest rung of the profession who did mechanically and perhaps obtusely follow legal authority.[90] But their juristic performance represents no more than one form or one level of *taqlīd*, an activity that stretched over a wide spectrum. The search for the school's authoritative principles and the attempt to apply them to individual cases emerged as one of the mainstays of *taqlīd*.[91] The characteristic

87 See, e.g., ʿAlī b. ʿAbbās al-Baʿlī Ibn al-Laḥḥām al-Ḥanbalī, *al-Qawāʿid wal-Fawā'id al-Uṣūliyya*, ed. Muḥammad al-Fiqī (Beirut: Dār al-Kutub al-ʿIlmiyya, 1403/1983); ʿIzz al-Dīn Ibn ʿAbd al-Salām, *Qawāʿid al-Aḥkām fī Maṣāliḥ al-Anām*, 2 vols. (Cairo: Maṭbaʿat al-Istiqāma, n.d.); Shihāb al-Dīn al-Qarāfī, *al-Furūq*, 4 vols. (Cairo: Dār Iḥyā' al-Kitāb al-ʿArabī, 1925–27).

88 The most well-known works in this area are Jalāl al-Dīn ʿAbd al-Raḥmān al-Suyūṭī's *al-Ashbāh wal-Naẓā'ir* (Beirut: Dār al-Kutub al-ʿIlmiyya, 1979), and Ibn Nujaym, *al-Ashbāh wal-Naẓā'ir*.

89 The genres of *qawāʿid* and *al-ashbāh wal-naẓā'ir* are yet to be investigated. However, beyond the fact that their emergence illustrates the growing tendency towards generalization, a fuller analysis of their nature and function lies beyond the scope of the present discussion.

90 The sources afford abundant references to incompetent practices of *taqlīd*. See Ibn ʿĀbidīn, *Sharḥ al-Manẓūma*, 13; Ḥaṭṭāb, *Mawāhib al-Jalīl*, VI, 60, 95, 96; Ibn Rushd, *Fatāwā*, III, 1274 ff., and passim; *al-Fatāwā al-Hindiyya*, III, 307.

91 This element of *taqlīd* has been shown to be evident in Ibn Rushd's typology of jurists. The ability to distinguish between those views that accord with the school's principles and those that do not turns out to be characteristic of both the second and, expectedly, the third groups. See chapter 1, section II, above.

listing of opinions pertaining to a single issue had a number of functions, not the least of which was the illustration of how each opinion was the result of the application of a different principle or of a different interpretation of the same principle. Connected with this listing of opinions was the defense of the authoritative doctrine of the school against other schools or the defense of a single authority over and against other authorities, from both within and without the school. And although the traditionally recognized authorities were, as a rule, followed, there were nonetheless exceptions to this rule, even though they remained, it must be stressed, within the purview of *taqlīd*. In fact, it is a salient feature of Islamic legal doctrine that the juristic authority embedded in the works of the immediate or near-immediate precursors was to come to constitute the chief source from which the jurists expounded their own doctrines, or at least on par with the teachings of the founders. *Taqlīd*, therefore, was not bound by any particular authority just because this authority was equated with an eponym or an early master. *Taqlīd* of the "moderns" (*muta'akhkhirūn*) was therefore as legitimate as – and in fact more frequently practiced than – that of the "ancients" (*mutaqaddimūn*).

Finally, we must not overlook an important aspect of *taqlīd* that epitomized its dynamic and vibrant nature, namely, its reenactment of the textual evidence and legal reasoning adopted by a master. As in the case of the search for principles, this reenactment of what was in effect an *ijtihād*ic activity had more than one function, including instruction in the principles, evidence, and reasoning behind legal cases, as well as defense of the great *mujtahid*s by vindicating the methods and outcome of their *ijtihād*.

# 5

# OPERATIVE TERMINOLOGY AND THE DYNAMICS OF LEGAL DOCTRINE

## I

We earlier concluded that the rise of *taqlīd* as a *modus operandi* was symptomatic of the *madhhab*'s final coming to maturity as an authoritative entity. It was the external expression of the internal juridical dynamics that came to dominate and characterize the *madhhab* both as an established and authorized body of doctrine and as a delimited hermeneutical enterprise. One of the functions of *taqlīd*, we have also seen, was the defense of the school as a methodological and interpretive entity, an entity that was constituted of identifiable theoretical and substantive principles.[1] But the school was also defined by its substantive boundaries, namely, by a certain body of positive doctrine that clearly identified the outer limits of the school, limits beyond which the jurist ventured only at the risk of being considered to have abandoned his *madhhab*.[2] An essential part of the school's authority, therefore, was its consistency in identifying such a body of doctrine. On the macro-level, this doctrine was formed of the totality of the founder's opinions, substantive principles, and legal methodology, whether they were genuinely his or merely attributed to him.[3] Added to this were the doctrines of jurists deemed to have formulated legal norms in accordance with the founder's substantive and theoretical principles. We have seen that the opinions of those jurists who departed from a school's principles, such as Muzanī and the Four Muḥammads, were excluded from the body of authoritative doctrine, even though this exclusion was by no means final and in fact remained the object of some controversy. Finally, and with the same intention of following a well-trodden methodological path, all later opinions, expressed

[1] Namely, those principles that were elaborated in legal theory (*uṣūl al-fiqh*) and those that governed the hermeneutical activity of *taqlīd* in substantive law (which we discussed in the previous chapter).

[2] See n. 5, below. [3] See chapter 2, above.

mostly as *fatwās*,[4] belonged to the inner limits of the school's doctrinal boundaries. At this macro-level, there appears to have been no question whatsoever as to what was the doctrinal constitution and substantive make-up of Mālikism, Ḥanafism, or any other school for that matter. This writer, for one, has never encountered an opinion whose school affiliation was contested.[5] The imposing authority of the founder, constructed and genuine, ensured that the school named after him was a highly consolidated and integral entity.

On the micro-level, however, plurality of opinion within a given school was literally the name of the game. Each school possessed a vast corpus of opinions attributed to the founder, his immediate followers, and later authorities. In other words, they represented the total sum of doctrinal accretions beginning with the founder down to any point of time in the history of the school. In the Mālikite school, it was determined that Ibn al-Qāsim and Saḥnūn were the most reliable transmitters of Mālik's doctrine, and so their *riwāyas* became the most authoritative source for Mālik's opinions.[6] As Ibn al-Qāsim never set his *riwāya* in writing, the doctrine he taught on behalf of Mālik was in turn transmitted by Asad Ibn al-Furāt (d. 213/828), Saḥnūn, Ibn Ḥabīb (d. 238/852), and ᶜUtbī (d. 255/868). These jurists did record their transmissions in written form; as a result, their works later came to be known as the "Mothers" (*ummahāt*) of Mālikite legal literature.[7] The varieties that emerged in these recensions, the disciples' attributions to Mālik of various opinions, often contradictory, plus the opinions that were formulated by jurists in response to the exigencies of the geographical locales in which they flourished – from Baghdad to Andalusia – all led to a multiplicity of opinion that strongly colored the discourse of all later Mālikite works.

The plurality of opinion in the Ḥanafite school was equally abundant. In addition to the problem that later Ḥanafites faced in dealing with the conflicting opinions attributed to Abū Ḥanīfa, the three figureheads of the school also frequently disagreed with each other. For the students in the Ḥanafite tradition this was a subject of careful study and research.[8] To add to the challenge, Ḥanafite scholars had to learn about and deal with

[4] Hallaq, "From *Fatwās* to *Furūᶜ*," 39 ff.

[5] This is applicable even in the case of the so-called irregular opinions (*gharīb*, *shādhdh*) which were not accepted as part of authoritative doctrine, but remained, though inoperative, within the boundaries of the school. That they were irregular in one school did not make them the property of another, however.

[6] Ḥaṭṭāb, *Mawāhib al-Jalīl*, I, 33–34; Ibn Farḥūn, *Dībāj*, 239–41, 263–68.

[7] See Ḥaṭṭāb's introduction to his *Mawāhib al-Jalīl*, I, 6–42, especially at 33–35.

[8] As attested in Abū Zayd ᶜUbayd Allāh b. ᶜUmar al-Dabbūsī's *Kitāb Ta'sīs al-Naẓar* (Cairo: al-Maṭbaᶜa al-Adabiyya, n.d.).

the three levels of doctrine, the *ẓāhir al-riwāya*, *nawādir*, and *nawāzil*,[9] which represented a massive array of doctrine. The last of this trilogy included a body of opinion culled from juristic writings extending across several centuries and emanating from a number of disparate and far-flung regions, from Transoxania to Egypt.

Geographically speaking, and with the exception of the more recently Islamicized lands of South-East Asia which produced no truly authoritative doctrine, Shāfiʿism was more limited than its counterparts. But the plurality and diversity of opinion in it was no less staggering. Shāfiʿī himself was well known for having elaborated two sets of doctrine, one during his earlier life, known as the "Old" doctrine (*al-qawl al-qadīm*), and the other later on in his career, known as the "New" doctrine (*al-qawl al-jadīd*). And like the three Ḥanafite masters, he too was notorious for holding at times more than one opinion even within the "New" doctrine. In addition, the Shāfiʿites had to deal with a vast array of doctrine formulated by the *aṣḥāb al-wujūh*, those jurists who, as we have seen,[10] formulated opinions by way of *takhrīj*. As in the Mālikite school, the Shāfiʿites had more than one venue for transmitting the doctrines of both Shāfiʿī and the *aṣḥāb al-wujūh*. In this case, there were two which came to be known as *ṭarīqa*s (lit., ways).[11] One of these, identified with the Iraqians, was headed by the distinguished Abū Ḥāmid al-Isfarāʾīnī (d. 406/1015), who gained renown as *Shaykh al-Ṭarīqa al-ʿIrāqiyya*. The other, associated with the Khurasanians, was headed by Abū Bakr al-Qaffāl al-Marwazī (d. 417/1026), who was also nicknamed *Shaykh al-Ṭarīqa al-Khurasāniyya*.[12] Differences between the two *ṭarīqa*s were serious and often highly contentious. Shihāb al-Dīn Ibn Abī Shāma (d. 665/1266), a Shāfiʿite himself, severely criticized his school for the major deficiency (*khalal*) represented by the doctrinal discrepancies and contradictory transmissions of the two *ṭarīqa*s.[13] Nor was this all that the Shāfiʿite legists had to cope with. As in all other schools, they had to take

9 For a discussion of these, see chapter 2, section III, above.

10 See chapter 2, section III, above.

11 No modern scholar, as far as I know, has thus far attended to this development in Shāfiʿism, a development that promises to reveal valuable information about the history of this school.

12 Subkī, *Ṭabaqāt*, III, 24, 150, 198–99; Ibn Qāḍī Shuhba, *Ṭabaqāt*, I, 175–76; Shāshī, *Ḥulyat al-ʿUlamāʾ*, I, 54–55. Subkī reports (*Ṭabaqāt*, II, 116) that al-Muʿāfa Abū Muḥammad al-Mūṣilī wrote a treatise in which he brought the two *ṭarīqa*s together. For more on the nature of these *ṭarīqa*s, see Nawawī, *al-Majmūʿ*, I, 69; Nawawī, *Tahdhīb*, I, 18–19.

13 Shihāb al-Dīn b. Ismāʿīl Ibn Abī Shāma, *Mukhtaṣar Kitāb al-Muʾammal lil-Radd ilā al-Amr al-Awwal* in *Majmūʿat al-Rasāʾil al-Munīriyya*, vol. III (Cairo: Idārat al-Ṭibāʿa al-Munīriyya, 1346/1927), 20.

into account the vast body of cumulative doctrine produced by those authorities who lived after the *aṣḥāb al-wujūh*.

The Ḥanbalites were also faced with a fairly wide spectrum of doctrine, similar in some respects to the doctrinal diversity of the Shāfiʿite school. Perhaps due to the fact that Ibn Ḥanbal did not leave a legal corpus that could be regarded with any certainty as having been fixed by him, he was often associated with two, three, and at times even more opinions on the same case.[14] In terms of multiplicity of opinion, he is said to outdo even Shāfiʿī.[15] Furthermore, Ḥanbalite doctrine underwent the same process of elaboration through *takhrīj* as did that of the Shāfiʿites. Abū Yaʿlā Ibn al-Farrā', for instance, is said to have written a large work exclusively dedicated to the *riwāyāt* and *wujūh* in Ḥanbalite doctrine, the former being Ibn Ḥanbal's opinions and the latter those of the *aṣḥāb al-takhrīj*.[16]

The multiplicity of doctrinal narrative resulted in the development of a technical vocabulary whose purpose was to distinguish between types of legal opinion. We have already seen that those opinions formulated by means of *takhrīj* were called *wujūh*, primarily in the Shāfiʿite and Ḥanbalite schools. The opinions of the founders were also given special terms that designated them as such. Thus, in the Mālikite school, they were called *riwāyāt*, whereas *aqwāl* were assigned to those opinions formulated by Mālik's followers, including such late figures as Ibn Rushd and Māzarī. But the Mālikites admit that these terminological distinctions were not always observed and thus were not consistent.[17] In the Shāfiʿite school, the designation *aqwāl* was reserved for Shāfiʿī's opinions alone, whereas the *ṭuruq* (pl. of *ṭarīqa*) represented "ways of transmitting school doctrine." Thus, a jurist might claim that there exist two *wajh* or *qawl* opinions with regard to a certain question, while another might reject this claim and insist that there is only one. Such a disagreement would represent the variations involved in identifying or transmitting the *ṭarīqa*.[18] But differences among the Shāfiʿite jurists could at times also be found with regard to the distinctions between *qawl* and *wajh*. In a particular case pertaining to dietary law, for instance, Nawawī was not certain whether it had three *wujūh* or three *aqwāl*, the difference here

[14] See, for example, Zarkashī, *Sharḥ*, II, 560.
[15] See the editor's introduction to ibid., I, 20–21.
[16] Ibid. [17] Ḥaṭṭāb, *Mawāhib al-Jalīl*, I, 40.
[18] Nawawī, *al-Majmūʿ*, I, 65–66; Shāshī, *Ḥulyat al-ʿUlamā'*, VIII, 59. The *ṭarīqa* could, moreover, be made up of a number of elements. Thus, a *madhhab* case may consist of, say, three *ṭuruq*, each in turn consisting of one, two, or even three *qawl* or *wajh* opinions. For examples, see Shāshī, *Ḥulyat al-ʿUlamā'*, I, 85–86 (for a case having six *ṭuruq*), 86, 257; VIII, 59, 142–43, 181, 237–38; Nawawī, *al-Majmūʿ*, IV, 44.

being a matter of attribution either to Shāfiʿī or to those who practiced *takhrīj*. Generally, however, the Shāfiʿite notion of *ṭarīqa* was shared by the Mālikites as well,[19] but not by the Ḥanafites who, as we have already seen, developed the tripartite distinction between *ẓāhir al-riwāya*, *nawādir*, and *nawāzil*.[20]

## II

This technical terminology of narrative was symptomatic of the staggering variety of opinion which resulted from a fundamental structural and epistemological feature in Islamic law, a feature that emerged early on and was to determine the later course of legal development. Its root cause was perhaps the absence of a central legislative agency – a role which could have been served by the state or the office of the caliphate, but was not. The power to determine what the law was had lain instead, from the very beginning, in the hands of the legal specialists, the proto-*fuqahā'*, and later the *fuqahā'* themselves. It was these men who undertook the task of elaborating on the legal significance of the revealed texts, and it was they who finally established a legal epistemology that depended in its entirety upon the premise of an individualistic interpretation of the law. This feature was to win for Islamic law, in modern scholarship, the epithet "jurists' law." The ultimate manifestation of this individual hermeneutical activity was the doctrine of *kull mujtahid muṣīb*, i.e. that every *mujtahid* is correct.[21] The legitimization of this activity, and the plurality that it produced, had already been articulated as a matter of theory by as early a figure as Shāfiʿī.[22] It was also as a result of this salient feature that juristic disagreement, properly known as *khilāf* or *ikhtilāf*, came to be regarded as one of the most important fields of learning and enquiry, a field in which the opinions of a veritable who's who of jurists were studied and discussed.[23]

This feature of what we might term *ijtihād*ic pluralism had already become an epistemological element that was integral to the overall structure of the law. Its permanency is evidenced by the fact that, even after

[19] Ḥaṭṭāb, *Mawāhib al-Jalīl*, I, 38–39.

[20] See chapter 2, section III, above.

[21] Shīrāzī, *Sharḥ al-Luma'*, II, 1043–45; Aḥmad b. ʿAlī Ibn Barhan, *al-Wuṣul ila al-Uṣul*, ed. ʿAbd al-Ḥamīd Abū Zunayd, 2 vols. (Riyadh: Maktabat al-Maʿārif, 1404/1984), II, 341–51.

[22] Muḥammad b. Idrīs al-Shāfiʿī, *al-Risāla*, ed. Aḥmad Muḥammad Shākir (Cairo: Muṣṭafā Bābī al-Ḥalabī, 1969), 560–600; Norman Calder, "*Ikhtilāf* and *Ijmāʿ* in Shāfiʿī's *Risāla*," *Studia Islamica*, 58 (1984): 55–81.

[23] Ibn ʿAbd al-Barr, *Jāmiʿ Bayān al-ʿIlm*, II, 45 ff.; Makdisi, *Rise*, 107–11.

the final evolution of the *madhhab*, plurality could not be curbed: not only the old multiplicity of opinion that had emerged before the rise of the *madhhab*s, but also the plurality which surfaced later on, at every juncture of Islamic history. In other words, plurality remained a feature that proved utterly intractable. Its eradication, which did occur during the nineteenth century, would have meant the destruction of the distinctive *structural and epistemological* features of Islamic law.[24]

If legal pluralism was there to stay – a fact which the jurists never questioned – then it had to be somehow curbed or at least controlled, for, as a matter of consistency and judicial process, doctrinal uncertainty was detrimental. Which of the two, three, or four opinions available should the judge adopt in deciding cases or the jurisconsult opt for in issuing *fatwās*? The discourse of the jurists, in the hundreds of major works that we have at our disposal, is overwhelmingly preoccupied by this problem: Which is the most authoritative opinion? No reader, even a casual one, can miss either the direct or oblique references to this difficult question. Of course, the problem was not couched in terms of plurality and pluralism, for that would have amounted to stating the obvious. Rather, the problem was expressed as one of trying to determine the soundest or most authoritative opinion, although without entirely excluding the possibility that subjectivity might influence the decision. It is no exaggeration to maintain therefore that one of the central aims of all legal works, large or small, was precisely to determine which opinion was sound and which less so, if at all. As in all legal systems, consistency and certainty are not only a desideratum, but indispensable. In short, it cannot be overstated that reducing the multiplicity to a single, authoritative opinion was seen as absolutely essential for achieving the highest possible degree of both consistency and predictability.

## III

The same system that produced and maintained legal pluralism also produced the means to deal with the difficulties that this pluralism presented. To draw a more complete picture of the mechanisms that were developed to increase legal determinacy, we must look at two distinct levels of discourse, one emanating from a theoretical elaboration of this

[24] A number of traditional substantive laws continue to occupy a place in the codes of modern Muslim states, but structurally, epistemologically, and hermeneutically, traditional Islamic law has largely been demolished. State codification, the abolishing of *waqf*s, and the introduction of modern law schools and western courts were some of the factors that finally led to the structural collapse of the traditional legal system.

issue, the other deriving from positive legal formulations. The two levels were conceptually interconnected, and formed a virtual symbiosis. Theory acknowledged the reality of *ijtihād*ic pluralism, while practice – partly in the form of a discursive construction of substantive law – provided material for theoretical formulations.

Legal theory was based on the premise that the activity of discovering the law was both purely hermeneutical and totally individualistic. The allowances that were given to personal *ijtihād* created, within the theory itself, the realization that, epistemologically and judicially, pluralism had to be subjected to a further hermeneutical process by which plurality was reduced to a minimum. Different opinions on a single matter had to be pitted against each other in a bid to find out which of them was epistemologically the soundest or the weightiest. This elimination by comparison was in theoretical discourse termed *tarjīḥ*, namely, weighing conflicting or incongruent evidence. Here, evidence should be understood as the components making up the opinion itself: the revealed text from which the legal norm was derived; its modes of transmission; the qualifications and integrity of the transmitters; and finally the quality of linguistic and inferential reasoning employed in formulating the opinion. We shall now offer a brief discussion of preponderance in light of the problems that these components present.

Before we proceed, a preliminary, general remark is in order. It is a cardinal tenet in Islamic legal theory that *tarjīḥ* is permitted only in dealing with probable cases, that is, cases that do not depend on textual evidence whose linguistic significance and modes of transmission are deemed to be certain. The Quranic verse that allots the female half the male's share of inheritance is not open to *tarjīḥ* since, by definition, it is conclusive and not subject to interpretation or the formulation of other opinions. Furthermore, the epistemic hierarchy of the legal sources settles *a priori* any dispute as to which opinion must be deemed preponderant. Thus, an opinion on which consensus was reached is superior since consensus enjoys the highest epistemic value, even if the other opinions are derived from ambiguous Quranic verses. This superiority is in effect guaranteed by two attributes which consensus enjoys and which other sources do not. First, it is safeguarded against abrogation, and second, it is not subject to varying interpretations, for the interpretation agreed on by consensus acquires certainty and, consequently, bars alternative interpretations.[25] The hierarchy then is as follows: consensus, Quran, multiply

[25] Shīrāzī, *Sharḥ al-Luma*ʿ, II, 665–66, 682, 726–37; Ṭūfī, *Sharḥ Mukhtaṣar al-Rawḍa*, III, 675.

transmitted traditions (*mutawātir*), solitary traditions (*āḥād*), and *qiyās*, the inferential methods used in legal reasoning. In this hierarchy, the Quran and the *mutawātir* are on a par in terms of epistemic value.[26]

We now turn to preponderance as it relates to the categories we outlined above, the first of which is the transmission of the traditions. We have said that the most reliable form of transmission is the *tawātur* which alone, by the admission of most theoreticians and jurists, engenders certainty. Other forms, however, do not. The solitary tradition, and all other types of traditions standing between it and the *mutawātir*,[27] were deemed, according to the majority, to engender probable knowledge. Any tradition that does not meet the conditions of the solitary should not, theoretically at least, be utilized in matters legal. The general principle that governs transmission is that the more numerous the persons involved in the transmission of a report, the more reliable the report will be.[28]

Another aspect of transmission relates to the quality of the tiers of transmission. Thus, a tradition whose transmission can be traced all the way back to a Companion who was a direct witness of what the Prophet said or did is deemed superior to a tradition whose transmission begins with a Follower.[29] Similarly, a tradition that lacks the name of a transmitter at any tier of its transmission would be outweighed by another whose transmission is uninterrupted.

The rectitude of the transmitters themselves was also of crucial importance. Thus, a tradition that was transmitted by persons known for their reliability, precision, and trustworthiness outweighed another that was transmitted by persons who enjoyed only some or none of these qualities. Degrees of reliability, precision, and trustworthiness were distinguished. The more perfect the qualities possessed by the transmitter, the more superior he was adjudged. Accordingly, a more precise transmitter

[26] Ṭūfī, *Sharḥ Mukhtaṣar al-Rawḍa*, III, 674–75. On the epistemology of the *mutawātir*, see Bernard Weiss, "Knowledge of the Past: The Theory of *Tawātur* According to Ghazālī," *Studia Islamica*, 61 (1985): 81–105; Wael B. Hallaq, "On Inductive Corroboration, Probability and Certainty in Sunnī Legal Thought," in Nicholas L. Heer, ed., *Islamic Law and Jurisprudence: Studies in Honor of Farhat J. Ziadeh* (Seattle: University of Washington Press, 1990), 9–24.

[27] Such as the *mashhūr* and *mustafīḍ*, which are epistemologically superior to the solitary traditions but said by the majority to yield only a high degree of probability. See Hallaq, "Inductive Corroboration," 21 f.

[28] Āmidī, *Iḥkām*, I, 229 f.; Abū Yaʿlā Ibn al-Farrā', *al-ʿUdda fī Uṣūl al-Fiqh*, ed. Muḥammad Mubārakī, 3 vols. (Beirut: Mu'assasat al-Risāla, 1980), III, 856–57; Ṭūfī, *Sharḥ Mukhtaṣar al-Rawḍa*, III, 690–91; Hallaq, "Inductive Corroboration," 9 ff.

[29] Ṭūfī, *Sharḥ Mukhtaṣar al-Rawḍa*, III, 692; Bernard Weiss, *The Search for God's Law: Islamic Jurisprudence in the Writings of Sayf al-Dīn al-Āmidī* (Salt Lake City: University of Utah Press, 1992), 735.

bestows greater strength on a tradition than another whose transmitter is less precise.[30]

There were numerous other factors which entered into considerations of *tarjīḥ* relative to transmitters. Oral learning and memorizing of a tradition renders it superior to another whose transmission was based on a written record. This preference for human memory makes any tradition which is dependent on writing less desirable. If at any stage of its transmission the tradition were committed to writing, and then once again transmitted orally from that point onward, then that tradition would be outweighed by another which had been continually transmitted by oral means and was hence devoid of such weakness. Similar to this is the preference given to a tradition purporting to contain a verbatim report of the Prophet's words. Such a tradition is considered far superior to another which conveys only the meaning or theme of what the Prophetic words said.[31] In the same vein, a tradition whose first transmitter reports that he heard the Prophet say something outweighs another based on a report in which the transmitter tells of what the Prophet wrote to someone on a certain matter.[32]

Chains of transmission that include legists are deemed superior to any that do not contain transmitters with such qualifications. Similarly, a transmitter of prestigious ancestry or one whose family converted to Islam at an early point in time is considered superior to another who is or happens to be the descendant of a more recent convert or whose family is not well known. The degree of closeness to the Prophet was also a consideration. Thus, as a transmitter, a close friend of the Prophet is deemed far superior to another who was not so close to him. It is perhaps the same logic which dictates that a Medinese transmitter is superior to another transmitter who hailed from or lived in another locale.[33] The last, but not the least, of these factors is the transmitter's conformity to the dictates of the tradition he narrates. If one or more of the transmitters of a tradition were known to have acted in accordance with its message, their transmission would be considered to outweigh another where the transmitters did not act pursuantly to what they have narrated.[34]

The circumstances which gave rise to a tradition also determined its strength. Thus, if a tradition was transmitted within the context of an event which is considered widely known, then it would outweigh another lacking such a context. Similarly, if the first transmitter was somehow implicated or involved in the event that gave rise to a tradition, then the

[30] Ṭūfī, *Sharḥ Mukhtaṣar al-Rawḍa*, III, 693; Shawkānī, *Irshād al-Fuḥūl*, 54–55.
[31] Shawkānī, *Irshād al-Fuḥūl*, 57; Weiss, *Search*, 736. [32] Bājī, *Iḥkām al-Fuṣūl*, 739.
[33] Shīrāzī, *Sharḥ al-Lumaʿ*, II, 657–60; Hallaq, *History*, 67–68. [34] Weiss, *Search*, 735.

tradition would be regarded as superior to another where the transmitter was merely an observer. This involvement may be one of two types. The first is a tradition in which the first transmitter reports that the Prophet said or did something that concerned the reporter personally, such as Maymūna's report that the "Prophet married me in Sarif[35] while he was in the state of *ḥalāl*." This tradition was considered superior to Ibn ʿAbbās's report of the same marriage with the difference that in this latter transmission the Prophet was said to be in a state of *iḥrām*.[36] The second type is a tradition whose object specifically pertains to the first transmitter, such as the tradition concerning menstruation. Some jurists considered the tradition whose first transmitter was a woman more reliable than one first transmitted by a man. Other jurists, however, begged to differ, arguing that if the man was a reliable, trustworthy, and precise transmitter, his report should outweigh a woman's transmission, even if he was not personally involved in the matter that gave rise to the tradition in the first place.[37]

Also subject to preponderance were the texts themselves (*matn*; pl. *mutūn*), irrespective of the mode of their transmission. The following are some types of *tarjīḥ* that apply in such cases:[38]

1. A tradition whose text consists of fixed and steadily reported language outweighs another whose language is inconsistent and confused. A text whose language is not fixed leads to varying interpretations and reveals the imprecision of its transmitter(s).
2. A text in which the legal norm is explicitly and completely expressed is superior to another in which the norm is elliptically stated or merely suggested.
3. Related to the previous category, a tradition or text whose *raison d'être* is the stipulation of a legal norm is considered better than another in which the legal norm is incidentally stated.
4. A text whose general language (*ʿāmm*)[39] has been particularized in a manner which the jurists have approved is superior to another in which particularization has proven to be controversial.

[35] A watering place located six miles away from Mecca.

[36] *Iḥrām* is a state into which the Muslim enters physically, spiritually, and temporally during the greater or lesser pilgrimage, i.e. *ḥajj* and *ʿumra*. During *iḥrām*, the pilgrim should not engage in sexual intercourse, lie, argue, hunt wild game, kill any creatures (even flies), use perfume, clip fingernails, or trim or shave hair. See Wael B. Hallaq, "Forbidden," *Encyclopaedia of the Qur'an* (Leiden: E. J. Brill, forthcoming).

[37] Bājī, *Iḥkām al-Fuṣūl*, 735, 742, 744–45.

[38] For these types, see ibid., 745 ff.; Shīrāzī, *Sharḥ al-Lumaʿ*, II, 660–62; Weiss, *Search*, 736.

[39] Words that equally designate two or more individuals of the genus to which they refer are deemed general. Particularization (*takhṣīṣ*) means the exclusion from the general of a part that was subsumed under that general. For more on the general and the particular, see Hallaq, *History*, 45–47.

5. A text containing a real usage (*ḥaqīqa*) outweighs another containing a metaphor (*majāz*).[40]
6. A text that is expressed in emphatic language outweighs another that is not.
7. A text that reflects the consensus of the entire community is superior to another which reflects the consensus of the scholars. The same logic also dictates that the consensus of the Companions be deemed superior to that of the Followers, which also means that the consensus of dead *mujtahid*s outweighs that of living *mujtahid*s.
8. A text that includes additional information outweighs another that omits this information.

It should be noted that the types of *tarjīḥ* involved in numbers 2, 3, 4, 5, and 6 – as well as all other types that relate to the linguistic structure of *ḥadīth* texts – are also applicable to the Quranic language. It is only in the area of the transmission of the Quranic text that questions of *tarjīḥ* are precluded, since this transmission was the surest form of *mutawātir*, thereby engendering certainty.

What we have surveyed in the foregoing paragraphs is, relatively speaking, no more than a few rules of *tarjīḥ*. The legal literature in general, and works of legal theory in particular, elaborated on this theme extensively, producing dozens of distinctions and types. Āmidī, for instance, lists a total of 173 forms.[41] What we have discussed here are some of the more important and representative ones. Using the same criteria, let us go on to discuss how *tarjīḥ* applies in *qiyās*, perhaps the most difficult and complex form of preponderance.

Preponderance relating to *qiyās* addresses the four categories of which *qiyās*, as an archetype, consists: (1) the new case (*farᶜ*) that requires a legal solution; (2) the original rule or case embedded in the primary sources, the Quran and the sunna; (3) the *ratio legis*, or the attribute common to both the new case and the original case; and (4) the legal norm, or the rule (*ḥukm*) attached to the original case, which, due to the similarity between the two cases, is transferred from that case to the new one.[42] Of these, the two most important categories are the original rule and the *ratio legis*, the latter in particular having been at the center of much debate. As these two categories are closely related, we shall deal with them as a unit.[43] The principal forms of *tarjīḥ* in *qiyās* are as follows:

40 Further on tropology, see ibid., 42–43.

41 See Weiss, *Search*, 734.

42 Hallaq, *History*, 83.

43 Shīrāzī, *Sharḥ al-Lumaᶜ*, II, 950–65; Bājī, *Iḥkām al-Fuṣūl*, 757–66; Imām al-Ḥaramayn al-Juwaynī, *al-Talkhīṣ fī Uṣūl al-Fiqh*, ed. ᶜAbd Allāh al-Nībālī and Shabbīr al-ᶜUmarī, 3 vols. (Beirut: Dār al-Bashā'ir al-Islāmiyya, 1417/1996), III, 322–30; Rāzī, *Maḥṣūl*, II, 470–88; Weiss, *Search*, 737–38.

1. An original rule that is certain outweighs another that is probable.
2. An original rule based on a *ratio legis* subject to consensus is superior to another based on a *ratio* that is subject to disagreement.
3. An original rule on which the jurists had agreed that it is not subject to abrogation (*naskh*) is superior to another whose abrogation is debatable.
4. A *qiyās* that was based on a probable original rule but was conducted according to the systematic rules of legal reasoning outweighs another whose original rule is certain but which did not conform to such systematic rules.
5. An original rule whose *ratio* was extracted from the revealed texts outweighs another that was inferred on the basis of a former *qiyās*. Epistemologically, the latter was considered a derivative of the former.[44]
6. A *ratio* that was clearly articulated in the texts as the cause or rationale of the rule outweighs another that was not articulated as such.
7. A certain *ratio* obviously outweighs a probable one, just as a highly probable *ratio* outweighs a merely probable one.
8. A *ratio* ascertained through a superior method of analysis outweighs another ascertained by a less convincing method, or by a method that is controversial.[45]
9. A *ratio* that includes a single determinate attribute outweighs another involving a complex *ratio*, namely, one which gives rise to a legal norm due to a number of aggregate attributes.
10. A *ratio* arising from considerations of public welfare outweighs another that was ascertained by other considerations.[46]
11. A *ratio* supported by a number of textual citations is superior to another that is supported by a single citation.
12. A *ratio* in the original text that is found to be identical to that found in the new case is considered superior to another which does not have this quality, such as when the *genus* of the *ratio* in the new case does not exactly correspond to that found in the original text.
13. A *ratio* having a number of applications to new cases outweighs another that may be extended to merely a few cases or only one.
14. A *ratio* that leads to a rule based on reasonable doubt outweighs another that does not lead to such a rule. Accordingly, a *ratio* that results in waiving capital punishment on the basis of reasonable doubt is superior to another that makes no allowance for such doubt.

[44] Rāzī, *Maḥṣūl*, II, 483.

[45] On the methods of ascertaining the *ratio*, see Weiss, *Search*, 594 ff.; Hallaq, *History*, 86 ff.

[46] On considerations of public welfare in ascertaining the *ratio legis*, see Hallaq, *History*, 88 ff.

## IV

Now, this theoretical account of preponderance represents, in general terms, the methodological terrain in which the jurists were trained to deal with all conceivable possibilities of conflict in textual evidence and in the methods of legal reasoning. Their knowledge of all the issues involved in preponderance equipped them for the world of positive law where theory met with legal practice. It is with this arsenal of legal knowledge of the theoretical principles of preponderance that the jurists tackled the problem of legal pluralism and plurality of opinion. These principles provided the epistemic and methodological starting point for the operative terminology of substantive law, to which the remainder of this chapter will be dedicated.

Yet, it is curious that in works of substantive law, the concept of *tarjīḥ* appears less frequently than do a number of other, epistemologically related, terms. Conversely, these terms, which we shall discuss in detail here, make no appearance in works of legal theory. This phenomenon is neither singular nor surprising, however, for it is common to nearly all branches of Islamic religious learning. The same methods of inference expounded and analyzed in works of Arabic logic are labeled by entirely different terminology than that in treatises on legal theory. This much is well known. But the terminology involved in the study and exposition of the science of *ḥadīth* differs from one group of specialists to another, notably, the traditionists and the jurists. Even when one and the same scholar – such as Ibn al-Ṣalāḥ or Nawawī – deals with *ḥadīth* for legal purposes, he employs a set of terms different from those he applies to the same traditions when approaching them as a *muḥaddith*.[47]

Some of the terms that have appropriated the function of *tarjīḥ* in works of substantive law are derivatives of the root *ṣ.ḥ.ḥ.*, a root which carries the notion of correcting, rectifying, or making something sound or straight. The term *ṣaḥīḥ* (sound or correct), one of the most frequently used derivatives of this root, largely took the burden of what was otherwise known in works of legal theory as *rājiḥ*, namely, the preponderant opinion. The linguistic and conceptual links between *ṣaḥīḥ*, or the verbal noun *taṣḥīḥ* (the act of making something *ṣaḥīḥ*), and *tarjīḥ* were not lost on those who wielded them, however. Even in works of substantive law, the jurists did at times, albeit inadvertently, make a connection between

[47] See Wael B. Hallaq, "The Authenticity of Prophetic Ḥadīth: A Pseudo-Problem," *Studia Islamica*, 89 (1999), 81 ff.

the two concepts. Pointing out the need to investigate the strength of the *wujūh* opinions in the Shāfiᶜite school, Ibn al-Ṣalāḥ argues that it is necessary to conduct *tarjīḥ* among these *wujūh* in order to know which of them is the *ṣaḥīḥ*.[48] Hence, in Ibn al-Ṣalāḥ's discourse, *tarjīḥ* is the means by which the *ṣaḥīḥ* or correct opinion becomes known. The organic connection between *taṣḥīḥ* and *tarjīḥ* is also obvious in *Taṣḥīḥ al-Furūᶜ*, by the Ḥanbalite Mirdāwī.[49] *Taṣḥīḥ*, the reasoning that leads to the *ṣaḥīḥ*, therefore presupposes the same epistemological criteria employed in *tarjīḥ*. Opinions are assessed on the strength of the textual evidence upon which they are constructed, as well as upon the extent of persuasiveness of the lines of legal reasoning and causation upon which they rest.

Perhaps the most obvious link made between *taṣḥīḥ* and *tarjīḥ* is to be found in Tāj al-Dīn al-Subkī's bio-bibliographical dictionary *Ṭabaqāt al-Shāfiᶜiyya al-Kubrā*. In the long biographical notice which he allots to his father, Taqī al-Dīn, Tāj al-Dīn devotes a section to those school opinions that his father had "corrected" (*mā saḥḥaḥahu*). It immediately becomes clear that *ṣaḥīḥ* and *taṣḥīḥ* are used synonymously with *tarjīḥ*. The section, we are told, includes only those cases that Subkī the father "rendered preponderant" (*rajjaḥa*) over and against the choices of Rāfiᶜī (d. 623/1226) and Nawawī, the two most authoritative jurists of later Shāfiᶜism. A reading of the cases listed (over two hundred in all) leaves no doubt that *tarjīḥ* and *taṣḥīḥ* were used interchangeably. It is furthermore revealing that these cases, which were formally listed as *taṣḥīḥāt* (pl. of *taṣḥīḥ*), are referred to in the biographical notice itself as *tarjīḥāt* (pl. of *tarjīḥ*). Upon reading what were described as *taṣḥīḥāt*, for instance, Ibn Ḥabīb is reported to have found "these *tarjīḥāt*" impressive.[50] *Taṣḥīḥ* and *tarjīḥ* appear here as entirely synonymous.

The conceptual link between *ṣaḥīḥ* and *tarjīḥ* is further illustrated in the following example from Nawawī, where he deals with the (im)permissibility of eating carrion when no other food is to be found:

> If a person finds himself far from an urban setting, then it is permissible for him to eat [carrion] until he is satiated. If he is not that far, then it is not permissible [for him to eat until satiation], but only enough to get him to his destination. This is the broad distinction made by our associates. Imām al-Ḥaramayn al-Juwaynī reported this distinction and rejected it. He argued that there surely must be further differentiation (*tafṣīl*). Thus, he and Ghazālī were reported to have made the [following] differentiation:

[48] Ibn al-Ṣalāḥ, *Adab al-Muftī*, 124. [49] Mirdāwī, *Taṣḥīḥ al-Furūᶜ*, I, 50.

[50] Subkī, *Ṭabaqāt*, VI, 186–96. The cases that Taqī al-Dīn subjected to *taṣḥīḥ* (=*tarjīḥ*) have been compiled in verse (see ibid., VI, 196–99).

> If a person finds himself in a desert and he fears that if he does not eat to the full he may starve to death, then we affirm that it is permissible for him to eat until he is satiated. But if he thinks that he can get to a town [where lawful food is to be had] before hunger strikes again, then we affirm that he should eat only enough to keep alive . . . Ghazālī's and Imām al-Ḥaramayn's differentiation is good, and it is the preponderant opinion (*rājiḥ*). Our associates have disagreed about the various possibilities of this case. Abū ʿAlī al-Ṭabarī in his *Ifṣāḥ*, Rūyānī [d. 307/919], and others found preponderant [the opinion] that it is permissible for him to eat until he is satiated. On the other hand, al-Qaffāl [al-Shāshī] and many others have found preponderant the opinion that it is permissible for him to eat only enough to keep alive and that it is forbidden for him to eat until sated. This [latter] is the correct (*ṣaḥīḥ*) opinion, but God knows best.[51]

Apart from the subjectivity that lies at the heart of *taṣḥīḥ* – a matter we shall take up later – this passage illustrates the juxtaposition of the two concepts of "preponderant" and "correct." Ghazālī's and Juwaynī's differentiation was found to be *rājiḥ* (preponderant), in comparison with the broad distinction that Nawawī observes in the works of their predecessors. At the same time, these latter were split into two allegedly preponderant opinions, the second of which is found by the author to be the *ṣaḥīḥ*. It is obvious that, for Ṭabarī and Rūyānī, the *rājiḥ* is nothing other than the *ṣaḥīḥ*. But in order to reserve for himself the decision on what is, in the final analysis, the correct of the two competing opinions, Nawawī asserts that the *ṣaḥīḥ of the two rājiḥ opinions* is the one that was adopted by Qaffāl.

Treatises on substantive law are replete with statements declaring certain opinions to be *ṣaḥīḥ*, more *ṣaḥīḥ*, or not at all.[52] The idea behind this juristic activity derives from the fundamentals of preponderance as expounded in works of legal theory and as outlined earlier in this chapter. But as an organic part of the environment of substantive law which includes as one of its essential components the school's authoritative and long-established positive doctrine, *taṣḥīḥ* was bound to take into account both the methodological and the substantive principles of the school. Thus, in realistic terms it acquires a complexity which exceeds that observed in the discourse of legal theory.

Despite (or perhaps because of) the fact that a staggering number of opinions are determined in terms of *ṣaḥīḥ* or non-*ṣaḥīḥ*, the authors of law books seldom bother to demonstrate for the reader the process by which an opinion was subjected to *taṣḥīḥ*. This phenomenon, I think, is

[51] Nawawī, *al-Majmūʿ*, IX, 43. [52] On the non-*ṣaḥīḥ* opinions, see n. 61, below.

not difficult to explain. *Taṣḥīḥ* usually involved a protracted discussion of textual evidence and lines of legal reasoning, such as those we saw in the previous chapter concerning the defense of the *madhhab*. Most works, or at least those available to us, do shy away from providing such self-indulgent detail. The Ḥanafite Ibn Ghānim al-Baghdādī, for instance, explains the problem in his introduction to *Majmaᶜ al-Ḍamānāt*, where he states: "Except for a few cases, I have not included the lines of reasoning employed in the justification of the rules, because this book is not concerned with verification (*taḥqīq*).[53] Our duty is rather limited to showing which [opinion] is *ṣaḥīḥ* and which is *aṣaḥḥ*."[54] The task of "verifying" the opinions was not only too protracted, but also intellectually demanding. It is precisely this achievement of "verifying" all available opinions pertaining to one case and declaring one of them to be the strongest that gave Nawawī and Rāfiᶜī such a glorious reputation in the Shāfiᶜite school, and Ibn Qudāma the same reputation in the Ḥanbalite school.[55] This was an achievement of a few during the entire history of the four schools.

In his magisterial *Majmūᶜ*, Nawawī sometimes, but by no means frequently, explains the reasoning involved in *taṣḥīḥ*. Consider the following examples, the first of which pertains to the types of otherwise impermissible food which a Muslim can eat should he find himself, say, in a desert where lawful food is not to be had:

> Our associates held that the impermissible foods which a person finds himself compelled to eat are of two types: intoxicating and non-intoxicating . . . As for the non-intoxicant type, all foods are permitted for consumption as long as these do not involve the destruction of things protected under the law (*itlāf maᶜṣūm*). He who finds himself compelled to eat is permitted to consume carrion, blood, swine meat, urine, and other impure substances. There is no juristic disagreement (*khilāf*) as to whether he is permitted to kill fighters against Islam and apostates and to eat them. There are two *wajh* opinions[56] [though] concerning the married fornicator

[53] Verification is the activity of the "verifiers" (*muḥaqqiqūn*), scholars who establish the solution to problems by means of original proof and reasoning. See Muḥammad b. ᶜAlī al-Tahānawī, *Kashshāf Iṣṭilāḥāt al-Funūn*, 2 vols. (Calcutta: W. N. Leeds' Press, 1862), I, 336 (s.v. *taḥqīq*); W. B. Hallaq, *Ibn Taymiyya against the Greek Logicians* (Oxford: Clarendon Press, 1993), 12 (n. 2).

[54] Baghdādī, *Majmaᶜ al-Ḍamānāt*, 3.

[55] In the Ḥanafite school, Marghīnānī, among others, acquired a similar status. In Mālikism, it was Ibn Rushd, Māzarī, and Ibn Buzayza, although in his *Mukhtaṣar* Khalīl was to bring together the fruits of these and other jurists' efforts.

[56] Opinions formulated by *aṣḥāb al-wujūh* or *aṣḥāb al-takhrīj*. See chapter 2, section III, above.

> (*zānī muḥṣan*),[57] rebels, and those who refuse to pray (*tārik al-ṣalāt*). The more correct of the two opinions (*aṣaḥḥ*) is that he is permitted [to kill and eat them]. Imām al-Ḥaramayn, the author [Shīrāzī],[58] and the majority of jurists (*jumhūr*) conclusively affirm the rule of permissibility. [In justification of permissibility] Imām al-Ḥaramayn maintained that this is because the prohibition [imposed upon individual Muslims] to kill these is due to the power delegated to governing authority (*tafwīḍan ilā al-sulṭān*), so that the exercise of this power is not preempted. When a dire need to eat arises, then this prohibition ceases to hold.[59]

Juwaynī's reasoning here was used by Nawawī to achieve two purposes: the first to present Juwaynī's own reason for adopting this *wajh* opinion, and the second to use the same reasoning to show why Nawawī himself thought this opinion to be the more correct of the two. Thus, the absolute legal power of the *sulṭān* to execute married fornicators, rebels, and prayer-deserters is preempted by the private individual's need to eat, should he or she face starvation.

Note here that Nawawī gives only the line of reasoning underlying the opinion that he considers to be more correct of the two, despite the fact that the other *wajh* opinion is admitted as *ṣaḥīḥ*. This was the general practice of authors, a practice which has an important implication: If another author thought the second, *ṣaḥīḥ*, opinion to be in effect superior to the one identified by Nawawī as the *aṣaḥḥ*, then it was the responsibility of that author to retrieve from the authoritative sources the line of reasoning sustaining that opinion and to show how it outweighed the arguments of Juwaynī and of others. In fact, this was the invariable practice since nowhere does one encounter a reprimand or a complaint that the author failed to present the lines of reasoning in justification of what he thought to be the less authoritative or correct opinion(s).

There was no need to present the evidence of non-*ṣaḥīḥ* opinions because they were by definition negligible – not worth, as it were, the effort.[60] These opinions became known as *fāsid* (void), *ḍaʿīf* (weak), *shādhdh* (irregular), or *gharīb* (unknown), terms that never acquired

[57] Since, unlike the unmarried fornicator whose punishment falls short of the death penalty, the married fornicator receives the full extent of this punishment. See Nawawī, *Rawḍat al-Ṭalibīn*, VII, 305–06.

[58] Since Nawawī's work is a commentary on Shīrāzī's *Muhadhdhab*, he refers to him as "the author" (*al-muṣannif*), a common practice among commentators.

[59] Nawawī, *al-Majmūʿ*, IX, 43–44.

[60] For example, in his *al-Majmūʿ*, I, 5, Nawawī states that he will overlook the lines of reasoning in justification of weak opinions even when these opinions are of the widespread (*mashhūr*) category.

any fixed meaning and remained largely interchangeable.[61] No particular value was attached to any of them, for just as in the study of *ḥadīth*, a *ḍaʿīf* report was dismissed out of hand. A premium, on the other hand, was placed upon the category of the *ṣaḥīḥ* and its cognate, the *aṣaḥḥ*. At first, it might seem self-evident that the *aṣaḥḥ* is by definition superior to the *ṣaḥīḥ*. But this is not the case. Claiming *ṣaḥīḥ* status for an opinion necessarily implies that the competing opinion or opinions are not *ṣaḥīḥ*, but rather *ḍaʿīf*, *fāsid*, *shādhdh*, or *gharīb*.[62] But declaring an opinion *aṣaḥḥ* means that the competing opinions are *ṣaḥīḥ*, no less. Thus, in two cases, one having a *ṣaḥīḥ* opinion and the other an *aṣaḥḥ* opinion, the former would be considered, in terms of authoritative status, superior to the latter since the *ṣaḥīḥ* had been taken a step further in declaring the competing opinion(s) weak or irregular, whereas the *aṣaḥḥ* had not been. In other words, the *ṣaḥīḥ ipso facto* marginalizes the competing opinions, whereas the *aṣaḥḥ* does not, this having the effect that the competing opinion(s) in the case of the *aṣaḥḥ* continue(s) to retain the status of *ṣaḥīḥ*. The practical implications of this epistemic gradation are that it was possible for the opinions that had competed with the *aṣaḥḥ* to be used as a basis for

[61] Subkī, *Fatāwā*, II, 10 ff.; Suyūṭī, *al-Ashbāh wal-Naẓā'ir*, 104; Nawawī, *Tahdhīb*, I, 94, 113, 164; Ibn Qāḍī Shuhba, *Ṭabaqāt*, I, 96; II, 93–94. Ibn ʿĀbidīn, *Sharḥ al-Manẓūma*, 38; Baʿlī, *al-Ikhtiyārāt al-Fiqhiyya*, 24; Mirdāwī, *Taṣḥīḥ al-Furūʿ*, I, 25, 31, 32; Ibn Rajab, *Dhayl*, I, 70, 157 ff.; ʿĪsā b. ʿAlī al-ʿAlamī, *Kitāb al-Nawāzil*, 3 vols. (Rabat: Wizārat al-Awqāf wal-Shu'ūn al-Islāmiyya, 1983), III, 6. When Taqī al-Dīn Subkī went against Rāfiʿī and Nawawī concerning a case of pledging real property and considered as *ṣaḥīḥ* an opinion contrary to another which they had considered as authoritative, it was possible for Tāj al-Dīn al-Subkī to declare that his father had rendered the opinions of the two masters weak (*wa-ḍaʿʿafa maqālatahum*). See his *Ṭabaqāt*, VI, 191.

In the Ḥanbalite school, Abū al-Khaṭṭāb al-Kilwadhānī (d. 510/1116) was said to have held a number of opinions not shared by the members of his school, opinions described as *tafarrudāt*. These opinions, also characterized as *gharā'ib* (pl. of *gharīb*), were corrected (*ṣaḥḥaḥa*) by later Ḥanbalites. See Ibn Rajab, *Dhayl*, I, 116, 120, 126–27.

It is to be noted that in some cases the opposite of the *ḍaʿīf* was the *qawī* (lit. strong) or the *aqwā* (stronger), terms that were rarely used and whose technical meaning remained unfixed. See, for instance, the Ḥanbalite Baʿlī, *al-Ikhtiyārāt al-Fiqhiyya*, 11. The same may be said of the term *ṣawāb* or its fuller expression *wa-hādhā aqrab ilā al-ṣawāb* (this is more likely to be true or correct), which was used infrequently to designate the status of an opinion. See, e.g., Kāsānī, *Badā'iʿ al-Ṣanā'iʿ*, I, 31. A very rare labeling of weak opinions is the term *quwayl* which is the diminutive of *qawl* (opinion). See the Ḥanbalite Zarkashī, *Sharḥ*, I, 63, 290.

[62] It is quite possible that the last two, and particularly the fourth, of this quartet may have referred to opinions lacking in terms of sufficient circulation, without any consideration of correctness or soundness. However, the connection that was made between authoritative status and level of acceptance meant that widely circulated opinions were correct whereas those that failed to gain wide acceptance problematic. See further on this issue below.

*iftā'* or court decisions, whereas those opinions that had competed with the *ṣaḥīḥ* could no longer serve any purpose once the *ṣaḥīḥ* had been identified (that is, unless a *mujtahid* or a capable jurist were to reassess one of these weak opinions and vindicate it as being more sound than that which had been declared earlier as *ṣaḥīḥ*. This, in fact, was one means by which legal change took place).[63]

This epistemic evaluation of *taṣḥīḥ* was usually helpful in assessing opinions between and among a number of jurists belonging to one school. At times, however, it is necessary to evaluate opinions within the doctrinal corpus of a single jurist, in which case the *ṣaḥīḥ* and the *aṣaḥḥ* would acquire different values. If a case has only two opinions and the jurist declares one to be *ṣaḥīḥ* and the other *aṣaḥḥ*, then the latter is obviously the more preponderant one. But if the case has three or more opinions, then the principles of evaluation as applied to the larger school doctrine would apply here too. It is to be noted, however, that these principles of evaluation were generally, but by no means universally, accepted. Disagreements about the comparative epistemic value of *taṣḥīḥ* persisted and were never resolved, a fact abundantly attested by the informative account penned by the last great Ḥanafite jurist Ibn ᶜĀbidīn (d. 1252/1836).[64]

In due course we shall discuss further the relative uses of operative terminology and the subjectivity that it involved. But before doing so, we should turn to the types of reasoning that form the basis of *taṣḥīḥ*. In the case of eating the flesh of apostates and married fornicators, the basis is a legal category derived from textual evidence which was construed to permit the killing of apostates and married fornicators. A further distinction between the two can still be made: The married fornicator becomes deserving of capital punishment on a purely criminal basis, namely, violating the sexual code of the Muslim community as enshrined in the injunctions of the revealed texts. Apostasy, on the other hand, is not, strictly speaking, a criminal act, but rather a matter of what we might call international law which acknowledges a sharp distinction between the territory of Islam and that of unbelievers who must be fought until death, conversion, or subjugation as *dhimmīs*.[65] That these apostates and married fornicators should be killed is not subject to dispute. Rather, the issue that becomes relevant in this case is the juristic basis upon which

[63] See chapter 6, below.

[64] See his splendid discussion in *Sharḥ al-Manẓūma*, 38 ff. which marshals a myriad of opinions from the early and late periods.

[65] Aḥmad Ibn Naqīb al-Miṣrī, *ᶜUmdat al-Sālik wa-ᶜUddat al-Nāsik*, ed. and trans. N. H. Keller, *The Reliance of the Traveller* (Evanston: Sunna Books, 1991), 602–03.

a private Muslim individual is permitted to eat the flesh of these people. Such considerations I call secondary, in the sense that they constitute not a legal category directly derived from the textual sources, but one that is based on an already formulated set of established rules. We should note in passing that much of the legal reasoning involved in works of substantive law and collections of *fatwās* belong to this type of secondary juristic considerations.

The second of the two cases presents a different sort of *taṣḥīḥ*:

> Is it permissible to drink date-wine, grape-wine or any other inebriant as medicine or for the purpose of quenching thirst [when water is nowhere to be found]? With regard to this question, there are four *wajh* opinions all of which are widespread (*mashhūra*). The correct one (*ṣaḥīḥ*) according to the majority of associates is that they are not permitted for either purpose. The second opinion is that they are permissible. The third is that they are permitted as a medicinal cure but not for quenching thirst. The fourth is the converse of the third [namely, that they are permitted for quenching thirst but not as a cure]. Rāfiᶜī said that the correct (*ṣaḥīḥ*) opinion according to the majority of jurists is that they are not permitted for either of the two purposes, the evidence for this being the tradition transmitted by Wā'il b. Ḥajar [who reported] that when Ṭāriq b. Suwayd al-Jaᶜfī asked the Prophet about wine, the latter prohibited him [from drinking it] and expressed his dislike for making it. Ṭāriq said: "I only make it as a medicinal cure," whereupon the Prophet said: "It is not a cure but a disease." Muslim transmitted this tradition in his *Ṣaḥīḥ*. The authoritative opinion of the school (*al-madhhab*)[66] is the first one, namely, that wines are not permitted for either of the two purposes. This opinion was corrected (*ṣaḥḥaḥa*) by Maḥāmilī and I shall present his argument momentarily[67] . . . Imām al-Ḥaramayn and Ghazālī opted (*ikhtārā*) for the opinion that wines are permitted for the purpose of quenching thirst. The former argued that "wine quenches thirst so that it is not of the same category as curative medicine. He who claims that wine does not quench thirst simply does not know, and his opinion is not to be considered authoritative; indeed, it is erroneous and fanciful. [Drinking in] wine taverns substitutes for drinking water." But this is not correct, since the widespread (*mashhūr*) opinion of Shāfiᶜī, of our associates and of physicians is that wine does not quench thirst but in fact intensifies it. It is a well-known habit of wine drinkers to consume large quantities of water. Rūyānī reported that Shāfiᶜī opined that it is prohibited if it is used for

[66] On the *madhhab*-opinion as an operative usage, see our discussion later in this chapter.

[67] Nawawī does not state Maḥāmilī's argument for *taṣḥīḥ* as an integral opinion but apparently chooses to reproduce it through Rūyānī, Abū al-Ṭayyib al-Ṭabarī, and Qāḍī Ḥusayn whom he discusses later in the same passage.

> the purpose of quenching thirst, his reasoning being that it makes one both hungry and thirsty. Al-Qāḍī Abū al-Ṭayyib [al-Ṭabarī] said: "I asked people knowledgeable in this matter and [concluded that] Shāfiʿī was right: It quenches the thirst for a while but thereafter it causes extreme thirst." In a lecture note, Qāḍī Ḥusayn maintained that "the physicians say that wine increases thirst and that wine-drinkers appreciate cold water." The conclusion of all that we have said is that wine is useless for the purpose of quenching thirst. And the conclusion based on the aforementioned tradition [from Wā'il] is that it is not beneficial as curative medicine. Therefore, its prohibition is established categorically.[68]

This passage presents us with two significant points: First, although the four *wajh* opinions are recognized as widespread (*mashhūra*), three of them are declared incorrect. Later, we shall discuss the *mashhūr* category of opinion and its relationship to other categories, but for now it suffices to say that despite the pedigree of these four opinions as both *mashhūr* and *wujūh*, three of them are rejected as incorrect. Yet this declaration was made *e contrario*: by declaring one to be a *ṣaḥīḥ* opinion, it is concluded that the others are not deemed to be *ṣaḥīḥ*. This assessment is to be contrasted with the preceding one with regard to consuming the flesh of apostates and married fornicators, where the fact that one opinion was declared "more correct" meant that the other was correct, nonetheless. But a declaration of an opinion as *ṣaḥīḥ* must be seen to be as much a condemnation of the other alternatives as it is a vote in favor of that opinion.

The other, more important, point to be made here is the basis of *taṣḥīḥ*. In the case of eating the flesh of married fornicators and apostates, the basis was purely hermeneutical in the sense that doctrinal considerations of established principles dictated a certain extension of these principles. Here, however, the basis of *taṣḥīḥ* is sensory perception and experience, gained by the observations of physicians and experts. The underlying question was one that required experiential knowledge of whether wine was, physiologically speaking, a substance that quenched or induced thirst. In this regard, it is interesting to note that the usual considerations of inebriation – which otherwise permeate all discussions of wine – were not here relevant.

*Taṣḥīḥ* may also be based on considerations of customary practices (*ʿāda*). Rāfiʿī and Nawawī held the opinion that wearing silk should be limited to the extent that it should only form a piece of a garment, specifically used as a trimming that is no wider than "four fingers," that

68 Nawawī, *al-Majmūʿ*, IX, 51–52.

is, the width of a palm without counting the thumb. The basis of this opinion was said to be social custom, presumably that which prevailed during the lifetimes of Rāfiʿī and Nawawī.[69] Taqī al-Dīn al-Subkī deemed this opinion to be the correct one, although our source does not give any account of the other opinions.[70]

Social need and necessity also appear as grounds for *taṣḥīḥ*. In fact, they are cited as grounds for abandoning an otherwise *ṣaḥīḥ* opinion in favor of another which would become on these very grounds the *ṣaḥīḥ*. The Ḥanafite jurist Ibn ʿĀbidīn argues this much:

> Not every *ṣaḥīḥ* [opinion] may be used as a basis for issuing *fatwā*s because another opinion may be adopted out of necessity (*ḍarūra*) or due to its being more agreeable to changing times and similar considerations. This latter opinion, which is designated as fit for *iftāʾ* (*fīhi lafẓ al-fatwā*), includes two things, one of which is its suitability for issuing *fatwā*s, the other is its correctness (*ṣiḥḥatihi*), because using it as the basis of *iftāʾ* is in itself [an act] by which it is corrected (*taṣḥīḥ la-hu*).[71]

These notions of *taṣḥīḥ* did not remain a matter of theory or an unaccomplished ideal. In his *al-Fatāwā al-Khayriyya*, Khayr al-Dīn al-Ramlī offers a substantial collection of questions which were addressed to him and which he answered with opinions that had been corrected (*ṣaḥḥaḥahu*) by the leading Ḥanafite scholars on the basis of considerations having to do with changing requirements of the age and of society.[72]

Needless to say, the basis of *taṣḥīḥ* may also be any of the considerations we have enumerated in the theory of preponderance. Illustrations of such considerations, especially those related to Sunnaic textual evidence, abound, and it suffices for our purposes here to refer the reader to those cases we cited in the preceding chapter as examples of defending the *madhhab*. Obviously, the purposes of *taṣḥīḥ* fundamentally differ from those of defending the *madhhab*, but the processes involved in both activities are very much the same: they are offshoots of *tarjīḥ* or adaptations thereof.

Preponderance, as we have seen, depends in part on corroboration by other members of a class, which is to say that it is subject to inductive corroboration by an aggregate body of the same type of evidence. Thus, a tradition transmitted by a certain number of channels and transmitters

[69] Although Rāfiʿī lived mostly in Qazwīn and Nawawī in faraway Syria.
[70] Subkī, *Ṭabaqāt*, VI, 188. [71] Ibn ʿĀbidīn, *Sharḥ al-Manẓūma*, 38–39.
[72] Khayr al-Dīn al-Ramlī, *al-Fatāwā al-Khayriyya*, printed on the margins of Ibn ʿĀbidīn's *al-ʿUqūd al-Durriyya fī Tanqīḥ al-Fatāwā al-Ḥāmidiyya*, 2 vols. (Cairo: al-Maṭbaʿa al-Maymūniyya, 1893), I, 3.

was considered to be superior to another transmitted by fewer channels and transmitters. Similarly, a *ratio legis* attested by more than one text was deemed to outweigh another supported by a single text. Consensus itself, epistemologically the most powerful sanctioning authority, depended on universal corroboration. Thus, what we have called inductive corroboration no doubt constituted a fundamental feature of legal thinking, both in the theory of preponderance and elsewhere in the law.[73]

It is perhaps with this all-important notion in mind that we might appreciate the controversy that found its way into the discourse on the *ṣaḥīḥ*. Tāj al-Dīn al-Subkī reports that in his magisterial work *al-Muḥarrar*, Rāfiʿī was rumoured to have determined opinions to be *ṣaḥīḥ* on the basis of what the majority of leading Shāfiʿites considered to fall into this category,[74] this majority being determined by an inductive survey of the opinions of individual jurists. Ramlī reiterated this perception of Rāfiʿī's endeavor and added that he did so because maintaining the authority of school doctrine is tantamount to transmitting it, which is to say that authority is a devolving tradition that is continually generated by a collectivity of individual transmissions. He immediately adds, however, that preponderance by number is particularly useful when two (or more) opinions are of the same weight.[75]

Be that as it may, *taṣḥīḥ* on the basis of number or majority appears to have become a standard, especially, if not exclusively, when all other considerations seemed equal. Ibn al-Ṣalāḥ maintained that if the jurist cannot determine which opinion is the *ṣaḥīḥ* because the evidence and reasoning in all competing opinions under investigation appear to him to be of equal strength, he must nonetheless decide which is the *ṣaḥīḥ* and preponderant opinion according to three considerations in descending order of importance: superior number or majority, knowledge, and piety.[76] Thus, an opinion would be considered *ṣaḥīḥ* if more jurists considered it to be such than they did another. The *taṣḥīḥ* of a highly learned jurist outweighs that of a less knowledgeable one, and that of a pious jurist is superior to another of a less pious one. In the same vein, an opinion held to be *ṣaḥīḥ* by a number of jurists would be considered superior to another held as such by a single jurist, however learned he may be. The same preference is given to a learned jurist over a pious one. Thus, *tashīh* operates both within and between these categories.

That number is important should in no way be surprising. The entire enterprise and concept of the *madhhab* is based on *group affiliation* to a set

[73] On this theme, see Hallaq, "Inductive Corroboration," 3–31.

[74] Subkī, *Ṭabaqāt*, V, 124. [75] Ramlī, *Nihāyat al-Muḥtāj*, I, 37.

[76] Ibn al-Ṣalāḥ, *Adab al-Muftī*, 126.

of doctrines, considered to have an authoritative core. Reducing plurality through number or any other means was certainly a desideratum. It is therefore perfectly reasonable to find the Mālikite Ḥaṭṭāb declaring, like many others, that the descending order of number, knowledge, and piety is a denominator common to all four schools.[77]

But this order and the principles that governed it did not guarantee the objective reality of the *ṣaḥīḥ*. Nor could the theory of preponderance ensure that a *ṣaḥīḥ* opinion would be accepted as such by either the contemporaries or successors of the jurist who undertook its *taṣḥīḥ*. The fact of the matter is that the *ṣaḥīḥ* and the entire activity of *taṣḥīḥ* were highly subjective. In the example concerning the extent to which a person is permitted to eat if he finds himself denied lawful food, we have seen that two groups of jurists differed as to which opinion outweighed the other, each group supporting a diametrically opposite position. In the other example of drinking wine as medicine or for the purpose of quenching thirst in circumstances of *ḍarūra*, the *ṣaḥīḥ* opinion was determined over and against three other widespread opinions. This is particularly significant for us, because "widespread" means an opinion held by a good, if not great, number of jurists. Even Rāfiᶜī, Nawawī, and Taqī al-Dīn al-Subkī at times abandon certain widespread opinions in favor of less popular ones.[78] In a number of cases, Nawawī himself declares as *ṣaḥīḥ* opinions those that Rāfiᶜī does not deem as such.[79] Similarly, in addressing the very same cases, he and Ibn ᶜAṣrūn (d. 585/1189) often consider the two conflicting opinions to be *ṣaḥīḥ*.[80] Ibn Qāḍī Shuhba remarks that Nawawī's *taṣḥīḥ* in his early works, especially in those cases where he goes against the *mashhūr*, are not to be considered reliable.[81]

The following case, about the lawfulness of eating game that was brought down out of the hunter's sight, whether by one of his arrows or by his hunting dog, nicely illustrates the relativity of the *ṣaḥīḥ*:

> Of the [existing] opinions, there are two that are more widespread (*ashhar*). The *aṣaḥḥ* of the two opinions according to the majority of the Iraqians and others is that [eating] the game is prohibited. According to Baghawī and Ghazālī, however, the *aṣaḥḥ* opinion is that it is permitted. This [latter] is the *ṣaḥīḥ* or the right opinion (*ṣawāb*).[82]

[77] Ḥaṭṭāb, *Mawāhib al-Jalīl*, VI, 91. See also Mirdāwī, *Taṣḥīḥ al-Furūᶜ*, I, 51; Nawawī, *al-Majmūᶜ*, I, 68.

[78] Subkī, *Ṭabaqāt*, III, 151.

[79] Ramlī, *Nihāyat al-Muḥtāj*, I, 45.

[80] Subkī, *Ṭabaqāt*, VI, 192.

[81] Ibn Qāḍī Shuhba, *Ṭabaqāt*, II, 199. The reference is particularly to his *Nukat al-Tanbīh* and *al-ᶜUmda fī Taṣḥīḥ al-Tanbīh*.

[82] Nawawī, *al-Majmūᶜ*, IX, 117.

Although we do not know the identity of the Iraqians or their number, it seems safe to assume that they were many more than two, and especially that certain "others" are said to have adopted this opinion as well. Nawawī, the author of this passage, sides with Baghawī and Ghazālī, a comparative minority. What is important here is that the subjectivity of *taṣḥīḥ* appears on two levels. Each side considered the opinion it adopted as the "more correct" of the opposing choices, while Nawawī engages in a further *taṣḥīḥ*, siding in this case with the minority opinion. His hermeneutic, the details of which he chooses not to reveal in this case, amounts in effect to an ordinary *taṣḥīḥ* for it involves the examination of evidence adduced by the two sides. But for these sides to claim to support the *aṣaḥḥ*, they had to conduct the same examination with regard to the evidence of the preexisting, hitherto uncorrected opinions.

The roots of this subjectivity are to be found in the very hermeneutic embodied in the theory of preponderance. The preceding example of hunting is a case in point. The *taṣḥīḥ* itself becomes, on the basis of the same theory, the object of yet another *taṣḥīḥ*. But the question that poses itself at this juncture is: What is the underlying cause of such hermeneutical variations and difference? Why would one jurist consider an *aṣaḥḥ* or a *ṣaḥīḥ* opinion to be less than what had been claimed for it by a another jurist? The answer, of course, is not easy to provide, for much more needs to be known about the socio-legal background of the jurist in question, and how this background relates to each of the cases he subjects to his interpretive methodology. The task is formidable. But that this background is of primary relevance is beyond a shadow of doubt. Ibn ʿĀbidīn's testimony in this regard is valuable. He explicitly argues that the jurists disagree with regard to *taṣḥīḥ* because of a variety of factors, among them the ever-changing social customs (*ʿādāt*) and conditions of people (*aḥwāl al-nās*). He was acutely aware of the law's responsiveness to social reality, a subject to which he dedicated a short treatise vindicating legal change as a response to corresponding social change.[83] *Taṣḥīḥ*, he also argues, differs (presumably between one jurist and another) due to the fact that what is considered suitable and agreeable to society changes according to the transformations that this society undergoes. Furthermore, economic and other transactions (*taʿāmul*) undergo change that needs to be accounted for in the law. Finally, Ibn ʿĀbidīn introduces a juristic category, namely, that *taṣḥīḥ* differs from one jurist to another because the evidence in favor of one opinion appears to be stronger than that which supports its

[83] See his *Nashr al-ʿUrf*, 114–47. See also chapter 6, section VIII, below.

counterpart (*mā qawiya wajhuhu*).[84] Whereas in all previous categories Ibn ᶜĀbidīn provides a perspicacious explanation of causality, he fails – or chooses not – to do so in the last instance, perhaps assuming the impossibility of an intellectual activity that is entirely independent of the social and other contexts in which it took place.

## V

In the course of the preceding discussion, we saw how *ṣaḥīḥ* and *aṣaḥḥ* opinions fared in connection with what we have termed widespread opinion, properly called the *mashhūr*. The most salient feature of the examples we have thus far presented is that the *mashhūr* was subjected to *taṣḥīḥ*, which means that the ultimate authority of doctrine did not derive from the procedure of *tashhīr* (declaring an opinion to be *mashhūr*) but rather from *taṣḥīḥ*.

This mode of authorization, however, was not a practice common to all four schools. It will be noticed that the examples we have adduced in this connection, and the jurists we have named, disclose an essentially Ḥanafite[85] and Shāfiᶜite approach to authorization through *taṣḥīḥ*, an approach which is, to some extent, different from that adopted by the Mālikites. The Ḥanbalites for their part seem to have adopted the Ḥanafite and Shāfiᶜite attitude toward this issue. Mirdāwī's work *Taṣḥīḥ al-Furūᶜ*, for instance, is a commentary on *Kitāb al-Furūᶜ* of Ibn Mufliḥ (d. 763/1361). A late author, Mirdāwī (d. 885/1480) had the benefit of hindsight, and was thus able to gauge the operative terminology prevalent in his school. It turns out that the highest form of authorization was the *taṣḥīḥ* which, he maintains, was known through having recourse to the doctrines of the leading jurists of the school, jurists whose task it was to establish which opinion was preponderant and *ṣaḥīḥ* and which not (note the interchangeability of the two terms). The *raison d'être* of Mirdāwī's own work, as the title indicates, is precisely the determination of the *ṣaḥīḥ* opinions which Ibn Mufliḥ did not, or could not, undertake. The aim of the book, therefore, and its central concern, was to accomplish the *taṣḥīḥ* of the *corpus juris* of the Ḥanbalite *madhhab* (*taḥrīr al-madhhab wa-taṣḥīḥihi*),[86] an achievement that would become the product of a

[84] Ibn ᶜĀbidīn, *Nashr al-ᶜUrf*, 130; Ibn ᶜĀbidīn, *Sharḥ al-Manẓūma*, 40.

[85] For further evidence of Ḥanafite *taṣḥīḥ*, see n. 101, below. See also the following: Ramlī, *al-Fatāwā al-Khayriyya*, I, 2–3; Samarqandī, *Tuḥfat al-Fuqahā'*, I, 29, 35, 67, 76, 90, 101, 102, 104, and passim; Kāsānī, *Badā'iᶜ al-Ṣanā'iᶜ*, I, 27, 31, 151, 151, 159; Baghdādī, *Majmaᶜ al-Ḍamānāt*, 3; Ibn ᶜĀbidīn, *Ḥāshiya*, I, 3–4; Ibn ᶜĀbidīn, *Sharḥ al-Manẓūma*, 38–40; Ibn ᶜĀbidīn, *Nashr al-ᶜUrf*, 130 and passim.

[86] Mirdāwī, *Taṣḥīḥ al-Furūᶜ*, I, 25, 50.

joint effort on the part of Ibn Mufliḥ and Mirdāwī. It is worth noting at this point that *taṣḥīḥ* was a desideratum of several later works emerging from the four schools, so Mirdāwī's work is in no way an exception to the rule.[87] We have already mentioned that the prestige and authority of Rāfiʿī and Nawawī in the Shāfiʿite school, of Ibn Qudāma in the Ḥanbalite school, and of Marghīnānī in the Ḥanafite school rest in good measure upon this achievement.

We have said that the highest form of authorization for the Mālikites was the *mashhūr*, although they resorted to *taṣḥīḥ* rather frequently. Indeed, one might say that the procedure, in comparison with the other three schools, was exactly reversed: the Shāfiʿite, Ḥanafite, and Ḥanbalite *taṣḥīḥ* of the *mashhūr* was matched by the Mālikite *tashhīr* of the *ṣaḥīḥ* or *aṣaḥḥ*. This explains a highly recurrent and authoritative statement made by many authors in the four schools, but which in Mālikism received a slightly different stress. The Ḥanafites, Ḥanbalites, and Shāfiʿites demanded that the jurisconsult and *qāḍī* not diverge from the *ṣaḥīḥ* opinions of the school, or as they might say, *al-qawl al-muṣaḥḥaḥ* (the corrected opinion). It is in this spirit that the Ḥanafite Ḥaṣkafī was commended for his ingenuity, despite the fact that he had never in his entire career issued a *fatwā* or passed a verdict that was not based on a *muṣaḥḥaḥ* opinion.[88] Compare this requirement with its Mālikite counterpart. Instead of prescribing knowledge of the *muṣaḥḥaḥ* opinion, they embraced the *mashhūr* which was to constitute the basis of *fatwā* and court decisions.[89] It was in this spirit too that Māzarī, a distinguished Mālikite *mujtahid*, was extolled for never having abandoned the *mashhūr* in his *fatwā*s despite attaining such epistemic preeminence.[90]

So what exactly is the *mashhūr*? Before addressing this question, it is important to point out that, in spite of its fundamental importance, the operative terminology of substantive law, strictly speaking, never found its way into the technical dictionaries which claimed to be able to furnish definitions for the entire range of the Muslim sciences, religious as well as rational.[91] We know that thousands of technical words were afforded definitions, explications, and clarifications, but neither the *mashhūr* nor the *ṣaḥīḥ*, nor for that matter any of the other operative terms we shall

[87] See, for instance, the Ḥanbalite Taqī al-Dīn Muḥammad al-Futūḥī Ibn al-Najjār, *Muntahā al-Irādāt*, 2 vols. (Cairo: Maktabat Dār al-ʿUrūba, 1961–62), I, 6.

[88] Ibn ʿĀbidīn, *Ḥāshiya*, I, 16.

[89] Ibn Farḥūn, *Tabṣirat al-Ḥukkām*, I, 46, 51; Ḥaṭṭāb, *Mawāhib al-Jalīl*, I, 32; VI, 91; ʿAlamī, *Nawāzil*, III, 6.

[90] Ibn Farḥūn, *Tabṣirat al-Ḥukkām*, I, 51; Ḥaṭṭāb, *Mawāhib al-Jalīl*, I, 32.

[91] Such as Tahānawī's *Kashshāf*, Aḥmadnagarī's *Jāmiʿ al-ʿUlūm*, and Jurjānī's *Taʿrīfāt*.

discuss, made an appearance there. This leaves us with a body of legal literature which, in employing this terminology, simply assumes that readers partake of, and fully understand, the inner layers of the tradition within which they were written. Our challenge then is to extract from various sources, and from scattered statements and legal cases, what each term meant and how it was variably used.

In the case of the Shāfiᶜites and Ḥanbalites,[92] the term *mashhūr* generally stood for an opinion that had gained wide circulation among the jurists. Its legitimacy, then, stemmed from the fact that many jurists deemed it correct, this being the epistemic foundation of historical narrative, including the transmission of *ḥadīth*. Yet, its wide acceptance did not guarantee its superiority or even its validity. Once subjected to *taṣḥīḥ*, a *mashhūr* could turn out to be a weak opinion, to be excluded, as we have seen in Nawawī, from the corpus of authoritative doctrine. But which corpus? There is no doubt that the *mashhūr* was characterized by the same uncertainty and subjectivity as that from which *taṣḥīḥ* suffered. One instance of this subjectivity can be seen in the fact that if the *mashhūr*'s *taṣḥīḥ* were rejected, then its authoritative status would remain intact. Ibn Qāḍī Shuhba in fact rejected Nawawī's *taṣḥīḥ* of the *mashhūr* which the latter had conducted in his early works.[93] But even if the *taṣḥīḥ* in a particular case or cases was accepted, it did not automatically mean that the *mashhūr* would be abandoned. According to the royal decrees of judicial appointment preserved in Qalqashandī, the Shāfiᶜite *qāḍī* was to adjudicate according to the preponderant opinion (*rājiḥ*), leaving aside that which was non-preponderant (*marjūḥ*). Qalqashandī however admits that in practice the *marjūḥ* remained valid and authoritative if it stemmed from the founding imam's doctrine or if it had been adopted by the majority of Shāfiᶜite jurists.[94] Later on, Nawawī was to reserve the term *mashhūr* for those of Shāfiᶜī's opinions that were considered stronger than certain others that he was said to have held.[95] Similarly, the Ḥanbalite Zarkashī seems to have attempted to reserve the term for Ibn Ḥanbal's opinions, but he was not entirely successful.[96] But the weight of the traditional meaning of *mashhūr* as simply a widespread opinion – without it necessarily belonging to Shāfiᶜī – did not make for greater

[92] For the Ḥanbalite use of the *mashhūr* and *tashhīr*, see Ibn al-Najjār, *Muntahā al-Irādāt*, I, 6; Mirdāwī, *Taṣḥīḥ al-Furūᶜ*, I, 23.

[93] Ibn Qāḍī Shuhba, *Ṭabaqāt*, II, 199.

[94] Aḥmad b. ᶜAlī al-Qalqashandī, *Ṣubḥ al-Aᶜshā fī Ṣināᶜat al-Inshā*, 14 vols. (Beirut: Dār al-Kutub al-ᶜIlmiyya, 1987), XI, 196.

[95] Ramlī, *Nihāyat al-Muḥtāj*, I, 42.

[96] Zarkashī, *Sharḥ*, I, 274, 326, 318, 612, 614, 618, and passim. However, in vol. I, 299, 317, 327, and passim, he used so to designate other jurists' opinions.

consistency in Nawawī's discourse. In the example cited above in which Nawawī pronounced on the legality of drinking wine as medicine or for the purpose of quenching thirst, we saw that he introduced four *wajh* opinions, none of which, by definition, were held by Shāfiᶜī, although all were said to have been of the *mashhūr* type.[97] In fact, even in the introduction to his work, he makes the remark that he will not expound the evidence or lines of legal reasoning of weak opinions, even though they may be of the *mashhūr* type.[98] Here, the reference is clearly to the general body of opinion, not to that of Shāfiᶜī's alone. To say that Nawawī contradicted himself on what precisely constitutes the *mashhūr* is to state the obvious. Nevertheless, the definition of the *mashhūr* as an opinion which acquired authority due to having gained wide circulation among the jurists remained the dominant conception among the Shāfiᶜites and Ḥanbalites.[99]

The Ḥanafites, on the other hand, do not seem to have used the term with any frequency, at least not in the technical sense of referring to a particular type of authoritative opinion. In Ḥaṣkafī's list of operative terms conventionally used by the Ḥanafites, the term makes no appearance.[100] A survey of some of the most important Ḥanafite works confirms this absence, both from the lists of operative terms presented by the authors (when they do so) in the opening pages of their works as well as from their overall contents.[101]

In the case of the Mālikite *mashhūr,* we are fortunate to have Ibn Farḥūn's revealing discussion. In his *Tabṣira*, he maintains that ultimate authority is embodied in Mālik's doctrine from which neither the jurisconsult nor the *qāḍī* may swerve. Some jurists, he remarks, argued that the final authority of Mālikite doctrine resides in Ibn al-Qāsim's work, especially if Mālik's authoritative doctrine cannot be determined. This hierarchy of doctrine, it is claimed, constituted the foundations of

97 For other examples, see Nawawī, *al-Majmūᶜ*, IX, 45, 192, 199, and passim; Subkī, *Ṭabaqāt*, III, 151.

98 Nawawī, *al-Majmūᶜ*, I, 5.

99 It is interesting that Zarkashī, for instance, often couples the term *mashhūr* with *maᶜrūf*, well known (e.g. *al-maᶜrūf al-mashhūr*, or the reverse order). See his *Sharḥ*, II, 534, 547, 589; VII, 398.

100 Ḥaṣkafī, *al-Durr al-Mukhtār*, I, 72–75.

101 See Marghīnānī, *Hidāya*; Qāḍikhān, *Fatāwā*; *al-Fatāwā al-Hindiyya*; Muḥammad b. Shihāb Ibn Bazzāz al-Kurdarī, *al-Fatāwā al-Bazzāziyya al-Musammātu bil-Jāmiᶜ al-Wajīz*, printed on the margins of *al-Fatāwā al-Hindiyya*, vols. IV–VI (repr.; Beirut: Dār Iḥyā' al-Turāth al-ᶜArabī, 1980); Ḥalabī, *Multaqā al-Abḥur*; Ibn ᶜĀbidīn, *Ḥāshiya*; Kamāl al-Dīn Ibn al-Humām, *Sharḥ Fatḥ al-Qadīr*, 10 vols. (repr.; Beirut: Dār al-Fikr, 1990). It is to be noted that the principal terms used in these works for the authorization of legal opinions are the *ṣaḥīḥ* and *aṣaḥḥ*.

juridical practice among Andalusian and Moroccan jurists.[102] With this background in mind, Ibn Farḥūn continues his discussion:

> Our foregoing discussion leads us to the conclusion that if Ibn al-Qāsim's opinions are to be found in the *Mudawwana*, then they are the *mashhūr* opinions of the school. In the technical usage of Moroccan jurists (*al-Maghāriba*), the *mashhūr* are the opinions found in the *Mudawwana*. But the Iraqians [of the Mālikite school] often disagree with the Moroccans as to which opinions are *mashhūr*, for they declare certain opinions *mashhūr* [when the Moroccans do not]. The practice of the more recent jurists (*muta'akhkhirūn*) is to consider *mashhūr* that which is deemed thus by the Egyptian and Moroccan jurists. Ibn Rāshid reported that he had heard that some scholars spurned the term *mashhūr* because the jurists may consider certain opinions as *mashhūr* though they have weak foundations (*laysa la-hu aṣl*). The fact is that reliable opinions are only those which are supported by [strong] evidence. Ibn Bashīr maintained that "there is disagreement about the *mashhūr*, consisting of two positions. The first is that the *mashhūr* is the opinion which is supported by strong evidence; the second is that it is the opinion held by many jurists. The correct position (*al-ṣaḥīḥ*) is the first. But this position is marred by the fact that the jurists at times declare one opinion to be *mashhūr* and the [competing] opinion *ṣaḥīḥ*." But nothing should mar this position because the *mashhūr* is the doctrine of the *Mudawwana*. There may be a sound tradition supporting the other opinion, and probably transmitted by Mālik, but which he did not use in support of that opinion due to a reason which prevented him from doing so, a reason not obvious to the [later] jurist. When this jurist finds a sound tradition to support the said opinion, he declares the opinion *ṣaḥīḥ*, a practice of frequent occurrence in the commentaries of Ibn al-ᶜArabī and Ibn ᶜAbd al-Salām on Ibn al-Ḥājib . . . Ibn Rāshid said that "the second position – that the *mashhūr* is that which is held by many – is also marred by the fact that in certain legal cases, we find the *mashhūr* to be those opinions which carry the legal norm of prohibition, whereas the majority [of jurists] hold those opinions which carry the legal norm of permissibility." [Here, Ibn Rāshid cites a custody case to prove his point.] However, Ibn Khuwayz Mindād maintained that the legal doctrines of the school show that the *mashhūr* is that which is supported by strong evidence and that Mālik, in questions subject to disagreement, sided with the opinions supported by strong evidence, not those held by many jurists.[103]

This passage contains both doctrinal and historical information. First, it speaks of fundamental uncertainty in the Mālikite school as to what

[102] Ibn Farḥūn, *Tabṣirat al-Ḥukkām*, I, 49.

[103] Ibid., I, 50. Ibn Khuwayz Mindād's assertion is not borne out by Mālik's *Muwaṭṭa'*, as we have seen in chapter 2, section II, above.

exactly the *mashhūr* was. Is its preponderance based on strength of evidence or on sheer weight of numbers? Ibn Farḥūn defended the former meaning of the *mashhūr*, but he in no way resolved the dispute. In fact, as far as I know, there was never to be a final resolution of this disagreement. Second, even if we disregard the issue of the *mashhūr*'s evidential and epistemic foundations, there was another major disagreement as to which opinion is *mashhūr* and which not. Ibn Farḥūn speaks of a Mālikite split on the matter, with the Iraqians standing on one side and the Moroccans on the other. Furthermore, this split may have widened in later centuries to include the Egyptians who joined the fray on the side of the Moroccans.

If *taṣḥīḥ*, whose foundations were relatively well defined and generally agreed upon, was nonetheless dealt with in a subjective fashion, then small wonder that the *mashhūr* was chronically prone to such treatment. Ibn Farḥūn himself admits this much, not only in the passage we have translated above, but also in his description of his colleagues' practices. He also quotes Ibn Rāshid who speaks of Ibn al-Ḥājib's confused use of the *mashhūr* and the *ashhar* (more widespread). At times, Ibn al-Ḥājib considered *ashhar* what others deemed *mashhūr*, a practice that was also associated with the Egyptian and Moroccan jurists, including Ibn al-ᶜArabī. In a rather clumsy justification of this practice, Ibn Rāshid maintained that Ibn al-Ḥājib did so "perhaps because the word *ashhar* is more elegant and shorter"![104] The fact that Ibn Rāshid had to resort to such an unconvincing explanation speaks of the uncertainty that engulfed the technical connotation of the *mashhūr*.

The severity of the problem led to attempts at finding a remedy, although these were largely unsuccessful. This is evidenced in the Mālikite creation of a hierarchy of the *mashhūr* doctrine based on juristic authority within the school. In this respect, Ḥaṭṭāb reflected the standard doctrine of the Mālikite school when he stated that, in those cases on which the *mashhūr* opinion cannot be determined through an examination of textual evidence and legal reasoning, recourse should be had to the later masters of the school. Thus, the *tashhīrāt* of Ibn Rushd take precedence over those of Ibn Buzayza, while the *tashhīrāt* of Ibn Rushd, Māzarī, and ᶜAbd al-Wahhāb are of equal weight.[105]

But how were these *mujtahid*s to determine which opinion was *mashhūr* and which not? Again, Mālik's doctrine emerges as the ultimate

[104] Ibn Farḥūn, *Tabṣirat al-Ḥukkām*, I, 51: "*fa-yuḥtamal an yakūn qaṣada hādhihi al-ᶜibāra li-rashāqatihā wa-qillati ḥurūfihā.*"

[105] Ḥaṭṭāb, *Mawāhib al-Jalīl*, I, 36.

frame of reference. Given that Mālik was known to have often held more than one opinion on a single case, the question becomes: Which opinion should be considered the *mashhūr*? The answer is fairly simple: it is the opinion that he held last, because those opinions that he held earlier in his life were deemed abrogated by later ones.[106] But what if the chronology of opinions cannot be established, which is frequently the case? In such cases, the *mujtahid*, and only the *mujtahid*, should determine which opinion is supported by the best evidence and most persuasive legal reasoning, and this he must do in light of his intimate knowledge of Mālik's methodology and principles. Whatever emerges as the best of all opinions must then be presumed to have been Mālik's last opinion, the *mashhūr*.[107] More often than not, however, it is the *muqallid* who needs to determine the status of the opinions. But since he lacks knowledge of the founder's methodology and principles, he must rely on Ibn al-Qāsim's recension of Mālik's doctrine, and this he does to the best of his knowledge of what Mālik's last doctrine is.[108]

## VI

But this is not all. Leaving the determination of the *mashhūr* to the *muqallid* increases subjectivity and creates further multiplicity of presumed authoritative opinions. Thus, in order to reduce plurality and increase the chances of determining authoritative opinions, the four schools resorted to other means, each of which was labeled with what we have called an operative term. Leaving aside any consideration of their order of importance, these terms were as follows: *rājiḥ*, *ẓāhir*, *awjah*, *ashbah*, *ṣawāb*, *madhhab*, *maftī bi-hi*, *maᶜmūl bi-hi*, *mukhtār*. It is with these concepts – which together with the *ṣaḥīḥ*, the *mashhūr*, and their derivatives

[106] That the last opinion of the imam abrogates an earlier one is a doctrine held by all the schools, although it figured more prominently in the Shāfiᶜite and Mālikite schools. But it too had its opponents, especially among the Mālikites. Abū ᶜAbd Allāh al-Tilimsānī argued that if a *mujtahid* arrives at two opinions for the same case, then they must be based on probability, and if so, they are equally subject to falsification. Therefore, the second opinion may turn out to be mistaken, just as the first opinion was determined to be so earlier. Tilimsānī reports that Ibn Abī Jamra also argued that the earlier opinion should not be considered invalid without it being subjected to the *mujtahid*'s scrutiny. See Tinbaktī, *Nayl al-Ibtihāj*, 441–43.

[107] Wansharīsī, *al-Miᶜyār al-Mughrib*, X, 44, on the authority of Abū Muḥammad ᶜAbd Allāh Ibn Satārī. See also the *fatwā* of Abū ᶜAbd Allāh al-Tilimsānī in Tinbaktī, *Nayl al-Ibtihāj*, 443.

[108] Wansharīsī, *al-Miᶜyār al-Mughrib*, X, 45–46, on the authority of Ibn Satārī and his teacher Abū al-Ḥasan al-Abyārī. See also Tilimsānī's *fatwā* in Tinbaktī, *Nayl al-Ibtihāj*, 443.

constituted the backbone of the operative discourse of substantive law – that we shall concern ourselves in the remainder of this chapter.

## *Rājiḥ*

We have seen that *tarjīḥ* is the most general of all concepts, representing as it does the effort through which one of two or more opinions is made preponderant (*rājiḥ*). As such, *tarjīḥ* was equated with *taṣḥīḥ* and *tashhīr*, and was used for that matter in connection with all other categories of operative terminology. This explains therefore Ḥaṭṭāb's remark that *tarjīḥ* is determined by the term (*lafẓ*) of *tashhīr*, *madhhab*, *ẓāhir*, *maftī bi-hi*, or *maᶜmūl bi-hi*.[109]

## *Ẓāhir*

In technical legal usage, the term indicates the meaning that is comprehended by the mind immediately upon hearing a particular term or expression that potentially has two or more meanings. Derived from a root suggesting the notion of strength, *ẓāhir* is applied to that meaning which is the predominant one among the many connotations of a word, i.e., the meaning that leaps out ahead of the rest. This term was usually cast in opposition to *naṣṣ*, which refers to the univocal language of the Quran and the Sunna.[110]

Insofar as legal preponderance was concerned, *ẓāhir* also meant the stronger or more prominent of the two (or more) opinions, or simply the strong opinion in contradistinction to a weak one. Nawawī and Ramlī reserved this term for weighing Shāfiᶜī's opinions. When faced with two conflicting opinions attributed to the latter – whether they were both the product of his New doctrine or one Old and the other New – they used the term to designate the preponderant opinion.[111] This of course was by no means always the case in the Shāfiᶜite school prior to Nawawī, although it is possible that some consistency in the use of the term was

[109] Ḥaṭṭāb, *Mawāhib al-Jalīl*, I, 36.

[110] Abū al-Walīd b. Khalaf al-Bājī, *Kitāb al-Ḥudūd fī al-Uṣūl*, ed. Nazīh Ḥammād (Beirut: Mu'assasat al-Zuᶜbī lil-Ṭibāᶜa wal-Nashr, 1973), 43, 48; ᶜAbd al-Nabī b. ᶜAbd al-Rasūl al-Aḥmadnagarı, *Jamiᶜ al-ᶜUlum fı Iṣṭilaḥat al-Funun al-Mulaqqab bi-Dustur al-ᶜUlamā'*, 4 vols. (repr.; Beirut: Mu'assasat al-Aᶜlamī lil-Maṭbūᶜāt, 1975), II, 286; Ibn ᶜĀbidīn, *Nashr al-ᶜUrf*, 128; Imām al-Ḥaramayn Pseudo-Juwaynī, *al-Kāfiya fī al-Jadal*, ed. Fawqiyya Maḥmūd (Cairo: Maṭbaᶜat ᶜĪsā Bābī al-Ḥalabī, 1979), 49; al-Sayyid Sharīf ᶜAlī b. Muḥammad al-Jurjānī, *al-Taᶜrīfāt* (Cairo: Maṭbaᶜat Muṣṭafā Bābī al-Ḥalabī, 1938), 124.

[111] Ramlī, *Nihāyat al-Muḥtāj*, I, 42.

encouraged due to Nawawī's tremendous influence. An earlier Shāfiᶜite, Shāshī (d. 508/1114), used the term for both Shāfiᶜī's opinions and those of the *aṣḥāb al-wujūh*, foremost of whom was Ibn Surayj.[112] Regarding one case especially, he reports the existence of two *wajh* opinions, one by Ibn Surayj and the other anonymous. He leans toward the latter in this instance, declaring it the *ẓāhir* of the Shāfiᶜite *madhhab*, namely, the strongest, soundest, or most authoritative doctrine of the school.[113] In another case, he also reports two *wajh* opinions, one *ẓāhir al-naṣṣ* and the other *aẓhar*.[114] Although it is possible that Shāshī is using the term in its usual sense, namely, that the opinion is based on clear Sunnaic or Quranic language, it is more likely that he is referring to Shāfiᶜī's *naṣṣ* which is the latter's authoritative opinion on a certain matter. Despite this fact, he still finds the second opinion the weightier.

The Mālikites and Ḥanbalites do not seem to have used this term as frequently as the Shāfiᶜites and Ḥanafites. The Ḥanbalite Mirdāwī, for instance, does not enumerate it among the *tarjīḥ* terms of his school, although he and other Ḥanbalite jurists did occasionally use it.[115] The same appears to have been the situation in the Mālikite school.[116] The lesser importance of this term in these two schools may be attributed to the fact that it was not linked to the teachings of any of the founding masters, as was the case with the Shāfiᶜites and the Ḥanafites. The latter two schools by contrast made frequent use of the term, linking it, as we have seen, to the most authoritative category of Ḥanafite doctrine, the *ẓāhir al-riwāya*.[117] However, the use of this term was not confined to this category of doctrine, especially when used in the elative. When an opinion was established as preponderant, it was described as being the *aẓhar* (stronger) of the two.[118]

## <u>Awjah</u>, <u>ashbah</u>, AND <u>ṣawāb</u>

These terms were used only on occasion, and at great intervals. They lacked the relative technical rigor of the terms *ṣaḥīḥ* and *mashhūr*, and even that of *ẓāhir* and *aẓhar*. They were the later equivalent of the early

[112] Shāshī, *Ḥulyat al-ᶜUlamā'*, I, 75, 89, 97–98, 99, 168, 181, 187, 190, 191; VIII, 282.
[113] Ibid., VIII, 282: "*wa-hwa al-ẓāhir min madhhab al-Shāfiᶜī.*" For other cases declared as *ẓāhir al-madhhab*, see ibid., I, 63, 140, 168, 206, 255.
[114] Ibid., VIII, 127. [115] Mirdāwī, *Taṣḥīḥ al-Furūᶜ*, I, 23, 27, and passim.
[116] Ḥaṭṭāb, *Mawāhib al-Jalīl*, I, 36.
[117] See chapter 2, section II, above. For its uses in positive law, see, e.g., Abū al-Layth al-Samarqandī, *Fatāwā al-Nawāzil* (Hyderabad: Maṭbaᶜat Shams al-Islām, 1355/1936), 3, 11, 63, 84, and passim.
[118] Samarqandī, *Fatāwā*, 78.

non-technical terminology, such as *ajwad* (better), used at times by the Ḥanafite Ṭaḥāwī.[119] As a fairly non-technical term, *awjah* simply meant the stronger of two (or more) opinions, precisely as one might refer to such an opinion as the *aṣaḥḥ*, the *ashhar*, or the *aẓhar*. But there was a difference. While the *ashhar* was likely to be distinguished, within the same school, from the *aṣaḥḥ*, the use of *awjah* was in this respect ambiguous, for it does not seem to have implied, as did the others, a certain pedigree of opinion. The same might be said of the *ashbah*, a fairly non-technical term indicating something like "more or most likely," as in the pronouncement that such and such is the more likely of the two opinions. Of this trilogy, the more technical term is *ṣawāb*, along with its elative form *aqrab ilā al-ṣawāb*.[120] Though more technical, it pales into insignificance when compared with its counterparts, *ṣaḥīḥ*, *mashhūr*, etc. Ibn Taymiyya uses it in the sense of soundest or most correct, as when he says that the soundest *qiyās* in the school is such and such.[121] The Ḥanafite Kāsānī uses it in a more relative sense, as in his assessment of an opinion being "more likely to be sound."[122]

## *Madhhab*

On a number of occasions in this study, we have noted that the term *madhhab* acquired different meanings throughout Islamic history. Its earliest use was merely to signify the opinion or opinions of a jurist, such as in the pronouncement that the *madhhab* of so-and-so in a *particular* case is such-and-such.[123] Later on, the term acquired a more technical sense. During and after the formation of the schools, it was used to refer to the *totality* of the *corpus juris* belonging to a leading *mujtahid*, whether or not he was the founder of a school. In this formative period, the term also meant the doctrine adopted by a founder and by those of his followers, this doctrine being considered cumulative and accretive. Concomitant with this, if not somewhat earlier, appeared the notion of *madhhab* as a corporate entity in the sense of an integral school to which individual jurists considered themselves to belong. This was the personal meaning of the *madhhab*, in contrast to its purely doctrinal meaning which was expressed as loyalty to a general body of doctrine.

There was at least one other important sense of the term which deserves our attention here, namely, the individual opinion, accepted as the most

[119] Ṭaḥāwī, *Mukhtaṣar*, 394, 440, and passim. [120] Kāsānī, *Badā'iᶜ al-Ṣanā'iᶜ*, I, 31.
[121] Baᶜlī, *al-Ikhtiyārāt al-Fiqhiyya*, 150.
[122] Kāsānī, *Badā'iᶜ al-Ṣanā'iᶜ*, I, 31: "*wa-hādhā aqrab ilā al-ṣawāb*."
[123] For example, see Shāfiᶜī, *Umm*, II, 102, 113, 136, 163, and passim.

authoritative in the collective doctrinal corpus of the school. In order to distinguish it from the other meanings of the word *madhhab*, we shall assign to it the compound expression *madhhab*-opinion.

Given the paucity of sources from the early period, it is difficult to establish the origins of this latter usage. It is certain, however, that it had become well established by the middle of the fifth/eleventh century. The period of its evolution must therefore be located some time during the preceding century or so, for evidently it could not have emerged prior to the middle of the fourth/tenth century, before the schools as doctrinal entities reached maturity.

In this doctrinal sense, the term *madhhab* meant the opinion adopted as the most authoritative in the school. Unlike the *ṣaḥīḥ* and the *mashhūr*, there were no particular or fixed criteria for determining what the *madhhab*-opinion was, since it might be based on general acceptance on the grounds of *taṣḥīḥ*, *tashhīr*, or some other basis. Yet, it was possible that the *madhhab*-opinion could be different, say, from a *ṣaḥīḥ* opinion.[124] However, the most fundamental feature of the *madhhab*-opinion remained its general acceptance as the most authoritative in the school, including its widespread practice and application in courts and *fatwā*s. This type of opinion is to be distinguished from the *mashhūr*, in that the latter is deemed widespread among a majority, but not the totality, of jurists belonging to a school. This explains why the *madhhab*-opinion could not be, as a rule, outweighed by another competing opinion.

A distinctive feature of the *madhhab*-opinion was its status as the normative opinion in legal application and practice. It is precisely here that an organic connection between *fatwā* and *madhhab*-opinion was forged – the *fatwā* being a reflection of litigation and the legal concerns of mundane social life.[125] Ḥaṭṭāb's commentary on the matter eloquently speaks of this connection: the term "*al-madhhab*," he remarked, was used by the more recent jurists (*muta'akhkhirūn*) of all the schools to refer to the opinion issued in *fatwā*s. He also remarked, conversely, that any *fatwā* issued on the basis of something other than the *madhhab*-opinion ought not to be taken into account (*lā yakūn la-hā iʿtibār*).[126] In these pronouncements by Ḥaṭṭāb, two important matters must be noted: First, that the connection between *fatwā* practice and the term *madhhab* (-opinion) is one that appeared among the *muta'akhkhirūn*, not among the *mutaqaddimūn*, i.e. the early jurists who flourished between the

124 Mirdāwī, *Taṣḥīḥ al-Furūʿ*, I, 50–51.
125 This has been demonstrated in Hallaq, "From *Fatwās* to *Furūʿ*," 31–38.
126 Ḥaṭṭāb, *Mawāhib al-Jalīl*, I, 24; VI, 91.

second/eighth and fourth/tenth centuries, a period in which the schools were formed;[127] second, that the *fatwā* practice defines the general body of *madhhab*-opinion in any given school.

But how did the jurist know which opinion constituted the standard basis of *fatwā*s or the *madhhab*-opinion? This became one of the most urgent questions, constituting a serious challenge to later jurists for whom the determination of the most authoritative school doctrine was essential. Nawawī provides an answer:

> You ought to know that law books of the school contain significant disagreements among the associates, so much so that the reader cannot be confident that a certain author's opinion expresses the *madhhab*-opinion until he, the reader, deciphers the majority of the school's well-known lawbooks . . . This is why [in my book] I do not exclude the mention of any of Shāfiʿī's opinions, of the *wajh* opinions, or other opinions even if they happen to be weak or insignificant . . . In addition, I also mention that which is preponderant, and show the weakness of that which is weak . . . and stress the error of him who held it, even though he may have been a distinguished jurist (*min al-akābir*) . . . I also take special care in perusing the law books of the early and more recent associates down to my own time, including the comprehensive works (*mabsūṭāt*), the abridgements (*mukhtaṣarāt*), and the recensions of the school founder's doctrine, Shāfiʿī . . . I have also read the *fatwā*s of the associates and their various writings on legal theory, biographies, *ḥadīth* annotation, as well as other works . . . You should not be alarmed when at times I mention many jurists who held an opinion different from that of the majority or from the *mashhūr*, etc., for if I omit the names of those constituting the majority it is because I do not wish to prolong my discussion since they are too many to enumerate.[128]

Nawawī did not live long enough to conclude his ambitious project, having completed only about a third of it by the time of his death. Yet for him to know what was the *madhhab*-opinion in each case, he felt compelled to investigate the great majority of what he saw as the most important early and later works. Hidden between the lines of this passage is the fundamental assumption that in order to identify the basis of *fatwā* practice one must know what the generally accepted doctrine was. In the final chapter, we shall see that jurists, in writing their works, continuously

[127] This periodization, which is determined by our independent investigation of the *madhhab* evolution and the construction of authority, agrees with the traditional distinction between the "early" and "later" jurists. See Ḥājjī Khalīfa, *Kashf al-Ẓunūn*, II, 1282.

[128] Nawawī, *al-Majmūʿ*, I, 4–5.

revised legal doctrine, weeding out opinions that had fallen out of circulation, and including those newer ones that had become relevant to legal practice. Only an intimate knowledge of the contents of the legal works written throughout the centuries could have revealed which opinions remained in circulation – i.e., in practice – and which had become obsolete. It is precisely this knowledge that became a desideratum, and this is why the subject of *khilāf* was so important. The study of *khilāf* was the means by which the jurist came to know what the *madhhab*-opinions were. Law students, for instance, are often reported to have studied law, *madhhaban wa-khilāfan*, under a particular teacher. The Mālikite Ibn ᶜAbd al-Barr emphatically states that for one to be called a jurist (*faqīh*), he must be adept at the science of *khilāf*, for this was par excellence the means by which the jurist could determine which opinions represented the authoritative doctrines of the *madhhab*.[129]

Although the determination of the *madhhab*-opinion was more an inductive survey than a hermeneutical–epistemological engagement, it nonetheless entailed some difficulties, not unlike those the jurists faced in deciding what the *ṣaḥīḥ* and the *mashhūr* opinions were. In his notable effort, Nawawī himself did rather well on this score, which explains his prestige and authority in the Shāfiᶜite school. Nonetheless, he and Rāfiᶜī are said to have erred in about fifty cases, claiming them to be *madhhab*-opinions when they were thought by many not to be so.[130] The following case from the *Fatāwā* of Taqī al-Dīn al-Subkī further illustrates the uncertainty involved:

> Two men die, one owing a debt to the other. Each leaves minor children behind. The guardian of the minors whose father was the lender establishes against the debtor's children the outstanding debt in a court of law. Should the execution of the judgment [in favor of the first party] be suspended until the defendants [i.e., the debtor's children] reach majority, or should the guardian take the oath [and have the debt be paid back]? . . . The *madhhab*-opinion is the latter. However, he who investigates the matter might think that the *madhhab*-opinion is that the judgment should await implementation [until the children reach majority], but this may lead to the loss of their rights. By the time the lender's children attain majority, the money may well have vanished at the hands of the debtor's heirs.[131]

Note here the ambiguity as to which of the two is the *madhhab*-opinion. Subkī identifies immediate execution of the judgment as the *madhhab*-opinion, while at the same time he also admits that anyone who investigates

[129] Ibn ᶜAbd al-Barr, *Jāmiᶜ Bayān al-ᶜIlm*, II, 43 f.
[130] Ramlī, *Nihāyat al-Muḥtāj*, I, 38. [131] Subkī, *Fatāwā*, I, 324.

the matter will find that the opposing opinion has the same status. Subkī does not even go so far as to claim that the one who espouses the latter is mistaken.

Be that as it may, the term *madhhab*, when referring to an individual opinion, was used to determine what the law on a particular case was. And the criterion for acquiring this status was general acceptance and the fact of its being standard practice in the school. But before proceeding to discuss the three remaining terms, which are closely related to the *madhhab*-opinion, we would do well to look at some of the contextual uses of this term:

1. *ʿAlā al-ṣaḥīḥ min al-madhhab*, that which is deemed *ṣaḥīḥ* according to the *madhhab* – an expression that indicates what the school as a body of legal doctrine and an aggregation of individual members generally accepts as the *ṣaḥīḥ*. Note here that the category of the *ṣaḥīḥ* is legitimized in a double-pronged manner: one is the hermeneutical preponderance of textual evidence and of lines of reasoning, the other the overwhelming support of those belonging to the school, itself based on a juristic preponderance. The expression may appear less frequently with the variation *ʿalā al-madhhab al-ṣaḥīḥ*.[132]
2. *Iqtiḍāʾ al-madhhab*, with the more frequent variant *yaqtaḍīhi al-madhhab*, that which the *madhhab* dictates. The following example illustrates the use of this expression: In a case pertaining to the observance of ritual purity, Ibn al-Ṣabbāgh held that the *madhhab* dictates that this observance be considered valid, but legal reasoning (*taʿlīl*) dictates that it be deemed invalid. Obviously, *madhhab*-opinion here was not based on systematic *qiyās* but rather on some other consideration which may have been *istiḥsān* or *istiṣlāḥ*.[133]
3. *Qiyās al-madhhab*, the authoritative, standard *qiyās* with regard to a particular case.[134] Consider the following example, from a Ḥanbalite source: "Is the minor's bequest valid? There are two *wajh* opinions. Al-Qāḍī said that according to *qiyās al-madhhab*, it is valid because Aḥmad [Ibn Ḥanbal] considered the minor's power of attorney (*wakāla*) and his sale transactions, if he has permission from his guardian, valid."[135] Accepted as the authoritative basis of the school, Ibn Ḥanbal's doctrine became the foundation of any case that could be deemed to have attributes justifying extension by analogy. But the authority of *qiyās al-madhhab* was no more universal or binding than were the *ṣaḥīḥ*, *mashhūr*, or the *madhhab*-opinions themselves. In this very case, Ibn Qudāma, a leading Ḥanbalite, rejected this *qiyās* altogether and considered the bequest of a minor invalid.[136]

132 See, for example, Shāshī, *Ḥulyat al-ʿUlamāʾ*, IV, 113; VIII, 177, 265, and passim; Baʿlī, *al-Ikhtiyārāt al-Fiqhiyya*, 15, 21; Abū ʿAlī Aḥmad b. Muḥammad al-Shāshī, *Uṣūl al-Shāshī* (Beirut: Dār al-Kitāb al-ʿArabī, 1982), 120.

133 Shāshī, *Ḥulyat al-ʿUlamāʾ*, I, 193.

134 Zarkashī, *Sharḥ*, II, 544; VII, 412.

135 Ibn al-Laḥḥām, *Qawāʿid*, 24.

136 Ibid. See also Shāshī, *Ḥulyat al-ʿUlamāʾ*, I, 94.

4. *Ẓāhir al-madhhab*, the dominant opinion in the school.[137]
5. *Mashhūr al-madhhab*, the opinion sanctioned as *mashhūr* by the collective school body.[138]
6. *Laysa bi-madhhab* (lit. not a *madhhab*-opinion), an expression used to dismiss an opinion as falling short of being the standard opinion of the school, even though it might be *ṣaḥīḥ*.[139]

## *Maftī bi-hi, maʿmūl bi-hi*

We have seen that the *madhhab*-opinions gained authoritative status due to the fact that they were predominantly used as the basis of issuing *fatwās*. The Shāfiʿite Ramlī declares that the jurist's most important task is to determine which opinions in his school are regularly applied (*mutadāwala*) in the practice of *iftāʾ* since this will determine the authoritative *madhhab*-opinions.[140] In his widely known work *Multaqā al-Abḥur*, the Ḥanafite Ḥalabī also considered his chief task to be the determination of which opinions were the most authoritative. It turns out that next to the *ṣaḥīḥ* and the *aṣaḥḥ*, the most weighty opinions were those "chosen for *fatwās*" (*al-mukhtār lil-fatwā*).[141] In the Mālikite school, the authoritative category of the *mashhūr* was in part determined by the common practice of *iftāʾ*. Ḥaṭṭāb maintains that *tashhīr* is determined, among other things, by the *maftī bi-hi*, the opinions predominantly adopted by the jurisconsults.[142] At the risk of repetition, it is important at this point to recall Ibn ʿĀbidīn's statement, which reflected the centuries-old practice of his school:

> Not every *ṣaḥīḥ* [opinion] may be used as a basis for issuing *fatwās* because another opinion may be adopted out of necessity (*ḍarūra*) or due to its being more agreeable to changing times and the likes of such considerations. This latter opinion, which is designated as fit for *iftāʾ* (*fī-hi lafẓ al-fatwā*), includes two things, one of which is its suitability for issuing *fatwās*, the other its correctness (*ṣiḥḥatihi*), because using it as the basis of *iftāʾ* is in itself [an act] by which it is corrected (*taṣḥīḥ la-hu*).[143]

Similarly, the rules that were applied, i.e. the *maʿmūl bi-hi*, acquired paramount importance as the authoritative doctrine of the school. Like the *maftī bi-hi*, the *maʿmūl bi-hi* formed the basis of *tashhīr* in the Mālikite

[137] Shāshī, *Ḥulyat al-ʿUlamāʾ*, I, 63, 140, 168, 255, and passim.
[138] Subkī, *Ṭabaqāt*, VI, 193.
[139] Shāshī, *Ḥulyat al-ʿUlamāʾ*, I, 140, 187, 188, 192; IV, 67–68 and passim.
[140] Ramlī, *Nihāyat al-Muḥtāj*, I, 36–37.
[141] Ḥalabī, *Mulatqā al-Abḥur*, I, 10; II, 194, 202, 207, 210, 211, and passim.
[142] Ḥaṭṭāb, *Mawāhib al-Jalīl*, I, 36. [143] Ibn ʿĀbidīn, *Sharḥ al-Manẓūma*, 38–39.

school,[144] the assumption being that the authoritative opinions of Mālik, Ibn al-Qāsim, and those of the later *mujtahid*s make up the foundations of dominant judicial practice. In his commentary on Nawawī's *Minhāj*, the Shāfiᶜite Ramlī purportedly included in his work only those opinions that were in predominant use, and whenever citing weaker opinions, he alerted the reader to this fact by distinguishing between the two types.[145] In the Ḥanafite school, the *madhhab*-opinion was organically linked both to *fatwā* and *ᶜamal* (practice). No *fatwā* was to be considered valid or at least authoritative unless it was backed by the judicial practice of the community (*ᶜalayhi ᶜamal al-umma*).[146] Ibn Ḥajar al-Haytamī summed up the entire issue when he said that "*ᶜalayhi al-ᶜamal*" was a *tarjīḥ* formula used to determine which opinions are correct and authoritative.[147] Conversely, an opinion that is not resorted to in judicial practice will become obsolete, and therefore negligible, if not altogether needless. Speaking of authorial practices, Ṭūfī argues that the author–jurist must not, as a rule, record those opinions that are not relevant to practice, for "they are needless."[148]

Since practice varied from one region to another, an opinion thought to have gained wide circulation in one region might not have been regarded as such in another, an added factor in the disagreement over which opinion was deemed authoritative in the school and which not. The Mālikite discourse on this matter perhaps best illustrates the difficulties involved. Ibn Farḥūn states that the commonly used formula "This is the prevailing practice in this matter" (*al-ladhī jarā al-ᶜamal bi-hi fī hādhihi al-mas'ala*) cannot be generalized to include all domains in which a particular school prevailed. Rather, such a formula would have been applicable only to that region or locale in which the practice had prevailed. This explains, he maintains, why the jurists attempted to restrict the applicability of the formula by adding to it expressions like "in such-and-such region" (*fī balad kadhā*). Otherwise, if they did not qualify the formula, then the opinion would be said to be universally applicable. The opinion's purported universality was in itself an argument in favor of its preponderance as the authoritative opinion of the school no matter where the opinion might be appealed to. Ibn Farḥūn also asserts that the principle of authorization by dominant practice is accepted by the Shāfiᶜites as well.[149] To

[144] Ḥaṭṭāb, *Mawāhib al-Jalīl*, I, 36. [145] Ramlī, *Nihāyat al-Muḥtāj*, I, 9.

[146] Ḥaṣkafī, *al-Durr al-Mukhtār*, I, 72–73. See also Ibn ᶜĀbidīn, *Sharḥ al-Manẓūma*, 38.

[147] Ibn Ḥajar al-Haytamī, *al-Fatāwā al-Kubrā al-Fiqhiyya*, 4 vols. (Cairo: ᶜAbd al-Ḥamīd Aḥmad al-Ḥanafī, 1938), IV, 293.

[148] Ṭūfī, *Sharḥ Mukhtaṣar al-Rawḍa*, III, 626: "*idh mā lā ᶜamala ᶜalayh lā ḥājata ilayh.*"

[149] Ibn Farḥūn, *Tabṣirat al-Ḥukkām*, I, 49.

the Shāfiᶜites he might as well have added the Ḥanafites who, as we have seen and as we shall further see in the next chapter, placed great stress upon dominant practice as a legitimizing factor. The Ḥanbalites, on the other hand, appear to have laid slightly less stress on it than any of the other schools, if we are to judge by what seems to have been a lower statistical frequency of explicit reference to practice in their works. But this is by no means correct in all cases. In his *Muntahā al-Irādāt*, for instance, Ibn al-Najjār considers practice (*ᶜalayhi al-ᶜamal*) to be a preponderating factor, standing on a par with *taṣḥīḥ* and *tashhīr*.[150]

## *Mukhtār, ikhtiyār*

Of relatively less frequent occurrence are the terms *mukhtār*, *ikhtiyār*, and the verb form *ikhtāra*,[151] indicating, respectively, the notions of chosen, choice, and to choose.[152] The most obvious implications of these terms are two, the first of which is that the jurist who is said to have chosen or made the choice is one who did not originally formulate the opinion but rather adopted it, directly or indirectly, from another jurist who did. This is the underlying significance of such statements as "Abū Ḥanīfa held such-and-such opinion, and this is the choice of Muzanī,"[153] statements which abound in the legal literature. Second, "choice," or any of its variants, suggests an act by which one opinion is deemed preponderant over the other(s). Thus, in substantive legal works it is reported that a *wajh* opinion formulated by Ibn Surayj constituted the choice (*ikhtiyār*) of al-Qāḍī Abū al-Ṭayyib al-Ṭabarī, just as one of Abū Ḥanīfa's opinions was chosen by Muzanī.[154] At times, the pedigree of the opinion is not mentioned, and the author confines himself to stating that it has been chosen, or for that matter adopted, by a certain distinguished jurist.[155]

150 Ibn al-Najjār, *Muntahā al-Irādāt*, I, 6.

151 In the majority of works, these terms do appear with less frequency than other operative terms. However, in a relatively very few works, they are used repeatedly, even surpassing the frequency with which terms such as *ṣaḥīḥ* and *aṣaḥḥ* are employed. See, for instance, the Ḥanbalite Zarkashī, *Sharḥ*, I, 290, 299, 300, 301, 304, and passim.

152 This is to be distinguished sharply from the very similar term *takhayyur* which in the pre-modern period meant the selective amalgamation of legal doctrines and opinions held by a number of jurists, not necessarily belonging to the same school. See Wael B. Hallaq, "Talfīḳ," *Encyclopaedia of Islam*, X, 161.

153 See next note, below.

154 Shāshī, *Ḥulyat al-ᶜUlamā'*, VIII, 266, 273. See also ibid., IV, 278, 377, 424, 467.

155 Ibid., I, 105, 155, 156, and passim; Qāḍīkhān, *Fatāwā*, I, 178, 204, and passim; Ibn Quṭlūbughā, *Tāj al-Tarājim*, 16–17.

That *ikhtiyār* and its varieties amount to formulas of *tarjīḥ* is quite obvious. Using any of them in conjunction with an opinion simply meant that the jurist who made the *ikhtiyār* found the opinion to be the preponderant one.[156] In his *Mukhtaṣar*, Khalīl used these variations as devices for the purpose of showing which opinions were considered to outweigh others. They stood in his discourse equal to such other terms as *tarjīḥ*, *arjaḥ*, *aẓhar*, *ṣaḥīḥ*, and *mashhūr*.[157] Given the subjectivity that engulfed operative terminology, *ikhtiyār* and *mukhtār* were relative. Thus, Khalīl often indicated that the opinion which a previous jurist had *chosen* was outweighed (*rujjiḥa*) by another opinion which he deemed preponderant.[158] In the same vein, and as with the other activities of *takhrīj*, *tarjīḥ*, *taṣḥīḥ*, and *tashhīr*, some jurists were more likely to engage in *ikhtiyār* than others. The Mālikites Māzarī, Ibn Rushd, and particularly Abū al-Ḥasan al-Lakhmī (d. 478/1085) are said to have been heavily involved in this activity, for all of them are also said to have been *mujtahid*s capable of *tarjīḥ*.[159]

The ability to engage in preponderance, which requires a considerable measure of *ijtihād*, was often connected with *ikhtiyār*. In this context, Ibn Abī Shāma's remark speaks for itself: "He who contemplates Nawawī's performance in his *Sharḥ al-Muhadhdhab*[160] realizes that the man no doubt reached the rank of *ijtihād*, especially in view of the fact that his *ikhtiyārāt* departed from the *madhhab*. This sort of thing can be done only by a *mujtahid*."[161] The same is reported of the Mālikite jurist Ibn Khuwayz Mindād and the Shāfiᶜites Muḥammad b. Naṣr and Sirāj al-Dīn al-Bulqīnī who had in their own *ikhtiyārāt* deviated from the authoritative doctrine of their schools.[162] Departure from school doctrine was not always a matter of incidental disagreement on certain legal cases. When Muḥammad al-Juwaynī, the father of Imām al-Ḥaramayn, deliberately aimed at distancing himself from the doctrines of the schools,[163] he was

[156] As we shall see, preponderance was an essential part of *ikhtiyār*. However, in rare instances, the term was used to mean a choice between two opinions of the same strength. For instance, if the jurist could not determine which of Shāfiᶜī's two opinions was preponderant, it was said that he should adopt one of the two at any rate, this act being characterized as *takhyīr*. See Baṣrī, *Muᶜtamad*, II, 861. See also how Ibn Farḥūn, *Dībāj*, 87, uses the terms interchangeably.

[157] Ḥaṭṭāb, *Mawāhib al-Jalīl*, I, 34–35. [158] Ibid.

[159] Ibid., I, 35, 40–41. See also Ibn Farḥūn, *Dībāj*, 87, in connection with Ibrāhīm b. ᶜAbd al-Ṣamad al-Tanūkhī (d. after 526/1131) who was also said to have engaged in *ikhtiyār* and *tarjīḥ* because he "had risen above the rank of *taqlīd*."

[160] Namely, *al-Majmūᶜ* whose subtitle is *Sharḥ al-Muhadhdhab*.

[161] Cited by Suyūṭī, *al-Radd*, 193.

[162] Ibid., 192–93; Nawawī, *Tahdhīb*, I, 94; Ibn Qāḍī Shuhba, *Ṭabaqāt*, IV, 50.

[163] See chapter 3, section II, above.

said to have made *ikhtiyārāt* in opposition to their authoritative doctrines and was accordingly described as a *mujtahid mutakhayyir*.[164]

## VII

The foregoing discussion has shown that operative terminology evolved as a response to the plurality and thus indeterminacy of legal rules. All operative terms had in common a single purpose, namely, the determination of *the* authoritative opinion on any given case, a determination which amounted in effect to reducing plurality to a single opinion. Epistemologically, this determination and the varied vocabulary that expressed it stood as the binary opposite of *ijtihād*. The latter created multiplicity, the former attempted to suppress, or at least minimize, it. *Ijtihād*, then, was causally connected with operative terminology, for it stood as its progenitor, historically and epistemologically.

This terminology evolved also in conjunction with a monumental development in Islamic legal history, that is, the rise of the *madhhab* as a doctrinal entity. Before the rise of the *madhhab*, jurists, in their capacity as *qāḍī*s and jurisconsults, had recourse to virtually any set of doctrines they liked, without being bound by any particular doctrine. This much has been demonstrated in chapters 2 and 3. Later, however, when the *madhhab* reached maturity, jurists had to confine themselves to those opinions accepted as the authoritative doctrine of the school. Only at that stage of development, the need to rank competing opinions arose. This ranking or, to put more precisely, authorization, required the development of what we have called operative terminology. We have seen that Fūrānī (d. 461/1068) was considered one of the first jurists to take it upon himself to weigh *wajh* opinions in an effort to conduct *taṣḥīḥ*.[165] Of course, we cannot take this narrative at its face value, for we know that others were already engaged in this activity some time before Fūrānī was even born. Muḥammad b. Waraqa al-Bukhārī (d. 385/995) is also said to have been in the habit of adopting those *wujūh* opinions that he considered to be *ṣaḥīḥ*.[166] Even earlier, jurists of all shades and colors did make distinctions between opinions, and did, albeit rarely, consider some opinions preponderant.[167] But it is no coincidence that Fūrānī, explicitly,

[164] Suyūṭī, *al-Radd*, 190. For other jurists known to have had *ikhtiyārāt*, see Ibn al-Farrā', *Ṭabaqāt*, II, 163; Ibn Qāḍī Shuhba, *Ṭabaqāt*, I, 57, 319; Ibn ʿĀbidīn, *Sharḥ al-Manẓūma*, 32.

[165] Subkī, *Ṭabaqāt*, III, 225; Ibn Qāḍī Shuhba, *Ṭabaqāt*, I, 266. See chapter 3, section II, above.

[166] Subkī, *Ṭabaqāt*, II, 168. [167] See, e.g. Ṭaḥāwī, *Mukhtaṣar*, 394, 440, and passim.

and Bukhārī, obliquely, have been associated with the earliest determination of the *ṣaḥīḥ*. Nor is it a coincidence that jurists who lived prior to Bukhārī were never associated with this activity, for the latter, as a systematic hermeneutical engagement, was a post-*madhhab* development.

A salient feature of operative terminology, which evolved as a response to the indeterminacy of legal rules, is its own indeterminacy. We have, I believe, conclusively shown that this terminology was engulfed by multilayered uses that rendered both the process and product of authorization subjective. It is no exaggeration to speculate that the jurists would have liked to develop objective criteria by which *the* authoritative opinion on any given case could be determined. In other words, what I wish to suggest is that if the jurists failed to develop such criteria, it was not because they did not want to. Yet their failure to develop this objective criteria, which would have reduced juristic disagreement on any particular case to one authoritative opinion, was a blessing, a *raḥma*, as they might have said. The very diversity of opinion that resulted from this failure allowed Islamic law to keep up with change, a theme which we will address more fully in our final chapter.

6

# THE JURISCONSULT, THE AUTHOR–JURIST, AND LEGAL CHANGE

## I

It is not our primary concern here to show that Islamic law underwent change at different points in its history or in particular regions under its jurisdiction, although there is sufficient justification to do so in light of the fact that modern Islamicist scholarship has, until recently, categorically denied that it experienced any noticeable, much less fundamental, development after the formative period. Instead, and going beyond the narrow confines of this issue, we will focus on explaining *how* change took place and *who* were the agents of this process. For in explaining the modalities of legal change, one can at the same time demonstrate, *a fortiori*, that not only did change take place but also that its means of accommodation were a fundamental, and indeed a structural, feature of Islamic law.

Before we proceed any further, a preliminary but important remark is in order; namely, that Muslim jurists and Islamic legal culture in general not only, as we shall see, experienced legal change in very concrete terms but were also aware of change as a distinct feature of the law. A society (or an individual, for that matter) may experience a certain phenomenon and even partake in it actively, yet may nevertheless fail to articulate the experience consciously and may thus remain unaware of the processes taking place and in which it is involved. This certainly was not the case with legal change in Islam. Muslim jurists were acutely aware of both the *occurrence* of, and the *need* for, change in the law, and they articulated this awareness through such maxims as "the *fatwā* changes with changing times" (*taghayyur al-fatwā bi-taghayyur al-azmān*) or through the explicit notion that the law is subject to modification according to "the changing of the times or to the changing conditions of society."[1]

[1] For a momentous discussion of this theme, see Ibn Qayyim al-Jawziyya, *Iʿlām al-Muwaqqiʿīn*, III, 14–70, and I, 110 f. See also Qāḍīkhān, *Fatāwā*, I, 2–3; Ramlī, *al-Fatāwā al-Khayriyya*, I, 3; Ibn ʿĀbidīn, *Nashr al-ʿUrf*, 114–46; Ibn ʿĀbidīn, *Ḥāshiya*, I, 69, and sources cited in nn. 104–11, below.

## II

Now, in determining the modalities and agents of legal change, which is the focus of the present enquiry, it is necessary to maintain a distinction between the four most important juristic roles that dominated Islamic legal culture, namely, the *qāḍī*, the *muftī*, the author–jurist, and the professor. These roles rarely stood independently of each other, for a jurist may combine two, three, or the entire set of roles, let alone other subsidiary ones.[2] It is remarkable that after the second/eighth century, the pillars of the legal profession usually excelled, or at least successfully engaged, in all four roles. Generally speaking, a jurist's career was not considered complete without his having fulfilled all these roles, although the role of *qaḍā'*, in the case of a number of distinguished legists, does not seem to have been seen as a prerequisite for crowning success. A typical example of an accomplished career is that of Kamāl al-Dīn Ibn al-Zamālikānī (d. 727/1326) who was considered, during the later part of his life, the leader of Syrian Shāfiᶜism. He is reported to have excelled as a *muftī* and professor, to have presided as a *qāḍī* in Aleppo, and to have authored several works of law.[3] Other typically distinguished careers are those of Ibn Surayj,[4] Taqī al-Dīn al-Subkī,[5] Sharaf al-Dīn al-Manāwī (d. 757/1356),[6] and Sirāj al Dīn al Bulqīnī (d. 805/1402),[7] all of whom were *qāḍī*s, distinguished *muftī*s, professors, and prolific authors.

The current state of knowledge in Islamic legal studies renders unnecessary any general comment on the nature of the offices of the jurisconsult, the judge, or the professor at law.[8] But a word on the author–jurist as a

2 In fact, a jurist may function in other subsidiary roles, such as that of notary. A notable example is the Ḥanafite Ṭaḥāwī, who functioned in this capacity as well as that of author–jurist and *qāḍī*. See Tamīmī, *al-Ṭabaqāt al-Saniyya*, II, 49–52.

3 Nuᶜaymī, *al-Dāris*, I, 31–32; Makdisi, *Rise*, 95, 159, 168.

4 Subkī, *Ṭabaqāt*, II, 87–96. 5 Ibn Qāḍī Shuhba, *Tabaqāt*, III, 47–53.

6 Ibid., III, 1. 7 Ibid., IV, 42–52.

8 On these offices or roles, see E. Tyan, *Histoire de l'organisation judiciaire en pays d'Islam*, 2nd ed. (Leiden: E. J. Brill, 1960), 100 ff., 219 ff.; E. Tyan, "Judicial Organization," in Majid Khadduri and Herbert Liebesny, eds., *Law in the Middle East* (Washington: D.C.: The Middle East Institute, 1955), 236–53, 259–71; Khalid Masud et al., eds., *Islamic Legal Interpretation: Muftis and their Fatwas* (Cambridge, Mass.: Harvard University Press, 1996), 8–15, 20–26; Makdisi, *Rise*, 148–59, 197–201, and passim; J. Nielsen, *Secular Justice in an Islamic State: Maẓālim under the Baḥrī Mamlūks, 662/1264–789/1387* (Istanbul: Nederlands Historisch–Archaeologisch Instituut, 1985), 3–6, 8–10, 19–27, 42–47, and passim; R. C. Repp, *The Müfti of Istanbul: A Study in the Development of the Ottoman Learned Hierarchy* (Oxford: Ithaca Press, 1986); J. H. Escovitz, *The Office of Qāḍī al-Quḍāt in Cairo under the Baḥrī Mamlūks* (Berlin: Klaus Schwarz Verlag, 1984), 131–62.

professional category seems required. As part of the veneration in Islam for the written word, it was deemed meritorious for the learned to write, since writing (*taṣnīf*)[9] was viewed as a religious act in the service of *ʿilm*.[10] The writing of treatises, short and long, was an essential part of any distinguished legal career. There is no complete biographical notice in the *ṭabaqāt* works of the jurists that does not include a list of the treatises written by the jurist under discussion. The mere absence of such a list from any biographical notice speaks volumes. A jurist who did not engage in *taṣnīf* was considered to be lacking in some way as a member of the legal profession. Zayn al-Dīn al-Khazrajī (d. 833/1429), for instance, is said to have failed to produce notable, successful students, a failure that was matched only by his inability to write anything of significance.[11] Others, however, are characterized by the sources as prolific authors, and as having gained merit by their practice of devoting at least one-third of night-time to *taṣnīf*.[12]

*Taṣnīf* as a legal activity was the exclusive domain of the author–jurist. Conversely, *as an act of writing, taṣnīf* was not a prerequisite either for the *qāḍī*, the *muftī*, or the professor. The *qāḍī*, for one, was not himself required, as part of his normal duties, to write down his decisions, much less the minutes of the court proceedings, since this task devolved upon the scribe (*kātib*) who was a permanent functionary of the court.[13] Even the formulation of the language in which court decisions and minutes were recorded was spared him, as this task was the province of the scribe as well. Nor was it part of the professor's function to write, although he had his teaching notes and supervised the writing, by his graduate students, of *taʿlīqa*s. That some jurists wrote treatises on law while being engaged in teaching should in no way mean that *taṣnīf* was part of their professional role as professors. This remained true even when they wrote *mukhtaṣar*s – short treatises used, *inter alia*, for pedagogical purposes. When they wrote such treatises, they were doing so as author–jurists, not as professors, for after all, most professors did not write *mukhtaṣar*s and yet many of them were highly successful teachers.[14]

9 Although the verb *ṣannafa* and the verbal noun *taṣnīf* were most common, other terms were used as well, e.g. *allafa* and *ta'līf*. See Ibn Farḥūn, *Dībāj*, 254, 334, 335, 338, 340, 341, 348, and passim.

10 Makdisi, *Rise*, 206 ff. On writing books in general, see J. Pedersen, *The Arabic Book*, trans. G. French (Princeton: Princeton University Press, 1984), 20–36.

11 Ibn Qāḍī Shuhba, *Ṭabaqāt*, IV, 96–97. 12 Ibid., I, 20, 108.

13 Wael B. Hallaq, "The Qāḍī's *Dīwān* (*Sijill*) before the Ottomans," *Bulletin of the School of Oriental and African Studies*, 61 (1998), 422 f., 426.

14 Makdisi, *Rise*, 208: "The working of students [*ishtighāl*] was distinguished from the function of the professor of law (*tadrīs*), and from the writing of books (*taṣnīf*)."

It may be argued that the *muftī* was an author–jurist because he *wrote* or *authored fatwās*. But this argument is at best incomplete and at worst misleading since the *muftī* may have been an author only in a very limited sense. The majority of *fatwās* consisted of a succinct statement of the law and rarely involved the elaboration of legal arguments, a practice highly discouraged.[15] Ibn al-Ṣalāḥ, himself the author of an influential manual on the art of *iftāʾ*, vehemently argues that *fatwās* should be kept short, to the point, and unreasoned, so that they would not fall into the category of *taṣnīf*.[16] Indeed, even the more extensive *fatwās* lacked the discursive strategies and forms of argumentation usually found in the works of the author–jurists. The fact that many *fatwās* consisted of very short answers – as short as "Yes" or "No" – is indicative of the very limited function of the *fatwā* as *authored* discourse. It was the custom that only the most distinguished *muftīs*, when faced with a problem of frequent occurrence or of fundamental importance, would rise to the occasion by writing a *risāla* in which lengthy and complex arguments were constructed. In such cases, the jurist would be exchanging the *muftī*'s hat for that of the author–jurist.[17] The art of writing the *risāla* and other forms of *taṣnīf* distinctly differed from that of *fatwā*.

It can safely be stated that, as a rule, accomplished jurists are portrayed in the biographical dictionaries as having been seriously engaged in teaching, writing, and issuing *fatwās*. Engaging in *qaḍāʾ*, however, was not necessarily regarded as the culmination of a successful legal career, since a number of first-rate jurists were never engaged in it, or at least are not reported to have done so. Even if they played this role, it is significant in itself that the biographers did not see it as worthwhile to record such an activity. For had it been an essential requirement, the biographers would surely have taken pains to stress this accomplishment, as they did in the cases of *taṣnīf*, *iftāʾ*, and *tadrīs* (teaching). One notable example of such a career is that of Abū ʿAmr Ibn al-Ṣalāḥ who was renowned as a *muftī*, a professor, and an influential author of legal and other works.[18] Ibn

[15] See Nawawī, *al-Majmūʿ*, I, 52, 57; Ibn al-Ṣalāḥ, *Adab al-Muftī*, 141; *al-Fatāwā al-Hindiyya*, III, 309.

[16] The argument was first articulated by Māwardī, but incorporated as part of Ibn al-Ṣalāḥ's discourse. Ibn al-Ṣalāḥ, *Adab al-Muftī*, 141: "*al-muftī ʿalayhi an yakhtaṣir jawābahu fa-yaktafī fī-hi bi-annahu yajūz aw lā yajūz, aw ḥaqq aw bāṭil, wa-lā yaʿdul ilā al-iṭāla wal-iḥtijāj li-yufarriqa bayna al-fatwā wal-taṣnīf*."

[17] Typical examples of such discourse may be found in Subkī, *Fatāwā*, I, 453–61; II, 309, 333–37, 477–83, and passim. (Note that in this work these writings are characterised as *mu'allafāt* [i.e. authored works], not *fatwās*; see especially I, 519 and II, 650.). See also Zayn al-Dīn Ibn Nujaym, *Rasāʾil*, ed. Khalīl al-Mays (Beirut: Dār al-Kutub al-ʿIlmiyya, 1980); Ibn ʿĀbidīn, *Majmūʿ Rasāʾil.*

[18] Nuʿaymī, *al-Dāris*, I, 20–21; Ibn Qāḍī Shuhba, *Ṭabaqāt*, II, 144–46.

al-Ṣalāḥ attained fame and distinction despite the fact that he never served in the capacity of a *qāḍī*.

In due course we shall see that the *qāḍī qua qāḍī*, by virtue of the nature of, and limitations imposed upon, his function, was of little if any consequence as an agent of legal change in the post-formative period.[19] I say *qāḍī qua qāḍī* because the four roles, including that of *qaḍāʾ*, were not always clearly distinguished from each other when they were present in the career of a single jurist – and this frequently was the case. Here, it is useful to recall sociology's theory of roles which acknowledges the participation of a role-set whenever any single role is engaged in.[20] Just as any social status involves an array of associated roles and does not stand, to any significant extent, independently of these roles, any or all of the juristic roles described above might come into play when a specific role is exercised. A modern-day professor of constitutional law, for example, must teach students, interact with her colleagues and the university administration, publish works of scholarship, and perform public duties when constitutional issues are debated. While still a professor, she might serve on a government sub-committee, preside as a judge, or work as an attorney. None of these roles can be kept entirely separate from the other ones, for as an author she might write a book on a fundamental issue of constitutional law, while as a member of a sub-committee she might prepare a report which heavily, if not totally, draws on her research for her monograph. The question that arises here pertains to the nature of her report: Is it a production of her work as a professor or as a member of the government sub-committee?

A similar question arises in the case of the *muftī* who engages in discourse that transcends the limits of the *fatwā* strictly so defined. A *muftī*, such as Taqī al-Dīn al-Subkī or Ibn Ḥajar al-Haytamī, might elect to address, in the form of a short treatise, a legal issue which had already elicited many *fatwā*s and which continued to be problematic and of general concern to the community or a segment thereof (*mā taʿummu bi-hi al-balwā*). In this case, how should the treatise be classified? Is it merely an extended *fatwā*, the work of the *muftī*? Or is it a *risāla*, the product of the author–jurist? Later on in this chapter we shall discuss the contributions of the *muftī* and the author–jurist at length. For now, we only need to assert that such questions of role-sets bear equally upon the *qāḍī*'s role

19 See n. 117, below.

20 For a discussion of role-set theory, see Stephen Cole, *The Sociological Orientation* (Chicago: Rand McNally College Publishing Co., 1979), 57–59; David Dressler, *Sociology: The Study of Human Interaction* (New York: Alfred A. Knopf, 1969), 355–58.

in legal change. According to the strict definition of the *qāḍī*'s profession (that is, the *qāḍī* as entirely dissociated from other roles), the institution of *qaḍā'*, after the formative period,[21] was, by and large, of marginal importance in legal change. The *qāḍī qua qāḍī* heard cases, determined certain facts as relevant, and, in accordance with these facts, rendered a judgment that was usually based upon an authoritative opinion in his school. Once rendered, his judgment was normally recorded in the *dīwān*, the register of the court's minutes.[22] At times, a copy of the record of the decision was given to one or both parties to a litigation, but such documents had no legal significance beyond the immediate and future interests of these parties. The court cases, however, were viewed as constituting a considerable part of practice, and the *qāḍī*'s *dīwān* amounted to a discursive reflection of this practice. But it was not the *qāḍī*'s function to assess or evaluate that *corpus juris* in which practice manifested itself. Such assessment and evaluation was the province of the *muftī* and perhaps more so that of the author–jurist. If a *qāḍī* was to assess the significance of court cases for legal practice, he would not be doing so as a *qāḍī*, but rather as a *muftī*, an author–jurist, or as both.

At any rate, such an assessment logically presupposed a repertoire of court cases, and thus represented a juristic activity that, materially speaking, came at the tail end of the adjudication process. We know, for instance, that Taqī al-Dīn al-Subkī drew heavily on his own experience as judge when he issued *fatwā*s and wrote several *rasā'il* on fundamental and highly relevant legal issues in his day. But it is important to realize that when he did so, it was by virtue of his role as a *muftī* and author–jurist, respectively. For it was in no way the function of the *qāḍī*, strictly speaking, either to engage in issuing *fatwā*s or to discourse, beyond the boundaries of his court, on legal issues.

If the *determination of what constitutes predominant practice* was not the *qāḍīs*' responsibility, then these latter, despite their participation in

21 A self-evident phenomenon of the formative period, legal change during the first three centuries in Islam does not constitute part of this enquiry (see preface). In this context, I submit that during that period, or for most of it, the *qāḍīs* contributed to the evolution of religious law in Islam. However, my contention here is that after the formative period (and probably before its end) it was the *muftī* and the author–jurist who played the most central role in legal change. Be that as it may, it is noteworthy that while legal change was integral to the formative period, the *qāḍī*'s role was one of constructing religio-legal norms on the basis of earlier (non-Islamic) legal traditions, not one whose sole focus was the hermeneutical manipulation of a mature and fairly well-rooted legal system. It was precisely this hermeneutical manipulation that constituted one of the main tasks of the *muftī* and author–jurist in their bid to effect legal change.

22 See Hallaq, "Qāḍī's *Dīwān*," 422 ff.

that practice,[23] could never have been directly involved in legal change. But could they have contributed to change insofar as they gradually but increasingly abandoned the authoritative doctrine in favor of another, one consisting of the practice that the author–jurist used, *ex post eventum*, as justification of legal change? In the previous chapter, we saw that predominant practice was one factor in effecting legal change. If what was once a minority opinion became frequently applied, and, later still, gained even wider circulation, it would likely be raised to the authoritative level of opinion known as the *ṣaḥīḥ* or the *mashhūr*, depending on the particular school involved. Now the question that poses itself here is: Did the *qāḍī*s participate in the practice through which an opinion was transformed from having a relatively marginal status to one having an authoritative status? This question in effect both implies and amounts to another: Did *qāḍī*s *qua qāḍī*s apply what was at the moment of decision other than the authoritative opinions to the cases they adjudicated? If the answer is negative, then it is difficult to argue that they played any role in legal change, for had they done so it would have been precisely in this sphere of juristic activity. But if the answer is in the affirmative, then a further question may be posed: Was it the *qāḍī*s *qua qāḍī*s who were responsible for departing from authoritative opinions in favor of less authoritative ones? Answers to these questions are by no means easy to give, since the present state of our knowledge of the processes involved in the *qāḍī*'s decision leaves much to be desired. Our answer must, therefore, remain tentative, based as it is on indirect evidence.

It is our contention that the *qāḍī qua qāḍī* was not, in the final analysis, free to depart from what is considered the authoritative opinion of the school. Even when there was no universal agreement on a certain question or case, it was not, generally speaking, the *qāḍī* who ultimately decided which of the two was the more authoritative. If *qāḍī*s were, from time to time, engaged in this latter activity, they were so engaged not necessarily in their role as *qāḍī*s but rather as jurists playing other roles, especially the *muftī* who had a central function in courts of law. Above, in chapter 3, and later on in the present chapter we show, on the basis of evidence from substantive legal works, that the *qāḍī* regularly turned to the *muftī* for legal advice. As early as the second/eighth century, it was already recognized that the *qāḍī* might or might not be a highly competent jurist,

[23] As we shall see in section VII below, the *qāḍī*s did at times deviate from established doctrine, thereby initiating what appears to us to have been, with the benefit of hindsight, the embryonic stages of legal change. But this initial participation would have amounted to very little without the intervention of the *muftī* and/or the author–jurist who articulated and legitimized that change.

which was not usually the case with the *muftī*. During this early period, and even later on, the *muftī* was mostly considered the ultimate hermeneutical authority, while the *qāḍī* largely fell short of this high expectation. Shāfiʿī already encouraged *qāḍīs* to seek legal counsel from learned jurists, i.e., the *muftīs* whom he considered in his discourse as *mujtahids*.[24] The Ḥanafite Jaṣṣāṣ perhaps represented the average position on this issue when he insisted that the *qāḍī*, in deciding which opinion is the soundest and most suitable for the case at hand, must seek the jurists' counsel by listening to their opinions.[25] Indeed, Islamic legal history abundantly attests to the centrality of the *muftī* to the *qāḍī*'s work. Suffice it here to adduce the vast bulk of *fatwās* that have been hitherto published. The majority of these show beyond doubt that they originated as *istiftā*'s requested by *qāḍīs* from *muftīs*[26] for the purpose of deciding court cases.

If the *qāḍī* was not responsible either for departing from authoritative opinions in favor of weaker ones or for determining that the predominant application of a weaker opinion should be given an authoritative status, then he, *qua qāḍī*, cannot, to any meaningful extent, be considered an agent of legal change. This assertion, however, should remain at this point tentative. For we know that *qāḍīs* gradually departed from certain authoritative doctrines of their school, and that this practice of theirs constituted the embryo of legal change. Yet it took no less than the *muftī* and the author–jurist to articulate and justify this change, and without their juristic endeavor, the first stages of legal change that had been initiated by the *qāḍīs*' practices would never – if at all – have come to fruition. Therefore, it is far less tentative to argue that if the *qāḍīs* contributed in some instances to legal change, their contribution must have been at best a necessary, but by no means sufficient, condition.

Nor can it be argued that the professor of law, again as an independent juristic role, was involved in legal change any more than the *qāḍī* was. Of course, some professors belonged to that rank of jurists who were engaged in articulating a legal reaction to social and other changes, but when they were engaged in this task, they were not acting as professors *qua* professors, but rather as *muftīs* and/or author–jurists. The professor taught law students and wrote what is usually considered condensed works for their benefit. In his *ḥalaqa*, he may have discussed certain cases of law in

24 Shāfiʿī, *Umm*, VI, 287.

25 Jaṣṣāṣ, *Adab al-Qāḍī*, 37–39, 42–43, 101–02, 105, 106. See also Ibn Māza, *Sharḥ Adab al-Qāḍī*, 76–77.

26 Some *istiftā*'s were requested by *muftīs* who were consulted by *qāḍīs* but who had to turn to more competent *muftīs*, apparently because they found the questions too difficult to answer, the point being that the final authority was the *muftī*, not the *qāḍī*.

terms of what we now – with the benefit of hindsight – call legal change, but articulating legal change was not part of his role as professor.

Having excluded the *qāḍī* and the professor as significant agents of legal change, we are therefore left with the *muftī* and the author–jurist. It is these two types of jurists – playing two distinct roles – who, we shall argue, undertook the major part, if not the entirety, of the task of articulating the law's reaction to social and other changes. We shall begin with the *fatwā* as a socio-legal tool, and then proceed to a discussion of the *muftī*'s role in modulating changes in the law. Since legal change is ultimately anchored in social reality, we will do well to discuss the social origins of the *fatwā* genre, the mechanism by means of which it became part of substantive law, and the role the *muftī* and author–jurist played in modifying the law. If we succeed in demonstrating that *fatwā*s emanated from and represented social reality, and that these *fatwā*s were regularly incorporated in positive legal works – the authoritative repertoire of the schools – then we shall have succeeded in showing that the law generally kept pace with the ever-changing social exigencies.

However, throughout the forthcoming discussion, it must remain clear that two distinct roles were involved, successively, in the transformation of the *fatwā* from the point of its social origin to its ultimate abode in substantive legal works. The first role, ending with the issuance and dissemination of the *fatwā*, was, *ipso facto*, that of the *muftī*, while the second, ending with the final incorporation of the *fatwā* in positive legal works, was that of the author–jurist. It is largely through this process of transformation that legal change was articulated and effected.

## III

In its basic form, a *fatwā* consists of a question (*su'āl, istiftā'*) addressed to a jurisconsult (*muftī*), together with an answer (*jawāb*) provided by that jurisconsult. When the question is drafted on a piece of paper – following the general practice[27] – the paper becomes known as *ruqʿat al-istiftā'* or, less frequently, *kitāb al-istiftā'*,[28] and once an answer is given on the same sheet of paper, the document becomes known as *ruqʿat al-fatwā*. *Fatwā*s issued by the major jurists were often collected and published as books,[29] and it is with these *fatwā*s that we are here concerned. The *fatwā* collections that have been edited to date may be classified into two categories:

[27] See Nawawī, *al-Majmūʿ*, I, 48, 57.
[28] For the use of these appellations, see *al-Fatāwā al-Hindiyya*, III, 309; Ibn al-Ṣalāḥ, *Adab al-Muftī*, 168–69.
[29] See par. 9 of the present section, below.

in the first, which includes Ibn al-Ṣalāḥ,[30] Wansharīsī, Subkī, Ibn Rushd, ᶜAlamī, and Nawawī,[31] the question and answer are preserved more or less in their original form and content; in the second, such as those of al-Shaykh al-Niẓām and Kurdarī,[32] the question and answer have undergone systematic alterations. Here, we shall refer to *fatwā*s of the former type as *primary* and those belonging to the latter as *modified*. Several indicators suggest that primary *fatwā*s were the outcome of a concrete and particular social reality:

1. All *fatwā*s begin with words such as "The Question: . . . ," followed at its end by "The Answer: . . ." Some jurists, such as Ibn Rushd, were in the habit of beginning their answer with the formula, "I have read your question and carefully considered it" (*taṣaffaḥtu su'ālaka wa-waqaftu ᶜalayh*) or some similar statement.[33] The presence of these formulae in *fatwā*s would be meaningless if we were to assume that the primary *fatwā*s were merely concocted in the jurists' imagination.
2. Nearly all *fatwā*s revolve around a person or persons in highly particular circumstances.[34] Neither modified *fatwā*s nor any other legal text (except perhaps court registers) provide the details that primary *fatwā*s do. The constant reference to actual reality and legal and other practices is a salient feature in a number of *fatwā* collections.[35]
3. *Fatwā*s are frequently supplemented either by an additional commentary by the jurisconsult who issued them or by another question submitted by the *mustaftī* on the same *ruqᶜa* (sheet), and to which question the jurisconsult provides an additional answer.[36]

[30] Abū ᶜAmr ᶜUthmān b. ᶜAbd al-Raḥmān Ibn al-Ṣalāḥ, *Fatāwā wa-Masā'il Ibn al-Ṣalāḥ*, ed. ᶜAbd al-Muᶜṭī Qalᶜajī, 2 vols. (Beirut: Dār al-Maᶜrifa, 1986).

[31] Muḥyī al-Dīn Sharaf al-Dīn b. Yaḥyā al-Nawawī, *Fatāwā al-Imām al-Nawawī al-Musammātu bil-Masā'il al-Manthūra*, ed. Muḥammad al-Ḥajjār (Medina: Dār al-Salām, 1985). For the *fatwā* collections of Wansharīsī, Subkī, Ibn Rushd, and ᶜAlamī, see the references, below.

[32] See the bibliography, below.

[33] Although this is the standard formula used by Ibn Rushd, some variations on it do occur. See his *Fatāwā*, I, 143 (*tasaffaḥtu, arshadanā Allāhu wa-iyyāk su'ālaka wa-waqaftu ᶜalayhi*), 160 (*taṣaffaḥtu raḥimanā Allāh wa-iyyāk su'ālaka hādhā wa-nuskhata al-ᶜaqd al-wāqiᶜ fawqah wa-waqaftu ᶜalā dhālika kullih*), 164–65, 166, 172, 177, 183 (*ta'ammaltu su'ālaka hādhā wa-waqaftu ᶜalayh*), and passim; ᶜAlamī, *Nawāzil*, I, 130 (*ta'ammala muḥibbukum mā saṭṭartumūh fawq, maᶜ al-rasm bi-yadi al-ḥāmil*), 145, 157, and passim.

[34] For a number of examples, see Subkī, *Fatāwā*, II, 26, 29, 30, 31, 34, 35, 40, 43, 50, 51, 61, 62, 67, and passim; Ibn Rushd, *Fatāwā*, I, 159 ff., 167–69, 171–73, 190 f., 196 f., 202 ff., 206; II–III, 1260–75, and passim; ᶜAlamī, *Nawāzil*, I, 46 f., 50 f., 53, 54, 57 f., 63, 74, 80 f., 94 f., 123 f., and passim.

[35] See sources cited in preceding note.

[36] See, e.g. Ibn al-Ṣalāḥ, *Fatāwā*, II, 416, 428; Uriel Heyd, "Some Aspects of the Ottoman Fetva," *Bulletin of the School of Oriental and African Studies*, 32 (1969), 42–43; Ibn Rushd, *Fatāwā*, I, 540–41.

4. Primary *fatwās* often refer to matters that are irrelevant to the law, but nonetheless stem from the real world. Questions concerned with such matters as a particular currency or weight (e.g. *dīnār Nāṣirī, dīnār Ṣūrī*) are examples in point.[37] But more important are the occasional references to the names of those involved in the matter that gave rise to the *fatwā*.[38] Their names are but rarely mentioned, however. Were the case otherwise, there would be little reason, if any, to doubt the verity of these *fatwās*. That names were so seldom recorded should not be taken to indicate that the *fatwās* were removed from social reality or that they were the creation of the jurists' imaginations. It was the common practice, as we shall see in due course, to omit names altogether, and whenever necessary to replace them with hypothetical names (most commonly Zayd and ᶜAmr).[39] Moreover, based upon his analysis of thousands of original Ottoman *fatwās* issued between the fifteenth and twentieth centuries, U. Heyd discovered that although the names of the petitioners are omitted from both the question and the answer, the verso of the *ruqᶜat al-fatwā* frequently contains notes referring not only to the names of the *mustaftīs* but also to their professions and even the town or quarter in which they resided.[40] As we shall see, the practice of omitting names was of particular significance and had an important function, for the *fatwā* was not merely an ephemeral legal opinion produced for a specific occasion or purpose but was also an authoritative statement of the law considered to transcend the individual case and its mundane reality.[41] This explains why the jurists, their disciples, and the courts as a rule made every effort to keep a record of the *fatwās* issued by the *muftīs*.[42]
5. The formulation of the question is often highly legalistic, a feature that makes it seem unlikely that the *fatwā* had its origin in a real situation. But *muftīs* commonly answered questions that had been drafted by persons learned in the law, including professional jurists.[43] Some jurisconsults reportedly were in the habit of refusing to answer questions unless they were formulated and handwritten by a learned legist residing in the same town as the *mustaftī*.[44] The formulator of the question, as stipulated by the manuals

[37] Ibn al-Ṣalāḥ, *Fatāwā*, II, 433, 434; Subkī, *Fatāwā*, II, 35. Also see n. 34, above.
[38] See, e.g. the references to Subkī's *Fatāwā*, in n. 34, above.
[39] Heyd, "Ottoman Fetva," 41; R. C. Jennings, "Kādī, Court, and Legal Procedure in 17th C. Ottoman Kayseri," *Studia Islamica*, 48 (1978), 134, 135.
[40] Heyd, "Ottoman Fetva," 38, 36, 41.
[41] Ibn Farḥūn, *Tabṣirat al-Ḥukkām*, I, 53, 56; Ibn Qayyim al-Jawziyya, *Iᶜlām al-Muwaqqiᶜīn*, I, 36, 38.
[42] See n. 52, below.
[43] Nawawī, *al-Majmūᶜ*, I, 57; Heyd, "Ottoman Fetva," 42–43, 51. See also David Powers, "*Fatwās* as Sources for Legal and Social History: A Dispute over Endowment Revenues from Fourteenth-Century Fez," *al-Qanṭara*, 11 (1990), 308; Ibn al-Ṣalāḥ, *Adab al-Muftī*, 169–71.
[44] See, e.g. the statement of Nawawī, *al-Majmūᶜ*, I, 57. Ibn al-Ṣalāḥ, *Adab al-Muftī*, 170–71, observes that the practice of *muftīs* rewriting the *istiftā'* was widespread.

that deal with the modalities of *iftā'* (*adab al-muftī wal-mustaftī*), must be adept in drafting the question; he must know which terms are legally appropriate and admissible and which must be avoided. His handwriting must neither be unduly large nor unduly small, and he must use language that does not lend itself to distortion.[45] In the Ottoman period, most shaykh al-Islāms refused to receive *istiftā'*s drafted by private persons. Abū al-Suʿūd, perhaps the most renowned shaykh al-Islām in all of Ottoman history, wrote a special treatise which contained instructions specifically directed to clerks and officials who were concerned with the art of drafting *fatwā* questions.[46] Many distinguished *muftī*s, such as the illustrious Abū Isḥāq al-Shīrāzī, reportedly followed the practice of redrafting questions in their own words.[47] The *iftā'* manuals recommend that if the question is vague or unduly general, the *muftī* must interrogate the questioner about the case, reformulate the question accordingly, and only then provide an answer.[48]

6. Many primary *fatwā*s deal with disputes that revolve around one type of contract or another. Most of these *fatwā*s include a copy of the contract involved, and in his answer the *muftī* makes constant reference to the stipulations of the contract.[49] A reading of these contracts leaves no doubt that these disputes involved real people faced with real situations.
7. Since one of the main functions of the *fatwā* was to support the case of a party to a lawsuit, the common practice seems to have been to record the *fatwa*s in the court record (*dīwān al-qāḍī*).[50] Jennings and Heyd report that throughout the Ottoman period *fatwā*s were recorded *in toto* in the *sijill*s of the court, and many were preserved in the *fetvakhane*.[51] This fact, together with the interest of the *muftī*s and their disciples in copying down *fatwā*s,[52]

[45] Nawawī, *al-Majmūʿ*, I, 57.
[46] Heyd, "Ottoman Fetva," 50–51.
[47] Nawawī, *al-Majmūʿ*, I, 48.
[48] Ibid.
[49] See Arabic quotations in n. 18, above; ʿAlamī, *Nawāzil*, I, 40, 127, 167, and passim; Ibn Rushd, *Fatāwā*, I, 171–73, 289–90, 323 ff., 331, 346, and passim; Bāʿalawī, *Bughyat al-Mustarshidīn*, 274; for *waqf* documents in *fatwā*s, see Subkī, *Fatāwā*, I, 462–63, 465–68, II, 60, 62 ff., 158 ff.; Powers, "*Fatwā*s as Sources," 298–99 and passim.
[50] For the reliance of the *qāḍī* on the jurisconsult's *fatwā*, see Ibn ʿĀbidīn, *Ḥāshiya*, V, 359, 360, 365; Muḥammad Amīn Ibn ʿĀbidīn, *al-ʿUqūd al-Durriyya fī Tanqīḥ al-Fatāwā al-Ḥāmidiyya*, 2 vols. (Cairo: al-Maṭbaʿa al-Maymūniyya, 1893), I, 3; David S. Powers, "On Judicial Review in Islamic Law," *Law and Society Review*, 26, 2 (1992), 330–31, 332 ff. For the importance placed on keeping not only a record of the court proceedings but also a private record for the *qāḍī*, see Muḥammad b. ʿĪsā Ibn al-Munāṣif, *Tanbīh al-Ḥukkām ʿalā Maʾākhidh al-Aḥkām* (Tunis: Dār al-Turkī lil-Nashr, 1988), 67, 68; Ibn Abī al-Damm, *Adab al-Qaḍā'*, 71, 75–76. See also Ibn ʿĀbidīn, *Ḥāshiya*, V, 370.
[51] Jennings, "Kādī, Court," 134; Heyd, "Ottoman Fetva," 51–52.
[52] On *muftī*s discussing *fatwā*s with their students, and students copying the *fatwā*s of their *muftī* teachers, see Nawawī, *al-Majmūʿ*, I, 34, 48; Ḥājjī Khalīfa, *Kashf al-Ẓunūn*, II, 1218, 1219–20, 1221, 1222, 1223; Ibn Rushd, *Fatāwā*, III, 1517; *al-Fatāwā al-Hindiyya*, III, 309.

explains the survival of a great number of not only individual *fatwās* but also entire collections of these documents.[53]

8. Some *fatwās* seem hypothetical, dealing with "academic" issues, or issues addressing purely theoretical concerns. Careful examination of the sources, however, reveals that these *fatwās* are rooted in real situations, mostly legal disputes between individuals. A case in point is a typical question about the qualifications of *muftīs*. Although such a question echoes the highly theoretical discussions found in works of legal theory (*uṣūl al-fiqh*), the question itself emanates from actual legal disputes where one of the parties attempted to disqualify the *muftī* who had issued a *fatwā* that favored the other party.[54] The same motivation may be attributed to a question concerning whether or not a certain opinion was held by an acknowledged legal authority. Again, such questions were designed to obtain, in the form of a *fatwā*, either a confirmation or a rebuttal of another *fatwā* in which that opinion was expressed. We thus have good reason to believe that such *fatwās* constituted an integral part of court proceedings.[55]
9. The *fatwās* of distinguished jurisconsults were often collected in volumes and arranged, it seems, in the order in which they were issued.[56] In his *Fatāwā*, Nawawī remarks that in arranging his material he followed the order in which the questions were asked, and he expresses the hope that other scholars might at a later time rearrange them according to the conventional order of *fiqh* books, a task subsequently undertaken by Ibn Ibrāhīm al-ʿAṭṭār.[57] Ibn Rushd's *fatwās*, now available to us in a critical edition, are not arranged in any thematic or logical sequence. One *fatwā* deals with a real property dispute, the next with marriage or homicide. The haphazard

[53] In *Kashf al-Ẓunūn*, II, 1283 ff., Ḥājjī Khalīfa records no less than 160 titles of *fatwā* collections, while in his *Muḥāḍarāt fī Tārīkh al-Madhhab al-Mālikī* (Rabat: Manshūrāt ʿUkāz, 1987), 105–10, ʿUmar al-Jīdī lists at least 80 titles of Mālikite *fatwā* works.

[54] Ibn Rushd, *Fatāwā*, III, 3, 1274–75; Powers, "Judicial Review," 330 ff.

[55] See, e.g. Subkī, *Fatāwā*, II, 44, 83 ff., 325 ff., 422, and passim; Powers, "*Fatwās* as Sources," 298–300, 306–25, 330–31, 332; Powers, "Judicial Review," 330 ff.

[56] The fact that *fatwās* were answered in the order in which they were asked was found noteworthy. Ḥājjī Khalīfa (*Kashf al-Ẓunūn*, II, 1223) cites Ibn Nujaym's preface to his *al-Fatāwā al-Zayniyya* as follows: "I have answered questions in the order they have been asked since I sat for *iftā'* in the year 965 (1557 A.D.). Thereafter, I decided to arrange them according to the order of *fiqh* works. They number 400, not to mention those which I have not managed to copy down." Ibn ʿAbd al-Salām's *al-Fatāwā al-Mūṣiliyya*, we are told, represents questions to which Ibn ʿAbd al-Salām provided answers while he was residing in Mūṣil. The *Fatāwā* of Abū ʿAbd Allāh al-Khayyāṭī are reported to be "answers to questions he was asked about." In his *al-Fatāwā al-Nasafiyya*, Najm al-Dīn al-Nasafī is reported to have included the answers "to all the questions he was asked throughout his life, in addition to those given by others" (ibid., II, 1219, 1223, 1230). See further nn. 57–59, below.

[57] Ḥājjī Khalīfa, *Kashf al-Ẓunūn*, II, 1230; Nawawī, *Fatāwā*, 11. Ghazālī's *fatwās*, for instance, remained largely unknown and did not draw the attention of jurists. See Ḥājjī Khalīfa, *Kashf al-Ẓunūn*, II, 1227.

ordering of many *fatwā* collections suggests that the *fatwā*s were copied down in the chronological order in which they were issued. Clearly, this arrangement proved unsatisfactory in a tradition with a strong inclination toward systematic ordering of legal subject matter. We know, for instance, that Muḥammad b. Hārūn al-Kinānī and ʿAbd al-Raḥmān al-Qaysī rearranged Ibn Rushd's *fatwā*s according to *fiqh* topics, and that the latter rearranged Ibn al-Ḥājj's *fatwā*s in the same manner.[58] Kinānī and Muḥammad b. ʿUthmān al-Andalusī also abridged Ibn Rushd's *fatwā*s, and in the process apparently rearranged the order of the subjects treated therein.[59]

10. Analyses of *fatwā*s in the Ottoman and other periods and locales suggest that the manuals on the art of *iftā'* were highly practical and pragmatic. Heyd's description of the Ottoman practice of *iftā'* (with the exception of a few matters relating to the highest political echelons) corresponds with the prescriptions in these manuals. Moreover, even without the support of the Ottoman and other evidence, a reading of this genre leaves the distinct impression that they were the product of real situations and actual judicial practice. The prescriptions are heavily geared toward ensuring orderly, efficient, and fair practices on the part of both the jurisconsult and the questioner. Considerable attention is paid to a variety of matters revolving around curbing abuse of the system and stemming the forgery of *fatwā* documents.[60] Such issues would have no existential justification in these manuals if the *fatwā*s were merely a product of the jurists' idealistic and speculative mental constructions.

Finally, we note a significant feature in the practice of *iftā'* which acquired considerable importance in the Islamic tradition following the first century of the Hijra. This feature finds expression in the dictum that no *fatwā* should be issued with regard to a problem that has not yet occurred in the real world.[61] It might be argued that the repeated emphasis on this dictum suggests that the legal profession needed to curb the practice of asking about hypothetical cases. But the evidence afforded by our primary *fatwā*s does not support this contention, though it might be conceded that a rather small number of these *fatwā*s may have originated as hypothetical cases. There are at least three reasons why the assumption of the hypothetical origins of *fatwā*s is not tenable. First, the ethical and religious consequences of speculating on hypothetical cases were made so grave that violation of this dictum could have been neither normative nor frequent. The dictum was enshrined not only as a central legal postulate but also, and perhaps more importantly, as a religious tenet.

[58] See the editor's introduction to Ibn Rushd's *Fatāwā*, I, 89.

[59] Ibid. For other cases of rearrangement and abridgment, see Ḥājjī Khalīfa, *Kashf al-Ẓunūn*, II, 1223, 1229.

[60] Ibn al-Ṣalāḥ, *Adab al-Muftī*, I, 73, 74, 78–81.

[61] Tyan, *Histoire*, 219; *al-Fatāwā al-Hindiyya*, III, 309.

Second, a very great number of *fatwās* were destined for the courtroom,[62] where hypothetical musings have no place. It was not in the interest of any party to a dispute to misrepresent the case, for such a misrepresentation could result in the judge ignoring the *fatwā* altogether. We may assume that misrepresentation of the case in the *istiftā'* was occasionally attempted in order to solicit a *fatwā* in favor of the petitioner.[63] But since we may also assume that people generally do not act against their own best interests, instances of misrepresentation could not have been very abundant and, furthermore, would have been unlikely to escape the scrutiny of the judge whose task it was to investigate the facts of the case.

Third, in all the primary *fatwā* collections available to us, the majority of *fatwās* were solicited by judges and *muftīs*.[64] Those solicited by judges obviously point to litigation as their source, whereas those solicited by *muftīs* usually involve difficult questions of law which arose in most instances as court cases, and which the *muftī* addressed to another *muftī* of higher caliber. (Note, significantly, that the final appeal for hermeneutical engagement is still to a *muftī*.)

## IV

Once the *fatwā*, consisting of a rule based on concrete social reality, was issued, it was often incorporated into works of positive law (*furū*ᶜ).[65] Technically, these works constituted the highest authority as compilations of the law. Although they contained a hierarchy of doctrinal authority, they represented on the whole the standard legal doctrine of the schools. There is no question that the rules and principles within them were as

[62] On the importance of *fatwās* in the courtroom, see n. 38, above, and R. C. Jennings, "Limitations of the Judicial Powers of the Kādī in 17th C. Ottoman Kayseri," *Studia Islamica*, 50 (1979), 157 ff., 176 ff., 179; Jennings, "Kādī, Court," 134 ff.; Ibn ᶜĀbidīn, *Ḥāshiya*, V, 359, 360, 365; Ibn ᶜĀbidīn, *al-ᶜUqūd al-Durriyya*, I, 3; Ibn al-Ṣalāḥ, *Adab al-Muftī*, I, 71.

[63] Such attempts were often countered by *muftīs* who, when suspecting misrepresentation, opened their *fatwā* with the qualifying phrase: "If the matter is exactly as you have described it, then . . ." (*idhā kāna al-amr kamā dhakartum* . . . ). Such statements, we assume, were intended to caution judges of a possible discrepancy between the actual facts of the case and the litigant's description of those facts. See, e.g. Ibn Rushd, *Fatāwā*, I, 166, 191, 192, 195, 307, and passim; ᶜAlamī, *Nawāzil*, I, 74, 78, 110, 354, and passim.

[64] See, for instance, the *fatwā* collections of Taqī al-Dīn al-Subkī, Ibn Rushd, and Wansharīsī.

[65] Which *fatwās* were incorporated and which were not is a question we will discuss in due course.

a rule valid, although, as we saw in the preceding chapter, validity was subject to a hierarchical classification of doctrine that was set in motion and manipulated by what we have called operative terminology. On the whole, however, the *furūᶜ* works contained the "canonized" version of the law, and as such became the standard, authoritative reference for the legal profession.

In the opening pages of the preceding chapter we also saw that the legal opinions of the later followers of the four schools were considered part and parcel of the authoritative doctrine contained in *furūᶜ* works. In discussing the function of *fatwā*s in positive law we need only cite one example, in this case Ḥanafite legal doctrine. But it must be clear that what is said of this school is, *mutatis mutandis*, equally true of the other three.

The third of the three levels of Ḥanafite positive doctrine consists of what was termed *wāqiᶜāt* or *nawāzil*, namely, cases of law that were not addressed by the early masters and which were solved by later jurists.[66] Clearly, these cases were new and the jurists who were "*asked about them*" and who provided solutions for them "were many."[67] Ḥājjī Khalīfa reports that the first work known to have brought together these cases is *Kitāb Fatāwā al-Nawāzil* of Abū al-Layth al-Samarqandī (d. 383/993),[68] a work which, according to Samarqandī himself, consisted of *fatwās* (*taḥallā bi-masā'il al-fatāwā*).[69] Here we have the first explicit reference to the fact that substantive law included the *fatwā*s of later jurists. It is significant that, despite all attempts to maintain the integrity of each of the three levels of doctrine, the jurists were not always successful in doing so. We are told that after Abū al-Layth al-Samarqandī many jurists compiled works in which *fatwās* – belonging to the third level of *furūᶜ* doctrine – were brought together, but that some of the later jurists combined these *fatwās* with doctrines belonging to the other two levels of Ḥanafite legal doctrine, i.e. *ẓāhir al-riwāya* and *nawādir*. *Fatāwā Qāḍīkhān* and *al-Khulāṣa* are two examples in point.[70] It is also significant that some jurists found it noteworthy and commendable that in his *al-Muḥīṭ* Raḍī al-Dīn al-Sarakhsī recorded first the authoritative doctrines of the founding masters, then the *nawādir*, followed by the *fatwās*.[71] The fact that such highly regarded works as *Fatāwā* Qāḍīkhān (also known

[66] See chapter 2, section III, above. [67] See Ibn ᶜĀbidīn, *Ḥāshiya*, I, 69.

[68] *Kashf al-Ẓunūn*, II, 1281. See also Ibn ᶜĀbidīn, *Ḥāshiya*, I, 69. The work is said to contain the *fatwās* of Ibn Rustam, Muḥammad b. Samāᶜa, Abū Sulaymān al-Jūzajānī, Abū Ḥafṣ al-Bukhārī, Muḥammad b. Salama, Muḥammad b. Muqātil, and Abū Naṣr al-Qāsim b. Sallām.

[69] Samarqandī, *Fatāwā*, 1. [70] Ibn ᶜĀbidīn, *Ḥāshiya*, I, 69. [71] Ibid.

as *al-Fatāwā al-Khāniyya*)[72] did not maintain the strict categorization of Ḥanafite legal doctrine is quite telling, and demonstrates that while it was generally seen as desirable that the *ẓāhir al-riwāya* and *nawādir* be kept separate from the *fatwā*s, in practice the importance of the latter overrode such concerns.

That *fatwā*s were regularly incorporated into *furūᶜ* works is supported by a substantial body of evidence. Consider the following:

1. In his commentary on Nasafī's work, Ibn Nujaym states that he aimed to incorporate not only other commentaries on *Kanz al-Daqā'iq* but also the *fatwā*s of a number of jurisconsults. It turns out that he was able to draw on no less than twenty *fatwā* collections for this task.[73]
2. Nawawī reports that in his *Muhadhdhab*, Shīrāzī included "*al-fatāwā al-maqṭūᶜāt*," which I take to mean *fatwā*s that had come to be considered as having undisputed authority in his school. Likewise, in his own commentary on *al-Muhadhdhab*, Nawawī indicates that he incorporated the "*fatwā*s of our associates."[74]
3. In his commentary on Nawawī's *Minhāj*, a widely used work, Shihāb al-Dīn al-Ramlī assimilated not only the doctrines of many Shāfiᶜite jurists but also the *fatwā*s of his father, under whom he had studied, and which the father had endorsed after having reviewed them.[75] Ramlī's commentary became the standard reference for students, judges, and *muftī*s.[76]
4. In his gloss on Ramlī's commentary on Nawawī's *Minhāj*, Nūr al-Dīn al-Shabrāmallisī incorporated the *fatwā*s of Tāj al-Dīn al-Subkī, of his father Taqī al-Dīn, and of Bulqīnī. Shabrāmallisī speaks of these *fatwā*s as having a highly authoritative status in the Shāfiᶜite school.[77]
5. The Mālikite jurist Muḥammad al-Ḥaṭṭāb remarks that the *Mukhtaṣar* of Khalīl b. Isḥāq "clarified the cases issued as *fatwā*s." And in his commentary on the work, Ḥaṭṭāb included countless *fatwā*s issued by a number of distinguished jurisconsults, such as Ibn Rushd and Burzulī.[78]

[72] By Ḥasan b. Manṣūr al-Ūzajandī Qāḍīkhān. See the bibliography.

[73] These include *al-Muḥīṭ* of Sarakhsī; *al-Dhakhīra* of Ibn Māza; *al-Badā'iᶜ*, *al-Ziyādāt*, and *al-Fatāwā* of Qāḍīkhān; *al-Ẓahīriyya* of Muḥammad b. Aḥmad al-Ḥanafī; *al-Walwālijiyya* of Isḥāq b. Abī Bakr al-Walwālijī; *al-Khulāṣa* of Sirāj al-Dīn Ibn al-Mulaqqin; *al-Bazzāziyya* of Ibn Bazzāz al-Kurdarī; *al-ᶜUmda* and *al-ᶜUdda* of al-Ṣadr al-Shahīd; *Ma'āl al-Fatāwā* and *Multaqaṭ al-Fatāwā* of Nāṣir al-Dīn al-Samarqandī; *al-Ḥāwī al-Qudsī* of Najm al-Dīn al-Qazwīnī; *Qunyat al-ᶜĀlim* of Muḥammad b. Masᶜūd; and *al-Sirājiyya* of Sirāj al-Dīn al-Awshī. See Zayn al-Dīn, Ibn Nujaym, *al-Baḥr al-Rā'iq: Sharḥ Kanz al-Daqā'iq*, 8 vols. (Cairo: al-Maṭbaᶜa al-ᶜIlmiyya, 1893), I, 2–3.

[74] Nawawī, *al-Majmūᶜ*, I, 3, 5. [75] See his *Nihāyat al-Muḥtāj*, I, 9–10.

[76] Ibid., I, 2.

[77] See his *Ḥāshiya ᶜalā Nihāyat al-Muḥtāj: Sharḥ al-Minhāj*, printed on the margins of Ramlī, *Nihāyat al-Muḥtāj*, I, 41–42 (Beirut repr.).

[78] See his *Mawāhib al-Jalīl*, VI, 32, 36, 37, 48, 49, 55, 75, 93, 94, 285, 287 ff., 326, 331 f., and passim.

6. In a specialized *furūᶜ* treatise, dealing with the bindingness of contracts and of other transactions (*iltizām*), Ḥaṭṭāb draws heavily on a number of collections of primary *fatwā*s, chief among which are those of Ibn Rushd, Burzulī, and Ibn al-Ḥājj.[79]
7. In another specialized work on damages (*ḍamānāt*), the Ḥanafite jurist Muḥammad b. Ghānim al-Baghdādī acknowledged that he drew on "reliable *fatwā* collections" (*al-kutub al-muᶜtabara fī al-fatwā*).[80]
8. The Mālikite jurist Ibn Salmūn al-Kinānī incorporated in his *al-ᶜIqd al-Munaẓẓam lil-Ḥukkām*, a *furūᶜ* work intended for the use of judges, "individual *fatwā*s" (*nawāzil fardiyya*).[81]
9. In his *Ḥāshiya ᶜalā Radd al-Muḥtār*, Ibn ᶜĀbidīn relies heavily on the *fatwā* literature, which he includes in his work because, *inter alia*, he "feared [that] the *ruqᶜa*s of the *fatwā*s might be lost."[82] This statement suggests that Ibn ᶜĀbidīn had in his possession original *fatwā* documents. Furthermore, he remarks that in addition to his free use of *fatwā*s (*uṭliqu fī al-fatāwā*) in his work, he constantly referred to the writings of those jurists who committed themselves to the study and issuance of *fatwā*s, including Ibn al-Humām, Ibn Amīr al-Ḥājj, al-Ramlī, Ibn Nujaym, Ibn Shalabī, Ismāᶜīl al-Ḥāʾik, and Ḥānūtī.[83]

## V

Now, if *fatwā*s did make inroads into works of positive law, three questions become pertinent: First, how were these *fatwā*s incorporated into *furūᶜ* works? Second, what types of *fatwā*s were deemed appropriate for such incorporation? And third, why were they incorporated?

To answer the first question, we must invoke again our distinction between primary and modified *fatwā*s, or between primary and modified *fatwā* collections. We have seen that *fatwā*s originate in a question – posed by a layman or a legist – to which an answer is provided by a jurisconsult. Some of these primary *fatwā*s found their way into the *furūᶜ* works through one of two channels, one direct, the other indirect. Two examples of a direct channel are the *fatwā*s of Ibn Rushd which made

[79] See his *Taḥrīr al-Kalām fī Masāʾil al-Iltizām*, ed. ᶜAbd al-Salām Muḥammad al-Sharīf (Beirut: Dār al-Gharb al-Islāmī, 1984), 79–80, 85 f., 88, 89, 93, 99, 105, 106, 113, 114 f., 177, 182, 192, 207, 224, 231, and passim. Note that the *fatwā*s collected by Burzulī, as yet unedited, belong to a number of jurists.

[80] See his *Majmaᶜ al-Ḍamānāt*, 2.

[81] 2 vols. (Cairo: al-Maṭbaᶜa al-Amīriyya al-Sharafiyya, 1301/1883), I, 2.

[82] The fear of losing *fatwā*s appears to have been widespread. See, e.g., Bāᶜlawī, *Bughyat al-Mustarshidīn*, 3, who, despite having completed his work, continued to append to it new *fatwā*s issued by himself and by other jurisconsults "for fear they might be lost."

[83] See his *Ḥāshiya*, I, 3–4.

their way into the *furūᶜ* works entitled *Mawāhib al-Jalīl* and *Taḥrīr al-Kalām*, both by Ḥaṭṭāb,[84] and the *fatwā*s of Ramlī's father which were incorporated in Ramlī's commentary on Nawawī's *Minhāj*.[85]

Primary *fatwā*s were regularly collected either by the jurisconsults themselves or by their students or associates (*aṣḥāb*). These collections may be limited exclusively to a single *muftī* or they may include the primary *fatwā*s of a number (sometimes a large number) of *muftī*s. Examples of the first type are Ibn Rushd, Nawawī, and Subkī's *fatwā* collections, and of the second, Wansharīsī, ᶜAlamī, and Burzulī's works.[86] As a rule, the primary *fatwā*s found in both types of collection are generally unedited, although exceptions to this rule may be found.[87]

The other channel was less direct, involving a lengthy process of collecting, editing, and abridging primary *fatwā*s for inclusion in collections that were not concerned with the *fatwā*s of particular jurisconsults, but rather with gathering *fatwā* material in order to constitute a work of *fiqh*. To these we have referred as modified *fatwā*s. Abū al-Layth al-Samarqandī and Nāṭifī, for instance, are said to have collected in their works – *Kitāb al-Nawāzil* and *Majmaᶜ al-Nawāzil wal-Wāqiᶜāt*, respectively – the *fatwā*s of the founding imams as well as *fatwā*s issued by jurisconsults such as Muḥammad b. Shujāᶜ al-Thaljī, Muḥammad b. Muqātil al-Rāzī and Jaᶜfar b. ᶜAlī al-Hinduwānī.[88] Similarly, Ḥusām al-Dīn al-Bukhārī is reported to have included in his *al-Wāqiᶜāt al-Ḥusāmiyya* not only the *fatwā*s contained in Abū al-Layth al-Samarqandī's and Nāṭifī's works but also those issued by later *muftī*s.[89] To this genre belong a great number of collections, of which we have in print *al-Fatāwā al-Khāniyya* by Qāḍīkhān, *al-Fatāwā al-Bazzāziyya* by Muḥammad al-Bazzāzī al-Kurdarī, and *al-Fatāwā al-Hindiyya*, compiled by a group of scholars under the supervision of the Ḥanafite jurist al-Shaykh al-Niẓām.[90] It is clear from the sources that the individual *fatwā*s in these collections underwent considerable editing and abridgment. Of this we will have something to say presently. The point, however, is that the *fatwā*s in these collections were incorporated into the commentative *furūᶜ*

[84] See nn. 79–80, above. [85] See n. 75, above. [86] See the bibliography, below.

[87] See, e.g. the editorial notes on Ibn Rushd's *Fatāwā*, where Burzulī seems to have edited or abridged some of Ibn Rushd's *fatwā*s (I, 177, 185, 207, 211, 231, and passim).

[88] Ḥājjī Khalīfa, *Kashf al-Ẓunūn*, II, 1220, 1281; Ibn ᶜĀbidīn, *Ḥāshiya*, I, 69.

[89] Ḥājjī Khalīfa, *Kashf al-Ẓunūn*, II, 2, 1228; N. Aghnides, *Mohammedan Theories of Finance* (New York: Columbia University Press, 1916), 184.

[90] On the latter, see Joseph Schacht, "On the Title of the *Fatāwā ᶜAlamgīriyya*," in C. E. Bosworth, ed., *Iran and Islam* (Edinburgh: Edinburgh University Press, 1971), 475–78.

works, as attested in the case of Ibn Nujaym, who assimilated no less than twenty such *fatwā* collections into his *al-Baḥr al-Rā'iq*.[91]

Just as primary *fatwās* underwent considerable transformation during the process of their assimilation into *furūᶜ* works, so they underwent a similar transformation in their passage from primary to modified *fatwās*. The path from the primary to the secondary or modified stage involved two practices, *tajrīd* and *talkhīṣ*;[92] and it seems that the term "*tanqīḥ*" was used to lump these two practices together.[93] *Tajrīd*, which may be rendered as "to make abstract," involved stripping a primary *fatwā* of a number of elements essential neither to a *furūᶜ* work nor to a modified *fatwā* collection. Although jurisconsults generally did not state the line of reasoning that led them to the opinion expressed in a *fatwā*,[94] some did include relatively detailed statements of legal reasoning.[95] *Tajrīd* referred to the process of omitting such details,[96] as well as any real or hypothetical names which happened to be mentioned. It also involved the omission of all words and phrases irrelevant to the law, such as religious formulas, the phrases "He was asked . . ." and "He answered . . ." and any introductory words indicating that the jurisconsults had carefully read and studied the *fatwā*. And since many *fatwās* contained legal documents, especially contracts, it was the function of *tajrīd* to omit these documents too. But because the complete omission of a document might distort the facts and law in the *fatwā* (*ṣūrat al-fatwā*), a second practice was resorted to, namely, *talkhīṣ* (abridgment).

[91] See n. 73, above.

[92] On *tajrīd*, see Nawawī, *al-Majmūᶜ*, I, 1, 57; Ḥājjī Khalīfa, *Kashf al-Ẓunūn*, II, 1887. On *talkhīṣ*, see the introduction to Ibn Rushd's *Fatāwā*, I, 89; Bāᶜlawī, *Bughyat al-Mustarshidīn*, 2. *Talkhīṣ* is also attested in Ibn Ziyād's work *Kitāb Ghāyat Talkhīṣ al-Murād min Fatāwā Ibn Ziyād*, printed on the margins of Bāᶜalawī's *Bughyat al-Mustarshidīn*, 79 ff.

[93] As expressed in Ibn ᶜĀbidīn's title, *al-ᶜUqūd al-Durriyya fī Tanqīḥ al-Fatāwā al-Ḥāmidiyya*. See also previous note.

[94] The practice of including arguments and lines of reasoning leading to the opinion was not recommended. See Nawawī, *al-Majmūᶜ*, I, 52, 57; Ibn al-Ṣalāḥ, *Adab al-Muftī*, 141; *al-Fatāwā al-Hindiyya*, III, 309. It is noteworthy that Ibn al-Ṣalāḥ enjoins a short, unreasoned answer so that the *fatwā* would not be confused with *taṣnīf*, the product of the author–jurist, not the *muftī*.

[95] See. e.g. Ibn Rushd, *Fatāwā*, I, 357 ff., 446 ff., 461, 617; II, 1196 ff.; Subkī, *Fatāwā*, II, 187 ff. *Fatwās* that included statements of legal reasoning were ordinarily issued upon the request of a judge or another *muftī*. In such cases, the *fatwās* were considered to be the product of *taṣnīf*, not necessarily *iftā'*. See previous note.

[96] See, e.g. Ibn ᶜĀbidīn, *al-ᶜUqūd al-Durriyya*, I, 2; Ḥājjī Khalīfa, *Kashf al-Ẓunūn*, II, 1887; Nawawī, *al-Majmūᶜ*, I, 57. See also Ḥaṭṭāb, *Mawāhib al-Jalīl*, VI, 94 (l. –12): "*mujarrad aqwāl Mālik*."

To illustrate the processes of *tajrīd* and *talkhīṣ*, we shall discuss a *fatwā* first issued by Ibn Rushd and later incorporated into the works of Ḥaṭṭāb and Ibn Salmūn al-Kinānī, two author–jurists. The Arabic text of the primary *fatwā*[97] contains 248 words, whereas the secondary, modified version[98] comprises only 110:

> [Ibn Rushd], may God be pleased with him, was asked about two men who fought each other; the name of the first is Abū al-Walīd and of the second ᶜAbd al-Malik. Abū al-Walīd inflicted upon ᶜAbd al-Malik a wound with a knife belonging to him, so ᶜAbd al-Malik, in the company of a relative named ᶜUmar, pursued Abū al-Walīd, who had injured him. On their way, ᶜAbd al-Malik and ᶜUmar met the brother of Abū al-Walīd whose name was Muḥammad. ᶜUmar held Muḥammad, the brother of Abū al-Walīd, and said to ᶜAbd al-Malik, "Strike to kill." Thus, he wounded Muḥammad. Each of the two parties inflicted injuries upon the other [in the process]: ᶜAbd al-Malik wounded Abū al-Walīd, and Muḥammad, the brother of Abū al-Walīd, wounded both ᶜAbd al-Malik and ᶜUmar, who held him. The injuries which the parties inflicted upon each other were confirmed by witnesses, but the testimony concerning the injury Muḥammad inflicted on both ᶜAbd al-Malik and ᶜUmar was inconsistent with the [actual] wound. Muḥammad died as a result of the injury. Abū al-Walīd sought to avenge his brother's death at the hands of ᶜAbd al-Malik and ᶜUmar, but he could procure no witnesses to take an oath against them, though he claims to have [as witnesses] two paternal cousins in another town. Should ᶜAbd al-Malik be executed on the basis of these [testimonial] oaths before he is healed of the injuries inflicted upon him by Abū al-Walīd? Or should the execution be delayed until he recovers?
>
> [Ibn Rushd] answered as follows: I have read your question and carefully considered it. The fact that an injury was inflicted by Muḥammad upon ᶜAbd al-Malik and his relative ᶜUmar is acknowledged, although no witnesses may have seen the [actual] wound; the injury is confirmed if other witnesses testify that an injury was inflicted upon him. ᶜAbd al-Malik should not be executed on account of the oaths until he recovers from his wounds, because this would abridge the rights of his relatives insofar as the punishment of his murderer is concerned.[99] Rather, all three assailants – Abū al-Walīd, ᶜUmar, and ᶜAbd al-Malik – should be jailed. If ᶜAbd al-Malik recovers from his wounds, and if Abū al-Walīd brings his cousins to take an oath, and they do take an oath against ᶜUmar and ᶜAbd al-Malik,

[97] Ibn Rushd, *Fatāwā*, I, 575–77. [98] In Ḥaṭṭāb, *Mawāhib al-Jalīl*, VI, 271.

[99] For, if he dies as a result of his wounds, his relatives are entitled to avenge his death. Were ᶜAbd al-Malik to be executed immediately, therefore, it would become impossible to establish that death would have resulted from the injury, thereby denying the rights of his relatives.

> then they both [ᶜUmar and ᶜAbd al-Malik] should be executed on the basis of these oaths, for that is sufficient grounds for their execution. If ᶜAbd al-Malik dies as a result of the wounds inflicted upon him, Abū al-Walīd, together with his cousins, may take an oath against ᶜUmar and they are entitled to have him executed. Likewise, the relatives of ᶜAbd al-Malik may take an oath against Abū al-Walīd, and on the basis of these oaths can have him executed. God is He who bestows peace.

From this point on, the *fatwā* is appropriated by the author–jurist who subjects it to the imperatives of his discourse. In the sections treating of penal law in his *Mawāhib al-Jalīl*, Ḥaṭṭāb produces an abridged version of the *fatwā* as a case of law (*farᶜ*) subsumed under the category of injuries. Having already cited Ibn Rushd with regard to another case, he states:

> In his *nawāzil*,[100] Ibn Rushd also said: A man inflicted a wound upon another and the brother of the former was also wounded by the latter, together with a relative of his. The relative held him and said to the other, "Strike to kill." The second man who was injured died. His brother wanted to avenge his death. Can the injured man, and his relative, be executed on the basis of testimonial oaths before the wounds inflicted upon him have healed, or should he be imprisoned until he recovers?
>
> He answered: The injured man should not be executed until the wounds inflicted upon him have healed, because this would abridge the rights of his relatives insofar as the punishment of his murderer is concerned.[101] Rather, all three assailants should be jailed. If the first man injured recovers from his wounds, then the brother of the dead man will take an oath together with one of his cousins against him as well as against his relative, and accordingly they will be executed on the basis of these oaths.[102]

In the edited version, not only are the names of the disputants omitted but also several details deemed by Ḥaṭṭāb to be devoid of legal relevance. The fact that the wounds were inflicted "with a knife belonging to" Abū al-Walīd, and the fact, repeated twice, that Muḥammad was the brother of Abū al-Walīd, are deleted in Ḥaṭṭāb's recension. Also omitted is the fact that the witnesses did not attest to the actual wound and that the witnesses testifying on behalf of Abū al-Walīd were unavailable because they resided in another town. Note also that the *istiftā'* appears to have been formulated by a person who was not particularly adept in legal matters. This is evidenced in the fact that repetition and irrelevant details

[100] I.e. *fatwā*s. The two terms are synonymous and were used interchangeably. Strictly speaking, the term *nawāzil* (sing. *nāzila*) refers to problems befalling the *mustaftī*, whereas the term *fatwā*s signifies the solution to such problems. But such distinctions do not seem to have been maintained in legal discourse.

[101] See n. 99, above. [102] Ḥaṭṭāb, *Mawāhib al-Jalīl*, VI, 271–72.

constantly surface in the text of the question. But Ḥaṭṭāb's exercise of *tajrīd* and *talkhīṣ* transforms the *fatwā* from a case of law pertaining to a particular and highly contextualized situation into an abstract case fit for inclusion in a standard *furūᶜ* work.

We now come to our second question: What types of *fatwā* were incorporated in *furūᶜ* works? To answer this question, we must first draw attention to a central fact that determined the nature of works treating substantive law, be they *furūᶜ* or primary and modified *fatwā* collections. The overriding concern of the authors of these works was the incorporation of law cases that were deemed relevant and necessary to the age in which they were writing. This is evidenced not only in the incorporation in their *furūᶜ* works of the latest *fatwā*s, but also in the untiring insistence of virtually all these author–jurists on the necessity of including in their works cases deemed to be relevant to contemporary needs and of wide occurrence (*mā taᶜummu bi-hi al-balwā*), and to exclude those of little or no relevance to the community and its needs.[103] In his *Fatāwā*, Qāḍīkhān includes only those cases that were of frequent occurrence (*yaghlubu wuqūᶜuhā*) or much needed (*tamissu al-ḥāja ilayhā*) and around which the problems arising in the community revolve (*tadūru ᶜalayhā wāqiᶜāt al-umma*). These cases belong either to the early masters or to the later jurisprudents (*al-mashāyikh al-muta'akhkhirīn*).[104] Zaylaᶜī informs us that he chose to comment on *Kanz al-Daqā'iq* because he thought it to be a superior abridgment containing "cases that are needed" (*mā yuḥtāju ilayhi min al-wāqiᶜāt*). And in his commentary, he declares, he added law cases that were needed and that belonged to the later jurisprudents.[105] Ramlī states that in his commentary on Rāfiᶜī's *Muḥarrar*, Nawawī incorporated cases that were needed and that Rāfiᶜī had neglected to include (*zāda . . . mā akhalla bihi min al-furūᶜ al-muḥtāj ilayhā*).[106] Ibn al-Ṣalāḥ is widely reported, with approval, to have argued that when a *muftī* or a judge is

[103] On the exclusion of legal doctrines that are not "in circulation," see Ramlī, *al-Fatāwā al-Khayriyya*, I, 3; Abū ᶜAbd Allāh Muḥammad b. Ḥārith al-Khushanī, *Uṣūl al-Futyā fī al-Fiqh*, ed. Muḥammad Majdūb (Beirut: al-Muᶜassasa al-Waṭaniyyal lil-Kitāb, 1985), 44.

[104] Qāḍīkhān, *Fatāwā*, I, 2. For a similar approach, see ᶜAlamī, *Nawāzil*, I, 18. Ḥājjī Khalīfa, *Kashf al-Ẓunūn*, II, 1282–83, remarks that the term *muta'akhkhirūn* refers to the jurisconsults who flourished after the fourth/tenth century.

[105] ᶜUthmān b. ᶜAlī al-Zaylaᶜī, *Tabyīn al-Ḥaqā'iq: Sharḥ Kanz al-Daqā'iq*, 6 vols. (Būlāq: al-Maṭbaᶜa al-Kubrā al-Amīriyya, 1313/1895), I, 2. For similar statements, see Kurdarī, *Fatāwā*, IV, 2; Mūṣilī, *Ikhtiyār*, I, 6. Likewise, Nawawī, after completing the first three volumes of his *al-Majmūᶜ* and finding the material to be too imposing, decided to expand only on those cases that were of general relevance and to abridge in those that were not. See his *al-Majmūᶜ*, I, 6.

[106] Ramlī, *Nihāyat al-Muḥtāj*, I, 45.

faced with a problem for which there are two equally valid solutions in the school, he must resort to the chronologically later solution.[107]

That a chronologically later opinion must replace an earlier one of equal validity is a doctrine that finds considerable support in our sources. As summarized by the Ḥanafite jurist Qāḍīkhān, this doctrine was, *mutatis mutandis*, accepted in all four schools: He explains that if the solution to the case is found in *ẓāhir al-riwāya* without disagreement, then it must be adopted. If the case is, on the other hand, subject to disagreement, then it is to Abū Ḥanīfa's own doctrine, not that of his two disciples, that the jurisconsult must resort. But if their disagreement is relevant to the needs of a particular age, then the opinions of his two disciples must be followed on the grounds that the "conditions of people do change" (*li-taghayyur aḥwāl al-nās*). In matters of contracts and commercial transactions, Qāḍīkhān tells us, the later jurists resorted to the doctrines of Abū Yūsuf and Shaybānī rather than to those of Abū Ḥanīfa.[108] The same principle governs the choice between doctrines belonging to earlier and later centuries. Ibn ᶜĀbidīn remarks that a substantial segment of Ḥanafite legal doctrine was formulated at a later date by jurists who sometimes held opinions different from those of the founders.[109] The Shāfiᶜite legist Khayr al-Dīn al-Ramlī is said to have followed Ḥanafite doctrine in issuing his *fatwā*s, including the opinions of the major jurists who modified the early doctrines *due to the changing of the times or to the changing conditions of society* (*li-ikhtilāf al-ᶜaṣr aw li-taghayyur aḥwāl al-nās*).[110] Apparently for the same reasons, Shihāb al-Dīn al-Ramlī included in his *furūᶜ* work, *Nihāyat al-Muḥtāj*, the doctrines of the later jurists, including Nawawī, Jalāl al-Dīn al-Maḥallī, Rāfiᶜī, and his own father.[111]

We must emphasize that the process of assimilating later *fatwā*s was selective, and only those *fatwā*s that added new material to the current body of legal doctrines were included. In compiling the *fatwā*s of his father Khayr al-Dīn, Muḥyī al-Dīn al-Ramlī considered for inclusion only those which he could not find in contemporary works and which had become much needed and oft-referred to in his own time.[112] The Mālikite jurisprudent Khushanī followed the same practice in his *Uṣūl*

[107] See, e.g. Bāᶜalawī, *Bughyat al-Mustarshidīn*, 8–9, on the authority of Abu Bakr al-Ashkhar. Ibn al-Ṣalāḥ states his opinion in his *Adab al-Muftī*, 123.

[108] Qāḍīkhān, *Fatāwā*, I, 2–3. [109] Ibn ᶜĀbidīn, *Ḥāshiya*, I, 69.

[110] Ramlī, *al-Fatāwā al-Khayriyya*, I, 3.

[111] Ramlī, *Nihāyat al-Muḥtāj*, I, 9–10. See also Ḥaṭṭāb, *Mawāhib al-Jalīl*, I, 31; Baghdādī, *Majmaᶜ al-Ḍamānāt*, 2.

[112] Ramlī, *al-Fatāwā al-Khayriyya*, 3.

*al-Futyā*, excluding those *fatwā*s that had gone out of currency or contained opinions that were considered irregular (*gharīb*).[113] We can thus safely assume that such *fatwā*s, as well as *fatwā*s that merely cited earlier authorities with regard to the same facts and with no qualification or addition (a practice known as *al-iftā' bil-ḥifẓ*),[114] were excluded as candidates for incorporation in both *fatwā* collections and *furū*ᶜ works. In fact, *al-iftā' bil-ḥifẓ* was not, strictly speaking, considered to constitute *iftā'* proper,[115] and was thus *ab initio* precluded from the recorded literature of *fatwā*.

Another category of *fatwā* excluded from positive legal works is that which contained weak opinions, based on unauthoritative legal doctrines (*al-ra'y al-ḍa*ᶜ*īf*). We have no evidence that such *fatwā*s, and *fatwā*s that merely relayed an established doctrine, ever found a place in the primary *fatwā* collections. Thus, our sources indicate that the primary *fatwā*s that appeared in these collections and those that were incorporated in *furū*ᶜ works were those that had been issued in response to new or partly new facts and situations. These novel circumstances, in turn, gave new significance to the statements of law, and this qualified them as new cases of law.

Let us now turn to our third, and most important, question: Why were these *fatwā*s incorporated in the *furū*ᶜ works? We must state at the outset that one of the most important functions of *furū*ᶜ works was to provide the jurisconsults with a comprehensive coverage of substantive rules, foremost among which were those that attained an authoritative status. These works were expected to offer solutions for all conceivable cases so that the jurisconsult might draw on them for the authoritative doctrine, and to include the most recent as well as the oldest cases of law that had arisen in the school. This explains why *fatwā*s were incorporated into these works, for they represented the oldest and most recent material relevant to the needs of society and responsive to the changes it had undergone over time. Primary *fatwā*s then provided a continuous source from which the law derived its ever-expanding body of material. This is why *ᶜilm al-fatwā* was often equated, and often used synonymously, with *fiqh*,[116] for *fiqh* was deemed largely the sum total of *fatwā*s that had entered the body of *furū*ᶜ.

113 Khushanī, *Uṣūl al-Futyā*, 44.

114 See, e.g. Ḥaṭṭāb, *Mawāhib al-Jalīl*, I, 33 (ll. 8–10).

115 Bāᶜalawī, *Bughyat al-Mustarshidīn*, 7; Ibn ᶜĀbidīn, *Ḥāshiya*, V, 366; Hallaq, "*Iftā'* and *Ijtihād*," 34, 336, n. 1.

116 See, e.g. Ghazālī's statement to this effect, quoted in Ḥājjī Khalīfa, *Kashf al-Ẓunūn*, II, 1281.

To say this is in fact to argue that it was the *muftī* and the author–jurist – not the *qāḍī* or anyone else – who were responsible for the development of the legal doctrine embodied in *furūᶜ* works. Thus far there is no good reason to disagree with the findings of such scholars as Schacht and G. H. Juynboll concerning the important role that early judges played in the formation of Islamic substantive law.[117] But after the second/eighth century, their contribution appears to have come to a halt, while the elaboration of law seems to have become almost exclusively the province of the *muftī* and the author–jurist.[118]

Although it was the common practice for judges to retain a record of court proceedings,[119] their decisions do not appear to have attracted the attention of the jurists who were concerned with elaborating and establishing the *furūᶜ* doctrines of their school. True, questions arising in judicial disputes (*muḥākamāt* or *ḥukūmāt*) were intensely discussed by *fuqahā'*, but these discussions seem always to have been connected with *fatwā*s that were issued specifically for such occasions.[120] The relationship between *fatwā*s and the *muḥākamāt* is explained by the fact that the judge depended heavily upon the *muftī*'s opinions,[121] for, as we have seen, judges commonly made recourse to the *muftī*s' opinions.[122] In fact, the judge's dependence upon the *fatwā* was so great that a *muftī* was often attached to the court; in later periods of Islamic history, his *fatwā* was considered binding.[123] Some legists went so far as to espouse the view that the decision of an ignorant and foolish judge remains valid as long as it is based on a jurisconsult's *fatwā*.[124]

The stipulation that the judge must resort to the *muftī* for legal advice underscores the fact that it is the *muftī*, not the *qāḍī*, who is the ultimate

117 Schacht, *Introduction*, 25 ff., summarizing his findings in his *Origins*; G. H. A. Juynboll, *Muslim Tradition: Studies in Chronology, Provenance and Authorship of Early Hadith* (Cambridge: Cambridge University Press, 1983), 77–95; G. H. A. Juynboll, "Some Notes on Islam's First *Fuqahā'* Distilled From Early *Hadīt* Literature," *Arabica* 39 (1992): 287–314.

118 Needless to say, this transformation still awaits investigation.

119 See Hallaq, "The Qāḍī's *Dīwān*," 422–29.

120 See Subkī, *Fatāwā*, II, 44, 183 ff., 325 ff., 422, and passim; Powers, "Judicial Review," 330–31, 332; Powers, "*Fatwā*s as Sources," 298–300, 306–25, 330–31, 332.

121 Ibn ᶜĀbidīn, *al-ᶜUqūd al-Durriyya*, I, 3; Ibn ᶜĀbidīn, *Ḥāshiya*, V, 359, 360, 365.

122 *Al-Fatāwā al-Hindiyya*, III, 312, 313; Ibn ᶜĀbidīn, *Ḥāshiya*, V, 360, 365. See also nn. 50, 51, 55, 62, above, as well as next note.

123 See Tyan, *Histoire*, 224; Rudolph Peters, "Murder on the Nile: Homicide Trials in 19th Century Egyptian Shariᶜa Courts," *Die Welt des Islams*, 30 (1990), 99. Similarly, the fact that the Chief Muftī of the Ottoman empire (Shaykh al-Islām) was in charge of the administration of the court system is significant.

124 *Al-Fatāwā al-Hindiyya*, III, 307.

expert on the law. This conclusion is reinforced by a number of considerations: First of all, the final goal of the methodology of *uṣūl al-fiqh* is *ijtihād*, performed by the *mujtahid*. As we saw in chapter 3, it was the *muftī*, not the *qāḍī*, who was equated with the *mujtahid*. Indeed, in the discourse of *uṣūl al-fiqh*, the terms *mujtahid* and *muftī* were used synonymously.[125] Second, throughout most of its history, and with the exception of the Ottoman period, the office of *iftā'* was largely independent of governmental interference; unlike judgeship, it was considered immune from political corruption. This is why many jurists regarded the duty to issue *fatwā*s obligatory (*farḍ kifāya*), whereas accepting the office of *qāḍī* was viewed with suspicion.[126] Formulating the law could not have been the responsibility of an institution that was commonly perceived as marred by worldly temptations and various sorts of corruption. This suspicion of *qāḍī*s was sanctioned by a divine message, delivered through the medium of the Prophet: "On the Day of Resurrection the judges will join the Sultans, but the *ᶜulamā'* [=*muftī*s] will join the Prophets."[127]

Third, the decisions of the *qāḍī*s do not appear, to any noticeable extent, to have been taken into account in *furūᶜ* works, whereas, as we have seen, *fatwā*s provided the primary source material for the elaboration and expansion of *furūᶜ*. If occasional court cases entered works of positive law, they did so through the *muftī*'s or the author–jurist's intervention. Fourth, it was held that the decision of the judge is particular (*juz'ī*, *khāṣṣ*) and that its import does not transcend the interests of the parties to a dispute, whereas the *fatwā* of the jurisconsult is universal (*ᶜāmm*, *kullī*) and thus applicable to all similar cases.[128]

125 Hallaq, "*Ifta'* and *Ijtihād*," 34 ff.; see also *al-Fatāwā al-Hindiyya*, III, 308: "It is the unshakable opinion of the legal theorists that the *muftī* is the *mujtahid*" (*istaqarra ra'yu al-uṣūliyyīn anna al-muftī huwa al-mujtahid*). See also Ibn ᶜĀbidīn, *Ḥāshiya*, V, 365, who equates the *muftī* with the *mujtahid* and asserts that the *qāḍī* is not required to be qualified as a *mujtahid*, "for it is sufficient for him to act upon the *ijtihād* of others." For a fuller treatment of the issue, see chapter 3, above.

126 *Al-Fatāwā al-Hindiyya*, III, 311: "*al-dukhūl fī al-qaḍā' rukhṣa wal-imtināᶜ ᶜanhu ᶜazīma.*"

127 Ibid., III, 310, where several jurists are cited to support the opinion that no jurist should accept a judgeship unless he is coerced to do so. See also ᶜAlī b. Yaḥyā al-Jazīrī, *al-Maqṣad al-Maḥmūd fī Talkhīṣ al-ᶜUqūd*, ed. A. Ferreras (Madrid: Consejo Superior de Investigaciones Científicas, 1998), 456. On the other hand, Nawawī (*al-Majmūᶜ*, I, 40) cites the widely accepted dictum that the *muftī*s are the heirs of the prophets. See also Brinkley Messick, *The Calligraphic State: Textual Domination and History in a Muslim Society* (Berkeley: University of California Press, 1993), 143–4.

128 Ibn Qayyim al-Jawziyya, *Iᶜlām al-Muwaqqiᶜīn*, I, 38: "*al-ḥākim ḥukmuhu juz'ī khāṣṣ lā yatᶜaddā ilā ghayri al-maḥkūmī ᶜalayh wa-lahu, wa'l-muftī yuftī ḥukman ᶜāmman kulliyan anna man faᶜala kadhā tarattaba ᶜalayhi kadhā wa-man qāla kadhā lazimahu kadhā.*"

Furthermore, the crucial role played by the *fatwā* in the formation of substantive law is nowhere more evident than in the dialectical relationship between *fatwā* and *madhhab*, the established and authoritative legal doctrine of the school. In chapter 5 we have shown that the *madhhab* as the authoritative doctrine of the school was defined by the practice of *iftā'*: what *fatwā*s commonly determined to be the law was the *madhhab*-opinion.[129] In his *Nihāyat al-Muḥtāj*, Ramlī, who draws on several *fatwā* collections, declared that he limited his work solely to the doctrines that were widely accepted and applied in the *madhhab* (*muqtaṣiran fī-hi ᶜalā al-maᶜmūl bihi fī al-madhhab*).[130] In legal jargon, Ramlī argues, the term *madhhab* signifies nothing more than the school's doctrine as determined by means of *fatwā*, for the latter "is more important for the *faqīh* than anything else."[131]

The dialectical relationship between *fatwā* and *madhhab* also meant that the *fatwā* must conform to the *madhhab*. In fact, it was a fundamental legal tenet that no *fatwā* would be deemed admissible if it were found to be at variance with the authoritative legal doctrine of the school. This did not mean that new problems could not elicit new solutions, but rather that in issuing legal opinions the jurisconsult must abide by the established doctrine if he finds a precedent; otherwise, he must resort to the revealed texts, and, on their basis, must apply, in a careful and prudent manner, the substantive principles established in *qawāᶜid*[132] and the methodology prescribed in *uṣūl al-fiqh*.[133] A *fatwā* would thus be inadmissible if it did not accord with a doctrine that had been subject to *tarjīḥ*, *taṣḥīḥ*, or *tashhīr*.[134] When Zaqqāq was asked about the duration of *ᶜidda* in the case of menstruating women, he fixed it at three months, dismissing as unworthy of the jurisconsult's attention – because it failed to accord with the *mashhūr* of the *madhhab* – a *fatwā* issued by a certain Dāwūdī fixing the duration at six months.[135]

The dialectical relationship between *fatwā* and *madhhab* is underscored by the terminology used to identify the processes of authorizing and

[129] Ḥaṭṭāb, *Mawāhib al-Jalīl*, I, 24; Ramlī, *Nihāyat al-Muḥtāj*, I, 36–37. See also chapter 5, section VI, above.
[130] See his *Nihāyat al-Muḥtāj*, I, 9.
[131] Ibid., I, 36–37. See also Ḥaṭṭāb, *Mawāhib al-Jalīl*, I, 24 (ll. 9–10).
[132] On *qawāᶜid*, see Jīdī, *Muḥāḍarāt*, 59 ff. See also chapter 4, nn. 87–89, above.
[133] Ḥaṭṭāb, *Mawāhib al-Jalīl*, VI, 96.
[134] ᶜAlamī, *Nawāzil*, III, 6; Ḥaṭṭāb, *Mawāhib al-Jalīl*, I, 32; VI, 91; Bāᶜalawī, *Bughyat al-Mustarshidīn*, 274; Ibn ᶜĀbidīn, *Ḥāshiya*, V, 359.
[135] ᶜAlamī, *Nawāzil*, I, 309–310. See also Ḥājjī Khalīfa (*Kashf al-Ẓunūn*, II, 1225) who remarks that *al-Fatāwā al-Sūfiyya* of Mawlā Birkilī (or Biriklī) is unauthoritative (*laysat min al-kutub al-muᶜtabara*) because it does not conform to the accepted principles of *fiqh*.

sanctioning legal opinions and doctrines. When a *fatwā* is declared to be in conformity with the *madhhab*, its status is indicated by terms such as "this is the *madhhab*" (*wa-ʿalayhi al-madhhab*) or "this is the preferred view" (*al-rājiḥ fil-madhhab*), "this is the view that is followed" (*al-ladhī ʿalayhi al-ʿamal*). On the other hand, when a *madhhab* doctrine is declared to be authoritative, the jurists employed the expression "this view is resorted to in *fatwā*" (*wa-ʿalayhi al-fatwā*, or *al-maftī bihi*).[136] Khalīl's highly acclaimed *Mukhtaṣar* contains the authoritative opinions of the Mālikite school, and these, it turns out, are the opinions commonly issued in *iftā*ʾ.[137]

The crucial role of the *muftī* in elaborating and developing the legal doctrine of *furūʿ* did not escape the attention of Muslim legal scholars. As we have seen, the *muftī* and his *fatwā* were deemed to stand at the center of the legal profession. Indeed, the chief goal of the traditional *madrasa* educational system was the training of *muftī*s.[138] The Sharīʿa system and its proper functioning depended on what was perceived to be a true reflection of God's commands, and on the consistency with which these commands, that is, the law, were applied. Determining the law in its social settings was the responsibility of the *muftī*. When he issued a *fatwā* in which he questioned or reversed the decision of a *qāḍī*, the party to the dispute obtaining this *fatwā* had valid grounds to turn to another *qāḍī* for a new trial.[139] The significant contribution and active participation of the *muftī* in the legal process are fully attested in the chapters of *furūʿ* works dealing with courts and evidence (*kitāb al-aqḍiya wal-shahādāt*). The rules and principles governing the court were the product of the *fatwā*s which were incorporated into, and became part of, these works. Even specialized treatises dealing with judges and courts (*adab al-qaḍā*ʾ) were, in their own composition, partly dependent on the *fatwā*s issued with regard to these matters.[140]

## VI

The foregoing facts and arguments demonstrably show that it was through the medium of *fatwā*s that law maintained contact with social reality, and developed and changed in light of that reality. But without

136 Ibn ʿĀbidīn, *Ḥāshiya*, I, 72; Ḥaṭṭāb, *Mawāhib al-Jalīl*, I, 36. Further on this, see chapter 5, section VI, above.

137 Ḥaṭṭāb, *Mawāhib al-Jalīl*, I, 2: "*ukhtuṣira bi-tabyīn mā bi-hi al-fatwā*."

138 Makdisi, *Rise*, 148.

139 See, e.g. Ibn Farḥūn, *Tabṣirat al-Ḥukkām*, I, 122; Powers, "Judicial Review," 332.

140 See, e.g., the *fatwā*s included in Kinānī's *al-ʿIqd al-Munaẓẓam*, I, 33, 43 ff., 71 f., 79 f., 81, 83, 88, 93, and passim; Ibn Farḥūn, *Tabṣirat al-Ḥukkām*, I, 46, 53, 54, 112, 123, 126, 146, and passim.

the contributions of the author–jurist, the full legal potential of *fatwās* would never have been realized, for it was he who finally integrated them into the larger context of the law, and it was he who determined the extent of their contribution to legal continuity, evolution, and change. The authority of the author–jurist stemmed from the fact that he was qualified to determine which opinions and *fatwās* were worthy of incorporation into his text, in which he aspired to assemble the authoritative doctrine of the school. Thus, like the *muftī*, and certainly not unlike the founding imam, the author–jurist's authority was primarily – if not, in his case, exclusively – epistemic.

Before we deal with the author–jurist as an agent of change, we shall first present a case study of a *fatwā* which had its origin in a concrete social reality and which was later appropriated, in various ways, by the author–jurists. The case involves an intentional homicide which took place in the Andalusian city of Cordoba in 516/1122.[141] The full text of the *fatwā*,[142] including the question as addressed to Ibn Rushd (d. 520/1126), runs as follows:

> Question: Concerning the murder of someone who leaves behind minor children and agnates who are of age. Should the minors be allowed to attain the age of majority, thus barring the agnates from seeking punishment?
>
> Regarding the case of intentional homicide which occurred in Cordoba – may God bring it back to Islamic dominion[143] – in the year 516, Abū al-Walīd Ibn Rushd – our master, the eminent jurist, erudite scholar, imam, fair-minded judge – said:
>
> Some of those who seek and investigate knowledge have asked me to explain a *fatwā* which I have issued concerning a man who was killed intentionally by another and who had minor children and agnates of age. [I held that] the children must be allowed to attain the age of majority and that the agnates are not entitled to take the *qasāma* oath[144] or have him executed. For the children's right to take the oath, to have him executed, or to pardon him overrides the right of the agnates. This is contrary to the authoritative doctrine governing this matter, a doctrine held by Mālik and others who follow him.
>
> [Those seekers of knowledge] did not understand what lay behind my opinion, and they thought that the jurisconsult must not abandon the authoritative doctrine applicable to the case. But what they thought is

[141] For a more detailed analysis of the *fatwā*, see Hallaq, "Murder in Cordoba."

[142] Ibn Rushd, *Fatāwā*, II, 1196–1203; Wansharīsī, *al-Miʿyār al-Mughrib*, II, 319 ff.

[143] This invocation must have been interpolated into the text at a later stage, probably after 541/1146, when Cordoba was seized by Alfonso VII. See B. Reilly, *The Contest of Christian and Muslim Spain* (Oxford and Cambridge, Mass.: Blackwell, 1992), 212, 218.

[144] On the *qasāma*, see n. 159, below.

incorrect, for the jurisconsult must not follow a doctrine, nor issue legal opinions according to it, unless he knows that it is sound. No learned person disagrees with this, for God – may He be exalted – said: "Ask the people of Remembrance if you do not know;"[145] and the Prophet asked Muᶜādh b. Jabal, when he dispatched him to Yemen to govern and teach, "According to what will you judge?" Muᶜādh said: "According to God's Book." The Prophet then asked: "What if you do not find [in the Book what you need]"? Muᶜādh replied: "Then according to the Sunna of God's Prophet." The Prophet asked: "What if you do not find [in the Sunna that which you seek]"? Muᶜādh answered: "I exercise my own legal reasoning." The Prophet then said: "Thank God for guiding the Prophet's deputy to that which the Prophet approves." The Prophet thus approved independent legal reasoning where the Book and the Sunna were silent. But he did not approve of a learned person turning to another learned person in order to adopt an opinion which the latter had reached by exercising his own legal reasoning. Whatever is approved by the Prophet is surely approved by God; and whatever God approves is the truth which should neither be set aside nor violated. The doctrine contrary to which I have issued a legal opinion runs counter to the fundamental principles of Islamic jurisprudence; in this doctrine, *qiyās* was set aside on certain grounds in favor of *istiḥsān*, as we shall explain later. Accordingly, sound reasoning requires one to abandon the [traditional] doctrine in favor of that which is more appropriate, especially in view of the fact that the killer was intoxicated when he committed the crime.

Some jurists hold that an intoxicated person who commits a murder while inebriated is not to be punished [by death]. Although we do not subscribe to this opinion, taking it into account is nonetheless necessary, in line with the Mālikite principle – whose validity we uphold – that divergent opinions must be taken cognizance of.

The way to establish the validity of our opinion with regard to this matter is to mention the relevant texts in the Quran and the Sunna on which the case is based. All jurists agree that the principal text governing this case is God's statement: "Whoso is slain unjustly, We have given power unto his heir, but let him [i.e. the heir] not commit excess in slaying [the murderer]."[146] In other words, [God has] empowered the heir to redress his rights.

The jurists, however, disagree as to whether or not the heir has the right to forgo the execution of the murderer and instead opt for blood-money, with or without the consent of the murderer. Their disagreement stems from their varying interpretation of God's statement: "And for him who is forgiven (*ᶜufya lahu*) somewhat by his [murdered] brother, prosecution according to established custom and payment unto him in kindness."[147]

[145] Quran 16:43. [146] Quran 17:33. [147] Quran 2:178.

Is it the agnate who forgives? Or is it the murderer?[148] Those jurists who espouse the view that it is the heir who has the right to pardon the murderer and instead receive blood-money, whether the latter agrees or not, unqualifiedly require that the minor children of the person killed be allowed to attain the age of majority. According to these jurists, it is not lawful to allow the agnates to seek the punishment [of the murderer] since this will abrogate the right of the minor children to receive blood-money upon their coming of age, whether the murderer agrees to this or not. This is analogous to the legal rights [of the parties] in non-penal cases subject to consensus. One of these latter is the case of preemption: all agree that a minor's preemptive right, established by a single witness, may not be transferred, due to his minor age, to his closest relatives. His right is preserved until he reaches the age of majority, at which point he will take an oath, thereby laying claim to the property. The same [principle] governs other rights. If a boy claims that a man has destroyed his goods or that he killed his beast or slave, and if he procures a single witness, then he would be entitled to compensation when he becomes of age. This is the doctrine of Ashhab,[149] and it is one of the two opinions held by Ibn al-Qāsim.[150] This doctrine is also transmitted by Muṭarrif[151] and Ibn al-Mājishūn[152] on the authority of Mālik. And it is the doctrine adopted by Shāfiʿī and the Syrian Awzāʿī.

From the Prophetic example, they adduce in support of their argument a sound tradition recorded in al-Bukhārī on the authority of Abū Hurayra. According to this tradition, the Prophet said: "He whose relative was murdered has the choice of either receiving monetary compensation or meting out punishment [to the murderer]."[153] The Prophet has also reportedly said: "He whose relative was murdered has the choice of either killing [the murderer] or pardoning [him in exchange for] receiving blood-money."[154]

From the perspective of rational argumentation, they hold that the murderer must seek to preserve his own life by means of his wealth, and if

[148] In other words, is pardoning or payment of blood-money in lieu of execution a right that may be exercised by the agnate of the victim or does the murderer have to agree or disagree to the payment of blood-money in lieu of execution?

[149] Abū ʿAmr Ashhab b. ʿAbd al-ʿAzīz al-Qaysī (d. 204/819), a traditionist and jurist, was one of Mālik's most distinguished students. See Fuat Sezgin, *Geschichte des arabischen Schrifttums*, 8 vols. (Leiden: E. J. Brill, 1967–), I, 466.

[150] Ibn al-Qāsim Abū ʿAbd Allāh ʿAbd al-Raḥmān al-ʿUtaqī (d. 191/806) was a student of Mālik. See ibid., I, 465.

[151] Muṭarrif b. ʿAbd Allāh al-Hilālī (d. 220/835) was a student of Mālik. See Ibn Farḥūn, *Dībāj*, 345.

[152] ʿAbd al-Malik b. ʿAbd al-ʿAzīz al-Madanī Ibn al-Mājishūn (d. 212/827) was a student of Mālik and a leading jurisconsult. See Khayr al-Dīn al-Ziriklī, *al-Aʿlām*, 8 vols. (Beirut: Dār al-ʿIlm lil-Malāyīn, 1980), IV, 160.

[153] See Abū ʿAbd Allāh Muḥammad al-Bukhārī, *Kitāb al-Jāmiʿ al-Ṣaḥīḥ*, ed. M. L. Krehl and T. W. Juynboll, 4 vols. (Leiden: E. J. Brill, 1908), IV, 318.

[154] Ibid.

he does not, blood-money must be taken from him, coercively if need be. Mālik said: "Blood-money must be taken from him, even coercively, and his [right to his own] wealth must not be protected, for he will derive no benefit from his wealth if he is executed."

There are those who espouse the view that the heir can obtain blood-money from the murderer only if the latter consents – a view held by Mālik, according to Ibn al-Qāsim's recension, and by a group of his followers, and it is one of the two opinions held by Ibn al-Qāsim. Analogy (*qiyās*), according to this view, also dictates that the minor children should be allowed to attain the age of majority, because their right to punish or to pardon, or to settle with him, overrides the right of their agnates. This is also analogous to cases involving rights, cases that are subject to consensus. But we gather from what has been related to us on their authority that their recourse to juristic preference (*istiḥsān*) and their setting aside of analogy led them to the view that the minors must not be awaited till they attain the age of majority unless they are close to reaching that age. This is the crux of their view. According to them, the minor children are entitled to blood-money only upon the consent of the murderer; they are entitled only to punish the murderer or pardon him, and these [decisions] can be taken by the agnates. Underlying their juristic preference is giving precedence to punishment over pardoning, because it constitutes a deterrence and restrains people from committing murder. For God, the exalted, has said: "And there is life for you in retaliation."[155] However, pardoning overrides punishment, for God has said: "The guerdon of an ill-deed is an ill the like thereof. But whosoever pardons and amends, his wage is the affair of God,"[156] and "Verily, whoso is patient and forgiving – lo! that is of the steadfast heart of things."[157] He also said: "And vie one with another for forgiveness from your Lord, and for a Paradise as wide as are the heavens and the earth, prepared for those who ward off [evil]. Those who spend [of that which God has given them] in ease and in adversity, those who control their wrath and are forgiving toward mankind; God loves the good-doers."[158] Such statements abound in the Quran.

Indeed, the people of learning hold the view that the imam must encourage the victim's relatives to pardon [the murderer] before they take the oath.[159] They will take the oath and have the murderer punished only if they persist in their demand. Therefore, since pardoning is recommended

155 Quran 2:179. 156 Quran 42:40. 157 Quran 42:43. 158 Quran 3:133–34.

159 I.e. the *qasāma*, which would have served to confirm their entitlement to prosecution. Although fifty oaths are required (implying that fifty persons must take them), it is sufficient for two agnates each to swear twenty-five oaths. See Abū ʿAbd Allāh Muḥammad al-Auṣārī al-Raṣṣāʿ, *Sharḥ Ḥudūd Ibn ʿArafa al-Mawsūm al-Hidāya al-Kāfiya al-Shāfiya*, ed. Muḥammad Abū al-Ajfān and al-Ṭāhir al-Maʿmūrī, 2 vols. (Beirut: Dār al-Gharb al-Islāmī, 1993), II, 626 ff.; ʿUbayd Allāh b. Ḥasan Ibn al-Jallāb, *al-Tafrīʿ*, ed. Ḥusayn al-Dahmānī, 2 vols. (Beirut: Dār al-Gharb al-Islāmī, 1987), II, 2, 207–08.

(*mustaḥabb*)[160] – and in this case pardoning is a right that belongs to the minor children upon their becoming of age – they must be allowed to attain the age of majority. If they wish, they will pardon, thereby seeking to attain the heavenly reward. This reward, to which they have the right when they reach the age of majority, must not be abrogated by allowing the agnates to have the murderer punished.

From the preceding discussion we conclude that there are two, and only two, opinions which are relevant to this case: First, according to strict legal reasoning, and without resort to juristic preference, the minor children must be allowed to attain the age of majority, and the agnates must not share with them the right to have the murderer punished. Second, according to juristic preference, and without resort to strict legal reasoning, it is [the agnates] who have such a right. However, the weakness of juristic preference lies in the fact, which we have explicated, that pardoning overrides punishment. The only valid view, therefore, is that the minor children must be allowed to attain the age of majority.

Should someone argue that execution overrides pardoning, our response to him would be to refer to the Quranic verses we have already cited. If he argues that the import of these verses is applicable to non-penal cases, we reply: Our evidence that they are applicable to both penal and non-penal cases is the report narrated on the authority of Anas b. Mālik who said: "When a man brought the murderer of his kin to the Prophet, the latter asked him to pardon him [the murderer]. When he refused, the Prophet asked him to accept compensation. When he [again] refused, the Prophet said: 'Should we execute him? You will be like him if you have him killed,' thereupon the man released him." This is an unambiguous text pointing to the superiority of pardoning to punishment. The Prophet, after all, does not recommend[161] something unless it is superior. He pointed to this by saying "You will be like him if you have him killed." The import of this statement is that his heavenly reward will be waived if he inflicts punishment [on the murderer], instead of pardoning him. And the murderer, once punished, will have paid for his deed, because punishment represents an atonement for those who are punished, according to Quranic penal law (*ḥudūd*). Both men become equal in that the first will receive no reward and the second will have atoned for his crime. This is my interpretation of the Prophetic tradition. It is interpreted in other ways that are open to objections.

Even if we submit that punishment supersedes pardoning and that juristic preference is valid in that the minor children must not be awaited till they attain the age of majority (according to one of the two doctrines narrated on the authority of Mālik, Ibn al-Qāsim and those who followed

160 See next note.

161 "Recommendation" here is to be taken as referring to the category of "recommended," one of the five legal norms.

> them in this) juristic preference in the present case is invalid because, it is reported, the murderer was intoxicated at the time he killed the victim. There is neither doubt nor dispute that pardoning the intoxicated [murderer] overrides punishing him, for it is held that he must not be punished [by death]. Thus, if consensus dictates that pardoning the murderer overrides punishing him, then consensus is also concluded to the effect that the minor children must be allowed to attain the age of majority; any other view is invalid.
>
> I have demonstrated the validity of my opinion with regard to this matter – thanks be to God. A briefer explanation would have sufficed, but, as Mālik remarked in his *Muwaṭṭa'*, people like to know the truth and the arguments supporting it. God, who has no partner, is the bestower of success.

We know that the case fell within Mālikite jurisdiction, and that in accordance with a *fatwā* issued by a number of Mālikite jurisconsults, including the illustrious Ibn al-Ḥājj (d. 529/1134), the murderer, having admitted his guilt, was executed at the instigation of the victim's brother and his sons.[162] Here, the jurisconsults were acting perfectly within the authoritative legal doctrine (*naṣṣ al-riwāya, al-ma'thūr*) of the Mālikite school, according to which the agnates of the victim having the right to demand the death penalty are not the children of the deceased – since they have not yet attained the age of majority – but rather their paternal uncle and his sons. This doctrine, thus far undisputed in the Mālikite *madhhab*, was supported by Mālik himself and by a number of later influential jurists who flourished before the beginning of the sixth/twelfth century, when the actual incident took place.[163]

Ibn Rushd, however, categorically dismissed the established doctrine and held the unprecedented opinion that only the children are entitled, upon reaching the age of majority, either to demand the murderer's punishment or to opt for monetary compensation – let alone pardoning him altogether without receiving any compensation.[164] In the Mālikite tradition, this constituted a novel position. Yet Ibn Rushd's departure was not meant to introduce an alternative ruling designed to coexist with the authoritative ruling followed in the school. Rather, he goes as far as

[162] Wansharīsī, *al-Mi<sup></sup>ʿyār al-Mughrib*, II, 320 (l. 2); Kinānī, *al-ʿIqd al-Munaẓẓam*, II, 256.

[163] For a statement of the doctrine, see Ḥaṭṭāb, *Mawāhib al-Jalīl*, VI, 252. See also Ibn Rushd, *Fatāwā*, II, 1197; Abū ʿAbd Allāh Muḥammad al-Kharashī, *Sharḥ Mukhtaṣar Khalīl*, 5 vols. (Cairo: al-Maṭbaʿa al-ʿĀmira al-Sharafiyya, 1899), V, 263–64; Wansharīsī, *al-Miʿyār al-Mughrib*, II, 320.

[164] It is the standard legal doctrine that the agnates of the victim are entitled to punish the murderer by death or pardon him with or without monetary compensation. For further details, see Ibn al-Jallāb, *Tafrīʿ*, II, 207 ff.

to argue that the commonly accepted ruling which he rejects is simply inconsistent with the general legal and hermeneutical principles of the Mālikite school, for the ruling is derived by means of the controversial method of juristic preference (*istiḥsān*), and not by the commonly accepted juridical inference known as *qiyās*.[165] He simply points out that if the jurist were to resort to the latter methodology of reasoning, as he should, then he would be bound to reject the established doctrine.

At a later stage of the *fatwā*, Ibn Rushd introduces a new fact to the case. Now we are told that the murderer was inebriated when he committed the crime. Resorting to *qiyās*, Ibn Rushd seems to say, is the only way to solve the case, whether this fact is taken into consideration or not. Nonetheless, this added fact gives the jurisconsult an even better reason to follow *qiyās* and abandon *istiḥsān*. Some jurists held that a person who kills another while in a state of intoxication is not punishable by death due to the fact that he was not acting with full mental capacity.[166] Ibn Rushd maintains that although the Mālikīs do not follow this doctrine, the general principle behind it has always been taken into account in cases where intoxication is involved. Thus, Ibn Rushd insists on *qiyās* as the

[165] On the method of *qiyās*, see chapter 5, section III, above, and Hallaq, *History*, 83–104. It is to be noted that *istiḥsān* was not accepted by all jurists and remained a controversial method of reasoning. A number of Ḥanafite, Ḥanbalite, and Mālikite legists held that *istiḥsān* emanates from a special group of *ʿilal* (pl. of *ʿilla*) which require particularization (*takhṣīṣ*). Particularization takes place when a relevant legal fact (otherwise considered irrelevant in *qiyās*) is deemed to influence the relationship between the *ʿilla* and the ruling of the case, thus compelling the jurist to take it into consideration in his inference. A case in point is the consumption of the meat of an unlawfully slaughtered animal (*mayta*) which is prohibited in *qiyās*. According to *istiḥsān*, however, this prohibition is removed under circumstances of hardship or starvation, e.g. starving in the desert. The proponents of *istiḥsān* argue that the added legal fact which dictates the use of *istiḥsān* must ultimately be based on the revealed texts. Thus, according to these jurists, the dividing line between the two methods is that *qiyās* does not require the particularization of its *ʿilla* whereas *istiḥsān* does. Other jurists, however, insist that since the additional facts are based on textual evidence, the reasoning in *istiḥsān* does not involve any particularization of the *ratio legis*; for them *istiḥsān* represents nothing more than a legal inference that is preferred, on the strength of textual evidence, to another, i.e. *qiyās*. On *qiyās* and *istiḥsān*, see Bājī, *Iḥkām al-Fuṣūl*, 528 ff., 687 ff.; Ibn Qudāma, *Rawḍat al-Nāẓir*, 247 ff.; Muḥammad b. Aḥmad Abū Sahl al-Sarakhsī, *al-Uṣūl*, ed. Abū al-Wafā al-Afghānī, 2 vols. (Cairo: Dār al-Maʿrifa, 1393/1973), II, 199 ff., 208 ff.; Hallaq, *History*, 107–11; Hallaq, "Function and Character of Sunnī Legal Theory," 683–84; John Makdisi, "Legal Logic and Equity in Islamic Law," *American Journal of Comparative Law*, 33 (1985), 73–85; John Makdisi, "Hard Cases and Human Judgment in Islamic and Common Law," *Indiana International and Comparative Review*, 2 (1991), 197–202.

[166] See Taqī al-Dīn Ibn Taymiyya, *Mukhtaṣar al-Fatāwā al-Miṣriyya*, ed. ʿAbd al-Majīd Salīm (Cairo: Maṭbaʿat al-Sunna al-Muḥammadiyya, 1949), 463; Ibn Rushd, *Fatāwā*, II, 1198.

proper method of legal reasoning in this case, especially in light of the fact of intoxication which encourages, though it does not strictly dictate, its use.

We have already noted that *fatwās* which contained new legal opinions (*ijtihād*) were, as a rule, incorporated in manuals on positive law (*furūʿ*) as well as in commentaries and super-commentaries on such manuals. Ibn Rushd's *fatwā* on homicide was no exception. In his *Mukhtaṣar*,[167] Khalīl b. Isḥāq (d. 767/1365), with typical succinctness, repeats the standard Mālikite doctrine that minors' rights in the law of homicide are transferred to their agnates. Two commentators on the *Mukhtaṣar*, Mawwāq (d. 897/1491) and Kharashī (d. 1101/1689), passed over Ibn Rushd's opinion in silence, both being satisfied with making a brief statement of the authoritative doctrine in the school.[168] A third commentator, however, does take it into consideration. In his commentary on Khalīl's statement, Ḥaṭṭāb begins by discussing Ibn Rushd's divergent opinion. According to *qiyās*, he states, Ibn Rushd argues that the minor children must be allowed to attain the age of majority before punishment can be decided. "When he was asked about his *fatwā*, which takes exception to the authoritative doctrine, Ibn Rushd maintained that the questioner (*al-sā'il*) did not understand the import of the [*fatwā*], thinking that the jurisconsult must not diverge from the authoritative doctrine. But this is not so; the jurisconsult must not follow a legal doctrine unless he knows that it is sound. No learned person disagrees with this [principle]."[169] Ḥaṭṭāb emphasizes that Ibn Rushd's opinion stands at variance with the accepted principles of the Mālikite school.

> Against these principles, Ibn Rushd reasoned what amounts to the following: The minor's right must be protected, and his entitlement to it must be postponed until he becomes of age, just as he is entitled to a right [in cases] attested to by a single witness. He also held that the minor has the right to force the murderer to pay blood-money, according to the doctrines of Ashhab and the Two Brothers,[170] and in conformity with one of the two views held by Ibn al-Qāsim.[171]

[167] Khalīl b. Isḥāq, *Mukhtaṣar* (Jazā'ir: Dār Shihāb, 1988), 278.

[168] Kharashī, *Sharḥ Mukhtaṣar*, V, 263–64; Muḥammad b. Yūsuf al-Mawāq, *al-Tāj wal-Iklīl fī Sharḥ Mukhtaṣar Khalīl*, printed on the margins of Ḥaṭṭāb, *Mawāhib al-Jalīl*, VI, 251.

[169] Ḥaṭṭāb, *Mawāhib al-Jalīl*, VI, 251–52.

[170] The Two Brothers are Muṭarrif and Ibn al-Mājishūn. Ziriklī reports on the authority of a certain Marghīthī that it was Ibn ʿArafa who originally referred to the two Mālikite authorities as "the Two Brothers" because their doctrines substantially agreed with one another. See *Aʿlām*, VII, 43 (col. 3).

[171] Ḥaṭṭāb, *Mawāhib al-Jalīl*, VI, 252.

Ibn ʿArafa (d. 803/1400), Ḥaṭṭāb reports, considered this opinion to be weak (*ḍaʿīf*) and stated that the jurists "do not take it into consideration in these times of ours. Ibn Rushd is entitled to hold such an opinion only because he is a leading authority (*li-ʿuluwwi ṭabaqatihi*)."[172] One of Ibn Rushd's contemporaries, Ḥaṭṭāb further remarks, declared that his was not the doctrine practiced (*laysa al-ʿamal ʿalā hādhā*),[173] for it ran counter to Ibn al-Qāsim's doctrine. At this point, Ḥaṭṭāb makes the enigmatic statement that in a copy of Ibn Rushd's *fatwā* collection, it was written on the margin of the *fatwā* dealing with the present case of homicide: "This is not the doctrine practiced since it is at variance with that held by Ibn al-Qāsim." Who it was that wrote this statement we are not told. In order to further weaken the validity of Ibn Rushd's opinion, Ḥaṭṭāb enlists the critical comment of Ibn al-Ḥājib (d. 646/1248), who is reported to have said that on this question Ibn Rushd neither followed the established doctrine of his school nor justified, by way of reasoned arguments (*ḥujja*), his new opinion. Then, after allocating a few lines to a discussion of Ibn Rushd's *fatwā* and to the reactions it provoked from Mālikite jurists, Ḥaṭṭāb goes on to give a detailed account of the conventional doctrine that had dominated the Mālikite school since the second/eighth century.[174]

As reported by Ḥaṭṭāb, Ibn al-Ḥājib's comment concerning the absence of reasoned arguments in Ibn Rushd's *fatwā* seems curious, to say the least; for the *fatwā* is indeed thoroughly reasoned. The only plausible explanation for this seeming contradiction is that Ibn al-Ḥājib was speaking of an earlier *fatwā* in which Ibn Rushd had apparently stated his opinion so elliptically, and without setting forth his reasoning, that a second one proved necessary to vindicate the first. The plausibility of this explanation is strengthened by the fact that Wansharīsī, whose work is one of the most comprehensive *fatwā* collections we know, does not seem to be aware of the existence of the second, much longer, *fatwā*. Ibn al-Ḥājib too may have been unaware of this *fatwā*, and if this was the case, then we can understand why he should have made such a statement. But why does Ḥaṭṭāb quote Ibn al-Ḥājib's unfavorable statement approvingly when it is evident that he himself was familiar with the second, more closely reasoned, *fatwā*? The explanation may lie in Ḥaṭṭāb's attitude toward Ibn Rushd's opinion, which was thoroughly negative. He not only

172 Ibid., VI, 252–53.

173 On the importance of such statements in determining the standard doctrine of the school, see chapter 5, above.

174 Ḥaṭṭāb, *Mawāhib al-Jalīl*, VI, 252–53.

allocated disproportionately little space for recording the contents of the *fatwā*, but also managed to suppress the crucial passages containing Ibn Rushd's reasoning. The arguments based on the Quran, the Sunna, and consensus are passed over in silence. More importantly, Ḥaṭṭāb hardly mentions Ibn Rushd's recommendation of the highly regarded method of *qiyās* or his objections to the controversial method of *istiḥsān*, by means of which the authoritative doctrine of the school was justified.

Furthermore, no reference whatsoever is made to the significant fact that the murderer was inebriated at the time he committed the crime. All this effort to weaken Ibn Rushd's opinion perhaps reflects the great reluctance of Ḥaṭṭāb to abandon the widely accepted and long-held doctrine in his school. Like many jurists, Ḥaṭṭāb was disinclined to adopt a doctrine which he did not deem to be widespread (*mashhūr*) and which did not form the basis of general practice (*ʿamal*) in the Mālikite school.[175] By declaring Ibn Rushd's *fatwā* weak, he, like Ibn ʿArafa, was in effect practicing *tarjīḥ*, whereby one opinion (in this case the traditional doctrine prevailing in the school) is chosen as superior to another. At the same time, he was also practicing *taṣḥīḥ* which amounts to declaring an opinion "more sound" than another.[176]

While Ḥaṭṭāb plainly rejects Ibn Rushd's opinion as weak, Ibn Salmūn al-Kinānī (d. 767/1365) presents it as being of equal validity to the opinion expressed by Ibn al-Ḥājj, which represented the standard doctrine of Mālikism. The manner in which Kinānī arranges his material as well as the fuller and more accurate account he gives of Ibn Rushd's *fatwā* reveal a favorable attitude towards a dissenting voice. Whereas Ḥaṭṭāb begins by a relatively brief, and definitely unrepresentative, discussion of Ibn Rushd's *fatwā*, and ends with a substantial body of arguments in favor of the conventional doctrine (and, one suspects, in refutation of Ibn Rushd's opinion), Kinānī follows the opposite procedure: He first briefly presents the traditional opinion advocated by Ibn al-Ḥājj and then goes on to give a fairly detailed account of Ibn Rushd's *fatwā*. In Kinānī, Ibn Rushd appears to have the last word on the matter.

Having stated Ibn al-Ḥājj's *fatwā* in favor of assigning to the agnates the right to have the murderer punished, Kinānī remarks that Ibn Rushd disagreed with this opinion, arguing that the right belongs to the minor children. "In his *masā'il*,"[177] Kinānī continues,

[175] For *mashhūr* and *ʿamal*, and their importance in determining the authoritative doctrines of the schools, see chapter 5, above.
[176] On *tarjīḥ* and *taṣḥīḥ*, see chapter 5, above.
[177] *Masā'il* and *nawāzil* are generally synonymous with *fatwās*.

Ibn Rushd said: In this case I held that the minor children must be allowed to attain the age of majority and that the agnates are not entitled to take the *qasāma* oath or have him executed, although this is contrary to the authoritative doctrine governing this matter, a doctrine held by Mālik and his followers. [I held this] on the following grounds: The jurists disagreed as to whether or not the heir has the right to forgo the execution of the murderer and instead opt for blood-money, with or without the consent of the murderer. Those jurists who espouse the view that it is the agnate who has the right to pardon the murderer and instead receive blood-money, whether the latter agrees or not, unqualifiedly require that the minor children of the person killed be allowed to attain the age of majority. According to these jurists, it is not lawful to allow the agnates to seek the punishment [of the murderer] since this will abrogate the right of the minors insofar as their entitlement to receive blood-money. This is analogous to those legal rights subject to consensus, such as preemption, etc.

There are those who espouse the view that the heir can obtain blood-money from the murderer only after the latter's consent – a view held by Mālik, according to Ibn al-Qāsim's recension, and by a group of his followers, and it is one of the two opinions held by Ibn al-Qāsim himself. Analogy (*qiyās*), according to this view, also dictates that the children must be allowed to attain the age of majority, because their right to punish or to pardon [the murderer], and to be reconciled with him, overrides the right of their agnates. This is also analogous to cases subject to consensus. But we gather from what has been related to us on their authority that their recourse to juristic preference (*istiḥsān*) led them to the view that the minors must not be awaited [until they attain majority] unless they are close to reaching that age. Underlying [their] juristic preference is giving punishment precedence over pardoning. But pardoning overrides punishment. Indeed, learned people hold the view that the imam must encourage the victim's relatives to pardon [the murderer] before they take the oath. Therefore, since pardoning is recommended (*mustaḥabb*) – and pardoning is a right that belongs to the minor children – the children must be allowed to attain the age of majority. Their right, acquired by the [heavenly] reward to which they are entitled, must not be abrogated by allowing the agnates to have the murderer punished.

We conclude that there are two, and only two, opinions which are relevant to this case. First, according to strict legal reasoning, and without resort to juristic preference, the minors must be allowed to attain the age of majority, and the agnates must not share with them the right to have the murderer punished. Second, according to juristic preference, and without resort to strict legal reasoning, [the agnates] have such a right. However, the weakness of juristic preference lies in the fact, which we have explicated, that pardoning overrides punishment. The only valid view, therefore, is that the minor children must be allowed to attain the age of majority.

> Even if we submit that punishment supersedes pardoning, in the present case this is inapplicable because, it is reported, the murderer was intoxicated. There is no doubt that pardoning the intoxicated [murderer] has precedence [over executing him], for it is held that he must not be punished. Thus, if pardoning the murderer overrides punishing him, then scholarly agreement (*ittifāq*) is also attained to the effect that the minor children must be allowed to reach majority; any other view is invalid.

It is to be noted that Kinānī's abridgment in the original Arabic text consists of 320 words, whereas the original text of the *fatwā* comprises 1,218 (this is to be contrasted with Ḥaṭṭāb's abridgment of a mere 90 words). We have mentioned earlier that authors of law manuals and commentators, when drawing on the literature of *iftā'*, followed the practices of *talkhīṣ* (abridging) and *tajrīd* (abstracting), whereby facts and arguments in the primary *fatwā* are reduced to a minimum, and details irrelevant to the law in the case are omitted. In the case under consideration, there are at least five types of material which are subject to *talkhīṣ* and *tajrīd.*

First, details concerning the locale and time in which the case occurred (Cordoba in the year 516/1122), as well as the fact that the victim was the father of *three* children, are omitted, for such details have no bearing whatsoever upon the law of the case. Second, Kinānī omits all Quranic verses and Prophetic traditions cited by Ibn Rushd, as well as his interpretation of this evidence. However, all the central arguments drawing on this body of textual material are retained. Third, stylistically, a number of phrases and clauses are deleted, for Kinānī seems to assume that they are obvious to his readers. For example, the adjective "minor" is almost always dropped before the word "children." Similarly, the phrase "from the murderer, whether he consents or not" is suppressed after the words "taking blood-money." Fourth, details of the positive law (*furū'*) cases which Ibn Rushd employed in his analogy with the case under discussion (notably preemption) are taken as obvious and are thus omitted. Fifth, Ibn Rushd's somewhat polemical introduction relating to the duty of the jurisconsult to follow what he deems to be the sound opinion, and not necessarily the prevalent opinion in the school, is left out. But although this introduction does not advance any point of law relevant to the case being considered, and its omission is therefore justifiable, there remains the question of why Ḥaṭṭāb retains it and gives it such prominence in his discussion. We suggest that Ḥaṭṭāb's inclusion of this part was quite deliberate and had a purely "ideological" function; namely, to underscore the fact that Ibn Rushd deviated from the established doctrine of the school. Reproducing this introduction reinforces his charge that Ibn

Rushd was quite prepared to abandon the *madhhab*, and furthermore demonstrates that his disagreement (*khilāf*) was not sufficiently widespread (*mashhūr*) to make his opinion one with which the jurists had to contend.

Now, in line with this analysis, it may be argued that Kinānī's omission of this introduction was, on the other hand, motivated by two considerations, the first being, obviously, its irrelevance to the law in the case in question, and the second Kinānī's wish to play down, if not suppress, the fact that Ibn Rushd deviated from the school's doctrine.

But what Kinānī retains in his account of Ibn Rushd's *fatwā* is, unlike Ḥaṭṭāb's truncated summary, more crucial than what he has omitted. The two central arguments in the *fatwā*, suppressed by Ḥaṭṭāb, are effectively reproduced; namely, the insistence on *qiyās* (and not *istiḥsān*) as the sole method of reasoning applicable to the case under consideration, and the fact that the murderer was intoxicated at the time he committed the crime. That Ḥaṭṭāb did not care to mention the matter of intoxication may be explained by the fact that, like Ibn al-Ḥājj and the majority of jurists, he did not deem inebriation a mitigating circumstance in cases of homicide. Kinānī, on the other hand, seems to have ranged himself with Ibn Rushd in taking intoxication to be a factor that relaxes the death penalty, which explains why he upheld Ibn Rushd's *qiyās* and, in an indirect way, gave it preference over the traditional doctrine.

Ḥaṭṭāb and Kinānī, irrespective of their particular approaches to Ibn Rushd's *fatwā*, functioned here as author–jurists who transposed the *fatwā* from the discursive field of the jurisconsult to that of positive law works, the field of the author–jurist. The end result of this process of incorporation signaled the formal entrance of the opinion embedded in the *fatwā* into the school's corpus of legal doctrine. The *fatwā* may, of course, have been authoritative for future cases without having been subjected to this process, but it would not have gained a formal place in the school's doctrine. For without undergoing this process, it would continue to stand on the periphery of the school. That it, like many other *fatwās*, became part of the commentary on an authoritative work (in this case Khalīl's *Mukhtaṣar*) sketching the outline of the school's authoritative doctrine meant that the opinion expressed in it had attained a definite place in the school's doctrine, and therefore in *khilāf*. And once an opinion was admitted as part of the discursive field of *khilāf*, its legitimacy as a valid opinion (though not necessarily as *ṣaḥīḥ* or *mashhūr*) was guaranteed.[178]

[178] Among others, for instance, Ẓāhirite opinions were, generally speaking, not counted in the discourse of *khilāfiyyāt*. See Ibn al-Salāh, *Fatāwā*, I, 32–33.

But the most important fact about Ibn Rushd's *fatwā*, as we have seen, is that it introduced a new option in Mālikite criminal law. It certainly did not replace the traditional doctrine, but it did provide an alternative which could be adopted by *muftīs* and *qāḍīs* in their daily administration of justice. In accepting Ibn Rushd's opinion in preference to the traditional school doctrine, Kinānī, as an author–jurist, in effect sanctioned legal change in this sphere of criminal law.

## VII

Thus far, we have been concerned with the process of legal change insofar as the *fatwā* was appropriated by the author–jurist for that end. In the remaining sections of this chapter we shall focus our attention exclusively on the contribution of the author–jurist as an agent of legal change, without particular regard to the *muftī* and his *fatwā*. Admittedly, legal change was also implemented by another means, namely, the discourse of the author–jurist on the basis of general legal practice which may have been expressed in a number of ways, including the *fatwā*, judicial opinion, and other types of juristic discourse. Here, the function of the author–jurist in legal change is to legitimize tendencies in general legal practice, tendencies that would otherwise remain lacking in formal recognition and therefore in sanctioned legitimacy.

In illustration of this process of legal change, we shall discuss the modalities of written communication prevalent among the *qāḍīs*, a subject that occupies space in both *adab al-qāḍī* works and *shurūṭ* manuals. The usual Arabic designation for this type of communication is *kitāb al-qāḍī ilā al-qāḍī*[179] and it takes place when "a *qāḍī* of a particular locale writes to a *qāḍī* of a different locale regarding a person's right that he, the first *qāḍī*, was able to establish against another person, in order that the receiving *qāḍī* shall carry out the effects of the communication in his locale."[180] The practical significance of this mode of writing is all too obvious, and the jurists never underestimated the fundamental need for

[179] There are other designations such as *al-kitāb al-ḥukmī*, *al-mukātaba al-ḥukmiyya*, *nuṣūṣ al-takhāṭub bayna al-quḍāt*, and *al-mukātaba bayna al-quḍāt*. See Ḥalabī, *Multaqā al-Abḥur*, II, 74; Ibn Abī al-Damm, *Adab al-Qaḍā'*, 343, 441, 447; Ibn al-Munāṣif, *Tanbīh al-Ḥukkām*, 174. However, *kitāb al-qāḍī ilā al-qāḍī* is unquestionably the most common of all. See Ibn Abī al-Damm, *Adab al-Qaḍā'*, 242.

[180] See Abū al-Walīd Sulaymān b. Khalaf al-Bājī, *Fuṣūl al-Aḥkām wa-Bayān mā Maḍā ʿalayhi al-ʿAmal ʿinda al-Fuqahā' wal-Ḥukkām*, ed. al-Bātūl b. ʿAlī (Rabat: Wizārat al-Awqāf wal-Shu'ūn al-Islāmiyya, 1410/1990), 269.

such a practice.[181] It was by means of such a written instrument that justice could be done in a medieval society which was geographically widespread and mobile. A debt owed to a person in a remote town or village might not be paid by the debtor without the intervention of the long arm of the court. Similarly, this instrument could mediate the return to the master of a slave who had fled to an outlying village. The use of this instrument, in effect, brought together otherwise dispersed and independent jurisdictional units into a single, interconnected juridical system. Without such a legal device, one jurist correctly observed, rights would be lost and justice would remain suspended.[182]

Now, one of the central conditions for the validity of such written instruments is the presence of two witnesses who will testify to the documentary transfer from one *qāḍī* to another. This condition was the common doctrinal denominator among all four schools. All the so-called founders, co-founders, and their immediate followers subscribed to, and indeed insisted upon, this requirement. The early Mālikites, such as Ibn al-Qāsim (d. 191/806), Ashhab (d. 204/819), Ibn al-Mājishūn (d. 212/827), and Muṭarrif (d. 282/895), never compromised the requirement of two witnesses.[183] It is reported that Saḥnūn used to know the handwriting of some of his deputy judges, and yet still insisted upon the presence of two witnesses before whom he broke the seal and unfolded the *kitāb*.[184]

[181] Abū al-Qāsim ᶜAlī b. Muḥammad al-Simnānī, *Rawḍat al-Quḍāt wa-Ṭarīq al-Najāt*, ed. Ṣalāḥ al-Dīn al-Nāhī, 4 vols. (Beirut and Amman: Mu'assasat al-Risāla, 1404/1984), I, 330; Ibn al-Humām, *Sharḥ Fatḥ al-Qadīr*, VII, 285–86; Marghīnānī, *Hidāya*, III, 105; Wansharīsī, *al-Miᶜyār al-Mughrib*, X, 60 ff.; Sarakhsī, *Mabsūṭ*, XV, 95; ᶜAbd al-Wahhāb al-Baghdādī, *al-Maᶜūna*, ed. Ḥumaysh ᶜAbd al-Ḥaqq, 3 vols. (Riyadh: Maktabat Nizār al-Bāz, 1415/1995), III, 1511; Ḥalabī, *Multaqā al-Abḥur*, II, 73, n. 1 (citing al-ᶜAynī). Ibn Qudāma, *Mughnī*, XI, 458; Ibn Qudāma, *al-Kāfī*, IV, 302; Shams al-Dīn Abū al-Faraj ᶜAbd al-Raḥmān Ibn Qudāma, *al-Sharḥ al-Kabīr ᶜalā Matn al-Muqniᶜ*, printed with Muwaffaq al-Dīn Ibn Qudāma, *Mughnī*, XI, 467; Ibn al-Munāṣif, *Tanbīh al-Ḥukkām*, 156; Māwardī, *Adab al-Qāḍī*, II, 89; ᶜAlā' al-Dīn ᶜAlī b. Khalīl al-Tarābulusī, *Muᶜīn al-Hukkām fī-mā Yataraddad bayna al-Khasmayn min al-Aḥkām* (Cairo: Muṣṭafā Bābī al-Ḥalabī, 1393/1973), 118.

[182] Ibn al-Munāṣif, *Tanbīh al-Ḥukkām*, 152–53; Baghdādī, *Maᶜūna*, III, 1511. See also sources cited in the previous note.

[183] Ibn Farḥūn, *Tabṣirat al-Ḥukkām*, II, 37; Kinānī, *al-ᶜIqd al-Munaẓẓam*, II, 201–02; Yaᶜqūb b. Ibrāhīm Abū Yūsuf, *Ikhtilāf Abī Ḥanīfa wa-Ibn Abī Laylā* (Cairo: Maṭbaᶜat al-Wafā', 1357/1938), 159. A few of the "legal specialists" who predated the schools of law, such as Ḥasan al-Baṣrī and ᶜUbayd Allāh b. Ḥasan al-ᶜAnbarī, are said to have admitted handwriting, without testimonial evidence, as valid proof. See Shāshī, *Ḥulyat al-ᶜUlamā'*, VIII, 151. Of the later jurists, it is reported that Abū Saᶜīd al-Iṣṭakhrī held what seems to have been a unique view, that acquaintance with the *qāḍī*'s handwriting and seal are sufficient for the acceptance of the *kitāb*. Simnānī, *Rawḍat al-Quḍāt*, I, 331.

[184] Ibn al-Munāṣif, *Tanbīh al-Ḥukkām*, 155–56. Nonetheless, see n. 189, below.

It appears that some time during the fifth/eleventh century[185] the Mālikite school underwent a dramatic change in the practice of the *qāḍīs*' written communications, a change that had no parallel among the other three schools. At around this time, the Andalusian and Maghrebi *qāḍīs* apparently began to admit the validity of such written instruments without the testimony of witnesses.[186] Authentication through the attestation of the *qāḍī*'s handwriting (*al-shahāda ʿalā al-khaṭṭ*) was sufficient to validate the document.[187] In other words, if a *qāḍī* felt reasonably certain that the document before him was in the handwriting of another *qāḍī*, then that would constitute sufficient proof of its authenticity.

It is highly probable that the practice initially started in eastern Andalusia, and spread later to the west of the peninsula and the African littoral.[188] The earlier Ẓāhirite acceptance of this doctrine and practice may represent the forerunner of this Mālikite development. Ibn Sahl, who died in 486/1093, reports that the eastern Andalusian *qāḍīs* were not only satisfied with handwriting and the seal, but accepted the *kitāb* as true and authentic even if the *qāḍī* wrote nothing in it but the *ʿunwān*, a short statement that includes the names of the sending and receiving *qāḍīs*.[189]

[185] A somewhat earlier date still is not to be excluded, especially if Ẓāhirite doctrine and practice may be accepted as a forerunner. The Ẓāhirites did admit the *kitāb* on the basis of the attestation of handwriting.

[186] The change appears with all likelihood to have taken place both in the eastern and western parts of the Muslim world. For the east, see the royal decrees of judicial appointment in Qalqashandī, *Ṣubḥ al-Aʿshā*, XI, 192, 201, and n. 190, below. But Qalqashandī's evidence belongs to a period after the 660s/1260s, when under the Mamlūks a chief justice was appointed to each of the four schools.

[187] For a detailed account of the law pertaining to *al-shahāda ʿalā al-khaṭṭ*, see Ibn Farḥūn, *Tabṣirat al-Ḥukkām*, I, 284–93.

[188] For North Africa, particularly Tunis, see Ibn ʿAbd al-Salām and Ibn Rāshid's weighty statements in Wansharīsī, *al-Miʿyār wal-Mughrib*, X, 61–62. This Ibn ʿAbd al-Salām, who was a Mālikite, is not to be confused with his Shāfiʿite namesake, a highly distinguished jurist who flourished in the east.

[189] Ibn Sahl's comment on the evidence of handwriting is cited in Wansharīsī, *al-Miʿyār al-Mughrib*, X, 61. The Mālikite Ibn ʿAbd al-Salām, as quoted by Wansharīsī (ibid., X, 62), reveals something about the origins of the doctrine which admits the practice of authenticating the *kitāb* through handwriting. He argues that this later doctrine and practice utterly deviate from the authoritative doctrines of the school's founding fathers, and was originally based on a faulty interpretation of the practice of Saḥnūn and Ibn Kināna, who used, on some occasions, to accept the written instruments of persons whom they knew intimately, and in whom they placed their personal trust and confidence. This exceptional and provisional practice, Ibn ʿAbd al-Salām says, was taken by later generations of judges and jurists to constitute a general principle (*aṣl*), on the basis of which an entire doctrine had come to be constructed. It is in this sense that we should understand the statement of Ibn Hishām al-Qurṭubī (d. 606/1209), who attributed a similar doctrine to Ibn al-Mājishūn and Muṭarrif. In his *Mufīd al-Ḥukkām*, he argued that in certain (but by no means all) cases a *qāḍī* should admit

Although this had never been the case before, it was to become the standard doctrine, acknowledged to be a distinctly Mālikite entity by the other schools as well as by the political authorities of the day.[190] The early Mālikite scholars considered a *qāḍī*'s *kitāb* invalid if its authentication depended solely on identification of the handwriting.[191] Muṭarrif and Ibn al-Mājishūn rejected the authenticity of a *kitāb* even though two witnesses might testify that they had seen the issuing *qāḍī* write it with his own hand.[192] They insisted, as did all the other jurists, that the witnesses attest to the fact by declaring that the issuing *qāḍī*, whom they knew, had made them testify on a certain day in his courtroom (*majlis*) in a particular city or village; that the instrument (the witnesses would at this time point to the document) was his *kitāb*; and that it bore his seal. At this point, the witnesses would be required to reiterate the contents of the document. Nothing short of this testimony would suffice.

Writing in around 600 A.H. (ca. 1200 A.D.), Ibn al-Munāṣif portrays a vivid picture of the onset of procedural change in the Maghreb and Andalusia:

> In the regions with which we are in contact, the people [i.e., jurists] of our age have nowadays agreed to permit the *kitāb*s of *qāḍī*s in matters of judgments and rights on the basis of sheer knowledge of the *qāḍī*'s handwriting without his attestation to it, and without a recognized seal. They have demonstrably acquiesced in permitting and practicing this [matter]. I do not think there is anyone who can turn them away from it, because it

the validity of another *qāḍī*'s *kitāb* if he, the former, was certain (*lam yashikk*) that the written communication was undoubtedly that of the latter. See Alfonso Carmona González, "La Correspondencia Oficial entre Jueces en el *Mufīd* de Ibn Hishām de Córdoba," in *Homenaje al Prof. Jacinto Bosch Vilá*, I (Granada: Universidad de Granada, 1991), 505–06. Similarly, see María Arcas Campoy, "La Correspondencia de los Cadies en el *Muntajab al-Aḥkām* de Ibn Abī Zamanīn," *Actas del XII Congreso de la UEAI (Malaga, 1984)* (Madrid: Union Européenne d'Arabisants et d'Islamisants, 1986), 62. I am grateful to Maribel Fierro for drawing my attention to these two articles.

190 See Qalqashandī, *Ṣubḥ al-Aʿshā*, XI, 192, 201, where one royal decree of judicial appointment, probably issued some time after the middle of the seventh/thirteenth century, acknowledges *al-shahāda ʿalā al-khaṭṭ* as being a distinctly Mālikite institution that is beneficial and conducive to the welfare of society (*qubūlu al-shahādati ʿalā al-khaṭṭi . . . fa-hādhā mimmā fī-hi fusḥatun lil-nāsi wa-rāḥatun mā fī-hā ba'sun . . . wa-hwa mimmā tafarrada bi-hi huwa* [i.e., the Mālikite *madhhab*] *dūna al-baqiyya wa-fīhi maṣlaḥa*). See Bāʿalawī, *Bughyat al-Mustarshidīn*, 266. The Shāfiʿite and Ḥanafite schools stand in diametrical opposition to the Mālikites on this issue. See Ibn Abī al-Damm, *Adab al-Qaḍā'*, 76.

191 Ibn Farḥūn, *Tabṣirat al-Ḥukkām*, I, 287.

192 Ibn al-Munāṣif, *Tanbīh al-Ḥukkām*, 155.

[the practice] has become widespread in all the regions, and because they have colluded to accept and assert it.[193]

That the change took place during the decades preceding Ibn al-Munāṣif's time may be inferred not only from his reaction to it as a novelty but also from the urgency with which he felt the need to justify the new practice. "We have established that Mālik's school, like other schools, deems the *qāḍīs' kitābs* which have been attested by witnesses lawful, and that these [instruments] could not be considered admissible merely on the evidence of handwriting." Yet, Ibn al-Munāṣif continues, "people and all judges [of our times and regions] are in full agreement as to their permissibility, bindingness, and putative authority; therefore we need to investigate the matter" by means of "finding out a good way to make this [issue] rest on a sound method and clear foundations to which one can refer and on the basis of which the rules of Sharīᶜa may be derived."[194] It is precisely here that the contribution of Ibn al-Munāṣif as an author–jurist lies.

Our author argues that the new practice is justified on the basis of *ḍarūra* (necessity), a principle much invoked to explain and rationalize otherwise inadmissible but necessary legal practices and concepts, including, interestingly enough, the very concept and practice of *kitāb al-qāḍī ilā al-qāḍī.* The principle of *ḍarūra* finds justification in Quran 2:185: "God wants things to be easy for you and does not want any hardship for you."[195] Ibn al-Munāṣif argues that it is often difficult to find two

[193] Ibid., 156: "*wa-qad asfaqa al-yawma ahlu ᶜaṣrinā fī al-bilād al-latī yantahī ilayhā amrunā fī dhālika ijāzata kutubi al-quḍāti fī al-aḥkāmi wal-ḥuqūqi bi-mujarradi maᶜrifati khaṭṭi al-qāḍī, dūna ishhādihi ᶜalā dhālika wa-lā khātamin maᶜrūfin, wa-taẓāharū ᶜalā jawāzi dhālika wal-ᶜamali bi-hi, fa-lā yastaṭīᶜu aḥadun fī-mā aẓunnu ṣarfahum ᶜan dhālika li-intishārihi fī kulli al-jihāt wa-tawāṭīhim ᶜalayhi bil-qabūli wal-ithbāt.*" With a minor variation in the opening line, this revealing statement was cited as an authoritative attestation to the practice by Wansharīsī, *al-Miᶜyār al-Mughrib*, X, 62.

[194] Ibn al-Munāṣif, *Tanbīh al-Ḥukkām*, 164–65 in conjunction with p. 156, both passages having the same theme: "*wa-idhā qarrarnā min madhhabi Mālikin wa-ghayrihi jawāza kutubi al-quḍāti bil-ishhādi ᶜalayhā wa-manᶜa al-qabūli bi-mujarradi maᶜrifati al-khaṭṭi, wa-anna al-nāsa al-yawma wa-kāffata al-ḥukkāmi mutamālūna ᶜalā ijāzati dhālika wa-iltizāmihi wal-ᶜamali bi-hi fa-lā budda an nuḥaqqiqa fī dhālika*" (164–65); "*wa-lā budda . . . min al-tanqībi wal-talaṭṭufi fī isnādi dhālika ilā wajhin ṣaḥīḥin wa-aṣlin wāḍiḥin yaṣluḥu al-maṣīru ilayhi wa-bināᶜu aḥkāmi al-sharīᶜati ᶜalayh*" (156). The first part of this statement was cited, with minor variations, by Wansharīsī, *al-Miᶜyār al-Mughrib*, X, 64.

[195] The textual justification of attesting handwriting operates on two levels: one direct, the other oblique. The Quranic verse (2:185) is indirect in the sense that it occasions a principle, *ḍarūra*, by which the practice is in turn justified. But Ibn al-Munāṣif (*Tanbīh al-Ḥukkām*, 165) also resorts to Prophetic *sīra* to validate the practice directly on textual basis, citing the Prophet's letters to the Byzantine emperor Hiraql

witnesses who can travel from one town to another, probably quite remote, in order to attest the authenticity of the conveyed document. Attesting handwriting thus became the solution to this problem. For without this solution, Ibn al-Munāṣif averred, either justice would be thwarted or the witnesses would have to endure the hardship of travel; and both results would be objectionable. Furthermore, since the ultimate goal is to prove the authenticity of the *qāḍī*'s *kitāb* against forgery and distortion, any means that achieves this end must be considered legitimate. If, therefore, the receiving *qāḍī* can establish beyond a shadow of doubt that the document in question – written by the hand of the sending *qāḍī* and set by his seal – truly belongs to the *qāḍī* who claims to have sent it to him, then the document possesses an authenticating power equal to, if not better than (*ḍāhā*), another document that has been attested and conveyed by two just witnesses.[196]

From all this two distinct features emerge in the context of the attestation to handwriting. First, the pervasive practice on the popular and professional legal levels – as vividly described by Ibn al-Munāṣif – appears to amount to a socio-legal consensus. The practice was so entrenched that any notion of reversing it would seem utterly unfeasible. True, this sort of consensus does not possess the backing of the traditional mechanisms of law, but its putative force – in its own locale and context – is nonetheless equal to that of traditional *ijmā*ʿ. Second, the justification of the practice squarely rests on the principle of necessity, sanctioned as a means by which undue hardship and harm are to be averted. Now, what is most interesting about these two features is that they both also played a most central role in introducing the *kitāb al-qāḍī ilā al-qāḍī* into the realm of formal legal discourse. Consensus was emblematic of its extensive existence in the world of practice, and the principle of necessity was instrumental in bringing it into the realm of formal legitimacy. Ibn al-Munāṣif, as an author–jurist, thus both articulates and formally sanctions legal change.

## VIII

Admittedly, however, Ibn al-Munāṣif does not steer his discourse beyond the dictates of the legal reality in which he lived. As we have said, he articulates and gives a formal sanction for what he observed on the ground. But the tools of the author–jurist did permit him to venture

(Heraclius) and the Sassanid Kisrā (Khusru Parviz). See also Aḥmad b. ʿAlī Ibn Ḥajar al-ʿAsqalānī, *Fatḥ al-Bārī bi-Sharḥ Ṣaḥīḥ al-Bukhārī*, ed. ʿAbd al-ʿAzīz Ibn Bāz et al., 13 vols. (Beirut: Dār al-Maʿrifa, 1980), XIII, 140–45.

196 Ibn al-Munāṣif, *Tanbīh al-Ḥukkām*, 165.

beyond these relatively narrow confines. One such tool, and an important one at that, is the appropriation and reworking of earlier discourse through the utilization of operative terminology.

Consider, for instance, the change that took place between the fifth/eleventh and seventh/thirteenth centuries with regard to claims of movable property sought to be redressed by means of *kitāb al-qāḍī ilā al-qāḍī*. In a section of his influential work *Adab al-Qaḍā'*, Ibn Abī al-Damm discussed this and other issues on the basis of Māwardī's treatise *Adab al-Qāḍī*. At first glance, the former appears to reproduce the latter's discussion not only verbatim but lock, stock, and barrel. However, a closer examination shows that the former borrowed from the latter selectively and only inasmuch as he needed to. If the movable property (e.g. a horse or a slave) possessed particular qualities which distinguished it from other similar properties, then the *qāḍī* must hear the testimony of witnesses and write what is in effect an open letter addressed to the locale in which the property was found.[197]

Māwardī, on the other hand, distinguished between two opinions (*qawlān*) with regard to a plaintiff who, at a court of law, claims the right to a movable property that was in the possession of an *absente reo*. In his view, the less acceptable of the two opinions was the one already mentioned by Ibn Abī al-Damm. Māwardī maintained that the authoritative doctrine of the Shāfiᶜites is that the *qāḍī* shall not decide on the right of ownership unless the property was physically present before the witnesses when they render their testimony. For allowing a testimony with regard to an absent property would raise the probability of error significantly because the property might be confused with another, similar, one. This opinion of the Shāfiᶜites, he asserted, has been put into normative practice (*maᶜmūl ᶜalayh*), which explains, in terms of authority, its superiority over the other opinion.[198]

It seems safe to assume that what was normative practice in Māwardī's time and place (Iraq in the fifth/eleventh century) was no longer so in Ibn Abī al-Damm's seventh/thirteenth-century Syria. It is with this consideration in mind that Ibn Abī al-Damm took exception to what Māwardī thought authoritative. Needless to say, this selective appropriation is emblematic of the creative reenactment of legal doctrine within the authoritative structure of the school. To say that Māwardī's discourse is used more as a mantle of authority than a real source of substantive legal doctrine is not only to state the obvious, but also to describe a common practice.

197 Ibn Abī al-Damm, *Adab al-Qaḍā'*, 346. 198 Māwardī, *Adab al-Qāḍī*, II, 107.

Selective appropriation and manipulation of earlier juristic discourse is the hallmark of the author's venture. To give adequate attention to this tool of change, we shall now turn to the issue of custom in the (later) Ḥanafite legal tradition. This issue illustrates a significant and fundamental transformation in the law, a transformation that was, no doubt, initially precipitated by legal praxis. Custom presented a major problem for later Ḥanafite jurists, since the school tradition of positive law and legal theory left little latitude for customary practices to establish themselves readily as authoritative entities. The difficulty is apparent in the fact that legal doctrine never succeeded in recognizing custom as an independent and formal legal source. Indeed, even when compared with the so-called supplementary sources – *istiḥsān*, *istiṣlāḥ*, etc. – custom never managed to occupy a place equal to that which these latter had attained in the hierarchy of legal sources. As a formal entity, it remained marginal to the legal arsenal of the four schools, although the Ḥanafites and Mālikites seem to have given it, at least outwardly, more recognition than did the other two schools, however informal this recognition might have been.

The failure of custom to occupy a place among the formal sources of the law becomes all the more striking since Abū Yūsuf, a foremost Ḥanafite authority and second only to Abū Ḥanīfa himself, seems to have recognized it as a source.[199] But for reasons that still await further research,[200] Abū Yūsuf's position failed to gain majority support and was

199 Ibn ʿĀbidīn, *Nashr al-ʿUrf*, 118.

200 Reasons that may well be related to legal developments during the second/eighth and third/ninth centuries when traditionalist groups were battling rationalist jurisprudence. The abandonment of certain rationalist theses seems to have become necessary in order to gain membership in mainstream Sunnism, just as traditionalism, especially its extreme anti-rationalist varieties, had to relinquish some of its fundamental doctrines to avoid being entirely marginalized, and perhaps even ousted altogether from within the pale of Sunnism. Ḥanafite jurisprudence was forced to substitute *ḥadīth* for *ra'y* during the third/ninth century, an accomplishment to be attributed to Muḥammad b. Shujāʿ al-Thaljī (d. 266/879). Another concession that the Ḥanafite jurists had to make was to reduce their reliance on rationalistic reasoning, a feature of Abū Ḥanīfa's influential legal doctrines. Abū Yūsuf's recognition of custom as a source of law must have stood as a flagrant violation of the traditionalist–rationalist synthesis which Sunnī Islam had reached by the end of the third/ninth century and beginning of the fourth/tenth. Indeed, it was this synthesis and the historical processes that lay behind them which led to what later became known as *uṣūl al-fiqh* and, perforce, to the exclusion therefrom of custom as a formal entity. On the traditionalist–rationalist conflict, see Melchert, *Formation of the Sunni Schools*, 1 ff. On the synthesis between the two camps, see Hallaq, "Was al-Shafiʿi the Master Architect?"; Hallaq, "Was the Gate of Ijtihad Closed?" 7–10. On Thaljī's contribution to the transformation of Ḥanafite jurisprudence, see the revealing biographical notice in Ibn al-Nadīm, *Fihrist*, 291; Qurashī, *al-Jawāhir al-Muḍī'a*, II, 221; Ibn Quṭlūbughā, *Tāj al-Tarājim*, 55–56.

in effect abandoned.[201] Instead, throughout the five or six centuries subsequent to Abū Yūsuf, the Ḥanafite school upheld the fundamental proposition that the textual sources unquestionably overrode custom.

The discourse of Ḥanafite texts during this period reflects their strong commitment to this proposition, since its vindication on the grounds that the textual sources are superior to custom was universally accepted.[202] While occasional references to custom remained part of the same discourse, it is nonetheless significant that such references appear fleetingly, as contingent entities intermittently relevant to the law. In Sarakhsī's highly acclaimed *Mabsūṭ*, for instance, both explicit reference and allusion to custom appear a number of times and in connection with a variety of topics.[203] In the context of rent, for instance, he states the maxim "What is known through custom is equivalent to that which is stipulated by the clear texts of revelation."[204] It is clear, however, that the maxim is not cited with the purpose of establishing a legal principle, but rather as a justification for a highly specific doctrine concerning the rent of residential property. If a house is rented, and the contract includes no stipulation as to the purpose for which it was rented, then the operative assumption – which the said maxim legitimizes – would be that it was leased for residential and not commercial or other purposes. The tendency to confine custom to very specific cases – which is evident in Sarakhsī's work – is only matched by its acceptance under the guise of other formal principles, such as *istiḥsān* and consensus. Custom was often treated in the law and law books *qua* custom, pure and simple, this being an unambiguous indication of the inability of jurists to introduce it into the law under the guise of established methodological tools.[205]

201 Until, that is, our author, Ibn ʿĀbidīn, not only rejuvenated interest in his position, but essentially revived it, as we shall see later.

202 Ibn Nujaym, *al-Ashbāh wal-Naẓā'ir*, 131 (on the authority of Ẓahīr al-Dīn b. Aḥmad); Suyūṭī, *al-Ashbāh wal-Naẓā'ir*, 93. For Marghīnānī's statement that "an explicit textual ruling is stronger than a custom and one does not abandon something stronger in favor of something weaker," see Gedeon Libson, "On the Development of Custom as a Source of Law in Islamic Law," *Islamic Law and Society*, 4, 2 (1997), 145.

203 See next note. For a biographical account of Sarakhsī, see Ibn Quṭlūbughā, *Tāj al-Tarājim*, 52–53.

204 Sarakhsī, *Mabsūṭ*, XV, 130: "*al-maʿlūm bil-ʿurf kal-mashrūṭ bil-naṣṣ*." See also XV, 85–86, 132, 142, 171; XII, 142 and passim.

205 It would, in this context, be instructive to explore the possible reasons that lie behind the incorporation of customary practices into law through these two distinctly different channels, namely, direct incorporation (= custom *qua* custom) and incorporation via formal and supplementary sources. Granting, as I do, the valid explanation in terms of chronological developments (whereby custom came into law as part of the evolutionary processes that gave rise to both positive law and legal theory), there remains the question as to why the supplementary and formal sources of law could not permit, under their own rubric, the total absorption of customary practices in the later period.

The incorporation into the law of custom *qua* custom seems to have increased some time after the sixth/twelfth century, although this incorporation was to remain on a case-by-case basis. While the cumulative increase in the instances of custom was evident, there was still no formal place for it in the methodological and theoretical scheme, no doubt because legal theory and methodology had become too well established to allow for a structural and fundamental change.

By the tenth/sixteenth century, it had become obvious that custom had to be accounted for in a manner that adequately acknowledged its role in the law but which did not disturb the postulates and basic assumptions of legal theory. This was no easy task. In the Ḥanafite school, Ibn Nujaym (d. 970/1563)[206] seems to have been one of the more prominent author–jurists to undertake the articulation of the relationship between law, legal theory, and custom. In his important work *al-Ashbāh wal-Naẓā'ir*, he dedicates a chapter to custom, significantly titled "Custom determines legal norms" (*al-ᶜĀda muḥakkima*).[207]

The first issue traditionally discussed in the exposition of legal sources is authoritativeness (*ḥujjiyya*), namely, a conclusive demonstration through textual support (*dalīl qaṭᶜī*) that the source in question is valid, admissible, and constitutes an authoritative basis for further legal construction. But all Ibn Nujaym can adduce in terms of textual support is the allegedly Prophetic report "Whatever Muslims find good, God finds it likewise,"[208] which is universally considered to be deficient. Ibn Nujaym acknowledges that the report lacks the final link with the Prophet, insinuating that it originated with Ibn Masᶜūd.[209] Al-Ḥaṣkafī al-ᶜAlā'ī also observes that after an extensive search he could find it in none of the *ḥadīth* collections except for Ibn Ḥanbal's *Musnad*.[210] Curiously, despite his obvious failure to demonstrate any authoritative basis for custom – a failure shared by the entire community of Muslim jurists – Ibn Nujaym proceeds to discuss those areas in the law where custom has traditionally been taken into account.[211]

[206] Brockelmann, *Geschichte*, II, 401–03.

[207] Ibn Nujaym, *al-Ashbāh wal-Naẓā'ir*, 129.

[208] "*Mā ra'āhu al-Muslimūna ḥasanan fa-hwa ᶜinda Allāhi ḥasan.*" [209] Ibid., 129–30.

[210] Ibn ᶜĀbidīn, *Nashr al-ᶜUrf*, 115; Suyūṭī, *al-Ashbāh wal-Naẓā'ir*, 89. This *ḥadīth* is also used by Shaybānī in justification of consensus. See W. B. Hallaq, "On the Authoritativeness of Sunnī Consensus," *International Journal of Middle East Studies*, 18 (1986), 431.

[211] An inductive survey of the instances of custom that have been incorporated into law appears to have been often offered as a substitute for a proof of authoritativeness (*ḥujjiyya*), although such a substitute clearly involved begging the question. It is perhaps the jurists' acute awareness of the pernicious effects of circularity that prevented them from claiming inductive knowledge to constitute a solution to the problem of *ḥujjiyya*.

After listing a number of legal cases acknowledged by the community of jurists as having been dictated by customary conventions, he argues that, in matters of usury not stipulated by the revealed texts, custom must be recognized. Those commodities that are measured by volume and/or by weight and which have been regulated by the revealed texts as lying outside the compass of usurious transactions are in no way affected by customary usage, of course. This, he maintains, is the opinion of Abū Ḥanīfa and Shaybānī, but not that of Abū Yūsuf, who, as we have seen, permitted the intervention of custom. Abū Ḥanīfa and Shaybānī's opinion, he further asserts, is strengthened by Ibn al-Ḥumām's arguments (*wa-qawwāhu fī Fatḥ al-Qadīr*)[212] in which the latter stresses, along with Ẓahīr al-Dīn (d. 619/1222),[213] that a clear text (*naṣṣ*) cannot be superseded by considerations of custom.[214]

Ibn Nujaym distinguishes between two types of custom, namely, universal (*ᶜurf ᶜāmm*) and local custom (*ᶜurf khāṣṣ*). The former prevails throughout Muslim lands, while the latter is in effect in a restricted area or in a town or village.[215] When the former does not contravene a *naṣṣ*, the authoritative doctrine of the Ḥanafite school is that it ought to be taken into consideration in legal construction. The contract of *istisnāᶜ* is but one example in point.[216] However, the Ḥanafites differed over whether local custom has any legal force. Najm al-Dīn al-Zāhidī (d. 658/1259),[217] for instance, refused to acknowledge that local custom had any such force, since the weight of local considerations is negligible. Others, such as the Bukhāran jurists, disagreed. Indeed, as quoted by Ibn Nujaym, Zāhidī gives us to understand that these jurists were the first in the history of the Ḥanafite school to advocate such an

212 *Fatḥ al-Qadīr* being Ibn al-Humam's (d. 681/1282) work which is a commentary on Marghīnānī's *Hidāya*.

213 Ẓahīr al-Dīn Abū Bakr Muḥammad b. Aḥmad, the author of the well-known *fatwā* collection *al-Ẓahīriyya*. See Qurashī, *al-Jawāhir al-Muḍīʾa*, II, 20.

214 Ibn Nujaym, *al-Ashbāh wal-Naẓāʾir*, 131.

215 Ibid., 137; Ibn ᶜĀbidīn, *Nashr al-ᶜUrf*, 132. On universal and local customs, see B. Johansen, "Coutumes locales et coutumes universelles," *Annales Islamologiques*, 27 (1993): 29–35.

216 *Istiṣnāᶜ* is a manufacturing contract whereby a sale is concluded with the condition of future delivery. The contract may also be one of hire, such as when a person gives a blacksmith a certain amount of metal so that the latter manufactures therefrom a pot or container, for a stipulated payment. Being of the same type as the *salam* contract, *istiṣnāᶜ* goes against the principles of *qiyās* which require the avoidance of risk (*gharar*) by ensuring that the object of sale or hire be in existence at the time of sale. See Sarakhsī, *Mabsūṭ*, XV, 84 ff.

217 For a biographical notice, see Ibn Quṭlūbughā, *Tāj al-Tarājim*, 73; Brockelmann, *Geschichte*, I, 382 (475).

opinion.[218] But Zāhidī emphatically states that the correct opinion (*al-ṣaḥīḥ*) is that local practices are effectively insufficient to establish themselves as legally admissible customs.

Ultimately, however, the question is not whether local custom can or cannot generate legal norms, for it was clear to the jurists that such customs cannot yield universal and normative legal rules, but only, if at all, particular ones. A universal rule simply cannot emanate from a local custom (*al-ḥukm al-ʿāmm lā yathbut bil-ʿurf al-khāṣṣ*).[219] This, Ibn Nujaym asserts, is the authoritative doctrine of the school (*al-madhhab*), although a good number of Ḥanafite jurists have issued *fatwā*s on the basis of local custom and in contravention of this doctrine. It is interesting that Ibn Nujaym finally takes the side of these jurists, in a conscious and bold decision to go against the *madhhab* doctrine.[220]

Ibn Nujaym's recognition of custom as an extraneous legal source represents only a later stage in a checkered historical process that began with the three founders of the Ḥanafite school. The religio-legal developments between the second/eighth and fourth/tenth centuries[221] appear to have led to the suppression of Abū Yūsuf's doctrine in favor of a less formal role for custom. Sarakhsī's recognition of custom on a case-by-case basis is but one illustration of the success of the thesis of divine origins of the law, a thesis that ensured the near decimation of Abū Yūsuf's doctrine and its likes. But the serious demands imposed by custom persisted. The practices and writings of the Bukhāran jurists, among others, were conducive to a process in which the informal role of custom as a source of law was expanded and given more weight. Ibn Nujaym's writings, in which he selectively but skillfully draws on earlier authorities, including the Bukhārans, typify the near culmination of this process.

The process reached its zenith with the writings of the last major Ḥanafite jurist, the Damascene al-Sayyid Amīn Ibn ʿĀbidīn (1198/1783–1252/1836), whose career spanned the crucial period that immediately preceded the introduction of Ottoman *tanẓīmāt*. There is no indication that Ibn ʿĀbidīn held an official post in the state, and he seems to have been distant from the circles of political power. His training and later career were strictly traditional: He read the Quran and studied language and Shāfiʿite law with Shaykh Saʿīd al-Ḥamawī. Later, he continued

[218] Ibn Nujaym states that these Bukhārans themselves formulated this opinion (*aḥdathahu baʿḍ ahl Bukhārā*), it being almost certain that their opinion is a reflection of their juridical practices. See his *al-Ashbāh wal-Naẓāʾir*, 138.

[219] Ibid., 137.

[220] Ibid., 138: "*lākin aftā kathīr min al-mashāyikh bi-iʿtibārihi, fa-aqūlu ʿalā iʿtibārihi.*"

[221] As briefly alluded to in n. 200, above.

his legal studies with Shaykh Shākir al-ᶜAqqād who apparently persuaded him to convert to Ḥanafism. With him he studied arithmetic, law of inheritance, legal theory, *ḥadīth*, Quranic exegesis, Ṣūfism, and the rational sciences. Among the texts he read with his shaykh were those of Ibn Nujaym, Ṣadr al-Sharīᶜa, Ibn al-Humām, and of other significant Ḥanafite authors.[222] His successful career brought him distinction in several spheres, not the least of which was his rise to prominence as a highly celebrated author and *muftī*. As a professor, he seems to have had an equally successful career, involving, among other things, the privilege of bestowing *ijāza*s on such important men as the Ottoman shaykh al-Islam ᶜĀrif Ḥikmat Bey.[223]

True, Ibn ᶜĀbidīn flourished before the *tanẓīmāt* started, but he was already witness to the changes that began to sweep the empire long before. When his legal education began, the *Nizām-i Cedid* of Selim III was well under way, and when his writing career reached its apex, Maḥmūd II and his men centralized, in an unprecedented but immeasurably crucial move, the major charitable trusts of the empire under the Ministry of Imperial Pious Endowments, which was established in 1826.[224] These significant developments, coupled with the changes that Damascene society experienced due to western penetration and intervention, already effected a new outlook that culminated not only in the *tanẓīmāt* reforms but also in a rudimentary rupture with traditional forms.[225] Ibn ᶜĀbidīn's writings do not mirror any clear sense of crises, either in epistemological or in cultural terms, but they do reflect a certain measure of subtle and latent impatience with some constricting aspects of tradition. This perhaps explains an insightful remark made nearly a century ago by one of the shrewdest commentators on Islamic law. Nicholas Aghnides has pointed out that Ibn ᶜĀbidīn's *magnum opus*, *Ḥāshiyat Radd al-Muḥtār*, "may be said to be the last word in the authoritative interpretation of Ḥanafite law. It shows originality in attempting to determine the status of present practical

222 For Ibn ᶜĀbidīn's biographical notices, see Khalīl Mardam Bīk (Bey), *Aᶜyān al-Qarn al-Thālith ᶜAshar fī al-Fikr wal-Siyāsa wal-Ijtimāᶜ* (Beirut: Mu'assasat al-Risāla, 1977), 36–39; ᶜAbd al-Razzāq al-Bīṭār, *Ḥulyat al-Bashar fī Tārīkh al-Qarn al-Thālith ᶜAshar*, ed. M. B. Bīṭār, 3 vols. (Damascus: Maṭbaᶜat al-Majmaᶜ al-ᶜIlmī al-ᶜArabī, 1963), III, 1230–39; Ziriklī, *Aᶜlām*, VI, 42.

223 Mardam, *Aᶜyān*, 37.

224 See Madeline C. Zilfi, "The *Ilmiye* Registers and the Ottoman *Medrese* System prior to the Tanzimat," in *Contributions à l'histoire économique et sociale de l'Empire ottoman* (Leuven: Editions Peeters, 1983), 309–27, at 312–13.

225 For a general history of Damascus during this period, see George Koury, "The Province of Damascus" (Ph.D. dissertation: University of Michigan, 1970); Yūsuf Naᶜīsa, *Mujtamaᶜ Madīnat Dimashq*, 2 vols. (Damascus: Ṭlās, 1986).

situations, as a rule, shunned by others."[226] This originality, which manifests itself even more acutely in his writings on custom, may be seen as representing a euphemism for a discursive attempt to twist and transform legal concepts within the fetters of an authoritative and binding tradition. Originality often does take such forms.

Some time in 1243/1827, Ibn ᶜĀbidīn wrote a short gloss on his *ᶜUqūd Rasm al-Muftī*, a composition in verse which sums up the rules that govern the office of *iftāʾ*, its functions, and the limits of the *muftī*'s field of hermeneutics.[227] In the same year, he authored a *risāla* in which he amplifies his commentary on one line in the verse, a line that specifically addresses the role of custom (*ᶜurf*) in law.[228] Having been written at the same time, cross-references between the two *risāla*s are many.[229] The disintegration of textual boundaries between the two treatises is further enhanced by constant reference to, and juxtaposition with, his supergloss *Ḥāshiyat Radd al-Muḥtār*. In the latter he also refers,[230] in the past tense, to his two *risāla*s, and in the two *risāla*s, in the same tense, to his *Ḥāshiya*.[231] This synchronous multiple cross-referencing suggests that Ibn ᶜĀbidīn composed his two *risāla*s during the lengthy process of writing the *Ḥāshiya*, which he never completed.

Establishing for these treatises a chronological order, or the absence thereof, is particularly important here because a correct analysis of Ibn ᶜĀbidīn's concept of custom depends on the relationship of his epistemological and authority-based assumptions in *Nashr al-ᶜUrf* to the hierarchy of authority which he sets forth in, and which governs the discourse of, his *Ḥāshiya*.[232] That *Nashr al-ᶜUrf* and *Ḥāshiya* were written simultaneously and that the former in fact represents a discursive extension of the latter, suggests that Ibn ᶜĀbidīn continued to uphold the structure of authority and epistemology as he laid it down in his *Ḥāshiya* and as it had been articulated in the Ḥanafite school for several centuries before him. It is precisely the resolution of the tension between this structure of authority and the role he assigned to custom in the law that presented Ibn ᶜĀbidīn with one of his greatest challenges.

The declared *raison d'ètre* of *Nashr al-ᶜUrf* is that custom presents the jurist with several complexities which Ibn ᶜĀbidīn's predecessors had not

226 Aghnides, *Mohammedan Theories*, 183. 227 Ibn ᶜĀbidīn, *Sharḥ al-Manẓūma*, 1–53.

228 Ibn ᶜĀbidīn, *Nashr al-ᶜUrf*, 114; the line runs as follows: "*wal-ᶜurf fī al-sharᶜ la-hu iᶜtibār / li-dhā ᶜalayhi al-ḥukm qad yudār.*"

229 Ibid., 114, 125, and passim; *Sharḥ al-Manẓūma*, 48 and passim.

230 Ibn ᶜĀbidīn, *Ḥāshiya*, IV, 364, 434, 519, and passim.

231 Ibn ᶜĀbidīn, *Nashr al-ᶜUrf*, 139 and passim; *Sharḥ al-Manẓūma*, 15.

232 Ibn ᶜĀbidīn, *Ḥāshiya*, I, 70 ff. See also *Sharḥ al-Manẓūma*, 16–18.

adequately addressed.[233] (In treating this presumably neglected area, Ibn ᶜĀbidīn seems to promise a certain measure of originality.) A careful reading of the *risāla* reveals that these complexities revolve around custom as a legal source as well as around its relationship to both the unambiguous revealed sources[234] and the authoritative opinions embodied in *ẓāhir al-riwāya*.

But before proceeding to unravel these complexities, Ibn ᶜĀbidīn attempts a definition of custom (*ᶜāda*). What is important about the definition is not so much its substance as the manner in which it is expounded. And it is this manner of discursive elaboration that characterizes, in distinctly structural ways, the methods and ways of the author–jurist. Here, as elsewhere in the *risāla*, the mode of discourse is selective citation and juxtaposition of earlier authorities, a mode that has for centuries been a common practice of the author–jurist. However conventional or novel they may be, arguments are presented as falling within the boundaries of authoritative tradition, for they are generally adduced as the total sum of quotations from earlier authorities, cemented together by the author's own interpolations, interventions, counter-arguments, and qualifications. Through this process, new arguments acquire the backing of tradition, represented in an array of voices that range from the highly authoritative to the not-so-authoritative. This salient feature of textual elaboration makes for a discursive strategy that we must keep in mind at all times, whether reading Ibn ᶜĀbidīn or other author–jurists.

Once a definition has been constructed, a necessary second step in the exposition of any legal source is to demonstrate its authoritativeness, and custom, if it must claim the status of a source, proves no exception to this rule. Here, Ibn ᶜĀbidīn falls back on Ibn Nujaym's by now familiar argument which is itself exclusively based on Ibn Masᶜūd's weak tradition. Realizing the weakness of the tradition and thus the invalidity of this argument, he remarks that custom was so frequently resorted to in the law that it was made a principle (*aṣl*), as evidenced in Sarakhsī's statement: "What is known through custom is equivalent to that which is stipulated by the clear texts of revelation."[235] But Ibn ᶜĀbidīn's compensatory argument does nothing to conceal the fact that custom could never find

[233] Ibn ᶜĀbidīn, *Nashr al-ᶜUrf*, 114.

[234] That is, the *naṣṣ*, as distinguished from ambiguous texts which are by definition capable of more than one interpretation. See Bājī, *Ḥudūd*, 42 ff. The ambiguous, equivocal texts did not present a challenge to custom because their hermeneutical effects were indeterminate.

[235] Sarakhsī, *Mabsūṭ*, XV, 130: "*al-maᶜlūm bil-ᶜurf kal-mashrūṭ bil-naṣṣ.*"

any textually authoritative vindication. Nor does justification in terms of frequent use in the law lead to anything but a *petitio principii*, namely, that custom should be used in the law because it is used in the law. Be that as it may, Ibn ʿĀbidīn states his piece and moves on, being scarcely, if at all, perturbed by his own, and tradition's, failure to persuade on this matter. Scarcely perturbed, because the focus of his agenda lay elsewhere: he, and the tradition in which he wrote, were cognizant of the theological and epistemological limitations that had been imposed on custom when legal theory was still in the process of formation. The challenge he now faced was to circumvent these limitations.

Thus, the real issue for Ibn ʿĀbidīn is one of more immediate and practical concern. It is one that is problematized through the introduction of two competing opinions on the relationship between custom and the doctrines of *ẓāhir al-riwāya*. In his *Qunya*, Zāhidī is reported to have maintained that neither the *muftī* nor the *qāḍī* should adopt the opinions of *ẓāhir al-riwāya* to the utter exclusion of custom. Both Hindī[236] and Bīrī[237] cited Zāhidī's argument, apparently approving its conclusion. These assertions, Ibn ʿĀbidīn argues, raise a problem, since the common doctrine of the school is that the opinions of *ẓāhir al-riwāya* remain binding unless the leading legal scholars (*al-mashāyikh*) decide to replace them by other opinions that have been subjected to *taṣḥīḥ*. The problem is accentuated in those areas of the law where the opinions of *ẓāhir al-riwāya* were constructed on the basis of revealed texts of an unambiguous nature (*ṣarīḥ al-naṣṣ*) and/or sanctioned by the conclusive authority of consensus. In these areas, custom does not, nor should it, constitute a source, for unlike the texts, it may simply be wrong. In what seems to be an attempt to accentuate this problematic, Ibn ʿĀbidīn invokes Ibn Nujaym's statement to the effect that custom must be set aside in the presence of a text, and conversely, that it may be taken into consideration only when no text governing the case in question is to be found.

Before Ibn ʿĀbidīn begins his treatment of this problematic, he introduces, in the footsteps of Ibn Nujaym, the distinction between universal and particular custom. Each of these two types is said to stand in a particular relationship with both the unambiguous revealed texts and *ẓāhir al-riwāya*, thereby creating what is in effect a four-fold classification. But Ibn ʿĀbidīn reduces them to a two-part discussion, one treating custom's relationship with the unambiguous revealed texts, the other its relationship with *ẓāhir al-riwāya*.

[236] In *Khizānat al-Riwāyāt*. See Brockelmann, *Geschichte*, II, 221 (286).
[237] Whom I could not identify.

In line with traditional juristic epistemology, it remains Ibn ᶜĀbidīn's tenet that whatever contravenes, *in every respect* (*min kulli wajh*), the explicit and unequivocal dictates of the revealed texts is void, carrying neither legal effect nor authority. The case of intoxicants affords an eloquent example of this sort of contravention. The key element in the formulation of this tenet is the clause "in every respect," a clause that quite effectively limits the boundaries of those texts that engender exclusive authority by removing from their purview all cases that posit no straightforward or direct contravention of these texts. A partial correspondence between the text and custom does not therefore render the latter inadmissible, for what is being considered in such cases is the corresponding part, not the differential. That part therefore particularizes (*yukhaṣṣiṣ*) the text, but does in no way abrogate it. However, in order for custom to have this particularizing effect, it must be universal. If universal custom can particularize a text, then it can, *a fortiori*, override a *qiyās* which is no more than a probabilistic inference. *Istiṣnāᶜ*, as we have seen, is a case in point.[238]

Turning to particular custom, Ibn ᶜĀbidīn makes the categorical statement that, according to the school's authoritative doctrine (*madhhab*), it is not taken into consideration (*lā tuᶜtabar*). But this rather forward statement of doctrine is undermined by Ibn ᶜĀbidīn's introduction of a succession of qualifying and opposing opinions expressed by other jurists. Before doing so, however, he states, on the authority of earlier jurists, the traditional school doctrine, thereby engaging in what amounts to polemical maneuvering. As might be expected, Ibn Nujaym's weighty attestation is given first, the intention being to introduce not so much an affirmation of the school's doctrine as Ibn Nujaym's partial qualification and exception that many jurists have issued *fatwās* in accordance with particular custom.[239] This is immediately followed by another, more drastic statement made by Ibn Māza who reported that the Balkh jurists, including Naṣīr b. Yaḥyā[240] and Muḥammad b. Salama,[241] permitted, among other things, a certain type of rent which is otherwise deemed prohibited. The permissibility of this type was justified on the grounds that the practice was not explicitly regulated by the texts and that it had become customary among the people of Balkh. The license of this exception in no way meant that the principles of rent were set aside. If this type of rent was permitted, it was deemed to be an exception, in the

[238] Ibn ᶜĀbidīn, *Nashr al-ᶜUrf*, 116. [239] See at n. 220, above.

[240] Muḥammad al-Mudarris, *Mashāyikh Balkh min al-Ḥanafiyya*, 2 vols. (Baghdad: Wizārat al-Awqāf, Silsilat al-Kutub al-Ḥadītha, 1979), I, 53, 76, and see index at II, 942.

[241] Ibid., I, 53, 89, and see index at II, 938.

same manner *istiṣnāᶜ* represents an exception to the principle that the object being sold must at the time of sale be in existence.

But Ibn Māza does not, in the final analysis, agree with the Balkh jurists. Having fully stated their case, he cautions that exceptions, made through particularization (*takhṣīṣ*) on the basis of a particular custom, are not deemed valid because the weight of such a custom is negligible, and that this engenders doubt (*shakk*) which does not exist in the case of *istiṣnāᶜ*, a pervasive practice that has been shown "to exist in all regions" (*fī al-bilād kullihā*). In support of Ibn Māza, Ibn ᶜĀbidīn interjects Ibn Nujaym's discussion of particular custom, which is in turn based on a series of citations from other jurists. Here he concludes that *qiyās* cannot be abandoned in favor of particular custom, although, as we have seen, some of Ibn Nujaym's authorities do recognize it. The commentators, Ibn ᶜĀbidīn argues, have upheld the rule that wheat, barley, dates, and salt are to be sold, without exception, by volume, while gold and silver are to be sold by weight. This rule is dictated by a well-known and explicit Prophetic tradition. Thus, the sale of wheat by weight and of gold by volume is unanimously considered null and void, whether or not it is sanctioned by custom. The explicit texts must always stand supreme. However, other commodities that carry no stipulations in the texts may be sold in accordance with the custom prevalent in a certain society.[242]

An apparently hypothetical interlocutor is made to state, on Qudūrī's authority, that Abū Yūsuf allowed custom to prevail over the Prophetic tradition concerning usury in the sale of certain commodities. Accordingly, gold might be sold in volume if custom dictated that it should be so.[243] This departure from the imperatives of the revealed texts therefore justifies the practice of usury and other unlawful matters as long as custom requires it.

Taking this to be a distortion of Abū Yūsuf's position, Ibn ᶜĀbidīn argues that what the master meant to do was to use custom as the *ratio legis* of the textual prohibition. If the Prophetic tradition dictated measurement by weight for certain commodities, and by volume for others, it was merely because it was the custom to do so at the time of the Prophet. Had custom been different, it is entirely conceivable that the Prophetic tradition might have permitted the sale of gold by volume, and that of barley by weight. Therefore, Ibn ᶜĀbidīn concludes, "if custom undergoes change, then the legal norm (*ḥukm*) must change too. In taking changing and unprecedented custom into consideration there is no violation of the texts; in fact, if anything, such consideration constitutes adherence to [the

[242] Ibn ᶜĀbidīn, *Nashr al-ᶜUrf*, 118. [243] Cf. Qudūrī, *Mukhtaṣar*, 87.

imperatives of] the texts."[244] At this point, Ibn ᶜĀbidīn hastens to add that certain pecuniary practices prevalent in his time – such as "buying *darāhim* for *darāhim*" or borrowing money on the basis of face value (or by count, *ᶜadad*) – do not in fact constitute violations of the texts, thanks to Abū Yūsuf's doctrine. "May God abundantly reward Abū Yūsuf for what he did for the people of these times of ours. He saved them from the serious affliction that is usury."[245]

The liberties granted with regard to borrowing money at face value and not by weight or volume were reached by means of *takhrīj*, representing a direct extension of Abū Yūsuf's doctrine.[246] This was originally Saᶜdī Afandī's *takhrīj*, confirmed later by Sirāj al-Dīn Ibn Nujaym (d. 1005/1596)[247] and others. Nābulusī,[248] however, thought the entire juristic construction needless since the coins struck by the state had a specific weight, and borrowing or exchange by denomination was effectively the same as representation of weight. Ibn ᶜĀbidīn introduces Nābulusī's argument only to disagree with it, apparently using it as a rhetorical pretext to bolster his arguments further. It may have been the case, he maintains, that in Nābulusī's time coins were equal in terms of weight and value; nevertheless, "in these times of ours" (*fī zamāninā*) each sultan struck currency of lower quality than that struck by his predecessor. The practice during Ibn ᶜĀbidīn's period involved the use of all sorts of currency, some containing a high ratio of gold and silver as well as those of a lower quality. When people borrow, for instance, they do not specify the type of currency but only the number, for when repayment becomes due, they may use any type of currency as long as the value of the amount paid equals that which had been borrowed.[249] Had it not been for Abū Yūsuf's doctrine, these types of transactions could have been said to involve usury because the weight of the coins borrowed was never identical to that with which repayment was made. If, on the other hand, such transactions were

[244] Ibn ᶜĀbidīn, *Nashr al-ᶜUrf*, 118: "*takūnu al-ᶜāda hiya al-manẓūru ilayhā fa-idhā taghayyarat taghayyara al-ḥukm, fa-laysa fī iᶜtibāri al-ᶜāda al-mutaghayyira al-ḥāditha mukhālafa lil-naṣṣ bal fī-hi ittibāᶜ al-naṣṣ.*"

[245] Ibid., 118: "*fa-law taᶜārafa al-nāsu bayᶜa al-darāhima bil-darāhima aw istiqrāḍahā bil-ᶜadad, ka-mā fī zamāninā, lā yakūn mukhālifan lil-naṣṣ. Fa-Allāh taᶜālā yajzī al-Imām Abā Yūsuf ᶜan ahl hādhā al-zamān khayra al-jazāʾ fa-laqad sadda ᶜan-hum bāban ᶜaẓīman min al-ribā.*"

[246] On *takhrīj* and its relationship to the doctrines of the schools' founders, see chapter 2, section III, above.

[247] In his *al-Nahr al-Fāʾiq*. See Brockelmann, *Geschichte*, Suppl. 2, 266.

[248] Probably Ismāᶜīl b. ᶜAbd al-Majīd al-Nābulusī (d. 1043/1633). See Brockelmann, *Geschichte*, Suppl. 2, 476.

[249] For a detailed discussion of fiscal issues in law, see Ibn ᶜĀbidīn, *Tanbīh al-Ruqūd ᶜalā Masāʾil al-Nuqūd*, in his *Majmūᶜ Rasāʾil*, II, 58–67.

to be regulated by Abū Ḥanīfa and Shaybānī's doctrines – which require the stipulation in the contract of the type of currency and the year of minting – the outcome would surely be objectionable since all pecuniary contracts and transactions would be deemed null and void. Their doctrines would thus lead to great difficulties (*ḥaraj ʿaẓīm*), since they would also necessarily entail the conclusion that "the people of our age are unbelievers." The only way out of this quandary, Ibn ʿĀbidīn asserts, is to go by Abū Yūsuf's doctrine which is left as the only basis of practice.[250]

In favoring Abū Yūsuf's weaker doctrine over and against the other one – also held by Abū Ḥanīfa and Shaybānī – there is an undeniable difficulty. Bypassing three authoritative doctrines by the most influential figures of the school in favor of a weak opinion certainly called for an explanation. Ibn ʿĀbidīn alludes to two possible solutions, one by upholding custom *qua* custom as a sufficient justification, the other by resorting to the notion of necessity (*ḍarūra*).[251] But Ibn ʿĀbidīn does not articulate the distinction between these two means of justification, for he immediately abandons custom in favor of necessity. This is to be expected. Rationalizing the relevance of Abū Yūsuf's doctrine and the need for it by means of custom amounts to rationalizing custom by custom, an argument involving the fallacy of a *petitio principii*. Falling back on necessity is thus left as the only logical choice.

Although the notion of necessity has been used to justify a number of departures from the stringent demands of the law, it is, like custom, restricted to those areas upon which the explicit texts of revelation are silent. Abū Yūsuf, for instance, was criticized when he held the opinion – which ran against the dictates of Prophetic Sunna – that cutting grass in the Sacred Precinct was permissible due to necessity. In this case, Ibn ʿĀbidīn does not seem to agree with Abū Yūsuf, his reasoning being that since the Prophet excluded from the prohibition the *idhkhir* plant,[252] we must conclude that the prohibition remains in effect, and that removal of the prohibition due to necessity is applicable only to that particular plant. More important, the hardship that may result from the prohibition against cutting the grass pales into insignificance when compared with the consequences of forcing a society to change its habits and customs.

250 Ibn ʿĀbidīn, *Nashr al-ʿUrf*, 119: "*fa-yalzam min-hu tafsīq ahl hādhā al-ʿaṣr, fa-yataʿayyan al-iftāʾ bi-dhālika ʿalā hādhihi al-riwāya ʿan Abī Yūsuf.*" (See also *ibid.*, 119–24, where similar arguments are made.)

251 Ibid., 120: "*wa-ʿalā kullin, fa-yanbaghī al-jawāz wal-khurūj ʿan al-ithm ʿinda Allāh taʿālā immā bināʾan ʿalā al-ʿamal bil-ʿurf aw lil-ḍarūra.*"

252 An aromatic plant that grew around Mecca and was used, when cut, in decorating houses and in funerals. See Ibn Manẓūr, *Lisān al-ʿArab*, IV, 302–03.

Ibn ᶜĀbidīn lists a number of cases in which hardship was mitigated due to necessity but then concludes that these cases are in no way comparable to the enormity of the hardship resulting from the imposition of a legal norm that contradicts prevailing social customs.

Having thus established necessity *a fortiori*, Ibn ᶜĀbidīn seeks to locate it in the hierarchy of school doctrine. Probably drawing on Ibn Nujaym, who argued that a good number of Ḥanafite jurists issued *fatwā*s on the basis of local custom, Ibn ᶜĀbidīn asserts that the acceptance of local custom[253] as a basis for a particular legal norm has become one of the opinions of the school, albeit a weak one (*qawl ḍaᶜīf*). Now, necessity renders the adoption of such an opinion permissible.[254] But this constitutes a serious departure from the mainstream doctrine of the school according to which the application of weak opinions is deemed strictly forbidden, since it violates, *inter alia*, the principles of consensus.[255] Furthermore, hermeneutically, weak opinions are considered void for they belong to the category of the abrogated (*mansūkh*), it being understood that they have been repealed by a sound or preponderant opinion (*rājiḥ*). The later Shāfiᶜites, however, adopted a less rigorous position on this matter than the Ḥanafites, and hence it is to them that Ibn ᶜĀbidīn turns for a way out of his quandary. In one of his *fatwā*s, the influential Taqī al-Dīn al-Subkī[256] states – concerning a case of *waqf* – that a weak opinion may be adopted if it is limited to the person and matter at hand and if it is not made transferable to other cases, either in courts of law or in *iftā*ʾ.[257]

But Ibn ᶜĀbidīn apparently finds that having recourse to a Shāfiᶜite authority is insufficient. To enhance Subkī's view, he refers the reader, among other things, to Marghīnānī's *Mukhtārāt al-Nawāzil*,[258] a well-known work which commentators on the same author's *Hidāya* often use in the writing of their glosses. There, Marghīnānī held the opinion that the blood seeping from a wound does not nullify ablution, an opinion that Ibn ᶜĀbidīn admits to be not only unprecedented, but also one that failed to gain any support among the Ḥanafites during or after Marghīnānī's time. Although he fully acknowledges that the opinion is

[253] It is worth noting that Ibn ᶜĀbidīn stresses the point that for a local custom to be considered a valid legal source, it must thoroughly permeate the society in which it is found. See *Nashr al-ᶜUrf*, 134.

[254] Ibid., 125: "*al-qawl al-ḍaᶜīf yajūzu al-ᶜamal bi-hi ᶜinda al-ḍarūra.*"

[255] Ibn ᶜĀbidīn, *Sharḥ al-Manẓūma*, 10–11, 48.

[256] For a biographical notice, see Subkī, *Ṭabaqāt*, VI, 146–227.

[257] Ibn ᶜĀbidīn's reference seems to be to Subkī's *Fatāwā*, II, 10 ff.; *Sharḥ al-Manẓūma*, 49: "*yajūz taqlīd al-wajh al-ḍaᶜīf fī nafs al-amr bil-nisba lil-ᶜamal fī ḥaqqi nafsihi, lā fī al-fatwā wal-ḥukm.*"

[258] Brockelmann, *Geschichte*, I, 378 (469); Marghīnānī, *Hidāya*, I, 3–9.

irregular (*shādhdh*), he nonetheless argues that Marghīnānī stands as an illustrious Ḥanafite, one of the greatest in the school and considered among the highly distinguished *aṣḥāb al-takhrīj*.[259] Therefore, he continues, his opinion ought to be considered sound and the application of a weak opinion must thus be allowed on a restricted basis when it is deemed necessary to do so.[260] Why only in a restricted sense? Because given its weak nature, it is not considered universal in the sense that a local custom gives rise to a legal norm that is applicable only to the city, town, or village where that custom is predominant.

It is to be noted here that Ibn ᶜĀbidīn's reasoning entails a fundamental leap which he does not address, much less justify. The restricted practice which has been deemed permitted by the four schools, usually termed *fī ḥaqqi nafsihi*, is a principle traditionally limited to the person exercising legal reasoning, the *mujtahid*. For example, a heretical *mujtahid* is allowed to apply his own legal formulations to himself (*fī ḥaqqi nafsihi*) but he is barred from issuing *fatwā*s for other Muslims.[261] Subkī himself appears to have made just such a leap in allowing the principle to apply to a *waqf* beneficiary, and Ibn ᶜĀbidīn went even further in imposing its application upon the inhabitants of a village, town, and even a city. It is quite interesting to observe that it is, in the final analysis, immaterial whether Ibn ᶜĀbidīn vindicates every step he takes in the construction of his arguments. Just as the anomalous opinions of Subkī and Marghīnānī were readily and unquestioningly brought into Ibn ᶜĀbidīn's discursive strategies to serve an end, so will Ibn ᶜĀbidīn's own conclusion be utilized to score further points in the future. The question that seems to matter most at this point – namely, whether local custom can lawfully give rise to a particular ruling – has been solved; and Ibn ᶜĀbidīn is responsible for it, in the face of opponents and proponents alike.

Thus far, local custom has been shown to be capable of yielding a particular rule in the locale in which it is predominant, even when contradicted by the dictates of a clear text.[262] What remains to be clarified is the relationship between custom and those opinions in *ẓāhir al-riwāya* derived from the texts by means of inferential reasoning. This is perhaps the most central theme of *Nashr al-ᶜUrf*, and an important one in *Sharḥ al-Manẓūma*.[263] Ibn ᶜĀbidīn avers in these two works that such opinions are arrived at by *mujtahid*s on the basis of a number of considerations, not

259 Ibn ᶜĀbidīn, *Sharḥ al-Manẓūma*, 49–50.
260 Ibid., 50. 261 Ibn al-Ṣalāḥ, *Adab al-Muftī*, 107.
262 Although the contradiction is seen in terms of particularization (*takhṣīṣ*). See paragraph ending with the cue for n. 238, above.
263 Ibn ᶜĀbidīn, *Nashr al-ᶜUrf*, 128 (l. 17); Ibn ᶜĀbidīn, *Sharḥ al-Manẓūma*, 46 f.

the least of which are the customary practices prevalent at the time when these opinions were formed. The need for taking customary practices into consideration explains the theoretical requirement that the *mujtahid* must possess precise knowledge of the habits and customs prevalent in the society that he serves.[264] The *mujtahid*'s reasoning, and the results it yields, therefore reflect a particular combination of law and fact, the latter being in part, if not entirely, determined by custom. If these practices differ from time to time, or from one place to another, they would lead the *mujtahid*s to different legal conclusions, depending on the time and place. This, Ibn ʿĀbidīn argues, explains why the later *mujtahid*s (*mashāyikh al-madhhab*) diverged in a number of areas from the rules that had been established by the school founders, the prevailing assumption being that had these founders faced the same customs that the later *mujtahid*s encountered, they, the founders, would have formed the same opinions as their later counterparts came to hold.

Here, Ibn ʿĀbidīn cites at least a few dozen cases in which *mashāyikh al-madhhab* differed with the founding masters.[265] One example in point is the regional and chronological variation in the law of *waqf*. In Anatolia, for instance, it is customary to dedicate cash or coins as *waqf*, when it is the authoritative doctrine of the school that movable property cannot be used as charitable trusts.[266] In "our region," Ibn ʿĀbidīn notes, such has never been the practice. An example of chronological change is the practice of dedicating a farmer's axe as *waqf*, which used to be customary in Syria during earlier periods "but unheard of in our times."[267] The change in the habits of a society must therefore lead to a correlative change in the law. But it is important to note, as Ibn ʿĀbidīn does, that such a legal change is not precipitated by a change in the law as a system of evidence or as a methodology of legal reasoning. Instead, it is one that is stimulated by changing times.[268]

The impressive list of cases compiled by Ibn ʿĀbidīn is intended to demonstrate that the jurisconsult "must not stubbornly adhere to the opinions transmitted in *ẓāhir al-riwāya* without giving due attention to society and the [demands of the] age it lives in. If he does, he will cause many rights to be lost, and will thus be more harmful than beneficial."[269]

[264] Ibn ʿĀbidīn, *Nashr al-ʿUrf*, 128–30. [265] Ibid., 126–28.

[266] On this practice, see J. E. Mandaville, "Usurious Piety: The Cash Waqf Controversy in the Ottoman Empire," *International Journal of Middle East Studies*, 10 (1979): 295–304.

[267] Ibn ʿĀbidīn, *Ḥāshiya*, IV, 364.

[268] Ibn ʿĀbidīn, *Nashr al-ʿUrf*, 126: "*wa-qad naṣṣa al-ʿulamāʾ ʿalā anna hādhā al-ikhtilāf (huwa) ikhtilāf ʿaṣr wa-awān lā ikhtilāf ḥujja wa-burhān.*"

[269] Ibid., 131; *Sharḥ al-Manẓūma*, 47.

"The jurisconsult must follow custom even though it might contradict the authoritative opinions of *ẓāhir al-riwāya*."[270] Both universal and local customs are included under these generalizations. "Even if local custom opposes the school doctrines (*al-naṣṣ al-madhhabī*) that have been transmitted on the authority of the school founder (*ṣāḥib al-madhhab*), it must be taken into consideration."[271]

Having reached this conclusion by what he takes to be an inductive survey of the law, Ibn ᶜĀbidīn goes on to say that the jurisconsult must treat both local and universal customs as equal insofar as they override the corpus of *ẓāhir al-riwāya*. The only difference between them is that universal custom produces a universal legal norm, whereas local custom effects a particular norm. Put differently, the legal norm resulting from a universal custom is binding on Muslims throughout Muslim lands, while local custom is binding in the village or town in which it prevails.[272] These conclusions Ibn ᶜĀbidīn seeks to defend and justify at any expense. Here, he introduces a statement reportedly made by Aḥmad al-Ḥamawī in his *Ḥāshiya ᶜalā al-Ashbāh*, a commentary on Ibn Nujaym's work. In this work, Ḥamawī remarked that from Ibn Nujaym's statement that "a local custom can never yield a universal legal norm" one can infer that "a local custom can result in a particular legal norm."[273] Obviously, there is nothing in the logic of entailment that justifies this inference. But Ibn ᶜĀbidīn accepts Ḥamawī's conclusion readily and unquestioningly.

The principles that justify the dominance of local custom over the school's authoritative doctrine also justify, with equal force, the continuous displacement of one local custom by another. If a local custom could repeal those doctrines that had been established by the school founders, then a later local custom, superseding in dominance its forerunner, can override both the forerunner and the *ẓāhir al-riwāya*. This much is clear from Ibn ᶜĀbidīn's statement that the local custom that overrides the school's authoritative doctrine includes both old and new local customs.[274] The legitimization of this continuous modification lies in Ibn ᶜĀbidīn's deep conviction that the founding fathers would have held the

[270] *Nashr al-ᶜUrf*, 131–32, restated at 133. [271] Ibid., 133.

[272] Ibid., 132: "*fal-ᶜurf al-ᶜāmm fī sā'ir al-bilād yathbut ḥukmuhu ᶜalā ahli sā'iri al-bilād wal-khāṣṣ fī balda wāḥida yathbut ḥukmuhu ᶜalā tilka al-balda faqaṭ.*"

[273] Aḥmad al-Ḥamawī, *Sharḥ al-Ashbāh*, printed with Ibn Nujaym's *al-Ashbāh wal-Naẓā'ir*, 137; Ibn ᶜĀbidīn, *Nashr al-ᶜUrf*, 132: "*qāla al-ᶜallāma al-Sayyid Aḥmad al-Ḥamawī . . . al-ḥukm al-ᶜāmm lā yathbut bil-ᶜurf al-khāṣṣ, yufham minhu anna al-ḥukm al-khāṣṣ yathbut bil-ᶜurf al-khāṣṣ.*"

[274] *Sharḥ al-Manẓūma*, 45; Ibn ᶜĀbidīn, *Nashr al-ᶜUrf*, 133: "*ammā al-ᶜurf al-khāṣṣ, idhā ᶜāraḍa al-naṣṣ al-madhhabī al-manqūl ᶜan ṣāḥib al-madhhab fa-hwa muᶜtabar . . . wa-shamala al-ᶜurf al-khāṣṣ al-qadīm wal-ḥādith.*"

same legal opinions had they encountered the same customs that the later jurists had to face.[275] This is one of Ibn ᶜĀbidīn's cardinal tenets which he nearly developed into a legal maxim.

Ibn ᶜĀbidīn's hermeneutical venture resulted in a conflict between his loyalty to the authoritative hierarchy of Ḥanafite doctrine and the demands of custom not only as a set of individual legal cases but more importantly as a source of law. For as a body of individual legal cases, custom was fairly successfully incorporated into law, a fact abundantly attested in the works of early jurists, and exemplified, as we have seen, in Sarakhsī's *Mabsūṭ*. But in attempting, as Ibn ᶜĀbidīn did, to raise the status of custom to that of a legal source, there arose a distinct difficulty in squaring this source not only with *ẓāhir al-riwāya* but also with the legal methodology that sustained both the doctrinal hierarchy and the theological backing of the law. That Ibn ᶜĀbidīn was entirely loyal to the hermeneutical imperatives of the Ḥanafite school and, at one and the same time, a vehement promoter of custom *as a legal source* makes his task all the more remarkable. Ultimately, through the discursive tools of the author–jurist, Ibn ᶜĀbidīn succeeded in constructing an argument that elevates custom to the status of a legal source, capable of overriding the effects of other sources, including the Quran and the Sunna.

Ibn ᶜĀbidīn's discourse on custom is instructive from a number of perspectives, not the least of which is the way it invokes the weak and minority positions in the tradition. These positions are made, by necessity, to juxtapose with the authoritative doctrine of the school, that which represents the dominant mainstream of legal doctrine and practice. The initial impulse that propelled the minority position was Abū Yūsuf's opinion which had largely been abandoned by Ibn Nujaym's time. Abū Yūsuf's opinion was revived through the device of necessity, a device that must have seemed handy when all other hermeneutical ventures appeared to have no prospect of success. Ibn ᶜĀbidīn's hermeneutics also entailed the manipulation of other minor opinions, such as those of Subkī and Marghīnānī. In this hermeneutical exercise, which turned the ladder of doctrinal authority right on its head, Ibn ᶜĀbidīn's skills as a polemicist, author, and textual strategist are not to be underestimated. Admittedly, however, they involved certain flaws in logical argumentation, flaws which were undoubtedly more a result of the strains inherent in Ibn ᶜĀbidīn's hermeneutically exacting venture than they were a reflection of his competence as a reasoner.

[275] Ibn ᶜĀbidīn, *Nashr al-ᶜUrf*, 128, 130: "*law kāna Abū Ḥanīfa ra'ā mā ra'aw, la-aftā bi-hi*" (at 130, l. 15); Ibn ᶜĀbidīn, *Sharḥ al-Manẓūma*, 14.

Ibn ʿĀbidīn's discourse is also instructive in that it contained a complex and multi-layered hermeneutical texture, a prominent feature in the author–jurist's enterprise. Functioning within the context of a school authority, Ibn ʿĀbidīn's discourse was dominated by the ever-present perception of a legal tradition within which he had to function and beyond which he could not tread. But the tradition was by no means so constraining. Rather, it offered multiple levels of discourse originating, chronologically, in centuries of legal evolution and, geographically, in far-flung regions dominated by Ḥanafite as well as other schools. This rich multiplicity afforded the author–jurist a large measure of freedom to include or exclude opinions at will. Opinions from distant and immediate predecessors were selectively cited and juxtaposed. They represented, at one and the same time, the dominant weight of the tradition and the means by which the tradition itself could effectively be manipulated. The author–jurist, the manipulator, cements the selected citations that make up the building blocks of his discourse through the medium of interpolations, interventions, counter-arguments, and qualifications. Although the manipulator's presence in the text that he produces seems more often than not to be minimal, it is he who decides how the tradition and its authority are to be used, shaped, and reproduced. It is a remarkable feature of the author–jurist's legal discourse that it was able to reproduce this varied and multi-layered tradition in a seemingly infinite number of ways. The interpretive possibilities seem astounding.

## IX

Our enquiry compels us to conclude that it was the *muftī* and the author–jurist who responded to the need for legal change by means of articulating and legitimizing that aspect of general legal practice in which change was implicit. The *qāḍīs*, as a community of legal practitioners, may have been involved in the application of newer or weak doctrines that differed from the established and authoritative doctrines of the school. But such a practice, assuming that it permeated all the schools, was merely a necessary – but by no means sufficient – condition for the implementation of change. In the entire process of change, the *qāḍīs*' contribution, whenever it was present, was only at an embryonic stage, and could not, in and by itself, have culminated in change. For in order to effect legal change in a formal and authoritative manner – which represents the full extent of the process of such change – the intervention of other agents was needed. These were the *muftī* and the author–jurist.

In the previous chapter, we noted that the *madhhab*-opinions gained authoritative status due to the fact that they were normatively used as the basis of *fatwās*. The *fatwā* thus acquired general, almost universal, relevance within the school, in contradistinction to the *qāḍī*'s ruling which was confined to the individual case at hand. And it was in such a capacity that the *fatwā* possessed the power to articulate and, in the final analysis, legitimize change. Ibn Rushd's *fatwā* pertaining to the murder in Cordoba illustrates a somewhat radical form of change in which a totally new opinion was introduced to the Mālikite *juris corpus*. But the *fatwā* was also instrumental to legal change in less radical ways. In its primary form, that is, before it had undergone the process of incorporation into works of positive law, the *fatwā* was authoritative, a fact evidenced in the "canonized" *fatwā* collections which were not affected by the contribution of the author–jurist *qua* author–jurist. Such collections, as we have seen, occupied a central place in the authoritative body of school doctrines. True, formally and in terms of the hierarchy of doctrine, they were second to many of the early masters' doctrines; yet, in the reality of practice they were nonetheless authoritative. Indeed, it is the ever continuous, diachronic substitution of such authoritative collections that reflected the fluidity of doctrine and thus the adaptability of the law. This explains not only the cumulative relevance of doctrine to the later jurists but also the diachronic significance of authoritative citations: the later the jurist, the more recent his authorities are, generally speaking, and the less his reliance on earlier doctrines.

The authoritative character of the *fatwā* as a universal statement of the law and as a reflection of legitimized legal practice made it a prime target of the author–jurist. An essential part of the *muftī*'s function was to articulate and legitimize legal change, but it was the author–jurist who was mainly responsible for setting the final seal on *fatwā*s by incorporating them into the school's works of positive law. This incorporation signified the final stage of legitimization, not as the exclusive doctrines of the school but rather as part of the school's *corpus juris*. We should not expect more, for it was rarely, quite rarely, the case that a single opinion governing a particular legal issue could for long stand as the exclusive doctrine of a school.

It is precisely here, in the multiplicity of opinions for each case, that the author–jurist was most creative in accommodating legal change. Ibn ᶜĀbidīn's discourse on custom is perhaps the most eloquent illustration in point. The multiple levels of discourse that were available to him, and on which he felt free to draw, enabled him in effect to turn the hierarchy of authoritative legal sources right on its head. Custom, in the end, was to override the authoritative doctrine of the school. It is no less than impressive that Ibn ᶜĀbidīn could have achieved this end while remaining within the hermeneutical boundaries of traditional Ḥanafite scholarship – a testimony to the Muslim jurist and to his ability to navigate so freely in what is seemingly a constrained tradition. The ability of the *muftī* and the author–jurist to articulate, legitimize, and ultimately effect legal change was not a contingent, *ad hoc* feature, but one that was structural, built into the very system that is Islamic law.

# SUMMARY AND CONCLUSIONS

The formation of the legal schools by the middle of the fourth/tenth century was achieved through the construction of a juristic doctrine clothed in the authority of the founding imam, the so-called absolute *mujtahid.* Juristic discourse and hermeneutics were the product of this foundational authority which was made to create a set of positive principles that came to define the school not so much as a personal entity of professional membership, but mainly as an interpretive doctrine to be studied, mastered, and, above all, defended and applied. Juristic authority, therefore, was to be sustained throughout the successive stages of legal history, each stage passing on its authoritative legacy to the next. But the transmission of authority in juristic typologies was progressively restrictive, reflecting not a growing rigidity in the law but rather the evolution of a relatively more determinate body of positive law. The perception of hierarchical ranking, in which the interpretive possibilities were, in diachronic terms, increasingly restricted, was thus a function of stability and determinacy, not of incompetence or unquestioning *taqlīd.* The hallmark of juristic excellence was not so much innovation as the ability to determine the authoritative school doctrine. This recognition of juristic competence in justifying and promoting continuity and thus stability, predictability, and determinacy was discursively attributed to the lower ranks of the juristic hierarchy, not because of a lower demand on the intellectual abilities of the jurist, but because justifying the tradition was an activity marked by insistence on the epistemic authority of the past, both recent and remote. For since a jurist could and did, admittedly, function at two or more levels of the juristic hierarchy, it was inconceivable that a jurist capable of *ijtihād* should have been incapable of *taqlīd.* Although the reverse of this progression is not readily obvious, the typologies do nonetheless permit the combination of a number of juristic functions in one professional career, with each function representing a different layer of interpretive activity.

But while we have accepted the structure of authority as an accurate description proffered by the juristic typologies, we have declined to admit to their historicity. It is revealing that the process of authority construction turns out to be incompatible with a scholarly reconstruction of history. But this incompatibility itself alerts us all the more readily to the precise nature of authorization and the lengths to which the jurists were willing to go in order to achieve it. The disregard shown, on the one hand, for the imams' debt to their predecessors and, on the other, the attribution to them of doctrines and opinions that were formulated by their successors were only two of the means by which the founding imams were fashioned into rallying points for their respective schools. Detaching them from their predecessors and successors was an *epistemological act* through which they were made into a species of "super-jurists," as it were, who – and this is important – had confronted the revealed texts directly and had single-handedly, by means of their own hermeneutical ingenuity, constructed a system of law. It is this, *primarily epistemic*, authority that was the object of construction.[1] The schools, therefore, could never have taken on the form and substance that they did without first having set in motion a process through which the authority of the imams was gradually and quite heavily augmented.

Our investigation into the activities of the *aṣḥāb al-wujūh*, or the *mukharrijūn*, also confirmed their importance as an essential element in the rise and final formation of the schools. Modern scholarship can no longer afford either to misunderstand[2] or to underestimate the significance of their contribution. They partook not only in the significant activity of constructing the imam's authority but also in helping to develop an interpretive methodology that came to characterize each school as a separate and unique juristic entity. One of the tasks of modern scholarship, therefore, will have to be a close and detailed scrutiny of their efforts, not only as active participants in the processes of authority construction but also as builders of the schools' *corpus juris*.[3] No less important are the juristic achievements of some of those who operated *outside* the hermeneutical limits of what came to be the school structure, for it is precisely these achievements that reveal to us how and why the schools arose in the manner they did and the complexities involved in this process.

As part of explaining *why* the four schools have managed to survive and even flourish, it is necessary for us to probe the question of *why* these *mukharrijūn* failed not so much to form their own schools (a process in which even the supposed founders of the *madhhab*s seem to have played hardly any role) but to become in their turn objects of the by now familiar process of authority construction. For it was the latter phenomenon which in the end determined that certain jurists and not others would go down in history as the originators of certain well-defined traditions of legal methodology and practice.

[1] Although it is highly likely that their religious and moral authority (two distinct but secondary types of authority) was likewise subjected to similar processes of construction and augmentation. The *manāqib* genre furnishes rich material for tracing these processes. See chapter 2, n. 1, above.

[2] See, for instance, chapter 1, n. 19, above.

[3] Among the foremost candidates who should command scholarly attention are Muzanī, Muḥammad b. Shujāᶜ al-Thaljī, Ibn ᶜAbd al-Ḥakam al-Miṣrī, Ibn al-Qāsim, Ḥarmala, Ibn Surayj, al-Qaffāl al-Shāshī al-Kabīr, the "Four Muḥammads," (especially Ṭabarī and Ibn al-Mundhir al-Nīsābūrī), Khiraqī, Abū Bakr al-Qaffāl al-Marwazī, and Abū Ḥāmid al-Isfarā'īnī.

It is certainly the success of the authority-construction process that has distorted, historically speaking, the juristic reality in which dozens of so-called absolute and affiliated *mujtahids* operated. The need to bestow authority on the so-called founders was matched only by the need to deemphasize their debt (whether direct or oblique) to the *mujtahids* who had preceded them. This act of intellectual, juristic, and hermeneutical expropriation constituted only one element in the process of school formation, for after all, the purpose of constructing the imam's authority was itself only one means, a tool, for building the school in its mature form.

The very act of hermeneutical expropriation was only one of the results of the need to limit the omnipresent plurality of legal opinion that emerged during the second/eighth century and most of the third/ninth, even though the proliferation of (independent) opinion continued to some extent for more than a century thereafter. The narrowing of juristic possibilities was no doubt a function of the tendency to increase the level of determinacy of positive legal doctrine, a fact represented in the highly applauded search, on the part of jurists, for those opinions considered to have achieved an authoritative status in the schools. The emergence of an authoritative body of legal doctrine was a post-formative phenomenon, or at the very least was symptomatic of the schools' evolution into doctrinal entities. Declaring an opinion to be authoritative amounted to a verdict passed on other opinions governing the same case under review. Such a declaration meant the existence of a standard yardstick by which the authoritative could be distinguished from the less authoritative, and this was precisely the significance of the school as a doctrinal entity.

The increasing abandonment of ubiquitous plurality in favor of the search for authoritative opinions amounted to a transition from what may be called the age of *ijtihād* to that of *taqlīd*. But *taqlīd*, it must be stressed, did not represent the unquestioning acceptance of earlier positions, for as we showed in chapter 4, this activity – and it *was* a juristic activity of the first order – involved highly complex modes of legal reasoning and rhetorical discourse.[4] Furthermore, *taqlīd* in and by itself was not a causal phenomenon, and this, I suggest, is a fundamental proposition. Instead, *taqlīd* was symptomatic of the rise of the schools as authoritative entities, that is, as objects of constructed authority. It was an expression of the complex dynamics that came to dominate the school as both a doctrinal entity and as a subject of hermeneutical engagement.

Part of the overarching activity of *taqlīd* also comprised a complex system of operative terminology whose purpose was, among other things, to curb the plurality of legal opinion by arguing in favor of those opinions deemed to be supremely authoritative. What constituted the authority of an opinion was no doubt a matter of some controversy. But two considerations stood as paramount:

[4] In the wide sense, defined and brilliantly analyzed by Chaim Perelman and L. Olbrechts-Tyteca in *The New Rhetoric: A Treatise on Argumentation* (Notre Dame: University of Notre Dame Press, 1969).

First, the soundness and persuasiveness of the lines of reasoning sustaining the opinion, and second, the degree to which the opinion succeeded in appealing to the community of jurists. Ultimately, these two considerations were not unrelated, and they did not stand wholly apart from yet other considerations. To be sure, widespread acceptance did not allude to any democratic principle, for the issue, in the final analysis, was an epistemological one. The soundness or persuasiveness of an opinion was put to the test of *ijmāʿ*ic review, although, technically speaking, the authority of *ijmāʿ* was never explicitly invoked in the context of operative terminology. But an underlying notion of this authority was constantly at play, nonetheless. Our two considerations therefore collapse into one larger, all-encompassing criterion.

However, a third consideration might also be subsumed under this criterion, namely, the degree to which an opinion was applied in the world of judicial practice. Again, the degree is ultimately adjudged as an epistemological matter, epistemology here having several dimensions, not excluding, for instance, sheer necessity as a ground for the dominant application, and therefore proclamation of an opinion as possessing supreme authority.

Operative terminology therefore served the interests of *taqlīd* in the sense – or rather in accordance with the multi-layered meanings – we have demonstrated. It reduced legal pluralism; it increased determinacy and predictability; and, above all, it promoted legal continuity and doctrinal–systemic stability. Operative terminology, which flourished after the formative period, permeated legal discourse and became a quintessential attribute of the system. And in view of the varied technical connotations of this terminology, no student of legal manuals can afford to gloss over such terms uncritically. In terms of modern research and methodology, operative terminology constitutes, without any exaggeration, one of the keys to unraveling the complexities that engulf the doctrinal history of Islamic law.

It may seem a curiosity that operative terminology served the interests of *taqlīd* as well as working so well as a tool of legal change. To put it differently, operative terminology as a mechanism of *taqlīd* also functioned as a tool for legitimizing and formalizing new developments in the law. Logically, this entails what may seem an astonishing but valid proposition, namely, that *taqlīd* embodied in itself the ability to accommodate legal change. But we need not restrict ourselves to drawing logical conclusions, for the evidence of our sources amply proves this much. In the extensive discourse of articulating operative terminology, and thereby in the very act of declaring certain opinions as authoritative, legal change was effected, insofar as this was needed. It should come as no surprise then that *taqlīd* functioned as a vehicle of legal change to the same extent as *ijtihād* did, if not more so. More, because *ijtihād* meant the introduction of new opinions which often lacked, *ipso facto*, an intimate, symbiotic relationship with the ongoing tradition. But through operative terminology, and therefore through *taqlīd*, familiar opinions once considered weak or relatively less authoritative had a better chance of rising to an authoritative position in the hierarchy of school doctrine.

Operative terminology and the discourse that surrounded it compel another conclusion, namely, that if this terminology was an integral part of Islamic law and its workings, then the mechanisms for accommodating legal change were structural features of that law. In other words, legal change did not occur only in an *ad hoc* manner, as it were, but was rather embedded in processes built into the very structure of the law. And since it was a structural feature, the jurists effected it as a matter of course. This inevitably suggests that the much-debated issue of whether change ever occurred in Islamic law is a product of our own imagination. For no medieval jurist lost much sleep over deciding in a given case that what had hitherto been considered by his predecessors a weak opinion had in fact much to recommend it as the most authoritative opinion in his school.

One of the conclusions reached in the course of this study was that the structural modalities of legal change lay with the jurisconsult and no less so with the author–jurist. It was, in other words, within the normal purview of these two offices or roles to modulate legal change, and this they did by means of articulating and legitimizing those aspects of general legal practice in which change was implicit. Through his *fatwā*, the jurisconsult created a discursive link between the realities of judicial practice and legal doctrine. Because the jurisconsult, by the nature of his function, was an agent in the creation of legal norms of universal applicability, his opinions were deemed to constitute law proper and as such were incorporated into the law manuals which were either *fatwā* collections or commentarial texts. In addition to *fatwā*s, the latter also included both the authoritative, traditional doctrine and the prevalent practices of the day. Both types of texts, as we have shown, possessed an authoritative doctrinal standing in the schools.

Texts produced by the jurisconsult and the author–jurist were authoritative in the sense that they provided contemporary and later jurists – whether notaries, judges, jurisconsults, or author–jurists – with normative rules that were advocated as standard doctrine. These texts, therefore, not only perpetuated the legal tradition but were also, at the same time, instrumental in legitimizing and formalizing legal change. It was the continual substitution of cases and opinions in the successive legal manuals and commentaries that reflected the fluidity of doctrine and thus the adaptability of the law. Positive legal principles persisted no doubt, but their case-by-case exemplification was in a state of constant flux. This phenomenon in turn reflects both the cumulative relevance of the doctrine to later jurists and the diachronic significance of authoritative citations: The later the jurist, the more recent his authorities are, and the less his reliance on earlier doctrines. Yet, the latter doctrines – especially those of the so-called founders – never faded away, and continued to serve not so much as a reservoir of positive rulings but rather as an axis of doctrinal authority and as archetypes for hermeneutically principled arguments that had generated these rulings.

While the jurisconsult's function in mediating legal change was central, the author–jurist, to some significant extent, determined which *fatwā*s were to be included in his text and which not. This authorial determination constituted, on the one hand, a device which checked the extent of the jurisconsult's contribution to the legal text, and sanctioned, on the other, those *fatwās* that were incorporated, whether or not the opinion expressed in them was subject to the author–jurist's approval. But the relationship between the jurisconsult *qua* jurisconsult and the author–jurist was also dialectical: The *fatwās* incorporated in the author–jurist's text themselves bestowed authority on the positive legal principles that they were intended to explicate in the first place. It is remarkable that the author–jurist was not subject to the control of other juristic or otherwise judicial functions and roles, and it is this fact that makes him, not necessarily a "law-maker" – as the jurisconsult was – but the chief legitimizer and formalizer of legal doctrine and legal change. His epistemic preeminence is furthermore enforced by his authorial dominance, manifested in his mastery of selective citations and juxtaposition of various authorities and of generating therefrom arguments through his own subtle interpolations, counter-arguments, and qualifications. The author–jurist therefore constantly adduced new arguments from old materials, without transcending the limits of discourse set by his school.

This is not to say, however, that the author–jurist's determination set the final seal on authoritative doctrines, for the system, as we have seen, was thoroughly pluralistic. Judges, jurisconsults, and the author–jurists themselves always had an array of opinions at their disposal. The author–jurist's legitimization did not therefore sanction rules as irrevocably authoritative, but was conducive to increasing determinacy in the diverse body of these rules. In a system that was and remained thoroughly pluralistic, this was no mean feat indeed.

At the end of the day, the solution to the very problematic created by the multiplicity of opinion in the formative and even post-formative periods turned out to be itself the salvation of the legal system during the later stages of its development. Without this multiplicity, therefore, legal change and adaptability would not have been possible. The old adage that in juristic disagreement there lies a divine blessing is not an empty aphorism, since critical scrutiny of its juristic significance proves it to be unquestionably true.

# BIBLIOGRAPHY

In classifying entries no account is taken of the letter *ʿayn*, the *hamza*, and the Arabic definite article *al-*.

## Primary sources

ʿAbbādī, Abū ʿĀṣim Muḥammad b. Aḥmad. *Ṭabaqāt al-Fuqahāʾ al-Shāfiʿiyya*, ed. Gosta Vitestam (Leiden: E. J. Brill, 1964).

ʿAbbādī, Aḥmad b. Qāsim. *al-Āyāt al-Bayyināt ʿalā Sharḥ Jamʿ al-Jawāmiʿ*, 4 vols. (Cairo: n.p., 1289/1872).

*Sharḥ ʿalā Sharḥ al-Maḥallī ʿalā al-Waraqāt*, printed on the margins of Shawkānī, *Irshād al-Fuḥūl.*

ʿAbd al-Bāqī, Fuʾād. *al-Muʿjam al-Mufahris li-Alfāẓ al-Qurʾān al-Karīm* (Cairo: Dār al-Kutub al-Miṣriyya, 1945).

Abū Yūsuf, Yaʿqūb b. Ibrāhīm. *Ikhtilāf Abī Ḥanīfa wa-Ibn Abī Laylā* (Cairo: Maṭbaʿat al-Wafāʾ, 1357/1938).

*Kitāb al-Kharāj* (Beirut and Cairo: Dār al-Sharq, 1405/1985).

Aḥmadnagarī, ʿAbd al-Nabī b. ʿAbd al-Rasūl. *Jāmiʿ al-ʿUlūm fī Iṣṭilāḥāt al-Funūn al-Mulaqqab bi-Dustūr al-ʿUlamāʾ*, 4 vols. (repr.; Beirut: Muʾassasat al-Aʿlamī lil-Maṭbūʿāt, 1975).

ʿAlāʾī. *See* Ḥaṣkafī, ʿAlāʾ al-Dīn Muḥammad ʿAlī.

ʿAlāʾī, Khalīl b. Kanīkaldhī Ṣalāḥ al-Dīn. *Ijmāl al-Iṣāba fī Aqwāl al-Ṣaḥāba*, ed. Muḥammad Sulaymān al-Ashqar (Kuwait: Manshūrāt Markaz al-Makhṭūṭāt wal-Turāth, 1407/1987).

ʿAlamī, ʿĪsā b. ʿAlī. *Kitāb al-Nawāzil*, 3 vols. (Rabat: Wizārat al-Awqāf wal-Shuʾūn al-Islāmiyya, 1983).

Āmidī, Abū al-Ḥasan ʿAlī Sayf al-Dīn. *al-Iḥkām fī Uṣūl al-Aḥkām*, 3 vols. (Cairo: Maṭbaʿat ʿAlī Ṣubayḥ, 1968).

*Muntahā al-Sūl fī ʿIlm al-Uṣūl* (Cairo: Maṭbaʿat Muḥammad ʿAlī Ṣubayḥ, n.d.).

Asnawī, Jamāl al-Dīn ʿAbd al-Raḥmān. *Nihāyat al-Sūl fī Sharḥ Minhāj al-Wuṣūl*, 3 vols. (Cairo: Muḥammad ʿAlī Ṣubayḥ, n.d.).

*Ṭabaqāt al-Shāfiʿiyya*, ed. ʿAbd Allāh al-Jubūrī, 2 vols. (Baghdad: Riʾāsat Dīwān al-Awqāf, 1970–71).
*Tadhkirat al-Tanbīh fī Taṣḥīḥ al-Tanbīh*, printed with Nawawī, *Taṣḥīḥ al-Tanbīh*.
*al-Tamhīd fī Takhrīj al-Furūʿ ʿalā al-Uṣūl*, ed. Muḥammad Ḥasan Haytū (Beirut: Muʾassasat al-Risāla, 1984).
ʿAsqalānī, Aḥmad b. ʿAlī Ibn Ḥajar. *al-Durar al-Kāmina fī Aʿyān al-Māʾa al-Thāmina*, 4 vols. (Hyderabad: Dāʾirat al-Maʿārif, 1350/1931).
*Fatḥ al-Bārī bi-Sharḥ Ṣaḥīḥ al-Bukhārī*, ed. ʿAbd al-ʿAzīz Ibn Bāz et al., 13 vols. (Beirut: Dār al-Maʿrifa, 1980).
*Lisān al-Mīzān*, 7 vols. (Beirut: Muʾassasat al-Aʿlamī lil-Maṭbūʿāt, 1390/1971).
Asyūṭī, Shams al-Dīn Muḥammad al-Minhājī. *Jawāhir al-ʿUqūd wa-Muʿīn al-Quḍāt wal-Muwaqqiʿīn wal-Shuhūd*, 2 vols. (Cairo: Maṭbaʿat al-Sunna al-Muḥammadiyya, 1374/1955).
ʿAynī, Abū Muḥammad Maḥmūd b. Aḥmad. *al-Bināya fī Sharḥ al-Hidāya*, 12 vols. (Beirut: Dār al-Fikr, 1980).
Bāʿalawī, ʿAbd al-Raḥmān b. Muḥammad. *Bughyat al-Mustarshidīn fī Talkhīṣ Fatāwā baʿḍ al-Aʾimma min al-ʿUlamāʾ al-Mutaʾakhkhirīn* (Cairo: Muṣṭafā Bābī al-Ḥalabī, 1952).
Baghdādī, ʿAbd al-Wahhāb. *al-Maʿūna*, ed. Ḥumaysh ʿAbd al-Ḥaqq, 3 vols. (Riyadh: Maktabat Nizār al-Bāzz, 1415/1995).
Baghdādī, al-Khaṭīb. *al-Faqīh wal-Mutafaqqih*, 2 vols. (Beirut: Dār al-Kutub al-ʿIlmiyya, 1975).
Baghdādī, Ibn Ghānim b. Muḥammad. *Majmaʿ al-Ḍamānāt* (Cairo: al-Maṭbaʿa al-Khayriyya, 1308/1890).
Bahūtī, Manṣūr b. Yūnus Ibn Idrīs. *Kashshāf al-Qināʿ ʿan matn al-Iqnāʿ*, 6 vols. (Beirut: ʿĀlam al-Kutub, 1983).
Bājī, Abū al-Walīd Sulaymān b. Khalaf. *Fuṣūl al-Aḥkām wa-Bayān mā Maḍā ʿalayhi al-ʿAmal ʿinda al-Fuqahāʾ wal-Ḥukkām*, ed. al-Bātūl b. ʿAlī (Rabat: Wizārat al-Awqāf wal-Shuʾūn al-Islāmiyya, 1410/1990).
*Kitāb al-Ḥudūd fī al-Uṣūl*, ed. Nazīh Ḥammād (Beirut: Muʾassasat al-Zuʿbī lil-Ṭibāʿa wal-Nashr, 1973).
*Iḥkām al-Fuṣūl fī Aḥkām al-Uṣūl* (Beirut: Dār al-Gharb al-Islāmī, 1986).
Baʿlī, ʿAlāʾ al-Dīn ʿAlī b. Muḥammad b. ʿAbbās. *al-Ikhtiyārāt al-Fiqhiyya min Fatāwā Shaykh al-Islām Ibn Taymiyya* (Beirut: Dār al-Fikr, 1369/1949).
Bannānī, ʿAbd al-Raḥmān b. Jād Allāh. *Ḥāshiya ʿalā Jamʿ al-Jawāmiʿ*, 2 vols. (Bombay: Molavi Mohammed B. Gulamrasul Surtis, 1970).
Bāṣābirīn, ʿAlī, *Ithmid al-ʿAynayn fī baʿḍ Ikhtilāf al-Shaykhayn* (Cairo: Muṣṭafā Bābī al Ḥalabī, 1952).
Baṣrī, Abū al-Ḥusayn. *al-Muʿtamad fī Uṣūl al-Fiqh*, ed. Muhammad Hamidullah et al., 2 vols. (Damascus: Institut Français, 1964–65).
Bayḍāwī, ʿAbd Allāh b. ʿUmar. *al-Ghāya al-Quṣwā fī Dirāyat al-Fatwā*, ed. ʿAlī Muḥyī al-Dīn Dāghī, 2 vols. (Cairo: Dār al-Naṣr lil-Ṭibāʿa al-Islāmiyya, 1400/1980).

*Minhāj al-Wuṣūl ilā ʿIlm al-Uṣūl*, printed with Ibn Amīr Ḥājj, *al-Taqrīr*.

Bayhaqī, Aḥmad b. al-Ḥusayn Abū Bakr. *Aḥkām al-Qur'ān*, 2 vols. (Beirut: Dār al-Kutub al-ʿIlmiyya, 1975).

*Manāqib al-Shāfiʿī*, ed. Aḥmad Ṣaqr, 2 vols. (Cairo: Maktabat Dār al-Turāth, 1971).

Bīṭār, ʿAbd al-Razzāq. *Ḥulyat al-Bashar fī Tārīkh al-Qarn al-Thālith ʿAshar*, ed. M. B. Bīṭār, 3 vols. (Damascus: Maṭbaʿat al-Majmāʿ al-ʿIlmī al-ʿArabī, 1963).

Bukhārī, Abū ʿAbd Allāh Muḥammad. *Kitāb al-Jāmiʿ al-Ṣaḥīḥ*, ed. M. L. Krehl and T. W. Juynboll, 4 vols. (Leiden: E. J. Brill, 1908). Trans. O. Houdas and W. Marçais, *Les traditions islamiques*, 4 vols. (Paris: Leroux, 1903–14).

Ḍabbī, Aḥmad b. Yaḥyā b. ʿUmayr. *Bughyat al-Multamis fī Tārīkh Rijāl Ahl al-Andalus* (Cairo: Dār al-Kutub al-Miṣriyya, 1989).

Dabbūsī, Abū Zayd ʿUbayd Allāh b. ʿUmar. *Kitāb Ta'sīs al-Naẓar* (Cairo: al-Maṭbaʿa al-Adabiyya, n.d.).

Daylamī, Shīrawayh b. Shahridār. *Kitāb Firdaws al-Akhbār*, 5 vols. (Beirut: Dār al-Kitāb al-ʿArabī, 1407/1987).

Fārisī, Abū ʿAlī. *Jawāhir al-Uṣūl fī ʿIlm Ḥadīth al-Rasūl* (Madina: al-Maktaba al-ʿIlmiyya, 1969).

Farrā', Muḥammad b. Abī Yaʿlā. *See* Ibn al-Farrā'.

Fāsī, Muḥammad b. al-Ḥasan al-Ḥujawī al-Thaʿālabī, *al-Fikr al-Sāmī fī Tārīkh al-Fiqh al-Islāmī*, 2 vols. (Madina: al-Maktaba al-ʿIlmiyya, 1397/1977).

*al-Fatāwā al-Hindiyya*, comp. and ed. al-Shaykh al-Niẓām et al., 6 vols. (repr.; Beirut: Dār Iḥyā' al-Turāth al-ʿArabī, 1400/1980).

Ghazālī, Abū Ḥāmid Muḥammad b. Muḥammad. *al-Mankhūl min Taʿlīqāt al-Uṣūl*, ed. Muḥammad Ḥasan Haytū (Damascus: Dār al-Fikr, 1980).

*al-Mustaṣfā min ʿIlm al-Uṣūl*, 2 vols. (Cairo: al-Maṭbaʿa al-Amīriyya, 1324/1906).

*al-Wajīz*, 2 vols. (Cairo: Maṭbaʿat al-Ādāb, 1317/1899).

Ḥājjī Khalīfa (Katip Celebi). *Kashf al-Ẓunūn ʿan Asāmī al-Kutub wal-Funūn*, 2 vols. (Istanbul: Maṭbaʿat Wakālat al-Maʿārif al-Jalīla, 1941–43).

Ḥalabī, Ibrāhīm b. Muḥammad. *Multaqā al-Abḥur*, ed. Wahbī al-Albānī, 2 vols. (Beirut: Mu'assasat al-Risāla, 1409/1989).

Ḥamawī, Aḥmad. *Sharḥ al-Ashbāh*, printed with Ibn Nujaym, *al-Ashbāh wal-Naẓā'ir*.

Ḥaṣkafī, ʿAlā' al-Dīn Muḥammad ʿAlī (al-ʿAlā'ī). *al-Durr al-Mukhtār*, printed with Ibn ʿĀbidīn, *Ḥāshiya*.

Ḥaṭṭāb, Muḥammad b. Muḥammad. *Mawāhib al-Jalīl li-Sharḥ Mukhtaṣar Khalīl*, 6 vols. (Ṭarāblus, Libya: Maktabat al-Najāḥ, 1969).

*Taḥrīr al-Kalām fī Masā'il al-Iltizām*, ed. ʿAbd al-Salām Muḥammad Sharīf (Beirut: Dār al-Gharb al-Islāmī, 1984).

Haytamī, Ibn Ḥajar. *al-Fatāwā al-Kubrā al-Fiqhiyya*, 4 vols. (Cairo: ʿAbd al-Ḥamīd Aḥmad al-Ḥanafī, 1938).

Ḥusām al-Shahīd. *See* Ibn Māza.

Ḥusaynī, Abū Bakr Hidāyat Allāh. *Ṭabaqāt al-Shāfiʿiyya*, ed. ʿĀdil Nuwayhid (Beirut: Dār al-Āfāq al-Jadīda, 1979).
Ibn ʿAbd al-Barr, Abū ʿUmar Yūsuf. *Jāmiʿ Bayān al-ʿIlm wa-Faḍlihi wa-mā Yanbaghī fī Riwāyatihi wa-Ḥamlihi*, 2 vols. (Cairo: Idārat al-Ṭibāʿa al-Munīriyya, n.d.).
Ibn ʿAbd al-Salām, ʿIzz al-Dīn. *Qawāʿid al-Aḥkām fī Maṣāliḥ al-Anām*, 2 vols. (Cairo: Maṭbaʿat al-Istiqāma, n.d.).
Ibn Abī al-Damm, Ibrāhīm b. ʿAbd Allāh. *Adab al-Qaḍā' aw al-Durar al-Manẓūmāt fī al-Aqḍiya wal-Ḥukūmāt*, ed. Muḥammad ʿAṭā' (Beirut: Dār al-Kutub al-ʿIlmiyya, 1987).
Ibn Abī al-ʿIzz, Ṣadr al-Dīn al-Ḥanafī. *al-Ittibāʿ*, ed. Muḥammad ʿAṭā' Allāh Ḥanīf and ʿĀṣim al-Qaryūṭī (Amman: n.p., 1405/1984).
Ibn Abī Shāma, Shihāb al-Dīn b. Ismāʿīl. *Mukhtaṣar Kitāb al-Mu'ammal lil-Radd ilā al-Amr al-Awwal*, in *Majmūʿat al-Rasā'il al-Munīriyya*, vol. III, 19–39.
Ibn Abī al-Wafā', ʿAbd al-Qādir al-Qurashī. *al-Jawāhir al-Muḍī'a fī Ṭabaqāt al-Ḥanafiyya*, 2 vols. (Hyderabad: Maṭbaʿat Majlis Dā'irat al-Maʿārif al-Niẓāmiyya, 1332/1914).
Ibn ʿĀbidīn, Muḥammad Amīn. *Ḥāshiyat Radd al-Muḥtār ʿalā al-Durr al-Mukhtār Sharḥ Tanwīr al-Abṣār*, 8 vols. (Beirut: Dār al-Fikr, 1399/1979).
*Majmūʿ Rasā'il Ibn ʿĀbidīn*, 2 vols. (n.p., 1970).
*Sharḥ al-Manẓūma al-Musammā bi-ʿUqūd Rasm al-Muftī*, in Ibn ʿĀbidīn, *Majmūʿ Rasā'il Ibn ʿĀbidīn*, I, 1–53.
*Nashr al-ʿUrf fī Binā' Baʿḍ al-Aḥkām ʿalā al-ʿUrf*, in Ibn ʿĀbidīn, *Majmūʿ Rasā'il Ibn ʿĀbidīn*, II, 114–47.
*Tanbīh al-Ruqūd ʿalā Masā'il al-Nuqūd* in Ibn ʿĀbidīn, *Majmūʿ Rasā'il Ibn ʿĀbidīn*, II, 58–67.
*al-ʿUqūd al-Durriyya fī Tanqīḥ al-Fatāwā al-Ḥāmidiyya*, 2 vols. (Cairo: al-Maṭbaʿa al-Maymūniyya, 1893).
Ibn Amīr al-Ḥājj. *al-Taqrīr wal-Taḥbīr: Sharḥ ʿalā Taḥrīr al-Imām al-Kamāl Ibn al-Humām*, 3 vols. (Cairo: al-Maṭbaʿa al-Kubrā al-Amīriyya, 1317/1899).
Ibn ʿAqīl, Abū al-Wafā' Muḥammad. *Kitāb al-Funūn*, ed. George Makdisi, 2 vols. (Beirut: Dār al-Mashriq, 1970–71).
Ibn ʿArafa, Muhammad. *Tafsīr*, ed. Ḥasan Mannāʿī, 2 vols. (Tunis: al-Sharika al-Tunisiyya, 1986).
Ibn Barhān, Ahmad b. ʿAlī. *al-Wuṣūl ilā al-Uṣūl*, ed. ʿAbd al-Ḥamīd Abū Zunayd, 2 vols. (Riyadh: Maktabat al-Maʿārif, 1404/1984).
Ibn Daqīq al-ʿĪd, Taqī al-Dīn. *Iḥkām al-Aḥkām: Sharḥ ʿUmdat al-Aḥkām*, ed. M. Fiqqī, 2 vols. (Cairo: Maṭbaʿat al-Sunna al-Muḥammadiyya, 1372/1953).
Ibn Farḥūn, Shams al-Dīn Muḥammad. *al-Dībāj al-Mudhahhab fī Maʿrifat Aʿyān ʿUlamā' al-Madhhab* (Beirut: Dār al-Kutub al-ʿIlmiyya, 1417/1996).
*Tabṣirat al-Ḥukkām fī Uṣūl al-Aqḍiya wa-Manāhij al-Aḥkām*, 2 vols. (Cairo: al-Maṭbaʿa al-ʿĀmira al-Sharafiyya, 1883).
Ibn al-Farrā', Muḥammad b. Abī Yaʿlā al-Baghdādī. *Ṭabaqāt al-Ḥanābila*, ed. M. H. al-Fiqī, 2 vols. (Cairo: Maṭbaʿat al-Sunna al-Muḥammadiyya, 1952).

*al-ʿUdda fī Uṣūl al-Fiqh*, ed. Muḥammad Mubārakī, 3 vols. (Beirut: Mu'assasat al-Risāla, 1980).
Ibn al-Ḥājib, Jamāl al-Dīn Abū ʿAmr. *Mukhtaṣar al-Muntahā al-Uṣūlī* (Cairo: Maṭbaʿat Kurdistān al-ʿIlmiyya, 1326/1908).
*Muntahā al-Wuṣūl wal-Amal fī ʿIlmayy al-Uṣūl wal-Jadal*, ed. Muḥammad al-Naʿsānī (Cairo: Maṭbaʿat al-Saʿāda, 1326/1908).
Ibn Ḥazm, ʿAlī b. Muḥammad. *al-Muḥallā bil-Āthār*, 12 vols. (Beirut: Dār al-Kutub al-ʿIlmiyya, 1988).
*Muʿjam al-Fiqh*, 2 vols. (Damascus: Maṭbaʿat Jāmiʿat Dimashq, 1966).
Ibn al-Humām, Kamāl al-Dīn. *Sharḥ Fatḥ al-Qadīr*, 10 vols. (repr.; Beirut: Dār al-Fikr, 1990).
Ibn al-Jallāb, ʿUbayd Allāh b. Ḥasan. *al-Tafrīʿ*, ed. Ḥusayn al-Dahmānī, 2 vols. (Beirut: Dār al-Gharb al-Islāmī, 1987).
Ibn Kathīr, Ismāʿīl b. ʿUmar. *al-Bidāya wal-Nihāya*, 14 vols. (Beirut: Dār al-Kutub al-ʿIlmiyya, 1985–88).
*al-Masā'il al-Fiqhiyya al-Latī Infarada bi-hā al-Imām al-Shāfiʿī*, ed. Ibrāhīm Ṣanduqjī (Madina: Maktabat al-ʿUlūm, 1986).
Ibn Khallikān, Abū al-ʿAbbās Shams al-Dīn. *Wafayāt al-Aʿyān wa-Anbā' Abnā' al-Zamān*, 8 vols. (Beirut: Dār Ṣādir, 1977–78).
Ibn al-Laḥḥām, ʿAlī b. ʿAbbās al-Baʿlī. *al-Qawāʿid wal-Fawā'id al-Uṣūliyya*, ed. Muḥammad al-Fiqī (Beirut: Dār al-Kutub al-ʿIlmiyya, 1403/1983).
Ibn Manẓūr, Jamāl al-Dīn. *Lisān al-ʿArab*, 15 vols. (repr.; Beirut: Dār Ṣādir, 1972).
Ibn Māza, ʿUmar b. ʿAbd al-ʿAzīz al-Ḥusām al-Shahīd. *Sharḥ Adab al-Qāḍī*, ed. Abū al-Wafā al-Afghānī and Muḥammad al-Hāshimī (Beirut: Dār al-Kutub al-ʿIlmiyya, 1414/1994).
Ibn Mufliḥ, Shams al-Dīn Muḥammad al-Maqdisī. *Kitāb al-Furūʿ*, ed. ʿAbd al-Sattār Farrāj, 6 vols. (Beirut: ʿĀlam al-Kutub, 1405/1985).
Ibn al-Mulaqqin, Sirāj al-Dīn Abī Ḥafṣ ʿUmar b. ʿAlī. *al-Bulgha fī Aḥādīth al-Aḥkām mimmā Ittafaqa ʿalayhi al-Shaykhān*, ed. Muḥyī al-Dīn Najīb (Damascus: Dār al-Bashā'ir, 1414/1994).
Ibn al-Munāṣif, Muḥammad b. ʿĪsā. *Tanbīh al-Ḥukkām ʿalā Ma'ākhidh al-Aḥkām* (Tunis: Dār al-Turkī lil-Nashr, 1988).
Ibn al-Mundhir, Muḥammad b. Ibrāhīm al-Nīsābūrī. *Kitāb al-Awṣat fī al-Sunan wal-Ijmāʿ wal-Ikhtilāf*, ed. Abū Ḥammād Ḍayf, 2 vols. (Riyadh: Dār Ṭuyiba, 1985).
*al-Ijmāʿ*, ed. ʿAbd Allāh al-Bārūdī (Beirut: Dār al-Jinān, 1986).
*al-Iqnāʿ*, ed. Muḥammad Ḥasan Ismāʿīl (Beirut: Dār al-Kutub al-ʿIlmiyya, 1418/1997).
*al-Ishrāf ʿalā Madhāhib Ahl al-ʿIlm*, ed. Muḥammad Sirāj al-Dīn, 2 vols. (Qaṭar: Idārat Iḥyā' al-Turāth al-Islāmī, 1406/1986).
Ibn al-Nadīm. *al-Fihrist* (Beirut: Dār al-Maʿrifa lil-Ṭibāʿa wal-Nashr, 1398/1978). Trans. B. Dodge, *The Fihrist of al-Nadim: A Tenth-Century Survey of Muslim Culture* (New York: Columbia University Press, 1970).

Ibn al-Najjār, Taqī al-Dīn Muḥammad al-Futūḥī. *Muntahā al-Irādāt*, 2 vols. (Cairo: Maktabat Dār al-ᶜUrūba, 1961–62).
Ibn Naqīb al-Miṣrī, Aḥmad. *ᶜUmdat al-Sālik wa-ᶜUddat al-Nāsik*, ed. and trans. N. H. Keller, *The Reliance of the Traveller* (Evanston: Sunna Books, 1991).
Ibn Naṣr, ᶜAbd al-Wahhāb b. ᶜAlī. *al-Muqaddima fī al-Uṣūl*, printed with Ibn al-Qaṣṣār, *al-Muqaddima fī al-Uṣūl*.
Ibn Nujaym, Zayn al-Dīn. *al-Ashbāh wal-Naẓā'ir* (Calcutta: al-Maṭbaᶜa al-Taᶜlīmiyya, 1260/1844).
*al-Baḥr al-Rā'iq: Sharḥ Kanz al-Daqā'iq*, 8 vols. (Cairo: al-Maṭbaᶜa al-ᶜIlmiyya, 1893).
*Rasā'il*, ed. Khalīl al-Mays (Beirut: Dār al-Kutub al-ᶜIlmiyya, 1980).
Ibn Qāḍī Shuhba, Taqī al-Dīn b. Aḥmad. *Ṭabaqāt al-Shāfiᶜiyya*, ed. ᶜAbd al-ᶜAlīm Khān, 4 vols. (Hyderabad: Maṭbaᶜat Majlis Dā'irat al-Maᶜārif al-ᶜUthmāniyya, 1398/1978).
Ibn al-Qāṣṣ, Abū al-ᶜAbbās Aḥmad b. Abī Aḥmad al-Ṭabarī. *Adab al-Qāḍī*, ed. Ḥusayn Jabbūrī, 2 vols. (Ṭā'if: Maktabat al-Ṣiddīq, 1409/1989).
Ibn al-Qaṣṣār, ᶜAlī b. Umar. *al-Muqaddima fī al-Uṣūl*, ed. Muḥammad al-Sulaymānī (Beirut: Dār al-Gharb al-Islāmī, 1996).
Ibn Qayyim al-Jawziyya, Shams al-Dīn Muḥammad b. Abī Bakr. *Iᶜlām al-Muwaqqiᶜīn ᶜan Rabb al-ᶜĀlamīn*, ed. Muḥammad ᶜAbd al-Ḥamīd, 4 vols. (Beirut: al-Maṭbaᶜa al-ᶜAṣriyya, 1407/1987).
Ibn Qudāma, Muwaffaq al-Dīn. *al-Kāfī fī Fiqh al-Imām Aḥmad b. Ḥanbal*, ed. Ṣidqī Jamīl and Yūsuf Salīm, 4 vols. (Beirut: Dār al-Fikr, 1992–94).
*al-Mughnī*, 12 vols. (Beirut: Dār al-Kitāb al-ᶜArabī, 1983).
*Rawḍat al-Nāẓir wa-Junnat al-Munāẓir*, ed. Sayf al-Dīn al-Kātib (Beirut: Dār al-Kitāb al-ᶜArabī, 1401/1981).
Ibn Qudāma, Shams al-Dīn Abū al-Faraj ᶜAbd al-Raḥmān. *al-Sharḥ al-Kabīr ᶜalā Matn al-Muqniᶜ*, printed with Muwaffaq al-Dīn Ibn Qudāma's *Mughnī*.
Ibn Quṭlūbughā, Zayn al-Dīn Qāsim. *Tāj al-Tarājim fī Ṭabaqāt al-Ḥanafiyya* (Baghdad: Maktabat al-Muthannā, 1962).
Ibn Rajab, ᶜAbd al-Raḥmān Shihāb al-Dīn. *Kitāb al-Dhayl ᶜalā Ṭabaqāt al-Ḥanābila*, 2 vols. (Cairo: Maṭbaᶜat al-Sunna al-Muḥammadiyya, 1952–53).
Ibn al-Rāmī al-Bannā'. *al-Iᶜlān bi-Aḥkām al-Bunyān*, ed. ᶜAbd al-Raḥmān al-Aṭram, 2 vols. (Riyadh: Dār Ishbīlyā, 1416/1995).
Ibn Rushd, Muḥammad b. Aḥmad (al-Ḥafīd). *Bidāyat al-Mujtahid wa-Nihāyat al-Muqtaṣid*, 2 vols. (Beirut: Dār al-Maᶜrifa, 1986). Trans. Imran Ahsan Khan Nyazee, *The Distinguished Jurist's Primer*, 2 vols. (Reading: Garnet Publishing, 1994).
Ibn Rushd, Muḥammad b. Aḥmad (al-Jadd). *Fatāwā Ibn Rushd*, ed. al-Mukhtār b. Ṭāhir al-Talīlī, 3 vols. (Beirut: Dār al-Gharb al-Islāmī, 1978).
*al-Muqaddimāt al-Mumahhidāt*, ed. Muḥammad Ḥujī, 3 vols. (Beirut: Dār al-Gharb al-Islāmī, 1408/1988).

Ibn al-Ṣalāḥ, Abū ᶜAmr ᶜUthmān b. ᶜAbd al-Raḥmān. *Adab al-Muftī wal-Mustaftī*, ed. Muwaffaq b. ᶜAbd al-Qādir (Beirut: ᶜĀlam al-Kutub, 1407/1986).

*Fatāwā wa-Masā'il Ibn al-Ṣalāḥ*, ed. ᶜAbd al-Muᶜṭī Qalᶜajī, 2 vols. (Beirut: Dār al-Maᶜrifa, 1986).

*Muqaddimat Ibn al-Ṣalāḥ wa-Maḥāsin al-Iṣṭilāḥ*, ed. ᶜĀ'isha ᶜAbd al-Raḥmān (Cairo: Dār al-Maᶜārif, 1989).

Ibn Taymiyya, Taqī al-Dīn. *Ibn Taymiyya against the Greek Logicians*, trans. Wael B. Hallaq (Oxford: Clarendon Press, 1993).

*Mukhtaṣar al-Fatāwā al-Miṣriyya*, ed. ᶜAbd al-Majīd Salīm (Cairo: Maṭba'at al-Sunna al-Muḥammadiyya, 1949).

Ibn Zinjawayh, Ḥamīd b. Makhlad Abū Aḥmad al-Azdī. *Kitāb al-Amwāl*, ed. Shākir Fayyāḍ, 3 vols. (Riyadh: Markaz al-Malik Fayṣal lil-Buḥūth wal-Dirāsāt al-Islāmiyya, 1406/1986).

Ibn Ziyād, ᶜAbd al-Raḥmān b. ᶜAbd al-Karīm. *Kitāb Ghāyat Talkhīṣ al-Murād min Fatāwā Ibn Ziyād*, printed on the margins of Bāᶜalawī, *Bughyat al-Mustarshidīn*.

Ījī, ᶜAḍud al-Dīn. *Sharḥ Mukhtaṣar al-Muntahā al-Uṣūlī*, ed. Shaᶜbān Muḥammad Ismāᶜīl, 2 vols. (Cairo: Maṭbaᶜat al-Kulliyyāt al-Azhariyya, 1973–74).

Ismāᶜīl Pāshā, Amīn b. Aḥmad. *Īḍāḥ al-Maknūn fī al-Dhayl ᶜalā Kashf al-Ẓunūn*, 6 vols. (repr.; Beirut: Dār al-Kutub al-ᶜIlmiyya, 1992).

Isnawī, Jamāl al-Dīn ᶜAbd al-Raḥmān. *See* Asnawī.

Jāḥiẓ, Abū ᶜUthmān ᶜAmr b. Baḥr. *Rasā'il*, ed. ᶜAbd al-Salām Hārūn, 2 vols. (Cairo: Maktabat al-Khānjī, 1964).

Jamāᶜīlī, ᶜAbd al-Ghanī ᶜAbd al-Wāḥid. *al-ᶜUmda fī al-Aḥkām fī Maᶜālim al-Ḥalāl wal-Ḥarām*, ed. Muṣṭafā ᶜAṭā (Beirut: Dār al-Kutub al-ᶜIlmiyya, 1986).

Jaṣṣāṣ, Abū Bakr Aḥmad b. ᶜAlī. *Sharḥ Kitāb Adab al-Qāḍī* (of Khaṣṣāf), ed. Farḥāt Ziadeh (Cairo: Qism al-Nashr bil-Jāmiᶜa al-Amrīkiyya, 1978).

Jazīrī, ᶜAlī b. Yaḥyā. *al-Maqṣad al-Maḥmūd fī Talkhīṣ al-ᶜUqūd*, ed. A. Ferreras (Madrid: Consejo Superior de Investigaciones Cientificas, 1998).

Jurjānī, al-Sayyid Sharīf ᶜAlī b. Muḥammad. *al-Taᶜrīfāt* (Cairo: Maṭbaᶜat Muṣṭafā Bābī al-Ḥalabī, 1938).

Juwaynī, Imām al-Ḥaramayn. *al-Burhān fī Uṣūl al-Fiqh*, ed. ᶜAbd al-ᶜAẓīm Dīb, 2 vols. (Cairo: Dār al-Anṣār, 1400/1980).

*Kitāb al-Ijtihād*, ed. ᶜAbd al-Ḥamīd Abū Zunayd (Damascus: Dār al-Qalam, 1408/1987).

*al-Talkhīṣ fī Uṣūl al-Fiqh*, ed. ᶜAbd Allāh al-Nībālī and Shabbīr al-ᶜUmarī, 3 vols. (Beirut: Dār al-Bashā'ir al-Islāmiyya, 1417/1996).

*al-Waraqāt fī ᶜIlm Uṣūl al-Fiqh*, printed with ᶜAbbādī, *Sharḥ* (Surabaya: Sharikat Maktabat Aḥmad b. Saᶜd b. Nabhān, n.d.).

Psuedo-Juwaynī, Imām al-Ḥaramayn. *al-Kāfiya fī al-Jadal*, ed. Fawqiyya Maḥmūd (Cairo: Maṭbaᶜat ᶜĪsā Bābī al-Ḥalabī, 1979).

Kāsānī, ᶜAlā' al-Dīn Abū Bakr Ibn Masᶜūd. *Badā'iᶜ al-Ṣanā'iᶜ fī Tartīb al-Sharā'iᶜ*, 7 vols. (Beirut: Dār al-Kitāb al-ᶜArabī, 1982).

Khalīl b. Isḥāq. *Mukhtaṣar* (Jazā'ir: Dār Shihāb, 1988).

Kharashī, Abū ᶜAbd Allāh Muḥammad. *Sharḥ Mukhtaṣar Khalīl*, 5 vols. (Cairo: al-Maṭbaᶜa al-ᶜĀmira al-Sharafiyya, 1899).

Khaṣṣāf, Abū Bakr Aḥmad b. ᶜUmar. *Kitāb Adab al-Qāḍī*, printed with Jaṣṣāṣ' commentary, ed. Farḥāt Ziadeh (Cairo: Qism al-Nashr bil-Jāmiᶜa al-Amrīkiyya, 1978); also in Ibn Māza, *Sharḥ Adab al-Qāḍī.*

Khushanī, Abū ᶜAbd Allāh Muḥammad b. Ḥārith. *Quḍāt Qurṭuba* (Cairo: Dār al-Kutub al-Miṣriyya, 1982).

*Uṣūl al-Futyā fī al-Fiqh*, ed. Muḥammad Majdūb (Beirut: al-Muᶜassasa al-Waṭaniyya lil-Kitāb, 1985).

Kinānī, ᶜAbd Allāh Ibn Salmūn. *al-ᶜIqd al-Munaẓẓam lil-Ḥukkām*, 2 vols. (Cairo: al-Maṭbaᶜa al-ᶜĀmīriyya al-Sharafiyya, 1301/1883).

Kurdarī, Muḥammad b. Shihāb Ibn Bazzāz. *al-Fatāwā al-Bazzāziyya al-Musammātu bil-Jāmiᶜ al-Wajīz*, printed on the margins of *al-Fatāwa al-Hindiyya*, vols. IV–VI (repr.; Beirut: Dār Iḥyā' al-Turāth al-ᶜArabī, 1980).

*Manāqib al-Imām al-Aᶜẓam Abī Ḥanīfa*, printed with Makkī, *Manāqib al-Imām.*

Laknawī, Abū al-Ḥasanāt ᶜAbd al-Ḥayy. *al-Fawā'id al-Bahiyya fī Tarājim al-Ḥanafiyya* (Cairo: Maṭbaᶜat al-Saᶜāda, 1324/1906; Benares: Maktabat Nadvat al-Maᶜārif, 1967).

*al-Nāfiᶜ al-Kabīr: Sharḥ al-Jāmiᶜ al-Ṣaghīr* (Beirut: ᶜĀlam al-Kutub, 1406/1986).

Maḥallī, Jalāl al-Dīn Muḥammad. *Sharḥ ᶜalā Matn Jamᶜ al-Jawāmiᶜ*, printed with Bannānī, *Ḥāshiya ᶜalā Jamᶜ al-Jawāmiᶜ.*

*Sharḥ al-Waraqāt* (of Juwaynī) (Cairo: Maṭbaᶜat Muḥammad ᶜAlī Ṣubayḥ, n.d.).

*Majmūᶜat al-Rasā'il al-Munīriyya*, 3 vols. (Cairo: Idārat al-Ṭibāᶜa al-Munīriyya, 1346/1927).

Makhlūf, Muḥammad b. Muḥammad. *Shajarat al-Nūr al-Zakiyya fī Ṭabaqāt al-Mālikiyya*, 2 vols. (Cairo: al-Maṭbaᶜa al-Salafiyya, 1950).

Makkī, Abū al-Mu'ayyad Muwaffaq al-Dīn b. Aḥmad. *Manāqib al-Imām al-Aᶜẓam Abı Ḥanıfa*, 2 vols. (Hyderabad: Maṭbaᶜat Majlis Dā'irat al-Maᶜārif al-Nizāmiyya, 1312/1894).

Mālik b. Anas. *al-Mudawwana al-Kubrā*, ed. Aḥmad ᶜAbd al-Salām, 5 vols. (Beirut: Dār al-Kutub al-ᶜIlmiyya, 1415/1994).

*al-Muwaṭṭa'* (Beirut: Dār al-Jīl, 1414/1993).

Manāwī, Shams al Dīn Muḥammad al Sulamī. *Farā'id al-Fawā'id fī Ikhtilāf al-Qawlayn li-Mujtahid Wāḥid*, ed. Muḥammad b. Ismāᶜīl (Beirut: Dār al-Kutub al-ᶜIlmiyya, 1415/1995).

Manjūr, Aḥmad b. ᶜAlī. *Sharḥ al-Manhaj al-Muntakhab ilā Qawāᶜid al-Madhhab*, ed. Muḥammad al-Shaykh and Muḥammad al-Amīn, vol. I. (n.p. [Saudi Arabia]: Dār ᶜAbd Allāh al-Shanqīṭī lil-Ṭibāᶜa wal-Nashr, n.d.).

Marāghī, ʿAbd Allāh Muṣṭafā. *al-Fatḥ al-Mubīn fī Ṭabaqāt al-Uṣūliyyīn*, 3 vols. (repr.; Beirut: Dār al-Kutub al-ʿIlmiyya, 1974).

Mardam Bīk (Bey), Khālīl. *Aʿyān al-Qarn al-Thālith ʿAshar fil-Fikr wal-Siyāsa wal-Ijtimāʿ* (Beirut: Mu'assasat al-Risāla, 1977).

Marghīnānī, Burhān al-Dīn ʿAlī b. Abī Bakr. *al-Hidāya: Sharḥ Bidāyat al-Mubtadī*, 4 vols. (Cairo: Muṣṭafā Bābī al-Ḥalabī, n.d.; repr. 1400/1980).

Mawāq, Muḥammad b. Yūsuf. *al-Tāj wal-Iklīl fī Sharḥ Mukhtaṣar Khalīl*, printed on the margins of Ḥaṭṭāb, *Mawāhib al-Jalīl*.

Māwardī, ʿAlī Muḥammad b. Ḥabīb. *Adab al-Qāḍī*, ed. Muḥyī Hilāl Sarḥān, 2 vols. (Baghdad: Maṭbaʿat al-Irshād, 1391/1971).

*al-Ḥāwī al-Kabīr fī al-Furūʿ*, ed. Maḥmūd Maṭarjī et al., 24 vols. (Beirut: Dār al-Fikr, 1994).

*al-Nukat wal-ʿUyūn*, ed. Sayyid b. ʿAbd al-Maqṣūd b. ʿAbd al-Raḥmān, 6 vols. (Beirut: Dār al-Kutub al-ʿIlmiyya, 1992).

Mirdāwī, ʿAlī b. Sulaymān b. Muḥammad. *Taṣḥīḥ al-Furūʿ*, printed with Ibn Mufliḥ, *Kitāb al-Furūʿ*.

Mūṣilī, ʿAbd Allāh b. Maḥmūd Mawdūd. *al-Ikhtiyār li-Taʿlīl al-Mukhtār*, 5 vols. (Cairo: Muṣṭafā Bābī al-Ḥalabī, 1951).

*al-Mukhtār lil-Fatwā*, printed with his *Ikhtiyār*, vol. II.

Muslim, Abū al-Ḥasan b. al-Ḥajjāj al-Qushayrī. *Ṣaḥīḥ*, ed. Muḥammad Fu'ād ʿAbd al-Bāqī, 5 vols. (Cairo: ʿĪsā Bābī al-Ḥalabī, 1374–75/1955–56).

Muzanī, Ibrāhīm. *Kitāb al-Amr wal-Nahy*, in Robert Brunschvig, "Le livre de l'ordre et de la défense d'al-Muzani," *Bulletin d'études orientales*, 11 (1945–46): 145–94.

*Mukhtaṣar*, published as vol. IX of Shāfiʿī's *Umm*.

Nābulusī, ʿAbd al-Ghanī b. Ismāʿīl al-Ḥanafī. *Nihāyat al-Murād fī Sharḥ Hadiyyat Ibn al-ʿImād*, ed. ʿAbd al-Razzāq al-Ḥalabī (Dubai: al-Ajfan & Al-Jabi, 1994).

Nasafī, Najm al-Dīn Ibn Ḥafṣ. *Ṭalibat al-Ṭalaba fī al-Iṣṭilāḥāt al-Fiqhiyya* (Baghdad: Maṭbaʿat al-Muthannā, 1311/1900).

Nawawī, Muḥyī al-Dīn Sharaf al-Dīn b. Yaḥyā. *Fatāwā al-Imām al-Nawawī al-Musammātu bil-Masā'il al-Manthūra*, ed. Muḥammad al-Ḥajjār (Madina: Dār al-Salām, 1985).

*al-Majmūʿ: Sharḥ al-Muhadhdhab*, 12 vols. (Cairo: Maṭbaʿat al-Taḍāmun, 1344/1925).

*Minhāj al-Ṭālibīn wa-ʿUmdat al-Muftīn* (Semarang: Maktabat Usahā Kaluwārkā, n.d.).

*Rawḍat al-Ṭālibīn*, ed. ʿĀdil ʿAbd al-Mawjūd and ʿAlī Muʿawwaḍ, 8 vols. (Beirut: Dār al-Kutub al-ʿIlmiyya, n.d.).

*Tahdhīb al-Asmā' wal-Lughāt*, 3 vols. (Cairo: Idārat al-Ṭibāʿa al-Munīriyya, 1927).

*al-Taqrīb wal-Taysīr li-Maʿrifat Sunan al-Bashīr al-Nadhīr*, ed. ʿAbd Allāh al-Bārūdī (Beirut: Dār al-Jinān, 1406/1986).

*Taṣḥīḥ al-Tanbīh*, ed. Muḥammad Ibrāhīm, 3 vols. (Beirut: Mu'assasat al-Risāla, 1417/1996).

Niẓām, al-Shaykh. *See al-Fatāwā al-Hindiyya.*

Nuʿaymī, ʿAbd al-Qādir b. Muḥammad. *al-Dāris fī Tārīkh al-Madāris,* ed. Jaʿfar al-Ḥusaynī, 2 vols. (Damascus: Maṭbaʿat al-Taraqqī, 1367/1948).

Nuʿmān, al-Qāḍī. *Kitāb Ikhtilāf Uṣūl al-Madhāhib,* ed. Muṣṭafā Ghālib (Beirut: Dār al-Andalus, 1973).

Qāḍīkhān, Fakhr al-Dīn Ḥasan b. Manṣūr al-Ūzajandī. *Fatāwā Qāḍīkhān,* printed on the margins of *al-Fatāwā al-Hindiyya,* vols. I–III.

Qaffāl, Abū Bakr Muḥammad. *See Shāshī.*

Qalqashandī, Aḥmad b. ʿAlī. *Ṣubḥ al-Aʿshā fī Ṣināʿat al-Inshā,* 14 vols. (Beirut: Dār al-Kutub al-ʿIlmiyya, 1987).

Qarāfī, Shihāb al-Dīn. *al-Furūq,* 4 vols. (Cairo: Dār Iḥyāʾ al-Kitāb al-ʿArabī, 1925–27).

*al-Iḥkām fī Tamyīz al-Fatāwā ʿan al-Aḥkām wa-Taṣarrufāt al-Qāḍī wal-Imām,* ed. ʿIzzat al-ʿAṭṭār (Cairo: Maṭbaʿat al-Anwār, 1967).

Qāsimī, Ibrāhīm b. ʿAbd Allāh. *Taqrīb Iṣṭilāḥ al-Muḥaddithīn min Afhām al-Ṭālibīn* (Kerala: Dār al-Hilāl lil-Kutub al-Islāmiyya, 1985).

Qudūrī, Aḥmad b. Muḥammad b. Jaʿfar. *Mukhtaṣar,* ed. Kāmil ʿUwayda (Beirut: Dār al-Kutub al-ʿIlmiyya, 1418/1997).

*al-Qurʾān al-Karīm* (Kuwait: Wizārat al-Awqāf wal-Shuʾūn al-Islāmiyya, 1402/1981). Trans. [1] Arthur J. Arberry, *The Koran Interpreted,* 2 vols. (London and New York: George Allen & Unwin Ltd., 1955); [2] Mohammed Marmaduke Pickthall, *The Meanings of the Glorious Koran* (New York: Mentor, n.d.).

Qurashī, Abū al-Wafāʾ Muḥammad. *al-Jawāhir al-Muḍīʾa fī Ṭabaqāt al-Ḥanafiyya,* 2 vols. (Hyderabad: Maṭbaʿat Majlis Dāʾirat al-Maʿārif, 1332/1913).

Rāfiʿī, Abū al-Qāsim ʿAbd al-Karīm b. Muḥammad. *Fatḥ al-ʿAzīz: Sharḥ al-Wajīz,* printed with Nawawī, *al-Majmūʿ.*

Rāfiʿī, Sālim ʿAbd al-Ghanī. *Mukhtaṣar al-Majmūʿ: Sharḥ al-Muhadhdhab,* 8 vols. (Jedda: Maktabat al-Sawādī, 1995).

Rāʿī, Shams al-Dīn Muḥammad b. Muḥammad al-Andalusī. *Intiṣār al-Faqīr al-Sālik li-Tarjīḥ Madhhab al-Imām Mālik,* ed. Muḥammad Abū al Ajfān (Beirut: Dār al-Gharb al-Islāmī, 1981).

Ramlī, Khayr al-Dīn. *al-Fatawa al-Khayriyya,* printed on the margins of Ibn ʿĀbidīn, *al-ʿUqūd al-Durriyya.*

Ramlī, Muḥammad Shams al-Dīn b. Shihāb al-Dīn. *Nihāyat al-Muḥtāj ilā Sharḥ al-Minhāj,* 8 vols. (Cairo: Muṣṭafā Bābī al-Ḥalabī, 1357/1938; repr. Beirut: Dār Iḥyāʾ al-Turāth al-ʿArabī, 1939).

Raṣṣāʿ, Abū ʿAbd Allāh Muḥammad al Anṣārī. *Sharḥ Ḥudūd Ibn ʿArafa al-Mawsūm al-Hidāya al-Kāfiya al-Shāfiya,* ed. Muḥammad Abū al-Ajfān and al-Ṭāhir al-Maʿmūrī, 2 vols. (Beirut: Dār al-Gharb al-Islāmī, 1993).

Rāzī, Fakhr al-Dīn. *al-Maḥṣūl fī ʿIlm al-Uṣūl,* 2 vols. (Beirut: Dār al-Kutub al-ʿImiyya, 1408/1988).

Saḥnūn, Ibn Saʿīd al-Tanūkhī. *See Mālik b. Anas, Mudawwana.*

Sakkākī, Muḥammad b. ᶜAlī. *Miftāḥ al-ᶜUlūm* (Cairo: al-Maṭbaᶜa al-Adabiyya, 1317/1899).
Ṣāliḥī, Muḥammad b. Yūsuf. *ᶜUqūd al-Jummān fī Manāqib al-Imām al-Aᶜẓam Abī Ḥanīfa al-Nuᶜmān* (Hyderabad: Maṭbaᶜat al-Maᶜārif, 1394/1974).
Samarqandī, Abū al-Layth. *Fatāwā al-Nawāzil* (Hyderabad: Maṭbaᶜat Shams al-Islām, 1355/1936).
*Khizānat al-Fiqh wa-ᶜUyūn al-Masā'il*, ed. Ṣalāḥ al-Dīn al-Nāhī, 2 vols. (Baghdad: Sharikat al-Ṭabᶜ wal-Nashr al-Ahliyya, 1965).
Samarqandī, ᶜAlā' al-Dīn. *Ṭarīqat al-Khilāf bayna al-Aslāf*, ed. ᶜAlī M. Muᶜawwaḍ and ᶜĀdil ᶜAbd al-Mawjūd (Beirut: Dār al-Kutub al-ᶜIlmiyya, 1413/1992).
*Tuḥfat al-Fuqahā'*, 3 vols. (Damascus: Dār al-Fikr, 1384/1964).
Ṣanᶜānī, Muḥammad b. Ismāᶜīl. *Irshād al-Nuqqād ilā Taysīr al-Ijtihād*, in *Majmūᶜat al-Rasā'il al-Munīriyya*, I, 1–47.
Sarakhsī, Muḥammad b. Aḥmad Abū Sahl. *al-Mabsūṭ*, 30 vols. (Cairo: Maṭbaᶜat al-Saᶜāda, 1324–31/1906–12).
*al-Uṣūl*, ed. Abū al-Wafā al-Afghānī, 2 vols. (Cairo: Dār al-Maᶜrifa, 1393/1973).
Shabrāmallisī, Nūr al-Dīn. *Ḥāshiya ᶜalā Nihāyat al-Muḥtāj: Sharḥ al-Minhāj*, printed on the margins of Ramlī, *Nihāyat al-Muḥtāj*.
Shāfiᶜī, Muḥammad b. Idrīs. *Kitāb Ibṭāl al-Istiḥsān*, in his *Umm*, VII, 487–500.
*Kitāb Ikhtilāf al-ᶜIrāqiyyīn*, in his *Umm*, VII, 161–250.
*Kitāb Ikhtilāf Mālik wal-Shāfiᶜī*, in his *Umm*, VII, 307–415.
*al-Risāla*, ed. Aḥmad Muḥammad Shākir (Cairo: Muṣṭafā Bābī al-Ḥalabī, 1969).
*al-Umm*, ed. Maḥmūd Maṭarjī, 9 vols. (Beirut: Dār al-Kutub al-ᶜIlmiyya, 1413/1993).
Shāh Walī Allāh, Aḥmad b. ᶜAbd al-Raḥīm. *ᶜIqd al-Jīd fī Aḥkām al-Ijtihād wal-Taqlīd*, ed. Muḥibb al-Dīn al-Khaṭīb (Cairo: al-Maṭbaᶜa al-Salafiyya, 1385/1965).
Shāshī, Abū ᶜAlī Aḥmad b. Muḥammad. *Uṣūl al-Shāshī* (Beirut: Dār al-Kitāb al-ᶜArabī, 1982).
Shāshī, Sayf al-Dīn Abū Bakr Muḥammad al-Qaffāl. *Ḥulyat al-ᶜUlamā' fī Maᶜrifat Madhāhib al-Fuqahā'*, ed. Yāsīn Darārka, 8 vols. (Amman: Dār al-Bāzz, 1988).
Shāṭibī, Abū Isḥāq Ibrāhīm. *al-Iᶜtiṣām*, ed. Muḥammad Rashīd Riḍā, 2 vols. (repr.; Riyadh: Maktabat al-Riyāḍ al-Ḥadītha, n.d.).
*al-Muwāfaqāt fī Uṣūl al-Aḥkām*, ed. Muḥyī al-Dīn ᶜAbd al-Ḥamīd, 4 vols. (Cairo: Maṭbaᶜat Muḥammad ᶜAlī Ṣubayḥ, 1970).
Shawkānī, Muḥammad b. ᶜAlī. *al-Badr al-Ṭāliᶜ bi-Maḥāsin man baᶜda al-Qarn al-Sābiᶜ*, 3 vols. (Cairo: Maṭbaᶜat al-Saᶜāda, 1348/1929).
*Irshād al-Fuḥūl ilā Taḥqīq al-Ḥaqq fī ᶜIlm al-Uṣūl* (Surabaya: Sharikat Maktabat Aḥmad b. Nabhān, n.d.).
*al-Qawl al-Mufīd fī Adillat al-Ijtihād wal-Taqlīd* (Cairo: Dār al-Maṭbaᶜa al-Salafiyya, 1974).

Shaybānī, Muḥammad b. al-Ḥasan. *Kitāb al-Aṣl al-Maʿrūf bil-Mabsūṭ*, ed. Abū al-Wafā al-Afghānī, 5 vols. (Beirut: ʿĀlam al-Kutub, 1990).

*al-Jāmiʿ al-Kabīr*, ed. Abū al-Wafā al-Afghānī (Cairo: Maṭbaʿat al-Istiqāma, 1937).

*al-Jāmiʿ al-Ṣaghīr* (Beirut: ʿĀlam al-Kutub, 1406/1986).

Shīrāzī, Abū Isḥāq Ibrāhīm b. ʿAlī. *al-Muhadhdhab fī Fiqh al-Imām al-Shāfiʿī*, 3 vols. (Beirut: Dār al-Kutub al-ʿIlmiyya, 1995).

*Sharḥ al-Lumaʿ*, ed. ʿAbd al-Majīd Turkī, 2 vols. (Beirut: Dār al-Gharb al-Islāmī, 1988).

*Ṭabaqāt al-Fuqahā'*, ed. Iḥsān ʿAbbās (Beirut: Dār al-Rā'id al-ʿArabī, 1970).

Shirbīnī, Muḥammad al-Khaṭīb. *Mughnī al-Muḥtāj ilā Maʿrifat Maʿānī Alfāẓ al-Minhāj* (Cairo: Muṣṭafā Bābī al-Ḥalabī, 1958).

Simnānī, Abū al-Qāsim ʿAlī b. Muḥammad. *Rawḍat al-Quḍāt wa-Ṭarīq al-Najāt*, ed. Ṣalāḥ al-Dīn al-Nāhī, 4 vols. (Beirut and Amman: Mu'assasat al-Risāla, 1404/1984.

Subkī, Tāj al-Dīn b. Taqī al-Dīn. *Ṭabaqāt al-Shāfiʿiyya al-Kubrā*, 6 vols. (Cairo: al-Maktaba al-Ḥusayniyya, 1906).

Subkī, Taqī al-Dīn ʿAlī. *Fatāwā al-Subkī*, 2 vols. (Cairo: Maktabat al-Qudsī, 1937).

*Takmilat al-Majmūʿ: Sharḥ al-Muhadhdhab*, 12 vols. (Cairo: Maṭbaʿat al-Taḍāmun, 1344/1925).

Suyūṭī, Jalāl al-Dīn ʿAbd al-Raḥmān. *al-Ashbāh wal-Naẓā'ir* (Beirut: Dār al-Kutub al-ʿIlmiyya, 1979).

*al-Minhāj al-Sawī fī Tarjamat al-Imām al-Nawawī*, printed with Nawawī, *Rawḍat al-Ṭālibīn*, I, 51–96.

*al-Radd ʿalā man Akhlada ilā al-Arḍ wa-Jahila anna al-Ijtihād fī Kulli ʿAṣrin Farḍ*, ed. Khalīl al-Mays (Beirut: Dār al-Kutub al-ʿIlmiyya, 1983).

Ṭabarī, Abū Jarīr Jaʿfar. *Ikhtilāf al-Fuqahā'* (Beirut: Dār al-Kutub al-ʿIlmiyya, 1980).

Tahānawī, Muḥammad b. ʿAlī. *Kashshāf Iṣṭilāḥāt al-Funūn*, 2 vols. (Calcutta: W. N. Leeds' Press, 1862).

Ṭaḥāwī, Abū Jaʿfar Aḥmad b. Muḥammad. *Mukhtaṣar*, ed. Abū al-Wafā al-Afghānī (Cairo: Maṭbaʿat Dār al-Kitāb al-ʿArabī, 1370/1950).

Ṭaḥṭāwī, Aḥmad b. Muḥammad. *Ḥāshiya ʿalā Marāqī al-Falāḥ: Sharḥ Nūr al-Īḍāḥ* (Būlāq: al-Maṭbaʿa al-Kubrā al-Amīriyya, 1318/1900).

Tamīmī, ʿAbd al-Qādir. *al-Ṭabaqāt al-Saniyya fī Tarājim al-Ḥanafiyya*, ed. ʿAbd al-Fattāḥ al-Ḥulw, 3 vols. (Cairo: Dār al-Rifāʿī lil-Nashr, 1983).

Ṭarābulusī, ʿAlā' al-Dīn ʿAlī b. Khalīl. *Muʿīn al-Ḥukkām fī-mā Yataraddad bayna al Khaṣmayn min al Aḥkām*, (Cairo: Muṣṭafā Bābī al-Ḥalabī, 1393/1973).

Tinbaktī, Aḥmad Bābā. *Nayl al-Ibtihāj bi-Taṭrīz al-Dībāj*, ed. ʿAbd all-Ḥamīd al-Harāma (Ṭarāblus, Libya: Kulliyyat al-Daʿwa al-Islāmiyya, 1989).

Tirmidhī, Abū ʿĪsā. *Ṣaḥīḥ*, 2 vols. (Cairo: al-Maṭbaʿa al-ʿĀmira, 1292/1875).

Ṭūfī, Najm al-Dīn. *Sharḥ Mukhtaṣar al-Rawḍa*, ed. ʿAbd Allāh al-Turkī, 3 vols. (Beirut: Mu'assasat al-Risāla, 1407/1987).

ʿUlaymī, Mujīr al-Dīn ʿAbd al-Raḥmān. *al-Manhaj al-Aḥmad fī Tarājim Aṣḥāb al-Imām Aḥmad*, ed. ʿAbd al-Qādir al-Arnā'ūṭ, 6 vols. (Beirut: Dār Ṣādir, 1997).

Ūzajandī, Ḥasan b. Manṣūr. *See* Qāḍīkhān.

Wansharīsī, Aḥmad b. Yaḥyā. *al-Miʿyār al-Mughrib wal-Jāmiʿ al-Muʿrib ʿan Fatāwī ʿUlamā' Ifrīqiyya wal-Andalus wal-Maghrib*, 13 vols. (Beirut: Dār al-Gharb al-Islāmī, 1401/1981).

Zarkashī, Shams al-Dīn Muḥammad b. ʿAbd Allāh al-Miṣrī. *Sharḥ al-Zarkashī ʿalā Mukhtaṣar al-Khiraqī*, ed. ʿAbd Allāh b. ʿAbd al-Raḥmān al-Jabrīn, 7 vols. (Riyadh: Maktabat al-ʿUbaykān, 1413/1993).

Zaylaʿī, Jamāl al-Dīn b. Yūsuf. *Naṣb al-Rāya li-Aḥādīth al-Hidāya*, 4 vols. (Cairo: Maṭbaʿat Dār al-Ma'mūn, 1357/1938).

Zaylaʿī, ʿUthmān b. ʿAlī. *Tabyīn al-Ḥaqā'iq: Sharḥ Kanz al-Daqā'iq*, 6 vols. (Būlāq: al-Maṭbaʿa al-Kubrā al-Amīriyya, 1313/1895).

Zinjānī, Shihāb al-Dīn Maḥmūd. *Takhrīj al-Furūʿ ʿalā al-Uṣūl*, ed. Muḥammad Ṣāliḥ (Beirut: Mu'assasat al-Risāla, 1404/1984).

Zurqānī, Muḥammad b. ʿAbd al-Bāqī. *Sharḥ al-Zurqānī ʿalā Muwaṭṭa' al-Imām Mālik*, 4 vols. (Beirut: Dār al-Kutub al-ʿIlmiyya, 1990).

## Secondary sources

Aghnides, Nicholas P. *Mohammedan Theories of Finance* (New York: Columbia University Press, 1916); reprinted in part as *Introduction to Mohammedan Law* (Solo: Ab. Sitti Sjamsijah, 1955).

Bāḥusayn, Yaʿqūb b. ʿAbd al-Wahhāb. *al-Takhrīj ʿInda al-Fuqahā' wal-Uṣūliyyīn* (Riyadh: Maktabat al-Rushd, 1414/1993).

Benn, Stanley I. "Authority," *Encyclopedia of Philosophy*, 8 vols. (New York: Macmillan Publishing, 1967), I, 215–18.

Berger, Peter and Thomas Luckmann. *The Social Construction of Reality: A Treatise in the Sociology of Knowledge* (New York: Anchor Books, 1967).

Berkey, Jonathan. *The Transmission of Knowledge in Medieval Cairo* (Princeton: Princeton University Press, 1992).

Bousquet, G.-H. "Le mystère de la formation et des origines du *fiqh*," *Revue algerienne, tunisienne et marocaine de legislation et de jurisprudence*, 63 (1947): 66–81.

Brockelmann, Carl. *Geschichte der arabischen Literatur*, 2 vols. (Leiden: E. J. Brill, 1943–49); 3 supplements (Leiden: E. J. Brill, 1937–42).

Brockopp, Jonathan E. "Early Islamic Jurisprudence in Egypt: Two Scholars and their *Mukhtasars*," *International Journal of Middle East Studies*, 30 (1998): 167–82.

Brunschvig, Robert. "Considérations sociologiques sur le droit musulman ancien," *Studia Islamica*, 3 (1955): 61–73; reprinted in his *Etudes d'islamologie*, II, 119–31.

*Etudes d'islamologie*, ed. Abdel Magid Turki. 2 vols. (Paris: G.-P. Maisonneuve et Larose, 1976).

Calder, Norman. "Exploring God's Law: Muḥammad ibn Aḥmad ibn Abī Sahl al-Sarakhsī on *zakāt*," in Christopher Toll and J. Skovgaard-Petersen, eds., *Law and the Islamic World: Past and Present* (Copenhagen: Det Kongelige Danske Videnskabernes Selskab, 1995), 57–73.

"*Ikhtilāf* and *Ijmā*ᶜ in Shāfiᶜī's *Risāla*," *Studia Islamica*, 58 (1984): 55–81.

"al-Nawawī's Typology of *Muftī*s and its Significance for a General Theory of Islamic Law," *Islamic Law and Society*, 4 (1996): 137–64.

*Studies in Early Muslim Jurisprudence* (Oxford: Clarendon Press, 1993).

Campoy, María A. "La Correspondencia de los Cadies en el *Muntajab al-Aḥkām* de Ibn Abī Zamanīn," *Actas del XII Congreso de la UEAI (Malaga, 1984)* (Madrid: Union Européenne d'Arabisants et d'Islamisants, 1986), 47–62.

Carmona, Gonzalez, Alfonso, "La Correspondencia Official entre Jueces en el *Mufīd* de Ibn Hishām de Córdoba," in *Homenaje al Prof. Jacinto Bosch Vilá*, I (Granada: Universidad de Granada, 1991): 497–509.

Chamberlain, Michael. *Knowledge and Social Practice in Medieval Damascus, 1190–1350* (Cambridge: Cambridge University Press, 1994).

Chehata, Chafik. *Etudes des Droit Musulman* (Paris: Presses Universitaires de France, 1971).

Cole, Stephen. *The Sociological Orientation* (Chicago: Rand McNally Publishing Co., 1979).

Coulson, N. J. *Conflicts and Tensions in Islamic Jurisprudence* (Chicago: University of Chicago Press, 1969).

*A History of Islamic Law* (Edinburgh: Edinburgh University Press, 1964).

Cuno, Kenneth M. "Ideology and Juridical Discourse in Ottoman Egypt: The Uses of the Concept of *Irṣād*," *Islamic Law and Society*, 6, 2 (1999): 136–63.

De George, Richard T. *The Nature and Limits of Authority* (Lawrence, Kans.: University of Kansas Press, 1985).

Dressler, David. *Sociology: The Study of Human Interaction* (New York: Alfred A. Knopf, 1969).

Dutton, Yasin. *The Origins of Islamic Law: The Qur'an, the Muwaṭṭa' and Medinan ᶜAmal* (Richmond: Curzon, 1999).

*Encyclopaedia of Islam*, new (2nd) ed. (Leiden: E. J. Brill, 1960).

*Encyclopaedia of the Qur'an* (Leiden: E. J. Brill, forthcoming).

*Encyclopedia of Philosophy*, 8 vols. (New York: Macmillan Publishing, 1967).

Escovitz, J. H. *The Office of Qāḍī al-Quḍāt in Cairo Under the Baḥrī Mamlūks* (Berlin: Klaus Schwarz Verlag, 1984).

Fadel, Mohammad. "Adjudication in the Mālikī Madhhab: A Study of Legal Process in Medieval Islamic Law" (Ph.D. dissertation: University of Chicago, 1995).

"The Social Logic of *Taqlīd* and the Rise of the *Mukhtaṣar*," *Islamic Law and Society*, 4 (1996): 193–233.

Fierro, Maribel. "The *Qāḍī* as Ruler," in *Saber Religioso Y Poder Político en el Islam* (Madrid: Agencia Española de Cooperación Internacional, 1994), 71–116.

Foucault, Michel. "What is an Author?" in J. V. Harari, ed., *Textual Strategies: Perspectives in Post-Structuralist Criticism* (Ithaca: Cornell University Press, 1979), 141–60.

Frantz-Murphy, Gladys. "A Comparison of the Arabic and Earlier Egyptian Formularies, Part II: Terminology in the Arabic Warranty and the Idiom of Clearing/Cleaning," *Journal of Near Eastern Studies*, 44 (1985): 99–114.

Gerber, Haim. "Rigidity Versus Openness in Late Classical Islamic Law: The Case of the Seventeenth-Century Palestinian Muftī Khayr al-Dīn al-Ramlī," *Islamic Law and Society*, 5, 2 (1998): 165–95.

Hafsi, I. "Recherches sur le genre *ṭabaqāt*," *Arabica*, 23 (1976): 227–65; 24 (1977): 1–41, 150–86.

Hallaq, Wael B. "The Authenticity of Prophetic Ḥadīth: A Pseudo-Problem," *Studia Islamica*, 89 (1999): 75–90.

"On the Authoritativeness of Sunnī Consensus," *International Journal of Middle East Studies*, 18 (1986): 427–54; reprinted in Hallaq, *Law and Legal Theory in Classical and Medieval Islam*.

"Considerations on the Function and Character of Sunnī Legal Theory," *Journal of the American Oriental Society*, 104 (1984): 679–89.

"From *Fatwās* to *Furūʿ*: Growth and Change in Islamic Substantive Law," *Islamic Law and Society*, 1 (February 1994): 17–56.

*A History of Islamic Legal Theories* (Cambridge: Cambridge University Press, 1997).

*Ibn Taymiyya against the Greek Logicians*, trans. Wael B. Hallaq (Oxford: Clarendon Press, 1993).

"*Iftā'* and *Ijtihād* in Sunnī Legal Theory: A Developmental Account," in Masud et al., eds., *Islamic Legal Interpretation*.

"On Inductive Corroboration, Probability and Certainty in Sunnī Legal Thought," in Nicholas L. Heer, ed., *Islamic Law and Jurisprudence: Studies in Honor of Farhat J. Ziadeh* (Seattle and London: University of Washington Press, 1990), 3–31; reprinted in Hallaq, *Law and Legal Theory in Classical and Medieval Islam*.

*Law and Legal Theory in Classical and Medieval Islam* (Aldershot: Variorum, 1995).

"Model *Shurūṭ* Works and the Dialectic of Doctrine and Practice," *Islamic Law and Society*, 2, 2 (1995): 109–34.

"Murder in Cordoba: *Ijtihād*, *Iftā'* and the Evolution of Substantive Law in Medieval Islam," *Acta Orientalia*, 55 (1994): 55–83.

"On the Origins of the Controversy about the Existence of Mujtahids and the Gate of Ijtihād," *Studia Islamica*, 63 (1986): 129–41; reprinted in Hallaq, *Law and Legal Theory in Classical and Medieval Islam*.

"A Prelude to Ottoman Reform: Ibn ᶜĀbidīn on Custom and Legal Change," proceedings of a conference held in Istanbul, May 25–30, 1999 (New York: Columbia University Press, forthcoming).

"*Qāḍīs* Communicating: Legal Change and the Law of Documentary Evidence," *al-Qanṭara*, 20 (1999): 437–66.

"The *Qāḍī's Dīwān* (*Sijill*) before the Ottomans," *Bulletin of the School of Oriental and African Studies*, 61 (1998): 415–36.

"Was the Gate of Ijtihād Closed?" *International Journal of Middle East Studies*, 16 (1984): 3–41; reprinted in Ian Edge, ed., *Islamic Law and Legal Theory* (The International Library of Essays in Law and Legal Theory, series ed. Tom D. Campbell) (Aldershot: Dartmouth Publishing Co., 1993); also reprinted in Hallaq, *Law and Legal Theory in Classical and Medieval Islam.*

"Was al-Shafiᶜi the Master Architect of Islamic Jurisprudence?" *International Journal of Middle East Studies*, 4 (1993): 587–605; reprinted in Hallaq, *Law and Legal Theory in Classical and Medieval Islam.*

Haram, Nissreen. "Use and Abuse of the Law: A Muftī's Response," in Masud et al., eds., *Islamic Legal Interpretation.*

Heer, Nicholas, ed. *Islamic Law and Jurisprudence: Studies in Honor of Farhat J. Ziadeh* (Seattle and London: University of Washington Press, 1990).

Heyd, Uriel. "Some Aspects of the Ottoman Fetva," *Bulletin of the School of Oriental and African Studies*, 32 (1969): 35–56.

*International Encyclopedia of the Social Sciences*, ed. D. L. Sills, 17 vols. (New York: Macmillan and Free Press, 1968).

Jackson, Sherman. *Islamic Law and the State: The Constitutional Jurisprudence of Shihāb al-Dīn al-Qarāfī* (Leiden: E. J. Brill, 1996).

Jennings, R. C. "Kādī, Court, and Legal Procedure in 17th C. Ottoman Kayseri," *Studia Islamica*, 48 (1978): 133–72.

"Limitations of the Judicial Powers of the Kādī in 17th C. Ottoman Kayseri," *Studia Islamica*, 50 (1979): 151–84.

Jīdī, ᶜUmar. *Muḥāḍarāt fī Tārīkh al-Madhhab al-Mālikī* (Rabat: Manshūrāt ᶜUkāẓ, 1987).

Johansen, Baber. "Casuistry: Between Legal Concept and Social Praxis," *Islamic Law and Society*, 2, 2 (1995): 135–56.

"Coutumes locales et coutumes universelles," *Annales Islamologiques*, 27 (1993): 29–35.

"Legal Literature and the Problem of Change: The Case of the Land Rent," in Chibli Mallat, ed., *Islam and Public Law* (London: Graham & Trotman, 1993), 29–47.

Juynboll, G. H. A. *Muslim Tradition: Studies in Chronology, Provenance and Authorship of Early Hadith* (Cambridge: Cambridge University Press, 1983).

"Some Notes on Islam's First *Fuqahā'* Distilled from Early *Ḥadīṯ* Literature," *Arabica*, 39 (1992): 287–314.

Kaḥḥāla, ᶜUmar. *Muᶜjam al-Mu'allifīn*, 15 vols. (Damascus: Maṭbaᶜat al-Taraqqī, 1957–61).

Khoury, Raif. *ʿAbdullāh b. Lahīʿa (97–174/715–790): Juge et grand maître de l'école égyptienne* (Wiesbaden: Harrassowitz, 1986).

Koury, George. "The Province of Damascus" (Ph.D. dissertation: University of Michigan, 1970).

Krawietz, B. "The Weighing of Conflicting Indicators in Islamic Law," in U. Vermeulen and J. M. F. van Reeth, eds., *Law, Christianity and Modernism in Islamic Society* (Leuven: Uitgeverij Peeters, 1998), 71–74.

Kress, Ken. "Legal Indeterminacy and Legitimacy," in Gregory Leyh, ed., *Legal Hermeneutics: History, Theory and Practice* (Berkeley: University of California Press, 1992), 200–15.

Levinson, Sanford. "The Rhetoric of Judicial Opinion," in Peter Brooks and Paul Gewirtz, eds., *Law's Stories: Narrative and Rhetoric in the Law* (New Haven and London: Yale University Press, 1996), 187–205.

Libson, Gedeon. "On the Development of Custom as a Source of Law in Islamic Law," *Islamic Law and Society*, 4, 2 (1997): 131–55.

Makdisi, George. *The Rise of Colleges: Institutions of Learning in Islam and the West* (Edinburgh: Edinburgh University Press, 1981).

Makdisi, John. "Hard Cases and Human Judgment in Islamic and Common Law," *Indiana International and Comparative Review*, 2 (1991): 191–219.

"Legal Logic and Equity in Islamic Law," *American Journal of Comparative Law*, 33 (1985): 63–92.

Makdisi, John and Marianne Makdisi. "Islamic Law Bibliography: Revised and Updated List of Secondary Sources," *Law Library Journal*, 87 (1995): 69–191.

Mandaville, J. E. "Usurious Piety: The Cash Waqf Controversy in the Ottoman Empire," *International Journal of Middle East Studies*, 10 (1979): 295–304.

Masud, Khalid M., Brink Messick, and David Powers, eds. *Islamic Legal Interpretation: Muftīs and their Fatwās* (Cambridge, Mass.: Harvard University Press, 1996).

Melchert, Christopher. *The Formation of the Sunni Schools of Law* (Leiden: E. J. Brill, 1997).

Meron, Y. "The Development of Legal Thought in Hanafi Texts," *Studia Islamica*, 30 (1969): 73–118.

Messick, Brinkley. *The Calligraphic State: Textual Domination and History in a Muslim Society* (Berkeley: University of California Press, 1993).

Motzki, H. *Die Anfänge der islamischen Jurisprudenz: ihre Entwicklung in Mekka bis zur mitte des 2./8. Jahrhunerts* (Stuttgart: Abhandlungen für die Kunde des Morgenlandes, 1991).

"The Prophet and the Cat: On Dating Mālik's *Muwaṭṭa'* and Legal Traditions," *Jerusalem Studies in Arabic and Islam*, 22 (1998): 18–83.

Mudarris, Muḥammad. *Mashāyikh Balkh min al-Ḥanafiyya*, 2 vols. (Baghdad: Wizārat al-Awqāf; Silsilat al-Kutub al-Ḥadītha, 1979).

Muranyi, Miklos. *Beiträge zur Geschichte der Ḥadīṯ- und Rechts gelehrsamkeit der Mālikiyya in Nordafrika bis zum 5. Jh. d. H.* (Wiesbaden: Harrassowitz, 1997).

*Materialien zur mālikitischen Rechtsliteratur* (Wiesbaden: Harrassowitz, 1984).
Naᶜīsa, Yūsuf. *Mujtamaᶜ Madīnat Dimashq*, 2 vols. (Damascus: Ṭlās, 1986).
Nielsen, J. *Secular Justice in an Islamic State: Maẓālim Under the Baḥrī Mamlūks, 662/1264–789/1387* (Istanbul: Nederlands Historisch–Archaeologisch Instituut, 1985).
Peabody, Robert. "Authority," *International Encyclopedia of the Social Sciences*, I, 437–77.
Pedersen, J. *The Arabic Book*, trans. G. French (Princeton: Princeton University Press, 1984).
Perelman, Chaim and L. Olbrechts-Tyteca. *The New Retoric: A Treatise on Argumentation* (Notre Dame: University of Notre Dame Press, 1969).
Peters, Rudolph. "Murder on the Nile: Homicide Trials in 19th Century Egyptian Sharīᶜa Courts," *Die Welt des Islams*, 30 (1990): 98–116.
Powers, David. "The Art of the Judicial Opinion: On *Tawlīj* in Fifteenth-Century Tunis," *Islamic Law and Society*, 5, 3 (1998): 359–81.
"*Fatwās* as Sources for Legal and Social History: A Dispute over Endowment Revenues from Fourteenth-Century Fez," *al-Qanṭara*, 11 (1990): 295–340.
"On Judicial Review in Islamic Law," *Law and Society Review*, 26 (1992): 315–41.
al-Qāḍī, Wadād. "Biographical Dictionaries: Inner Structure and Cultural Significance," in George N. Atiyeh, ed., *The Book in the Islamic World* (Albany: State University of New York Press, 1995), 93–121.
Reilly, Bernard F. *The Contest of Christian and Muslim Spain* (Oxford and Cambridge, Mass.: Blackwell, 1992).
Reinhart, Kevin A. "Transcendence and Social Practice: *Muftīs* and *Qāḍīs* as Religious Interpreters," *Annales Islamologiques*, 28 (1993): 5–28.
Repp. R. C. *The Müfti of Istanbul: A Study in the Development of the Ottoman Learned Hierarchy* (Oxford: Ithaca Press, 1986).
Robson, James. "Varieties of the *Ḥasan* Tradition," *Journal of Semitic Studies*, 6 (1961): 47–61.
Schacht, Joseph. "Classicisme, traditionalisme et ankylose dans la loi religieuse de l'Islam," in Robert Brunschvig and G. E. von Grunebaum, eds., *Classicisme et decln culturel dans l'histoire de l'Islam* (Paris: G.-P. Maisonneuve, 1957), 141–61.
"Foreign Elements in Ancient Islamic Law," *Journal of Comparative Legislation and International Law*, 32 (1950): 9–17.
*An Introduction to Islamic Law* (Oxford: Clarendon Press, 1964).
*The Origins of Muhammadan Jurisprudence* (Oxford: Clarendon Press, 1950).
"Zur soziologischen Betrachtung des islamischen Rechts," *Der Islam*, 22 (1935): 207–38.
"On the Title of the *Fatāwā ᶜAlamgīriyya*," in C. E. Bosworth, ed., *Iran and Islam* (Edinburgh: Edinburgh University Press, 1971), 475–78.
"Sur la transmission de la doctrine dans les écoles juridiques de l'Islam," *Annales de l'Institut d'Etudes Orientales*, 10 (1952): 399–419.

Sezgin, Fuat. *Geschichte des arabischen Schrifttums*, 8 vols. (Leiden: E. J. Brill, 1967– ).

*Shorter Encyclopaedia of Islam* (Leiden: E. J. Brill, 1974).

Siegal, Reva. "In the Eyes of the Law: Reflections on the Authority of Legal Discourse," in Peter Brooks and Paul Gewirtz, eds., *Law's Stories: Narrative and Rhetoric in the Law* (New Haven and London: Yale University Press, 1996), 225–31.

Toledano, Henry. *Judicial Practice and Family Law in Morocco* (Boulder: Social Science Monographs, 1981).

Tsafrir, N. "The Beginnings of the Ḥanafi School in Iṣfahān," *Islamic Law and Society*, 5, 1 (1998): 1–21.

Tyan, Emile. *Histoire de l'organisation judiciaire en pays d'Islam*, 2nd ed. (Leiden: E. J. Brill, 1960).

"Judicial Organization," in Majid Khadduri and Herbert Liebesny, eds., *Law in the Middle East* (Washington, D.C.: The Middle East Institute, 1955).

Vogel, Frank Edward. "The Closing of the Door of Ijtihād and the Application of the Law," *American Journal of Islamic Social Sciences*, 10 (1993): 396–401.

Watt, E. D. *Authority* (London and Canberra: Croom Helm, 1982).

Watt, W. M. "The Closing of the Door of Igtihād," *Orientalia Hispanica*, vol. I (Leiden: E. J. Brill, 1974), 675–78.

Weiss, Bernard. "Interpretation in Islamic Law: The Theory of *Ijtihād*," *American Journal of Comparative Law*, 26 (1978): 199–212.

"Knowledge of the Past: The Theory of *Tawātur* According to Ghazālī," *Studia Islamica*, 61 (1985): 81–105.

*The Search for God's Law: Islamic Jurisprudence in the Writings of Sayf al-Dīn al-Āmidī* (Salt Lake City: University of Utah Press, 1992).

Wensinck, Arent Jan. *Concordance et indices de la tradition musulmane*, 8 vols. (Leiden: E. J. Brill, 1936–88).

Wheeler, Brannon M. *Applying the Canon in Islam* (Albany: State University of New York Press, 1996).

Wiederhold, Lutz. "Legal Doctrines in Conflict: The Relevance of *Madhhab* Boundaries to Legal Reasoning in the Light of an Unpublished Treatise on *Taqlīd* and *Ijtihād*," *Islamic Law and Society*, 4 (1996): 234–304.

Zilfi, Madeline C. "The *Ilmiye* Registers and the Ottoman *Medrese* System Prior to the Tanzimat," *Contribution à l'histoire économique et sociale de l'Empire ottoman* (Leuven: Editions Peeters, 1983), 309–27.

Ziriklī, Khayr al-Dīn. *al-Aᶜlām*, 8 vols. (Beirut: Dār al-ᶜIlm lil-Malāyīn, 1980).

# INDEX

In classifying entries no account is taken of the letter *'ayn*, the *hamza*, and the Arabic definite article *al-*.


'Abbādī, Aḥmad b. Qāsim, 70–71, 72
'Abd al-Wahhāb al-Mālikī, 151
Abū Ḥafṣ, Aḥmad al-Bukhārī, 48, 181
Abū Ḥanīfa, 15, 17, 26, 27, 28, 29, 30, 31, 36, 37, 38, 39, 40 n., 45, 46, 47, 54 n., 55 n., 60, 62, 80, 86, 90, 91, 92, 99, 105, 107, 108, 109, 110, 111, 112, 115, 122, 162, 189, 215, 218, 227
Abū al-Su'ūd, Shaykh al-Islām, 21, 177
Abū Thawr, Ibrāhīm b. Khālid, 49, 59, 61
Abū Umāma, 106
Abū Yūsuf, 15, 17, 26, 27, 29, 30, 38, 39, 45 n., 47, 80, 90, 91, 92, 99, 105, 106, 107, 108, 109, 110, 111, 112, 115, 189, 215, 216, 218, 219, 225, 226, 227, 232
Abū Zur'a, 105–06
*'āda*, 141, 145, 215–32, 234
Aghnides, N., 220
*āḥād*, 128
'Ā'isha, 99–100, 102
'Alamī, 'Īsā b. 'Alī, 175, 184
'Alqama, 27, 107
Āmidī, Sayf al-Dīn, 68–69, 70, 71, 72, 73, 74, 75, 131
Anas b. Mālik, 105, 107, 199
Andalusī, Muḥammad b. 'Uthmān, 179
'Aqīlī, Abū Razīn, 100
'Aqqād, Shākir, 220
'Āqūlī, Ṭalḥa b. Ṭalḥa, 64
*aqwāl*, 124; *see* opinion
Arānī, Aḥmad b. 'Alī, 50
*arjaḥ*, *see tarjīḥ*
*aṣaḥḥ*, *see ṣaḥīḥ*
*aṣḥāb*, 3, 79 n., 80, 137, 184
*aṣḥāb al-imlā'*, 90
*aṣḥāb al-takhrīj*, *see takhrīj*
*aṣḥāb al-tarjīḥ*, 16
*aṣḥāb al-ṭuruq*, 10, 11
*aṣḥāb al-wujūh*, 10, 11, 49, 65, 123, 124, 136 n., 154, 237; *see also wujūh*
*ashbah*, 152, 154–55
*al-ashbāh wal-naẓā'ir*, 119
Ashhab, Abū 'Amr, 197, 202, 209
*ashhar*, *see mashhūr*
Asmā' bt. Abī Bakr, 107, 108
Asnawī, Jamāl al-Dīn, 72, 73
Aswad, 107
Aswānī, Muḥammad b. Aḥmad, 63 n.
'Aṭā' b. Rabāḥ, 105, 107
'Aṭṭar, Ibn Ibrāhīm, 178
author–jurist, *see muṣannif* and *taṣnīf*
*awjah*, 152, 154–55
Awzā'ī, 'Abd al-Raḥmān, 10, 40 n., 197
*aẓhar*, *see ẓāhir*

Bā'alawī, 'Abd al-Raḥmān, 84
Bāfaqīh, 84
Baghawī, Ḥusayn b. Mas'ūd, 144, 145
Baghdādī, Ibn Ghānim, 136, 183
Bājī, Abū al-Walīd, 67
Balkh jurists, 224, 225

Balkhī, Zakariyyā b. Aḥmad, 49
Bannānī, ʿAbd al-Raḥmān, 71–72
Baṣrī, Abū al-Ḥusayn, 66–67, 69
Baṣrī, Ḥasan, 107, 209 n.
Bayḍāwī, ʿAbd Allāh b. ʿUmar, 72, 73
Bayhaqī, Abū Bakr, 63, 100, 102, 107
Bīrī, 223
Bukhāran jurists, 218, 219
Bukhārī, Abū ʿAbd Allāh, 100, 102, 107, 108, 197
Bukhārī, Ḥusām al-Dīn, 184
Bukhārī, Muḥammad b. Waraqa, 65, 164–65
Bulqīnī, Sirāj al-Dīn, 163, 167, 182
Burzulī, Aḥmad b. Muḥammad, 6, 112, 182, 183, 184

Calder, Norman, 14 n., 56 n.
caliphate, 125
Companions, 3, 27, 34, 80, 86, 100 n., 106, 107, 108, 128, 131
consensus, 3, 4, 15, 33, 36, 37, 66, 77, 80, 81, 127, 131, 143, 204, 213, 216, 239
counsel, legal, 77, 78

Ḍabbī, Muḥammad Abū al-Ṭayyib, 49
Dabbūsī, Abū Zayd, 40
*ḍaʿīf*, 137, 138, 190, 203, 227, 228 ff.; *see* opinion
Dāraquṭnī, 107
*ḍarūra*, 142, 144, 160, 212, 227
disagreement, *see khilāf*
*dīwān*, 171, 177

Fārisī, Abū Bakr, 58
*fāsid*, 137, 138; *see* opinion
*fatwā*, 3, 4, 5, 6, 12, 13, 25 n., 65, 66, 67–74, 78, 82, 84, 114, 122, 125, 139, 140, 142, 147, 156, 157, 160, 161, 166, 169, 174–95, 201, 202–04, 206–08, 219, 221, 224, 228, 229, 234, 240
Fayrazān, ʿAbd al-Raḥmān Ibn Baṭṭa, 50
*fiqh*, 13, 178, 184, 190
Followers, 3, 27, 28, 80, 86, 108, 128, 131
founders of legal schools, *see imam*
Four Muḥammads, 59, 60, 61, 121, 237 n.
Fūrānī, ʿAbd al-Raḥmān al-Marwazī, 50, 65, 164
*furūʿ*, 15, 24, 81, 133, 180, 181, 182, 183, 184, 185, 188, 190, 191, 192, 194, 202, 206, 215, 217, 234

*gharīb*, 64, 122, 137, 138, 190
Ghazālī, Abū Ḥāmid, 64, 68, 134–35, 140, 144, 145, 178 n.

*ḥadīth*, 3, 8, 10, 24, 33, 36, 40, 41, 66, 67, 81, 100–01, 104, 107, 108, 128–31, 133, 138, 148, 157, 215 n., 217, 220, 225
Ḥāʾik, Ismāʿīl, 183
Ḥājjī Khalīfa, 181
al-Ḥakam, 28, 107
Ḥalabī, Ibrāhīm, 93, 160
*ḥalaqa*, 173
Ḥamawī, Aḥmad, 231
Ḥamawī, Saʿīd, 219
Ḥammād b. Abī Sulaymān, 27, 28, 29, 30, 36, 107
Ḥammāl, Mūsā b. Hārūn, 107
Ḥanafī, Aḥmad b. Muḥammad, 98
Ḥanafite law, 26, 27, 29, 47, 48, 54, 91, 104–45, 122, 147, 189, 216–33, 235; *see also* Ḥanafite school, Ḥanafites, *masāʾil al-nawādir*, *ẓāhir al-riwāya*
Ḥanafites, 14, 17, 19, 26, 27, 38, 42, 50, 51, 79, 80, 86, 93, 96, 98, 104, 106, 107, 109, 110, 111 ff., 122, 182, 183, 201 n., 218–19, 228; *see also* Ḥanafite law, Ḥanafite school, schools of law
Ḥanafite school, 29, 80, 93, 111, 112, 113, 122, 124, 136, 161, 181, 216, 217–21, 229, 232, 233; *see also* Ḥanafite law, Ḥanafites, schools of law
Ḥanbalite law, 44, 47, 60, 90–93, 96–99, 104–05, 109–12, 115–18, 122, 124, 147, 149, 154, 181, 182, 215; *see* Ḥanbalites, Ḥanbalite school

Ḥanbalites, xiv, 23 n., 40, 47 n., 51, 124, 138 n., 146, 148, 149, 154, 159, 162, 201 n., 215; *see also* Ḥanbalite law, Ḥanbalite school, schools of law
Ḥanbalite school, 41, 44, 49, 51, 61, 64, 138 n., 146, 147, 159; *see also* Ḥanbalite law, Ḥanbalites, schools of law
Ḥānūtī, 183
Ḥarb al-Kirmānī, 41
Ḥarbī, Ibrāhīm b. Isḥāq, 41
Ḥarmala, Abū Ḥafṣ al-Tujībī, 59, 237 n.
*ḥasan-ṣaḥīḥ*, 100–01
Hāshimī, ʿAbd al-Khāliq, 64
Ḥaṣkafī, ʿAlā al-Dīn, 147, 149, 217
Ḥaṭṭāb, Muḥammad, 6, 88–89, 112, 144, 151, 153, 156, 160, 182, 183, 184, 186–88, 202–04, 205–07
Haytamī, Ibn Ḥajar, 161, 170
Heyd, U., 176, 177, 179
Hindī, 223
Hinduwānī, Jaʿfar, 184
ḥukūmāt, *191*
Ḥulwānī, Shams al-A'imma, 15

Ibn ʿAbbās, ʿAbd Allāh, 28, 30, 105, 107, 130
Ibn ʿAbd al-Barr, Yūsuf Abū ʿAmr, 40, 87 n., 158
Ibn ʿAbd al-Ḥakam al-Miṣrī, 237 n.
Ibn ʿAbd al-Salām, al-ʿIzz, 20, 69, 112, 150, 178 n.
Ibn Abī al-Damm, 51, 81–83, 214
Ibn Abī Jamra, 152 n.
Ibn Abī Laylā, 28, 29, 38, 92
Ibn Abī Shāma, Shihāb al-Dīn, 87 n., 123, 163
Ibn ʿĀbidīn, Muḥammad, 54 n., 139, 142, 145, 146, 160, 183, 189, 216 n., 219–33, 235
Ibn Amīr al-Ḥājj, 183
Ibn ʿAqīl, Abū al-Wafā', 40 n.
Ibn al-ʿArabī, Abū Bakr Muḥammad, 150, 151
Ibn ʿArafa, Muḥammad, 113, 202 n., 203, 204
Ibn Arṭa'a, Ḥajjāj, 100–01
Ibn ʿAṣrūn, 144
Ibn ʿĀt, Aḥmad b. Hārūn, 88
Ibn al-Athram, Abū Bakr, 40, 41
Ibn Bashīr, 150
Ibn Baṭṭa, *see* Fayrazān
Ibn Buzayza, 136 n., 151
Ibn Daqīq al-ʿĪd, Muḥammad Taqī al-Dīn, 50, 70, 87 n.
Ibn Farḥūn, Ibrāhīm b. Nūr al-Dīn, 83–84, 111, 149–51, 161
Ibn al-Farrā', Abū Yaʿlā, 41, 124
Ibn al-Faṣīḥ, Aḥmad Fakhr al-Dīn, 16
Ibn al-Furāt, Asad, 122
Ibn Ḥabīb, ʿAbd al-Malik, 122, 134
Ibn al-Ḥaddād, Saʿīd b. Muḥammad, 59
Ibn al-Ḥājib, Jamāl al-Dīn, 69, 72, 150, 151, 203
Ibn al-Ḥājj, Muḥammad b. Muḥammad, 179, 183, 200, 204, 207
Ibn Ḥanbal, ʿAbd Allāh, 41
Ibn Ḥanbal, Aḥmad, 23 n., 39–42, 44, 49, 55, 58, 60, 100, 102, 107, 124, 148, 159, 217
Ibn Ḥanbal, Ṣāliḥ, 41
Ibn Ḥarbawayh, ʿAlī b. al-Ḥusayn, 49
Ibn Ḥazm, Muḥammad, 87 n.
Ibn al-Humām, Kamāl al-Dīn, 183, 218, 220
Ibn Jaʿfar, ʿAbd Allāh, 28
Ibn Kajj, Yūsuf b. Aḥmad, 50
Ibn Kalīl, Abū Bakr Aḥmad, 60
Ibn Kamāl Pāshāzādeh, Ahmad, 14–17, 18, 19, 20, 21, 23, 26, 48 n., 87, 99, 103
Ibn Khalaf, Dāwūd al-Ẓāhirī, 49, 107
Ibn Khuwayz Mindād, Muḥammad Abū Bakr, 150, 163
Ibn Khuzayma, Muḥammad b. Isḥaq al-Nīsābūrī, 59, 60
Ibn Lahīʿa, 100–01
Ibn Lubāba, Muḥammad b. ʿUmar, 88–89
Ibn Mahdī, ʿAbd al-Rahmān, 31
Ibn Māja, 100, 102, 107
Ibn al-Mājishūn, ʿAbd al-Malik, 197, 202, 209, 211
Ibn Masʿūd, ʿAbd Allāh, 27
Ibn Māza, al-Ḥusām al-Shahīd, 80
Ibn Miqdām, Ṣāliḥ b. Yaḥyā, 107

Ibn al-Mubārak, ʿAbd al-Allāh, 31
Ibn Mufliḥ, Shams al-Dīn, 146–47
Ibn al-Munāṣif, Muḥammad b. ʿĪsā, 211–13
Ibn al-Mundhir, *see* Nīsābūrī
Ibn al-Munkadir, Muḥammad, 101
Ibn Muqātil, Muḥammad, 48, 181 n., 184
Ibn al-Musayyib, Saʿīd, 33, 39
Ibn al-Najjār, Taqī al-Dīn, 162
Ibn Naṣr, *see* Marwazī, Muḥammad
Ibn Nujaym, Sirāj al-Dīn, 226
Ibn Nujaym, Zayn al-Dīn, 178 n., 182, 183, 185, 217–19, 220, 222, 223, 224, 225, 228, 231, 232
Ibn Qāḍī Shuhba, 50, 144, 148
Ibn al-Qāsim, ʿAbd al-Raḥmān al-ʿUtaqī, 36 n., 122, 149–50, 152, 161, 197, 198, 199, 202, 203, 205, 209, 237 n.
Ibn al-Qāṣṣ, Abū al-ʿAbbās Aḥmad, 45, 46, 47, 62
Ibn Qayyim al-Jawziyya, 87 n.
Ibn Qudāma, Muwaffaq, 51, 136, 147, 159
Ibn Qutayba, 40
Ibn Rabāḥ, ʿAṭāʾ, 28
Ibn Rāhawayh, Isḥāq, 107
Ibn Rāshid, Bahlūl, 150, 151
Ibn Rushd, Abū al-Walīd Muḥammad (al-Jadd), 2, 3, 4, 5, 6, 14, 17, 18–19, 23, 87, 89, 119 n., 124, 136, 151, 163, 175, 178, 179, 182, 183, 184, 186–87, 195–208
Ibn Rustam, Ibrāhīm, 48, 181 n.
Ibn al-Sāʿātī, Aḥmad b. ʿAlī, 16
Ibn al-Ṣabbāgh, Abū Naṣr, 50, 159
Ibn Sahl, ʿĪsā al-Asdī, 210
Ibn Saʿīd, Yaḥyā, 33
Ibn al-Ṣalāḥ, Abū ʿAmr, 2 n., 7–14, 16, 17, 18, 19, 20, 21, 23, 44, 48 n., 64, 84, 87, 103, 112, 133, 134, 143, 169, 170, 175, 188
Ibn Salama, Muḥammad, 48, 181 n., 224
Ibn Sallām, al-Qāsim, 48, 181 n.
Ibn Salmūn al-Kinānī, 6
Ibn Samāʿa, Muḥammad, 48, 181 n.
Ibn Shalabī, 183
Ibn Surayj, Abū al-ʿAbbās, 17, 46, 47, 49, 61, 62, 95, 154, 162, 167, 237 n.
Ibn Suwayd, Ṭāriq, 140
Ibn Taymiyya, Majd al-Dīn, 45
Ibn Taymiyya, Taqī al-Dīn, 45, 51
Ibn ʿUbayd, Faḍāla, 107
Ibn ʿUmar, Ibn ʿAbd al-ʿAzīz, 99–100, 102
Ibn Uways, 34
Ibn Yaḥyā, Naṣīr, 48, 224
Ibn Yaḥyā, Ṣāliḥ, 107
Ibn Yasār, Salmān, 33
Ibn al-Zamālkānī, Kamāl al-Dīn, 167
Ibn Zayd, Ḥammād, 31
Ibn Ziyād, Aḥmad, 59
Ibn Ziyād, al-Ḥasan, 26, 29, 48
Ibn al-Zubayr, ʿAbd Allāh, 107
*iftāʾ*, *see fatwā*
Ījī, ʿAḍud al-Dīn, 72
*ijtihād*, x, xi, 4, 5, 6, 7, 10, 11, 15, 16, 19, 20, 21, 22, 24–38, 43–44, 53, 54, 55, 56 n., 62, 63, 66–70, 74–85, 87–88, 99, 103, 120, 125, 127, 163, 164, 192, 202, 236, 238, 239; *see also mujtahid*
*ikhtilāf*, *see khilāf*
*ikhtiyār*, 140, 152, 160, 162–64, 162 n., 163, 164
*ʿilla*, 53, 66, 131, 132, 143, 159, 201 n.
*ʿilm*, 4, 168, 190
*imāms*, x, xi, 8, 11, 13, 15, 24, 25, 41, 42, 43, 44, 45, 52, 54 n., 55, 57, 60, 81, 86, 152 n., 230, 231, 236; *see also* Abū Ḥanīfa, Ibn Ḥanbal (Aḥmad), Mālik, schools of law, Shāfiʿī
ʿIṣām b. Yūsuf, 48
Isfarāʾīnī, Abū Ḥāmid, 123, 237 n.
Isfarāʾinī, Abū Isḥāq, 9, 10, 46 n., 63, 123
Isnawī, *see* Asnawī
Iṣṭakhrī, Abū Saʿīd, 49
*istiftāʾ*, 114, 173, 174, 176 n., 177, 187
*istiḥsān*, 46, 97, 159, 196, 198, 201, 204, 205, 207, 215, 216
*istiṣlāḥ*, 159, 215
*ittibāʿ*, 38, 87 n., 103; *see also taqlīd*

Jābir, 100–01, 102, 105, 107, 108
Jāḥiẓ, Abū 'Uthmān 'Amr, 31
Jarīrite school, 60 n.
Jaṣṣāṣ, Aḥmad b. 'Alī al-Rāzī, 77–78, 80, 93, 173
Jennings, R. C., 177
Jīlī, 'Abd al-'Azīz, 64
judge, *see qāḍī*
Jūrī, 'Alī b. Ḥusayn, 49
jurists' law, 125
Jurjānī, Muḥammad b. Yaḥyā, 50, 65
Juwaynī, Abū Muḥammad, 63, 163
Juwaynī, Imām al-Ḥaramayn, 13, 58, 63, 65, 67, 68, 70, 71, 72, 134–35, 137, 140, 163
Juynboll, G. H., 191
Jūzajānī, Abū Sulaymān, 48, 181 n.

Karkhī, Abū al Ḥasan, 15, 16, 21, 93, 110
Kāsānī, 'Alā' al-Dīn, 155
Kaysānī, Sulaymān b. Shu'ayb, 91
Khālid b. al-Walīd, 107
Khalīl b. Isḥāq, 136 n., 163, 182, 202, 207
Khallāl, Aḥmad Abū Bakr, 41
Kharashī, 202
Khaṣṣāf, Abū Bakr, 15, 77, 80
Khaṭṭābī, 107, 108
Khawārizmī, 'Abd Allāh, 50
Khayyāṭī, Abū 'Abd Allāh, 178 n.
*khilāf*, 3, 8, 24, 33, 37, 40, 57, 80, 125, 136, 158, 207
Khiraqī, 'Umar b. al-Ḥusayn, 49, 237 n.
Khushanī, Muḥammad, 189–90
Kilwadhānī, Abū al-Khaṭṭāb, 138 n.
Kināni, Ibn Salmūn, 183, 186, 204, 206, 207, 208
Kinānī, Muḥammad b. Hārūn, 179

Lakhmī, Abū al-Ḥasan, 163
legal theory, *see uṣūl al-fiqh*

*mabsūṭāt*, 157, 168
*madhhab*, *see* Ḥanafite school, Ḥanbalite school, *madhhab*-opinion, Mālikite school, schools of law, Shāfi'ite school
*madhhab*-opinion, 95–96, 105, 118, 124 n., 140, 152, 155–60, 193, 194, 195, 204, 207, 214, 219, 224, 234, 235
*muftī bi-hi*, 152, 153, 160–62, 194
Maḥallī, Jalāl al-Dīn, 70, 71, 189
Maḥāmilī, Aḥmad b. Qāsim, 51, 140
Maḥbūbī, Ṣadr al-Sharī'a, 16, 220
Mālik b. Anas, 3, 7, 17, 18, 31, 33, 34, 35, 36, 37, 39, 40, 45 n., 60, 62, 105, 106, 107, 108, 109, 122, 124, 149, 150, 151–52, 161, 195–200, 205; *see also imāms*
Mālikite law, 4, 5, 7, 34, 36 n., 47, 88–89, 112–13, 122, 136, 147, 149, 161, 196, 200, 202, 204, 208, 211, 234; *see also* Mālikites, Mālikite school, schools of law
Mālikites, 2, 4, 17, 18, 34, 36, 42, 47, 51, 59, 106, 107, 113, 124, 125, 146, 147, 151, 152 n., 154, 163, 200, 201 n., 203, 209, 211, 215; *see also* Mālikite law, Mālikite school, schools of law
Mālikite school, 2, 3, 4, 5, 6, 7, 31, 36, 111, 112, 113, 122, 123, 124, 150, 152 n., 160, 182, 194, 200, 210; *see also* Mālikite law, Mālikites, schools of law
*ma'mūl bi-hi*, 102 n., 152, 153, 160–62, 204, 214
*manāqib*, 237
Manāwī, Sharaf al-Dīn, 167
Maqdisī, 'Abd Allāh Abū al-Faḍl, 62
Maqdisī, Aḥmad b. Sahl, 40
*marfū'*, 100
Marghinani, Burhan al-Din, 16, 21, 27 n., 50, 147, 216 n., 228–29, 232
Marrūdhī, Abū Bakr, 41
Marwazī, Abū Bakr al-Qaffāl (al-Ṣaghīr), 123, 237 n.
Marwazī, Abū Ḥāmid, 65
Marwazī, Abū Isḥāq Ibrāhīm, 58
Marwazī, Muḥammad b. Naṣr, 59, 62, 163
*masā'il al-nawādir*, 48, 123, 125, 181, 182
*masā'il al-uṣūl*, 47

*mashhūr*, 84, 85, 128 n., 140, 141, 144, 146–52, 153, 154, 155, 156, 158, 159, 160, 162, 163, 172, 193, 204, 207
*ma'thūr*, *see naṣṣ al-riwāya*
Mawāq, Muḥammad b. Yūsuf, 202
Māwardī, Abū al-Ḥasan, 51, 67, 78–79, 80, 105, 214
Maymūnī, 'Abd Allāh, 41
Māzarī, Muḥammad b. 'Alī, 83, 84, 85, 124, 136 n., 147, 151, 163
*Miḥna*, 42
Mihrān, 105
Mirdāwī, 'Alī b. Sulaymān, 134, 146–47, 154
Mu'ādh b. Jabal, 196
*muftī*, xii, 2, 4, 5, 6, 7, 8, 18, 20, 23, 37 n., 66, 67, 73, 74, 76, 77, 78, 84, 85, 167, 169, 170, 171, 172, 173, 174, 176, 177, 178, 180, 182, 184, 185 n., 191, 192, 208, 220, 223, 231, 233, 234, 235, 240–41; *see also fatwā*
  types of, 8–14, 18, 236
*muḥākamāt*, 191
*mujtahid*, 2, 6, 7, 8, 9, 10, 11, 12, 13, 15, 17, 18, 19, 20, 21, 22, 23, 24–26, 28–31, 43, 44–53, 57, 59, 62, 63, 66–75, 77, 80, 81, 84, 85, 86, 88, 120, 125, 131, 139, 152, 155, 163, 164, 173, 192, 229, 230, 236, 238; *see also ijtihād*
*mukharrijūn*, 16, 65; *see also takhrīj*
*mukhtār*, *see ikhtiyār*
*mukhtaṣarāt*, 157, 168
*munāẓara*, 78
*muqallid*, 2, 5, 11, 13, 14, 16, 17, 23, 37, 39, 43, 67, 69–74, 75, 84, 86, 88, 89, 99, 114, 119, 152; *see also taqlīd*
*murajjiḥūn*, *see aṣḥāb al-tarjīḥ*
*muṣannif*, xii, 11, 23, 167–71, 174, 186, 191, 195, 208, 213, 215 ff., 220, 233, 234, 235, 240–41; *see also taṣnīf*
Mūṣilī, 'Abd Allāh b. Mawdūd, 16, 98, 109, 116–18
Mūṣilī, Abū Muḥammad, 123
Muslim, Abū al-Ḥasan, 100, 102, 108
*mustafīḍ*, 128
*mustaftī*, 175, 176, 177
Muṭarrif b. 'Abd Allāh, 197, 202, 209, 211
*mutawātir*, 128
Muṭawwi'ī, Abū Ḥafṣ 'Umar, 2 n.
*mutūn*, 15
Muzanī, Ibrāhīm, 39, 49, 58, 59, 61, 87 n., 95, 105, 106, 237 n.

Nābulusī, Ismā'īl, 226
Nakha'ī, Ibrāhīm, 27, 28, 29, 30, 36, 107
Nasafī, Najm al-Dīn, 178 n., 182
Nasā'ī, 100, 102, 107
Naṣrī, 'Uthmān b. 'Abd al-Raḥmān, 50
*naṣṣ*, 153, 218, 222 n.
  *al-naṣṣ al-madhhabī*, 231
  *naṣṣ al-riwāya*, 200
Nāṭifī, 50, 184
*nawādir*, *see masā'il al-nawādir*
Nawawī, Sharaf al-Dīn, 14, 20, 49, 64, 71, 84, 85, 96, 99, 101, 102, 103, 105, 106, 107, 108, 133, 134, 135, 136, 137, 138 n., 141, 142, 144, 145, 147, 148, 149, 153, 154, 157, 158, 161, 163, 175, 178, 182, 184, 188, 189
*nawāzil*, *see wāqi'āt*
Nīsābūrī, Ibn al-Mundhir, 47 n., 59, 60, 61, 237 n.

opinion
  authoritative, *see madhhab*-opinion, *mashhūr*, *ṣaḥīḥ*
  chosen, *see ikhtiyār*
  correct, *see ṣawāb*
  preponderant, *see tarjīḥ*
  school, *see madhhab*-opinion
  stronger, *see ashbah*, *awjah*, *qawī*, *ẓāhir*
  used in *fatwās*, *see maftī bi-hi*, *ma'mūl bi-hi*
  weak, *see ḍa'īf*, *fāsid*, *gharīb*, *shādhdh*
  widespread, *see mashhūr*

Pazdawī, Fakhr al-Islām, 15
positive law, *see furū'*
preponderance, *see tarjīḥ*
principles, positive law, *see uṣūl*

professor, 167, 168, 169, 170, 173–74, 220
Prophet Muḥammad, 27, 34, 52, 100, 101, 104, 106, 107, 108, 128, 129, 130, 196, 197, 225
Prophetic traditions, *see ḥadīth*

*qaḍā'*, *see qāḍī*
*qāḍī*, xii, 2, 5, 6, 23, 46, 60, 66, 76–85, 92, 104–05, 147, 148, 149, 164, 167–74, 177 n., 182, 183, 191–92, 194, 208–13, 223, 233, 234, 241
Qāḍī Ḥusayn al-Marwazī, 50, 140 n., 141
Qāḍīkhān, Fakhr al-Dīn, 15, 181, 182 n., 184, 188, 189
Qāḍī al-Nu'mān, 40
Qaffāl, *see* Marwazī, Abū Bakr
al Qaffāl al Shāshī (al Kabīr), 135, 237 n.
Qarāfī, Shihāb al Dīn, 43 n.
Qalqashandī, Aḥmad, 148
Qaṭṭān, Aḥmad b. Muḥammad, 64
*qawā'id*, 15, 119, 193
*qawī*, 138 n., 146
Qayrawānī, Ibn Abī Zayd, 112
Qaysī, 'Abd al-Raḥmān, 179
*qiyās*, 12, 15, 16, 46, 52, 66, 77, 81, 82, 128, 131, 132, 155, 159, 196, 198, 201, 205, 207, 224, 225
Qudūrī, Abū al-Ḥasan, 16, 50, 92–93, 225
Quran, 3, 4, 8, 15, 24, 30, 31, 38, 52, 66, 77, 80, 81, 98, 100, 107, 108, 127, 128, 131, 153, 154, 196, 198–99, 204, 206, 212, 219, 220, 232
*quwayl*, 138 n.

*raf'*, *see marfū'*
Rāfi'ī, Abū al-Qāsim, 58, 59, 84, 85, 134, 136, 138 n., 140, 141, 142, 143, 144, 147, 158, 188, 189
*rājiḥ*, *see tarjīḥ*
Ramlī, Khayr al-Dīn, 142, 189
Ramlī, Muḥyī al-Dīn, 189
Ramlī, Shihāb al-Dīn, 143, 153, 160, 161, 182, 183, 184, 188, 189, 193
*ra'y*, 215 n.
Rāzī, 'Alī b. Aḥmad, 16
Rāzī, Ibn Abī Ḥātim, 105
*risāla*, 169, 170, 171, 221, 222
*riwāya*, 41 n., 122, 124
roles, legal, 76 n., 170
Rūyānī, Abū al-'Abbās Aḥmad, 135, 140

Sa'dī Afandī, 226
*ṣaḥīḥ*, 63 n., 65, 108, 133–48, 150, 151, 152, 153, 154, 155, 156, 158, 159, 160, 163, 164, 165, 172, 193, 204, 207, 219, 223
Saḥnūn, 'Abd al-Salām b. Sa'īd al-Tanūkhī, 35, 36 n., 113, 122, 209
Sa'īd b. Jubayr, 107
Sajzī, Da'laj b. Aḥmad, 60
Samarqandī, Abū al-Layth, 181, 184
Samarqandī, 'Alā' al-Dīn, 40, 93, 110
Sarakhsī, Muḥammad Abū Sahl, 29, 30, 48, 92, 104–05, 107, 216, 219, 222, 232
Sarakhsī, Raḍī al-Dīn, 181
Sarakhsī, Shams al-A'imma, 15, 110
Sarakhsī, Ẓāhir, 49
*ṣawāb*, 138 n., 144, 152, 154–55
Ṣaymarī, 'Abd al-Wāḥid, 2 n., 64, 65
Schacht, Joseph, 56 n., 191
schools of law, x, xi, xii, xiii, xiv, 1, 2, 11, 12, 13, 15, 17, 21, 22–23, 34, 42, 49, 51, 52, 54, 55, 57–65, 68, 69, 70, 75, 77 n., 78, 79, 80, 81, 82, 83, 84, 87, 98, 103, 104, 107–09, 111, 118, 121, 122, 125, 136, 142, 143, 144, 155, 156, 157 n., 159, 163, 164, 165, 171, 172, 193, 233, 236 ff.
Selim III, Sultan, 220
Shabramallisı, Nur al-Dın, 182
*shādhdh*, 122 n., 137, 138, 229
Shāfi'ī, Muḥammad b. Idrīs, 10, 13, 15, 17, 36–39, 40 n., 45, 46, 47 n., 52, 53, 55, 58, 59, 60, 62, 66, 77, 78, 96, 99, 100–01, 102, 103, 104, 105, 112, 123, 124, 125, 140, 141, 148, 149, 153, 154, 157, 163 n., 173, 197; *see also imams*
Shāfi'ites, 7, 10, 18, 42, 46, 47, 51, 63, 93, 112, 123, 134, 143, 144, 147, 148, 149, 154, 161–62, 167, 182,

214, 228; *see also* schools of law, Shāfiʿite law, Shāfiʿite school
Shāfiʿite law, 14, 47, 58, 78, 93–96, 99–103, 105–06, 107–08, 108, 123, 147, 219; *see also* schools of law, Shāfiʿites, Shāfiʿite school
Shāfiʿite school, 17, 18, 46, 49, 50, 54, 60, 61, 64, 81, 85, 96, 111, 113, 124, 134, 147, 152 n., 153, 154, 158, 182; *see also* schools of law, Shāfiʿites, Shāfiʿite law
Shāh Walī Allāh, 112
Shāshī, Abū Bakr Muḥammad, 93–96, 99, 154
Shaybānī, Muḥammad b. al-Ḥasan, 15, 17, 26, 27, 38, 45 n., 46 n., 48, 62, 80, 90, 91, 93, 99, 105, 106, 107, 108, 109, 110, 111, 112, 115, 189, 218, 227
al-Shaykh al-Niẓām, 175, 184
Shiblī, Muḥammad b. ʿAbd Allāh, 98
Shīrāzī, ʿAbd al-Wāḥid, 64
Shīrāzī, Abū Isḥāq, 46 n., 52–53, 67, 95, 100–01, 102, 103, 105, 106, 137, 177, 182
Shīrāzī, Majd al-Dīn, 87 n.
Shirbīnī, Aḥmad, 72
Shurayḥ, Qaḍī, 107
*sijill, see dīwān*
Subkī, Tāj al-Dīn, 63 n., 65, 70–71, 134, 138 n., 143, 170, 182
Subkī, Taqī al-Dīn, 20, 40, 134, 138 n., 142, 144, 158–59, 167, 171, 175, 182, 184, 228, 229, 232
Sufyān al-Thawrī, 31
*ṣuḥba, see aṣḥāb*
Sunna, 4, 15, 30, 31, 32, 33, 34, 37, 66, 77, 80, 81, 98, 131, 142, 153, 154, 196, 197, 204, 227, 232
Suyūṭī, Jalāl al-Dīn, 14
Suwayd b. Ghafla, 107

*ṭabaqāt*, 1, 2, 15, 46 n., 50–51, 55, 60, 66, 77, 168
Ṭabarī, Abū ʿAlī, 135
Ṭabarī, Abū al-Ṭayyib, 2 n., 51, 65, 140 n., 141, 162
Ṭabarī, Muḥammad b. Jarīr, 40, 59, 60, 237 n.
*tābiʿūn, see* Followers
*tadrīs*, 168 n., 169
*tafarrudāt*, 58, 59, 60, 64, 138 n.
Taftāzānī, Saʿd al-Dīn, 72
Ṭaḥāwī, Abū Jaʿfar, 15, 40, 90, 91, 92, 110, 111, 112, 115, 116–18
*taḥqīq*, 136
*taḥrīr*, 146
*tajrīd*, 185–88, 206
*takhayyur, see ikhtiyār*
*takhrīj*, 10, 11 n., 12, 16, 19, 22, 41 n., 43–56, 65, 75, 81, 123, 124, 125, 136 n., 226, 229, 237
*al-takhrīj wal-naql*, 44, 45
*taʾlīf*, 168 n.
*taʿlīqa*, 90 n., 168
*talkhīṣ*, 185–88, 206
*tanqīḥ*, 185
Tanūkhī, Abū Ṭāhir, 50
Taqiyya b. al-Walīd, 107
*taqlīd*, ix, xi, 9, 16, 21, 22, 23, 27, 38, 55 n., 66, 67, 69–74, 84, 85, 86–88, 98, 99, 102, 103, 104, 107, 109, 113, 114, 115, 118–20, 121, 236, 238, 239; *see also muqallid*
*ṭarīqa*, 123, 124, 125, 142
*tarjīḥ*, 22, 84, 102 n., 127–32, 133, 134, 135, 142, 143, 148, 152, 153, 154, 157, 161, 163, 193, 204, 228
*tashhīr, see mashhūr*
*taṣḥīḥ, see ṣaḥīḥ*
*taṣnīf*, 23, 168, 169, 185 n.; *see also muṣannif*
*tawātur, see mutawātir*
Ṭāwūs, 105
Tilimsānī, Abū ʿAbd Allāh, 152 n.
Tirmidhī, Abū ʿĪsā, 100–01, 102
Thaljī, Muḥammad b. Shujāʿ, 93, 184, 215 n., 237 n.
Thawrī, 105
Ṭūfī, Najm al-Dīn, 40, 44, 45, 47 n., 50, 53, 102 n., 161
Ṭurṭūshī, Abū Bakr, 79 n.
Two Brothers, 202

*'urf*, *see 'āda*
*uṣūl* (positive law), 55, 89–99, 121 n., 222
*uṣūl al-fiqh*, 8, 11, 13, 15, 16, 24, 55, 67, 77, 81, 86–87, 99, 121 n., 127, 135, 178, 192, 193, 215 n., 217, 220
'Utbī, Abū 'Abd Allāh Muḥammad, 122

Wā'il b. Ḥajar, 140–41
*wajh*, *see wujūh*
Wansharīsī, Aḥmad b. Yaḥyā, 6, 175, 184
*wāqi'āt*, 48, 55, 123, 125, 181
Wazzānī, Mahdī, 6
*wujūh*, 65, 124, 134, 137, 140, 141, 146, 149, 154, 157, 164; *see also aṣḥāb al-wujūh*
*wuqū'*, 74

Yaḥyā al-Laythī, 35

Zāhidī, Najm al-Dīn, 218, 219, 223
*ẓāhir*, 152, 153–54, 155, 160, 163
Ẓahīr al-Dīn, Abū Bakr Muḥammad, 218
*ẓāhir al-naṣṣ*, 154
*ẓāhir al-riwāya*, 26, 47, 48 n., 123, 125, 154, 181, 182, 189, 221, 223, 229, 230, 231, 232
Ẓāhirite school, 207 n., 210
Zarkashī, Shams al-Dīn, 87 n., 148
Zarnajrī, Bakr b. Muḥammad, 64
Zayla'ī, 'Uthmān b. 'Alī, 188
Zufar, 26, 48, 99, 110, 111, 112
Zuhrī, Ibn Shihāb, 33, 39

Printed in the United States
154340LV00003B/29/A

9 780521 023931